E-Commerce and V-Business

E-Commerce and V-Business

Digital Enterprise in the Twenty-First Century

Second Edition

Edited by
Stuart Barnes

ELSEVIER

AMSTERDAM • BOSTON • HEIDELBERG • LONDON • NEW YORK • OXFORD
PARIS • SAN DIEGO • SAN FRANCISCO • SINGAPORE • SYDNEY • TOKYO
Butterworth-Heinemann is an imprint of Elsevier

Butterworth-Heinemann is an imprint of Elsevier
Linacre House, Jordan Hill, Oxford OX2 8DP, UK
30 Corporate Drive, Suite 400, Burlington, MA 01803, USA

First edition 2000
Second edition 2007

British Library Cataloguing in Publication Data
A catalogue record for this book is available from the British Library

Library of Congress Cataloguing in Publication Data
A catalogue record for this book is available from the Library of Congress

ISBN: 978-0-7506-6493-6

For information on all Butterworth-Heinemann publications
visit our website at http://books.elsevier.com

Typeset by Charon Tec Pvt Ltd (A Macmillan Company), Chennai, India
www.charontec.com

Printed and bound in Great Britain

07 08 09 10 11   10 9 8 7 6 5 4 3 2 1

Working together to grow
libraries in developing countries

www.elsevier.com | www.bookaid.org | www.sabre.org

ELSEVIER   BOOK AID International   Sabre Foundation

Contents

Section One:
Recognizing the Potential of E-Business   1

Section Two: Shaping the Virtual Organization 179

Contributors

Stuart Barnes, Norwich Business School, University of East Anglia, Norwich, UK

Ai-Mei Chang, Information Resources Management College, National Defense University, Washington DC, USA

Alina M. Chircu, Department of Information, Risk and Operations Management, McCombs School of Business, University of Texas, Austin, USA

Eduard Cristóbal, Department of Business Administration, University of Lleida, Lleida, Spain

Charles H. Davis, Faculty of Communication and Design, Ryerson University, Toronto, Canada

Albrecht Enders, Faculty of Business Administration, Economics and Social Sciences, Friedrich-Alexander-Universität Erlangen-Nürnberg, Nurenberg, Germany

Titus Faupel, Institute for Computer Science and Social Studies, Department of Telematics, University of Freiburg, Freiberg, Germany

Daniel Gille, Institute for Computer Science and Social Studies, Department of Telematics, University of Freiburg, Freiberg, Germany

Nigel Holden, Nottingham Business School, Nottingham Trent University, Nottingham, UK

Harald Hungenberg, Faculty of Business Administration, Economics and Social Sciences, Friedrich-Alexander-Universität Erlangen-Nürnberg, Nurenberg, Germany

Claudio Huyskens, Department for Media Management, University of Cologne, Cologne, Germany

Lucas D. Introna, Department of Organization, Work and Technology, Management School, Lancaster University, Lancaster, UK

Tawfik Jelassi, School of International Management, Ecole Nationale des Ponts et Chaussées, Paris, France

Robert B. Johnston, Department of Information Systems, University of Melbourne, Victoria, Australia

P. K. Kannan, The Robert H. Smith School of Business, University of Maryland, College Park, USA

Robert J. Kauffman, Carlson School of Management, University of Minnesota, Minneapolis, USA

Andreas Koening, Faculty of Business Administration, Economics and Social Sciences, Friedrich-Alexander-Universität Erlangen-Nürnberg, Nurenberg, Germany

Sherah Kurnia, Department of Information Systems, University of Melbourne, Victoria, Australia

Feng Li, The Business School, University of Newcastle upon Tyne, Newcastle upon Tyne, UK

Claudia Loebbecke, Department for Media Management, University of Cologne, Cologne, Germany

Horace Cheok Mak, Sterling Commerce, Melbourne, Australia

Frederic Marimon, Faculty of Economics and Social Sciences, Universitat Internacional de Catalunya, Barcelona, Spain

Peter Marshall, School of Information Systems, Faculty of Business, University of Tasmania, Hobart, Australia

Judy McKay, Faculty of Information and Communication Technologies, Swinburne University of Technology, Hawthorn, Victoria, Australia

Akos Nagy, Department of Information Systems and Management, Tilburg University, Tilburg, The Netherlands

David J. Pauleen, School of Information Management, Victoria University of Wellington, Wellington, New Zealand

Dimitra Petrakaki, Department of Organization, Work and Technology, Management School, Lancaster University, Lancaster, UK

Oliver Prokein, Institute for Computer Science and Social Studies, Department of Telematics, University of Freiburg, Freiberg, Germany

Eusebio Scornavacca, School of Information Management, Victoria University of Wellington, Wellington, New Zealand

Richard Vidgen, School of Management, University of Bath, Bath, UK

Florin Vladica, Electronic Commerce Centre, University of New Brunswick, Saint John, Canada

Bin Wang, College of Business Administration, University of Texas-Pan American, Edinburg, USA

Andrew B. Whinston, Center for Research in Electronic Commerce, McCombs School of Business, University of Texas, Austin, USA

Howard Williams, Department of Management Science, University of Strathclyde, Glasgow, UK

Judy Young, School of Information Systems, Faculty of Business, University of Tasmania, Hobart, Australia

List of figures

List of tables

Preface

AFTER THE DOT.COM BOMB: E-BUSINESS GOES MAINSTREAM

In its short life, e-business has made an incredible journey. From its roots in the financial industry and in interorganizational electronic document transfer in the 1970s and 1980s, to the 1990s with its remarkable plethora of Internet start-ups and massive market capitalizations, to the dot.com 'bomb' of March and April 2000, to the subsequent consolidation and integration of e-business into mainstream business today. Interestingly, in writing this book, things have come full circle; the first edition was published in 1999, before the bomb. Now e-business is again in recovery and growth, but it has changed somewhat; no longer are there the empty and ill-considered business models of the past – e-business is focusing on fundamental business drivers of value creation.

History tells us that our experiences with e-business are not new; other technological revolutions – such as the industrial revolution, the age of steam and the age of mass production – have all been through a similar cycle from irruption, to frenzy, to crash and beyond to synergy and maturity (Perez, 2002). If this reasoning is correct, then e-business is firmly in the synergy phase, which is typified by investments in established incumbents and fewer, larger companies. The emphasis is no longer on technological innovation, but instead on how to make technology easy to use, reliable, secure and cost efficient (Jelassi and Enders, 2005).

In simple terms, electronic commerce refers to transactions taking place over electronic networks, particularly the Internet. Such developments, especially in business-to-consumer markets, have been well documented. Firms in the music business, travel, online book trade, auction houses, apparel retailing and online stockbrokers are memorable examples. Evidence suggests that behaviour is gradually changing; consumers enjoy the convenience, ease and availability of price comparisons and incentives in online shopping, although multi-channel buying processes are still commonplace (eMarketer, 2006a). In some areas, such as planning vacations, more than half of all activity is now online (eMarketer, 2006b). Encouragingly, Internet spending for 2005 gained 22 per cent over 2004 spending; total Internet spending, including travel, hit $143.2 billion in 2005 (comScore, 2006).

Notwithstanding, the impact of the Internet goes much deeper. There is no doubt that electronic commerce is changing the way that businesses behave. One of the most important shifts is away from the traditional idea that any business is more or less a free-standing entity, which requires significant intellectual and cultural shifts in order to succeed (Chesbrough and Teece, 1996). A key concept that has emerged from the synergies between new technological developments and changing paradigms of corporate culture is that of virtualization, as underpinned by the resource-based theory of organization (Barney, 1991). Although numerous aspects are considered important in the definition of a virtual organization, it essentially involves virtual business (or v-business) relationships in which partners share complementary resources and technologies to achieve a common goal, such as creating a product or service (Kierzkowski, 2005; Walker, 2006; Walters, 2005). Confronted with a continuously changing competitive environment – due to issues such as globalization, rapid technological change and shifts towards mass customization and improved customer service – this new and flexible organizational model has provided an attractive proposition to organizations in the twenty-first century. Evidence suggests that it is becoming a popular and increasingly valued business model (Elliot, 2006; Lin and Lu, 2005; Thorne, 2005).

At the core, both e-commerce and v-business revolve around enabling, enhancing and transforming relationships between various parties (including businesses in various parts of the supply chain and in different supply chains, consumers, other stakeholders and even 'intelligent agents') in any given situation using information and communications technologies, typically facilitated by the Internet or Internet-related technologies (Andel-Ancion *et al.*, 2003). In a sense, these developments are two sides of the same coin, and are examined equally in depth in the two sections of this book.

A real test of any innovation may be that of 'embeddedness'. In the early stages of the introduction of an innovation, its 'visibility' is high, as the market learns about it and begins to adopt it; however, over time, the innovation gradually becomes assimilated to the degree where ultimately it is not considered differently at all – it just blends into the background. Successful innovations are not noticed, they just work; you don't need to explain to a teenager how to send text messages on their mobile phone – it is by now an 'embedded' technology. Is e-business an embedded technology? Well, it is fast becoming so. There are noticeably fewer 'pure' e-business degrees than when we published the first edition of this book. What was considered 'e-'business is now just business; e-business has been assimilated into other business and management degrees and also into computer science degrees to some extent. It is still there, but it has now become 'mainstream' – although probably not fully embedded yet; as we will see in the following chapters, both e-commerce and v-business still have a number of important challenges ahead.

FEATURES OF THE BOOK

This book explores these two important issues, electronic commerce and virtual business, in some depth. Although the literature around electronic commerce and virtual organizations has developed to some extent independently, they are, as we shall see, inextricably linked. This text has arisen from extensive investigation into the impacts of such important concepts upon business, each highly dependent upon recent technological developments. It has also arisen from a personal review of the available literature on this and related topics, based on our own experience, and in the context of recent developments in the field.

While the book will hopefully be of interest to executives who are concerned with some of the many complex and inter-related issues associated with managing e-commerce and virtual organizations, its primary audiences are senior undergraduates and Masters students studying business-related degrees. Students who are about to begin research in this area should also find the book of particular help in providing a rich source of material reflecting leading-edge thinking.

The collected papers in this book illustrate the wide variety of business opportunities afforded by e-commerce and virtual business. They describe and discuss the important issues that follow when an organization decides to pursue consumers electronically and to organize its operations virtually. The authors in this text have written the most recent and emerging research. We have chosen authors whose work sits well within the framework of the book and which brings in a good balance of theory and practical issues.

In the development of this book, we solicited articles from authors worldwide. In so doing our purpose was two-fold. First, we wanted the content of this book to have a worldwide appeal. Except for a handful of countries where political considerations are paramount, the Internet is a truly global phenomenon. We wanted our selection of authors to reflect this. Second, we wanted to present the different perspectives represented by writers from different parts of the globe.

It is, of course, impossible to cover all aspects of these emerging topics. Our focus has been on attempting to cover some of the more recent and possibly more important aspects, and from a management perspective. The implications are that whilst technological aspects are covered in some detail, this is always in a mode accessible to the manager.

STRUCTURE OF THE BOOK

The structure for this book reflects the two important topics upon which our discussion is focused. Thus, we have organized the book into two sections:

Section One: Recognizing the Potential of E-Business

This first section examines the nature and implications of doing business electronically. To some extent, this involves looking at some of the evolving business models that enable firms to take advantage of this phenomenon, particularly in business-to-consumer markets. Indeed, there is a strong recognition that electronic commerce changes the 'rules of the game'; being successful in the online environment involves rethinking many aspects of the organization such as strategy, structure, processes, applications and products. The theory in this section is strongly supported by recent case studies and empirical evidence.

Section Two: Shaping the Virtual Organization

This second section extends some of the thinking from the first section. In particular, it explores new and emergent business models for flexible organizing in business-to-business environments. Such models are almost inevitably facilitated by recent technological developments. In a turbulent business world, alliance, cooperation and sharing between organizations can be a valuable source of competitive advantage. However, creating a dynamic and synergistic organizational form is a very complex undertaking. To provide some direction, this section critically examines in detail the nature, possibilities and limitations of this type of organization. Again, the analysis is interwoven with original case study and other empirical material to consolidate and support the arguments given.

As you will now be aware, e-commerce and v-business are diverse and complex subjects. They are not simply concerned with technological issues, but incorporate aspects of strategic management, economics, operations management and behavioural science, among others. Such an interdisciplinary perspective is critical if the subject domains are to be understood fully. All too poignant pre-bomb examples of e-commerce offerings that overestimate technology and underestimate consumers exemplify this point (e.g. Boo.com). For this reason, as you have seen, we advocate a broad management viewpoint. The issues debated here are far too important to be left to technologists; although technology is an important enabler, the vision, strategy and management of the transition to bold new business models lies squarely in the hands of managers. To reap the real rewards of e-commerce and v-business, management competence is crucial.

We hope you find this book of interest and that it raises some important issues that will be relevant to consideration in your study, research or organizational context. As you do so, we all take one more step in the much-anticipated 'digital economy'.

REFERENCES

Andel-Ancion, A., Cartwright, P. A. and Yip, G. S. (2003). The digital transformation of traditional business. *Sloan Management Review*, 12 (3), 34–41.

Barney, J. (1991). Firm resources and sustained competitive advantage. *Journal of Management*, 17, 99–120.

Chesbrough, H. W. and Teece, D. J. (1996). When is virtual virtuous? Organizing for innovation. *Harvard Business Review*, January–February, 65–71.

comScore (2006). *Online Holiday Spending Boosts E-Commerce to Record Annual Sales of $143 Billion*. comScore Networks. http://www.comscore.com/press/pr.asp

Elliot, S. (2006). Technology-enabled innovation, industry transformation and the emergence of ambient organizations. *Industry and Innovation*, 13, 209–225.

eMarketer (2006a). Buyers still shop online, buy offline. *Emarketer.com*, 21 November. http://www.emarketer.com/Article.aspx?1004290&src=article_head_sitesearch

eMarketer (2006b). Over 50% of vacations now planned online. *Emarketer.com*, 22 November. http://www.emarketer.com/Article.aspx? 1004295

Jelassi, T. and Enders, A. (2005). *Strategies for E-Business: Creating Value Through Electronic and Mobile Commerce*. FT Prentice Hall.

Kierzkowski, Z. (2005). Towards virtual enterprises. *Human Factors and Ergonomics in Manufacturing*, 15, 49–69.

Lin, L. and Lu, I. (2005). Adoption of virtual organization by Taiwanese electronics firms. *Journal of Organizational Change Management*, 18, 184–200.

Perez, C. (2002). *Technological Revolutions and Financial Capital: The Dynamics of Bubbles and Golden Ages*. Edward Elgar.

Thorne, K. (2005). Designing virtual organizations? Themes and trends in political and organizational discourse. *Journal of Management Development*, 24, 580–606.

Walker, H. (2006). The virtual organization: a new organizational form? *International Journal of Networking and Virtual Organizations*, 3, 25–41.

Walters, D. (2005). Performance planning and control in virtual business structures. *Production Planning and Control*, 16, 226–239.

Section One

Recognizing the Potential of E-Business

The relativity of disruption: e-banking as a sustaining innovation in the banking industry[1]

Albrecht Enders, Tawfik Jelassi, Andreas Koening and Harald Hungenberg

INTRODUCTION

Clayton Christensen's disruptive innovation theory (DIT) is one of the most influential theories in the recent academic and management literature. This is reflected not only in his bestselling books *The Innovator's Dilemma* and *The Innovator's Solution*, but also in the discussion and follow-up work that his theory created among academics and managers alike.

Christensen suggests a broad definition of the concept of innovation. To him, innovation refers to all changes of 'processes by which an organization transforms labour, capital, materials and information into products or services of greater value' (Christensen, 1997). Thus, in addition to creating new processes and products, innovation also includes new types of business models.

The DIT recognizes two types of innovation: on the one hand, sustaining innovations generate growth by offering a better performance in existing markets. Usually, regardless of whether they are incremental or radical, these innovations are exploited successfully by the established players in an industry and do not lead to revolutionary changes in an industry's landscape.

On the other hand, compared to existing products and business models, disruptive innovations initially have a lower performance in the traditionally most important performance criterion (such as functionality, speed or size). Even though, in most cases, disruptive innovations are less complex from a technological viewpoint, they are usually brought to the markets successfully by new entrants. Christensen posits that this is due to the behaviour that incumbents and new entrants typically display. Managers in incumbent firms are unwilling to support disruptive innovations because: (1) they usually do not fulfil the needs of the firm's existing and most profitable customers; and (2) they offer a much lower profit margin than sustaining innovations do.

As Christensen points out throughout his publications, it is not always easy to apply the categories of disruptive and sustaining innovation in practice: 'Even people who deeply understood the theories [of disruptive innovation] struggled to use them in a repeatable and methodical fashion' (Christensen et al., 2004). One reason for these difficulties is the fact that 'disruption is a relative term' (Christensen and Raynor, 2003). This means that even though a particular innovation is disruptive to one player in an industry it might be sustaining to another. This implies that firms have to be careful when categorizing innovations, particularly if most companies and public opinion consider an innovation to be of a disruptive nature. For example, throughout the second half of the 1990s, the Internet was believed to be a disruptive innovation to almost all industries, while in reality it turned out to be of a sustaining nature in many industries. Thus, the Internet had a sustaining impact in that it strengthened the position of the established market leaders.

In the area of electronic retail banking there has been an ongoing dispute among academics regarding the disruptive nature of the new business models based on the Internet. In their book *The Innovator's Solution*, Christensen and Raynor state that 'Internet banking can only be deployed as a sustaining technology relative to the business model of retail banks' (Christensen and Raynor, 2003). Their underlying argument is that it is difficult to 'create a business model that would afford a disruptive online bank attractive profits at the discount prices required to win business at the low end [of the market]'. This view was supported by the failure of numerous pure online ventures such as Bank One's online subsidiary Wingspan during the collapse of the online e-business bubble in 2001 which put the previous academic research (Li, 2001; Useem, 1999) regarding the disruptiveness of e-banking into severe doubt.

However, more recently, there have again been numerous authors who claim that Internet-based banking might be a disruptive innovation in retail banking after all. Research conducted by Frei, Campbell and Hitt (Campbell, 2003; Campbell and Frei, 2004; Hitt and Frei, 2002) points in this direction, implying that it is possible to develop a viable disruptive e-business model in retail banking. Gary (2004) discusses the case of ING Direct that displays characteristics of a low-end disruption because of cost advantages vis-à-vis physical retail outlets. Other scholars (e.g. Boss *et al.*, 2000) conclude that the failures of pure online ventures were rather consequences of inadequate strategic implementation of an otherwise promising business model. Thus, currently, the question regarding the disruptiveness of e-banking in the retail banking industry remains open – and along with it its future competitive landscape.

The objective of this chapter is to address this question by conceptually analysing the case of Nordea Bank (Scandinavia), an incumbent that has over the last decade enjoyed extraordinary success in e-banking. Nordea presents an interesting real-world example because it is an important bricks-and-mortar bank in the Scandinavian region while it is also considered to be one of the most important e-banks in the world (Echikson, 2001).

The research employed is a case design (Carlile and Christensen, 2005; Eisenhardt, 1989; Yin, 1984) where the primary unit of analysis was the online organization of Nordea, the largest Scandinavian bank, which is described in more detail in later sections. The time frame of the analysis spans from the inception of computer-based banking services at Nordea in the early 1980s until 2004. We chose Nordea as a case example because the bank's online operations are highly successful and because the bank has maintained an integrated approach to its online and offline banking operations since its inception. Data for the case study were collected through an extensive personal interview with the head of e-banking at Nordea, Bo Harald, and telephone interviews with his management staff.

These conversations were followed up by e-mail exchanges to collect quantitative data from the internal accounting systems.

This chapter is structured as follows. The next section provides an overview of the disruptive innovation theory (DIT) and highlights the five strategic dimensions that are associated with it. The subsequent section introduces the case of Nordea and describes the e-banking activities of this bank. This is followed by a section that analyses these activities along the five strategic dimensions of the DIT and addresses the question of whether the Internet has been a sustaining innovation at Nordea. Finally, the last section summarizes the key findings of this chapter and discusses implications.

THE DISRUPTIVE INNOVATION THEORY

Before discussing in more detail the case example of Nordea, this section provides an initial overview of the disruptive innovation theory. The fundamental assumption of DIT is that in most cases, technological progress evolves faster than customers' demand for better performance. This means that technologies that do not fulfil, during their early development stages, customers' performance requirements continue to evolve and, at one point in time, overshoot the performance that customers can absorb (see Figure 1.1).

To illustrate this type of evolution, let us consider, for example, the PC industry. During the 1980s, desktop PCs were not good enough for many business applications. As a result, private and corporate users frequently upgraded their PC equipment and, in order to succeed, PC manufacturers had to provide higher performance. Nowadays, however, the PC processing power and functionalities have improved beyond the point where most users could utilize them. Using the DIT terminology, PC customers have become 'overserved'.

The driving force behind the above development is called 'resource dependence' (Bower, 1970; Christensen, 1997; Pfeffer and Salancik, 1978). Its theory states that it is actually customers and investors – not managers – who control the allocation of resources in an enterprise. It is so because companies that invest in projects that do not satisfy the needs of their best customers and do not suit the risk structure of their investors over the long run will not receive the necessary funding. This is also due to the fact that companies generally generate most of their profits with their most demanding customers who are willing to pay premium prices for more sophisticated products. At the same time, profit margins with customers in lower segments are generally much

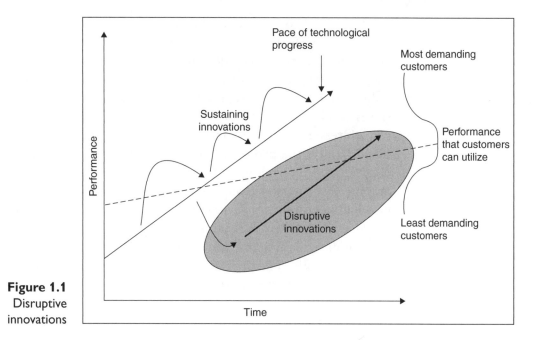

Figure 1.1
Disruptive
innovations

lower. Consequently, innovation efforts tend to revolve around the improvement of high-end products.

In Christensen's terminology, 'sustaining innovations' are those innovations that help established companies to generate higher margins by selling better products to the most demanding customers. Sustaining innovations can be incremental or radical. While incumbents are not always first to develop a sustaining innovation, they generally succeed in their large-scale commercialization efforts. This is due to the fact that compared to their start-up competitors, incumbents tend to have more financial resources, have a larger customer base and have the processes in place to push the innovation into the market.

In contrast to sustaining innovations, 'disruptive innovations' originate in segments that are unattractive for the incumbents, i.e. customers with the lowest demands. The key characteristic of disruptive innovations is that they are located in a different 'value-network' than sustaining innovations. A value-network is 'the specific context within which a firm identifies and responds to customers' needs, solves problems, procures inputs, reacts to competitors, and strives for profit' (Christensen, 1997). They show a lower performance in the dimensions that were valued in the old network, while at the same time offering performance value most important in a different value-network. This could either be a lower price (as is the case in discount grocery retailing), more convenience (as is the case in MP3 music players such as Apple's iPod), or more customizability (as is the case in Dell's build-to-order business model).

There are two potential markets for disruptive innovations. First, they can address those customers who are overserved by the functionality of their current provider. In the DIT terminology, this is called a 'low-end disruption' and illustrative examples include low-cost airlines, online book resellers (such as Amazon.com) or discount department stores (such as Wal-Mart or Target). Second, a disruptive innovation can address those customers who have hitherto been 'non-served', i.e. unable to use the product. For instance, the online auction Web site eBay allowed Internet users to auction off personal belongings to geographically dispersed groups of customers. Previously, this type of auction had been impossible to conduct. In the DIT terminology, this is called a 'new-market disruption'.

In summary, there are two important factors, which together may lead to disruptive innovations: (1) overlapping value-networks and (2) disruptive circumstances. More specifically:

- *Overlapping value-networks.* Disruptive innovations are located in a different value-network, where other performance criteria are the most important purchasing criteria for customers. However, the value-network of a disruptive innovation has a growing overlap with the traditional value-network (Adner, 2002). This means that even though in the beginning disruptive innovations only satisfy the low-end customers of the traditional value-network, they become attractive for more and more customers in the old value-network who ultimately switch over to the new value-network.
- *Disruptive circumstances.* Disruptive innovations only happen in disruptive circumstances. Either customers are overserved by established technologies or they are non-served customers, i.e. 'people who lack the ability, wealth, or access to conveniently and easily accomplish an important job for themselves' (Christensen *et al.*, 2004).

Under the assumption of the laws of resource dependence, increasingly overlapping value-networks in either low-end or new-market disruptive circumstances lead to so-called 'asymmetric motivation': incumbents have a high incentive to flee into higher-margin segments rather than to fight their customer base at the low end. Ultimately, their main customer base shrinks to the point where it is too small to sustain the organization and the incumbents therefore fail.

The potential for a low-end disruption is high if: (1) there is an overlap between the old value-network of the incumbents and the new value-network of the disruptive innovation; (2) if the overlap increases over time; and (3) if a substantial number of customers are overserved.

The potential for a new-market disruption is high if: (1) there is an overlap between the old value-network of the incumbents and the new value-network of the disruptive innovation; (2) if the overlap increases over time; and (3) if there are non-served customers.

A large fraction of the DIT literature discusses the question of how incumbents can react successfully if they concluded that a specific innovation has disruptive potential. Throughout his publications (e.g. Christensen, 1997; Christensen and Raynor, 2003; Christensen *et al.*, 2004), Christensen suggests considering the following strategic dimensions when deciding how to respond to a disruptive innovation: (1) organizational design; (2) structure of teams; (3) framing of the situation vis-à-vis the employees; (4) the strategy process; and (5) the design of the value chain. Let us examine each of these in turn:

- *Organizational design.* In order to exploit a disruptive innovation, incumbents should set up a separate organization. According to the resource dependence laws discussed above, the size of this new organization should fit the size of the market in order to enable it to be patient for growth while at the same time being impatient for profitability. Furthermore, the new organization should also use separate channels that fit into the value-network of the disruptive innovation: 'Disruptive products require disruptive channels' (Christensen and Raynor, 2003).

- *Structure of teams.* When deciding on the structure of the team that should be engaged to exploit the disruptive innovation, the CEO should evaluate the fit of the innovation with the organization's processes. If the innovation involves customary processes, teams coming from lower hierarchies of the organization can be successful. If the processes are entirely new, heavyweight teams that include senior staff are necessary to push through the new initiatives against organizational resistance (Christensen, 1997).

- *Framing of the situation vis-à-vis the employees.* As an incumbent, in order to receive the resources necessary to develop a disruptive innovation, the situation created by the innovation should first be framed as a threat to the organization. The management team will then feel obliged to allocate substantial resources to the project and employees will follow because both groups are afraid of losing the position in the marketplace. Once a separate organization has been founded, though, the situation should be framed as an opportunity. This is because individuals become more open and creative when they approach a new situation with this mindset. Being open-minded and creative is a central requirement for the emergent, opportunity-seeking strategy development typical for new players (Gilbert and Bower, 2002).

- *Strategy process.* This implies that in contrast to the planned marketing strategy, which is adequate for sustaining innovations in existing markets, disruptive innovations are best exploited through emergent strategies. This is because new markets, which are not yet defined, cannot be analysed using traditional market research instruments. Instead, companies trying to market disruptive innovations have to develop strategies 'by doing'. This approach also implies that they need the required resources to survive and to learn from early failure.

- *Design of the value chain.* When companies decide on their location in the value chain and their degree of vertical integration, they should try to be located in sustaining circumstances, i.e. in places of the value chain where the customer is underserved by the performance of the products offered. Under these circumstances, integrated business models usually have high transaction cost advantages over modular architectures (Christensen *et al.*, 2002).

In the following section, we present the key elements of Nordea's e-banking strategy as it has evolved over the last decade. This provides the basis for the subsequent analysis of Nordea's approach along the different dimensions of the DIT described above.

NORDEA CASE STUDY

Nordea Bank is the result of several mergers between banks from four Scandinavian countries. Domestic mergers in Finland were speeded up after a sustained economic crisis in the early 1990s, which was caused by the collapse of the Soviet Union and the general downturn of the global economy. In 1997, the Swedish company Nordbanken and the Finnish Merita bank merged to form MeritaNordbanken. In 1999, the Danish Unidanmark acquired TRYG and later on Vesta. In 2000, the Danish Unidanmark and the Swedish/Finnish MeritaNordbanken merged to form Nordic Baltic Holding, which then became Nordea after merging in 2000 with the Norwegian Christiana Bank Og Kreditkasse.

At the end of 2004, Nordea had almost 10 million private customers of which 4.1 million were active e-banking customers. Forty-five per cent of the total population in the Nordic countries have an account with Nordea; either a main account or a secondary one.

Over the last two decades, Bo Harald, Nordea's Vice President of Internet Banking Services, has been the main architect of Nordea's approach to e-banking. His job assignments pushed him to use computers to carry out some banking transactions. He said: 'While away from home, I started using the computer to authorize payments. The beginning of PC-banking in 1984 was a blessing for me. It became so much easier to do things from a distance' (Echikson, 2001).

Union Bank introduced electronic payment systems and started to phase out cheques in 1982. 'I think the secret of our success was to start early', says Bo Harald. 'We started back in 1982 with telephone voice commands. By 1984, we added PC banking with a dial-up modem. It was like black and white compared to the color Internet, but it was a start and it gave us the experience' (Echikson, 2001). Starting out early also helped to keep costs down. 'E-banking is not expensive if you start early and you build it up gradually', says Bo Harald. 'However, it can be very expensive if you wake up in the middle of when things are already happening because then you need to ask expensive consultants for advice and you end up buying all the expensive bells and whistles to outshine your competitors.'

The e-banking channel was developed from within the bank through a joint effort by managers with product responsibility and the IT department of the bank (Reinhardt and Lévesque, 2004). During its early stages, the e-banking initiative at Nordea was pushed primarily by Bo Harald, as head of IT at Nordea, and two managers from the product area. Support from top management was limited, though. Only after promising sales statistics were reported from the Helsinki region, where the e-banking project was launched, did top management embrace the e-banking strategy.

When building its customer base of online banking users, Nordea differentiated between two different customer types: Internet believers and non-Internet believers.

> ■ *Internet believers* have been online for years and have the know-how and trust to navigate the Internet, to shop online and to also do their banking online, i.e. they have a deeply ingrained e-habit. To them e-banking is a normal day-to-day activity; something that is not even worth talking about with their friends. From a marketing perspective, these customers

are therefore considered to be 'infertile' because they do not generally act as multipliers.

■ *Non-believers* are just starting to surf the Internet. It still requires substantial work in convincing these users to build up enough trust and know-how so that they start doing e-banking and create an e-habit. Friendly branch employees who are willing to take the time to explain the benefits of e-banking are best suited for taking away that insecurity. Once they are online, however, these customers tend to be amazed and proud of their accomplishments and want to pass the news on to their friends. After turning them into believers they take the next step and become preachers – a viral marketing effect where customers acquire more customers. This viral marketing effect has been one crucial lever for converting Nordea customers who used to go to physical branches into online customers.

After launching e-banking in 1984, Nordea has continued to introduce new customer interfaces such as those via Internet banking, TV banking, WAP (Wireless Application Protocol)-enabled mobile phones, digital TV and GPRS (General Packet Radio Service – a 2.5 generation mobile network standard) phones. Since the introduction of these new channels, usage patterns have shifted away from physical infrastructure to digital platforms as is shown in Figure 1.2. While the former decreased by a compounded annual growth rate (CAGR) of 6 per cent, the latter went up by 16 per cent annually with Internet payments displaying a particularly strong growth rate of over 21 per cent.

As a result of this shift to online channels the role of branch offices at Nordea has changed drastically over the last few decades (Shim, 2001). While in the past bank clerks spent most of their time keying in transactions manually, this number has drastically decreased during the last four years. Today, Nordea uses its branches primarily for establishing personal relationships with customers. Trust built up through personal relationships is important when customers need to make complex decisions (such as purchasing insurance or a pension scheme). In this sense, banking is local but it does not always require a fully equipped branch. Sometimes an office is enough; this may not offer the possibility to make transfers, but opens up the opportunity for fostering personal relationships.

In order to accelerate the migration away from physical banking transactions, such as cheque writing or transactions in branches, Nordea implemented pricing schemes that set incentives for customers to switch into the more cost-effective channel of online banking. In addition to using pricing as a way of channelling its business into the desired

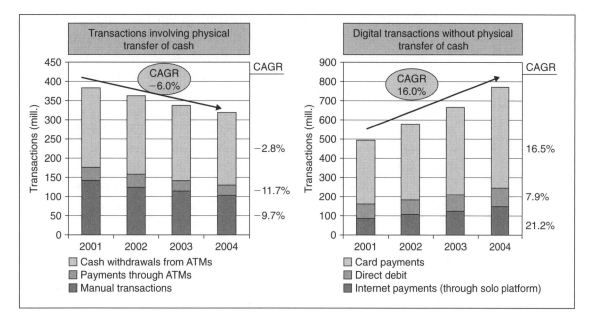

Figure 1.2
Cash transactions have decreased significantly while non-cash based payments have increased (source: Nordea)

distribution channel, Nordea adheres to the premise that when introducing new applications, added value should not be given away for free. For instance, customers pay a monthly fee for Internet banking. If further services are taken up such as brokerage, credit card reporting or WAP, customers are also charged for them.

However, enticing customers to move to the online channel created tension within the overall organization since branch-based banking was threatened by the new channel. To alleviate this tension, Nordea decided, unlike many other banks, to fully integrate its online banking within its physical banking operations, thereby eliminating possible competition between the two channels. In fact, branch employees were enticed to move branch customers over to the Internet. To ensure high motivation among employees, the e-banking channel was not set up as a separate profit centre, which reduced rivalry between the different channels. Instead, online revenues were credited to the bank branch the customer was affiliated to. The goal was to combine and leverage the cost efficiency and convenience of the online channel and the personal, trust-building atmosphere of personal relationships. Ultimately, the ability to leverage the branch network to move customers to the Internet, thereby eliminating the need for expensive marketing campaigns, was one of the main reasons Nordea managed to acquire a dominant position in the online banking world.

Nonetheless, as a result of this shift into online banking, the number of Nordea branches in Finland decreased significantly during the 1990s – down from 1300 in 1991 to 400 in 2000. The number of employees shrunk to less than half during the same time period, falling from 22 000 to 10 600. Nordea had to negotiate with trade unions at great length. The bank handed out generous packages to avoid actually having to lay off employees. A further argument was that the online channel had led to a great increase in customer satisfaction and that this would make Nordea a more competitive and stable institution in the future. In addition, labour unions were told that Finland was at the leading edge of Internet banking and that it was necessary to make changes in the organizational structure in order to maintain this lead. Finally, Nordea pointed out that it was problematic to have employees do manual, repetitive and low-paid work and that it would be much more valuable to educate these people to do a more creative and interesting job.

Regarding competition from pure e-banks that operate without any significant branch infrastructure, Nordea is not overly concerned. Bo Harald points out: 'We haven't lost a significant amount of business to pure e-players. They may be cheaper than us but an e-bank has no personal selling capabilities, no customer base, and it costs them a fortune to acquire customers. [...] I am convinced people value the safety of branches and a trusted relationship. I believe traditional banks will play a central place in the e-economy. They have trust. They have established brands' (Echikson, 2001).

Once Nordea had established a large customer base both on the private and the corporate level, the bank decided to leverage the competencies to also provide e-business solutions. This move into e-business was meant to differentiate the bank from its competitors, since all of them had started to offer e-banking services as well.

Nordea credits two factors for the success of its e-business services. First, the secure and economical log-on code has proven to be highly beneficial. The code is a combination of: (1) a nine-digit customer number; (2) a one-time code from a list or scratch card; and (3) a sign-out code that is chosen and sent out by the central server. For customers, this type of log-on code is highly convenient since they do not need to install software on their computer or carry around any password-generating devices. At the same time, the same code can be used in any computer, mobile phone, fixed line phone, or for TV banking, in addition to direct interaction with staff members in branches. This secure and convenient identification procedure provided the platform for the expansion into other e-business services.

Second, Nordea considers the support of sales staff as crucial for the success of its e-business services. The initial impetus was the bank's effort to move customers from the physical bricks-and-mortar branches into the e-banking channel. Once sales staff at the branch were convinced of the value of the online channel and had received the appropriate training for advising customers regarding the new channel, it became relatively easy to acquaint them with the subsequent e-business initiatives.

The main e-business services that Nordea currently offers to its private and corporate customers are based on reusing existing information and technology. They are described in the sections below.

Through Nordea's *e-identification services*, Nordea customers can identify themselves on the Web sites of other participating companies and governmental agencies. Discussions with insurance companies in Finland led to an agreement that customers who log into their services can be sent to the bank and log on just the way they would for a regular banking session. However, instead of getting to their online accounts, they are routed to the insurance company's service. The e-id is now especially widely used in the public sector and organizations. In fact, the Finnish Ministry of Finance has officially stated that if customers need strong identification, they can and should use the bank's identification standards.

Consider the case of a citizen who wants to access the state pension system to find out the status of her pension balance in order to decide how much she needs to save for retirement. Initially, she accesses the state pension system's Web site with links to all major banks in Finland that provide e-identification services. She then chooses her bank, accesses the respective Web site and identifies herself with her one-time password. Upon registering there, she can switch to other services, including the state pension service, while staying within the identified area. This state pension site is accessed 2000 times per day.

The e-identification service has proven to be so convincing that the Finnish Post Office has decided to stop its own identification service. Instead, the Post Office uses banks because it would be too expensive to have a reliable identification service only for its own services.

The *e-signature service* came about by 'accident'. When Nordea told executives from Sonera, the largest telecommunications operator in Finland, that customers could get a loan online, Sonera asked if it would also be possible to sign a phone contract using the same system. Nordea agreed with Sonera that they would send all customers interested in an online phone contract a link to Nordea's Solo Internet bank Web site where they could identify themselves and then sign the contract. This system was later extended to other businesses such as utilities that wanted to provide e-signatures for their contracts and has by now become a common e-signature standard in Finland.

Through Nordea's *e-billing services*, companies can send their invoices electronically to the bank, which then forwards them to customers with e-banking agreements, while those customers without e-banking accounts are automatically sorted out, and receive printed invoices via postal mail. Customers who get their invoice through their e-bank connection are notified and asked: 'Do you want to pay this bill?'; they can approve the payment with a mouse click and the bill is paid.

When e-commerce started to gain importance in the late 1990s, e-billing was introduced as a consequence of customers' unwillingness to pay with credit cards, as there was a lot of discussion around the issue of security. In addition, not all online shoppers had credit cards but they all owned a banking account. Based on this information, product developers at Nordea asked whether it would be possible to reuse the payment mechanisms used for bills for additional real-time e-commerce transactions between Nordea accounts. This service was first used in 1998 by Finland's main telephone companies, which started to send their invoices to their customers directly through the Internet.

In Sweden, Nordea is sending out invoice files to a Nordea switch, which are then distributed to private and large corporate customers (e.g. a telecoms company that sends invoices to its customers). As banks throughout Scandinavia increasingly start to provide e-billing services, real-time payments are also gaining in importance since they offer the opportunity to make business 'stateless'; buyers and sellers meet, close the deal, exchange payment, possibly exchange the already paid invoice if needed, and part without anything left in payables or receivables.

Through the *e-salary function*, companies can send income statements straight to the e-bank of their employees thereby eliminating the need for printed salary statements sent via postal mail. Introducing the e-salary functionality required only a small effort, since it essentially reuses the e-billing service.

The *e-payment function* is an adapted version of the invoicing function, which online merchants on the Solo platform can use for settling payments. Using this function, a customer can go to the Web site of any online store in the Solo marketplace and place an order. Then he clicks on a link to the e-payment system of Nordea where he requests to receive an electronic invoice. Upon approving the payment with a mouse click, the money is transferred immediately into the seller's account. The benefits of this method are two-fold: (1) merchants do not need to send out a paper invoice anymore; and (2) they do not need to worry anymore whether buyers will pay the invoice.

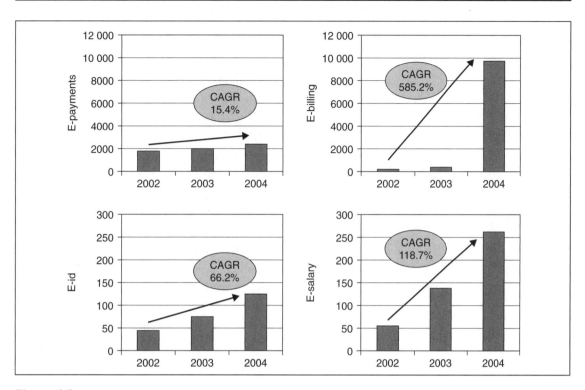

Figure 1.3
The evolution of the usage of e-business services (source: Nordea)

The evolution of the different e-business services between 2002 and 2004 is illustrated in Figure 1.3. The statistics refer to corporate and public service customers who want to start offering these services to their customers. For instance, the e-billing chart shows that in 2004 almost 10 000 companies, including large telecommunications or energy corporations, started sending e-invoices to their customers using the Nordea e-business platform. The compounded annual growth rate (CAGR) for e-payments, e-identification, e-salary and e-billing was respectively 15, 66, 119 and 585 per cent.

NORDEA EXAMINED USING THE DIT

The goal of this section is to analyse what type of innovation e-banking has been to the business model of Nordea. To do so, we systematically analyse the case of Nordea along the strategic dimensions presented earlier: (1) organizational design; (2) structure of teams; (3) framing of the situation vis-à-vis the employees; (4) the strategy process; and (5) the design of the value chain.

■ *Organizational design.* As stated in the case, Nordea exploited e-banking entirely in-house as a joint effort by managers with product responsibility and the IT department of the bank. From the beginning, Nordea tried to engage all bank employees in the new processes. Thus, the size of the organization was, from the beginning, large. Consciously, the management of Nordea chose traditional channels, i.e. the retail banking outlets, to promote and sell the new e-banking services. The fact that this organizational approach proved to be successful in the case of Nordea suggests that e-banking is a sustaining innovation.

■ *Structure of teams.* As the case points out, initially support from top management was limited. The e-banking strategy was only embraced on a larger scale after promising sales statistics had arrived from the Helsinki region where e-banking had first been tested. However, even though the support was limited, Bo Harald and his team were able to push e-banking through the entire organization at a relatively early stage of the development of the online banking technology. According to the DIT, this could be explained by the fit of the e-banking solutions with the established organizational processes, i.e. the similarity of the e-banking value-network with the established value-network.

■ *Framing of the situation vis-à-vis the employees.* Through intelligent framing and adequate incentive systems Nordea was able to convince employees of the benefits brought about by the new banking channels. There were strong incentives for branch employees to move customers into the e-banking channel. Branch employees also understood that the new technology would make their jobs more interesting, since mechanical work would be substituted by customer-related activities. At the same time, management saw the enormous cost-saving potential of e-banking which was combined with high potential for sustainable and predictable growth. Hence, the success Nordea had in framing this situation as an opportunity both for management and employees also suggests that e-banking is a sustaining innovation.

■ *Strategy process.* The strategy followed by Nordea was that of an integrated leader (Iansiti *et al.*, 2003). This means that Nordea started very early to use e-banking technologies inside the parent organization. By doing so, Nordea was able to leverage synergies between traditional retail banking and e-banking. Because of its early start with e-banking, Nordea could afford to be patient before expecting substantial growth rates from the new channel. As Bo Harald explains: 'Yes, everything takes time. There are no fast take-offs. Most products take five years before they take off. It was that way with foreign payments. It has been available for a while, but all of a sudden it has gone from almost 0% to 34% of all payments in the past year' (Echikson, 2001). For the following two reasons, DIT would suggest that this type of strategy process is typical for sustaining innovations. First, the patience shown by top management can be explained by the similarities of the value-networks of traditional branch banking and e-banking. Second, Nordea's e-banking strategy which targeted both low-end and high-end customers would be highly untypical for disruptive innovations – where incumbents are primarily motivated to target high-end customers with better performing products and services. Good examples for this broad strategy are the e-business solutions described in the last section that target the whole spectrum of the customer base.

■ *Design of the value chain.* Nordea has the integrated business model of a traditional retail bank. This means that customers can choose from a wide range of services (e.g. transactions, brokerage, savings, etc.) provided by one integrated supplier. DIT suggests that if a company is successful with an integrated value chain, then it is located in sustaining circumstances where customers are underserved with respect to the traditionally most-valued performance criteria (Apigian *et al*, 2005). Otherwise, customers would be buying from modular vendors that bundle the services of multiple product providers. Thus, the DIT would point to the sustaining nature of e-banking as the explanation for the success of Nordea's integrated approach.

CONCLUSIONS AND FURTHER RESEARCH

In this chapter we addressed a fundamental problem of the disruptive innovation theory which lies in the difficulty in categorizing new technologies into sustaining and disruptive innovations. To illustrate this problem, we used the example of e-banking, whose disruptive nature is debated intensely among researchers in the field. In our analysis, we first discussed the basic principles of the disruptive innovation theory and, based on the theory, outlined five main strategic dimensions that incumbent firms need to address when they face disruptive circumstances in their industry. Following the logic of DIT, in order to succeed in disruptive circumstances, incumbents need to take specific actions, such as creating a spin-out organization or using an emergent strategy process. By the same logic, however, if incumbents are successful in using sustaining approaches it can be assumed that the innovation is of a sustaining nature.

The description and the analysis of the Nordea case showed, first, that the bank integrated the new technologies successfully into its business model and, second, that all the actions taken by the bank were those that are only appropriate in sustaining circumstances. We therefore concluded that e-banking was a sustaining innovation for Nordea.

We posit that the main reason for the success of Nordea's approach is that the two value-networks of traditional retail banking and e-banking show substantial similarities. This argument follows the reasoning by Christensen and Raynor (2003). Regardless of the channel that is used, customers value the trustworthiness of a bank, its convenience and pricing (i.e. interest rates and fees).

Established banks have typically built up a brand name of trust over many decades. In addition, their branch network reassures online banking customers that if they should encounter any problems, they have a physical location to go to. Thus, it is sensible for a bank with a strong brand such as Nordea to extend its name into the online channel. As Christensen and Raynor (2003) point out, 'when customers aren't yet certain whether a product's performance will be satisfactory, a well crafted brand can step in and close some of the gap between what customers need and what they fear they might get if they buy the product from a supplier of unknown reputation'. Regarding convenience, most customers seem to value the availability of a physical branch that allows for face-to-face interaction with knowledgeable staff. Finally, the price dimension is closely related to the issue of trust. Banks with an established brand name and a sizeable customer base will typically find it much easier and more cost efficient to move their customers into the online channel than pure e-banks who need to build up a brand from scratch and attract customers (who typically already have accounts with other banks). On the basis of this assessment, it is unlikely that disruption will take place in the retail banking industry in the near to medium-term future.

Having stated this conclusion, it is important to look at the limitations of this research and to outline areas for future research activity. An interesting follow-up on this study would be the application of different methodological approaches to the analysis of the Nordea case. For instance, building on the work of Campbell and Frei (Campbell, 2003;

Campbell and Frei, 2004), it would be potentially insightful to analyse the cost structures of different business models and the profitability of different customer segments.

Furthermore, it would be useful to collect a broader sample both of pure e-banks and integrated clicks-and-mortar banks to challenge the conclusions presented in this chapter. In this context, it would be of particular interest to conduct a study across different continents and cultures since banking systems and processes differ from country to country. For instance, while the USA is a cheque-based society, Finland had an established gyro system even before the advent of the Internet. Since the services offered through the new e-banking channels were built to a large extent on this gyro system, the implementation of e-banking presented a sustaining innovation to Nordea. Thus, it is possible that the disruptiveness of the Internet to retail banking differs depending on the country at hand. A cross-country analysis would potentially allow us to resolve certain contradictions between our findings and the implications of Frei's research.

However, regardless of these limitations, it is useful to continue analysing e-banking using the toolset of the DIT. By doing so, we first expect to gain deeper insights into the banking industry itself and its evolution over time. Second, we hope to further develop the evaluation framework that was used in this chapter, which can then be transferred to other industries. This research should finally also help us strengthen our understanding of the disruptive innovation theory.

REFERENCES

Adner, R. (2002). When are technologies disruptive? A demand-based view of the emergence of competition. *Strategic Management Journal*, 23 (8), 667–688.

Apigian, C., Ragu-Nathan, T. S., Ragu-Nathan, B. and Kunnathur, A. (2005). Internet technology: the strategic imperative. *Journal of Electronic Commerce Research*, 6 (2), 123–145.

Boss, S., McGranahan, D. and Mehta, A. (2000). Will the banks control online banking? *The McKinsey Quarterly*, No. 3, 70–77.

Bower, J. L. (1970). *Managing the Resource Allocation Process*. Richard D. Irwin.

Campbell, D. (2003). *The Cost Structure and Customer Profitability Implications of Electronic Distribution Channels: Evidence from Online Banking*. Harvard Business School Working Paper, Boston.

Campbell, D. and Frei, F. (2004). The persistence of customer profitability: empirical evidence and implications from a financial service firm. *Journal of Service Research*, 7 (2), 107–123.

Carlile, P. R. and Christensen, C. (2005). *The Cycles of Theory Building in Management Research,* Harvard Business School Working Paper, Boston.

Christensen, C. (1997). *The Innovator's Dilemma.* Harper Business Essentials.

Christensen, C., Anthony, S. A. and Roth, E. A. (2004). *Seeing What's Next: Using the Theory of Disruptive Innovation to Predict Industry Change.* Harvard Business School Press.

Christensen, C. and Raynor, M. E. (2003). *The Innovator's Solution.* Harvard Business School Press.

Christensen, C., Verlinden, M. and Westermann, P. (2002). Disruption, disintegration and the dissipation of differentiability. *Industrial & Corporate Change,* 11 (5), 955–993.

Echikson, W. (2001). The dynamo of e-banking. *Business Week,* April 16.

Eisenhardt, K. M. (1989). Building theories from case study research. *Academy of Management Review,* 14 (4), 532–550.

Gary, L. (2004). *Taking Disruption to the Bank.* Strategy and Innovation Article No. S0409B. Harvard Business School Press.

Gilbert, C. and Bower, J. L. (2002). Disruptive change: when trying harder is part of the problem. *Harvard Business Review,* 80 (5), 95–101.

Hitt, L. M. and Frei, F. (2002). Do better customers utilize electronic distribution channels? The case of PC banking. *Management Science,* 48 (6), 732–748.

Li, F. (2001). The Internet and the deconstruction of the integrated banking model. *British Journal of Management,* 12 (4), 307–322.

Iansiti, M., McFarlan, F. W. and Westerman, G. (2003). Leveraging the incumbent's advantage. *Sloan Management Review,* 44 (4), 58–64.

Pfeffer, J. and Salancik, G. R. (1978). *The External Control of Organizations: A Resource Dependence Perspective.* Harper & Row.

Reinhardt, G. and Lévesque, M. (2004). A new entrant's decision on virtual vs. bricks-and-mortar retailing. *Journal of Electronic Commerce Research,* 5 (3), 136–152.

Shim, N. (2001). Strategies for competitive advantage in electronic commerce. *Journal of Electronic Commerce Research,* 2 (4), 164–171.

Useem, J. (1999). Internet defense strategy: cannibalize yourself. *Fortune,* 6 September, 121–134.

Yin, R. (1984). *Case Study Research.* Sage Publications.

CHAPTER 2

Online delivered content: concept and business potential[1]

Claudia Loebbecke and Claudio Huyskens

▮ INTRODUCTION

Electronically traded online delivered content (ODC) is data, information and knowledge traded on the Internet or through other online means (Dewan *et al.*, 2000). ODC includes online newspapers, magazines, blogs, music, podcasts, education, searchable databases, consulting, and eventually expertise and ideas.

When trading ODC, the full commercial cycle – offer, negotiation, order, delivery, payment – can be conducted via a network such as the

---

[1] For an earlier and shorter version of this chapter see Loebbecke (1999b).

Internet. In addition to the issues inherent in trading physical goods on the Web, trading ODC on the Internet raises concerns such as version control, authentication of the product, control over intellectual property rights (IPR) (Meisel and Sullivan, 2002; Waller *et al.*, 2002) and the development of profitable intra- and interorganizational business models (Werbach, 2000).

This chapter outlines the growing importance and possible business models for ODC. The chapter attempts to position electronic trading in ODC within the wider field of electronic commerce (Kalakota and Whinston, 1996; Loebbecke and Powell, 1999). It identifies its distinctive characteristics compared to other forms of trading content and to electronic trading in physical goods. Important ODC peculiarities are identified and analysed. Previous cases have already illustrated the initial application of the ODC concept (Loebbecke, 1999a). Current ODC offerings built from existing content are presented based on a current case of a medium-sized specialized publisher. The case shows how the coverage of value chain activities depends on the specific ODC offering. Financial impacts illustrate the success from adding ODC to the product or service portfolio. Finally, lessons learned from the case and some overall conclusions are outlined.

ONLINE DELIVERED CONTENT – THE CORE OF THE INTANGIBLE ECONOMY

A major characteristic of the Internet Economy (also commonly referred to as the Digital Economy or Information Society) is its shift to the intangible. The creation and manipulation of dematerialized content has become a major source of economic value (Wang *et al.*, 1998) and this development further accelerates under the current buzzword of Web 2.0. This move to the intangible affects all sectors and activities. It profoundly transforms economic relationships and interactions, the way firms and markets are organized and the way in which transactions are carried out. It also leads to dissemination and reconfiguration of value chains (see Figure 2.1). However, the intangible economy is not limited to the Internet. Analogue technologies such as radio and television are also to be considered integral parts – and these are used to an increasing degree. Driven by technological convergence, further media integration is under way.

To some extent the intangible economy runs squarely against the conventional logic of economics. Intangible goods are not limited by

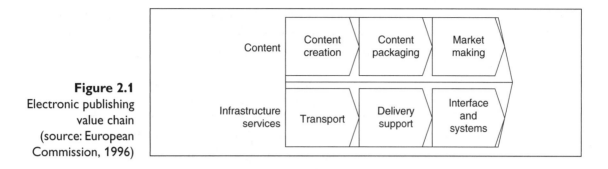

Figure 2.1
Electronic publishing
value chain
(source: European
Commission, 1996)

physical constraints and are not limited to traditional economic characteristics, such as 'durable', 'lumpy', 'unique' and 'scarce'. Instead, intangible goods can simultaneously be 'durable and ephemeral, lumpy and infinitely divisible, unique and ubiquitous, scarce and abundant' (Gelfand, 2004; Goldfinger, 1998). The business of purely intangible goods is radically different from conventional electronic commerce areas, which focus on trading or preparing to trade physical goods or hybrids between physical and intangible goods. Trading intangible goods has demanded adaptations in the way business is conducted. As a consequence, new business models have emerged and traditional business processes have been changed.

Classical economic theory does not usually address the issue of information, content or knowledge as a tradable good. The value of information is traditionally seen as derived exclusively from reducing uncertainty. In the Internet economy, however, information/content is simultaneously a production asset and a good.

From a supplier's perspective, the growing importance of intangible assets and the resulting complexity can be seen in the huge differences between book value and stock market values. These differences can partly be explained by the crucial role attributed to brands, content, publishing rights and intellectual capital, which may emerge via, be embedded in, or be stimulated by, ODC. The implied problem of pricing the value of information/content has so far received most attention in the context of managerial accounting when discussing the issues of: (1) consistent value measuring; and (2) the negligibility of costs for acquiring and creating intangible assets. In the rest of the chapter the concept of intangible assets will not be further pursued. However, suppliers' perspectives allow helpful insights into accounting and measuring aspects of intangible goods, and thus can well contribute to developing business models for electronically trading intangible goods and especially ODC.

The following focuses on intangible goods in general and ODC as one of its core representatives. The inherent logic of dematerialization is outlined in the context of ODC peculiarities.

Online delivered content – a special kind of intangible good

ODC is a particular kind of intangible good. In the literature, the term 'intangibility' refers to two rather different concepts. Levitt (1981) suggests that the terms 'goods' and 'services' be replaced by 'tangibles' and 'intangibles', and hence observes that, in their production and delivery mode, intangible products are highly people-intensive. This does not really match with a more recent interpretation of 'intangibility' aiming at non-material goods (but not services), often expressible in bits and bytes (Meinkoehn, 1998). While today most products contain intangible aspects such as know-how or brand recognition, this chapter considers ODC to be a counterexample of 'all products have elements of tangibility and intangibility' (Levitt, 1981: 101). ODC – by definition – has no tangible components.

Consequently, electronic infrastructure requirements for electronic trading (including delivery) in ODC are significantly higher than for electronic trading of tangible goods not delivered via the infrastructure (usually the Web). However, taking into account that no physical infrastructure is needed, the total infrastructure requirements for trading in ODC are comparatively low (and independent of the distance to be bridged).

Online delivered content – a special kind of experience good

Another common approach for clustering products is grouping them into 'search goods' and 'experience goods' (Peterson *et al.*, 1997). The quality of search goods can be determined without actually using them. With experience goods quality is learned from experiencing the product, i.e. from using the good. Most forms of ODC belong to the group of experience goods – the quality of content is only learned from using/consuming it. However, treating ODC as an experience good (i.e. letting potential clients 'experience' ODC) implies giving the actual content away for free (i.e. not trading it) and, in all likelihood, counting on receiving revenue via some synergy mechanisms. Unfortunately, once a potential customer has experienced ODC, he has no more reason to buy it. Suppliers of ODC try to solve this dilemma by shifting ODC as much as possible into the category of search goods. Possible steps for this are establishing strong brand reputation for Web sites, publishers, and so on, or offering abstracts, sample chapters or reviews as triggers to buy the whole product.

TOWARDS A FRAMEWORK OF ONLINE DELIVERED CONTENT

The above definition of ODC is derived from investigating the range of instances covered by Choi *et al.*'s (1997) description of the 'core of electronic commerce', also termed 'fully digital business'. They differentiate three dimensions: 'products', 'agents' (or players) and 'processes', which all are divided into 'physical' and 'digital'. This is shown in Figure 2.2.

The distinction between *physical* and *digital products* appears self-evident. According to Choi *et al.* 'anything that one can send and receive over the Internet has the potential to be a digital product' (1997: 62). Similarly, *agents* (or players) are 'sellers, buyers, intermediaries and other third parties such as governments and consumer advocacy groups' (p. 17). Physical players show up in person, digital players communicate via an electronic interface. For instance, electronic

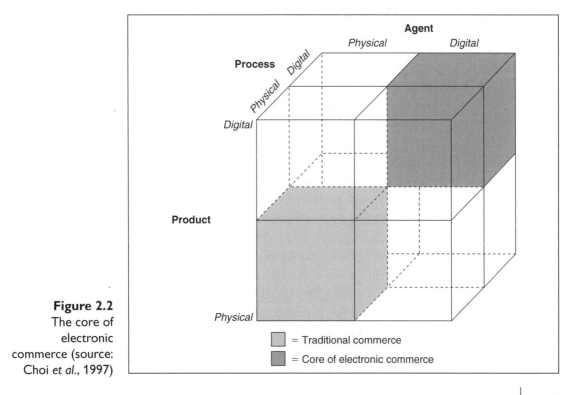

Figure 2.2
The core of electronic commerce (source: Choi *et al.*, 1997)

shoppers are considered to be digital players. The distinction between physical and digital processes depicted on the third axis seems to be as easy as the product dimension: 'visiting a store is a physical process, whereas searching on the Web is a digital process' (p. 17).

Regarding the product dimension, Choi *et al.*'s list of examples ranges from information in general, letters, postcards, credit card information, airline or concert tickets, to 'hybrid digital products' such as smart appliances. A good example for the latter is a Web-based navigation system that includes map information, and combined with Global Positioning (GPS) data and target specifications acts as a smart appliance. A more unusual, futuristic example is an intelligent toothbrush – this could take a sample of one's saliva, analyse selected aspects, transfer data to a connected server and start blinking in case of any unwanted bacteria.

In this context, the term 'digital' is clear. However, the term 'product' needs further clarification. As illustrated below, only some of the products falling under Choi *et al.*'s definition of digital products are also ODC.

To achieve this additional clarification of ODC, the introduction of a new dimension referring to the value of the digital product is suggested. It distinguishes 'bundled' or 'supported' versus 'unbundled' or 'stand-alone' digital products.

Traditionally, intangible goods were always bundled with some physical means. For centuries, content and physical medium were tightly linked, with the stronger value component being on the content side. Hence, the overall products were unique or reproducible only on a comparatively small scale (e.g. a theatre performance required a stage). Later storage and replication technologies have loosened the link between content and physical medium. As a result, goods with identical content appear in different forms and packages. For instance, certain songs appear on many different CD-ROMs, USB-enabled storage devices, and so on; news items can be printed in newspapers and magazines, shown on television, presented on a radio network or be distributed via an online network like the Internet. Thus, the importance of bundling content to a specific medium has decreased significantly with the emergence of the Internet.

The term 'ODC', as defined and applied here, is limited to 'unbundled', 'stand-alone' products consisting just of content/information. Hence, the term ODC implies that *only* the content is the object of a transaction – no physical product is shifted among suppliers, customers or other players.

The distinction between *physical* and *digital players* is more problematic. Even if players use a software-based agent, they are still a 'physical' legal entity (person, company or institution). Online shoppers are also to be viewed as physical shoppers – just not located inside the store. Following Choi *et al.*'s (1997) concept there cannot be any combination of a physical player executing a digital process; the example of the online shopper shows that running a digital process also makes the player digital. Since this still implies physical players (who may be supported by software/a digital agent), this dimension will be omitted when clarifying the term ODC.

Concerning 'processes', we concur with Choi *et al.*'s differentiation of *physical* and *digital processes*. In the following, the focus is only on those 'digital' processes that are part of a complete 'digital' cycle executed – or at least executable – over the electronic infrastructure. Offline processes refer to those cases in which certain 'sub'processes (e.g. product selection, production, market research, searches, ordering, payment, delivery or consumption) are not executed via the infrastructure.

Thus, the dimensions underpinning the proposed definition of ODC are as follows (see Figure 2.3). The 'product dimension' taken from Choi *et al.* is retained. A distinction between 'bundled and unbundled value' of the product traded is added. The 'agent/player dimension' is dropped, as it has no relevance to digital players. Finally the 'process dimension' is kept, stressing that digital processes are those in which *all* subprocesses are executed online. Strictly speaking, the idea of

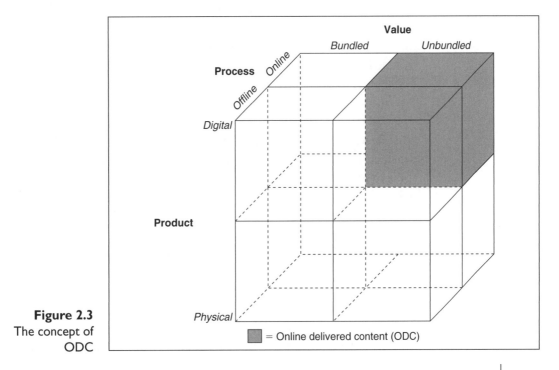

Figure 2.3
The concept of
ODC

unbundled value is implied in 'online processes' if the complete trading cycle also comprises product/value delivery. From a practical point of view, however, it is useful to stress the concept of unbundled product value separately. The following three examples further illustrate the ODC concept.

A first example is *music*. ODC refers to music that can be downloaded from virtual music stores such as Apple's iTunes on the Web. Afterwards, with several restrictions, it can be added to storage media such as MP3 players, hard disks or optical media such as CD or DVD (Pachet, 2003). ODC does *not* include the ordering of suitable storage media to be delivered to one's home, since ODC – by definition – refers *only* to the content and excludes the need for any physical medium.

A second example refers to *databases* offered by online bookstores and various kinds of content offered on Web pages maintained by television stations. The information/content contained in those Web sites is a form of ODC, even if it is not usually traded separately (Loebbecke *et al.*, 1998). Possibilities for commercializing such content could be 'pay per view', 'pay per page' or 'pay per time' concepts. By trying to sell such content (instead of offering it for free and counting on positive impact on other product lines such as books or TV programmes) suppliers would rely on the actual value that potential customers associate with it (regarding pricing issues and limits of cross-subsidizing – see the next section).

The third example to be mentioned – *tickets to planes, trains or concerts* – is actually a counterexample. It shows that even though information is increasingly detached from traditionally physical products, not all this information automatically converts to ODC. The example illustrates the difference between digital products as analysed by Choi *et al.* (1997) and ODC as introduced above. Choi *et al.* suggest 'digital products are not limited to information or "infotainment" products. All paper-based products, like posters, calendars, and all sorts of tickets … can be converted into or replaced by digital counterparts' (1997: 20). While in the early days of the Web tickets were subject to security constraints and still physically printed (Loebbecke, 2003), today, train, plane or concert tickets can be ordered and received online. Current technology already allows individuals to either print tickets on their own printer or show up with an authorization code replacing the printed ticket. Thereby individuals have been taking over certain functions that travel agencies or event agencies used to genuinely fulfil in the past. *However*, for consumers this is not the full delivery cycle. Consumers do not pay for the piece of paper called a ticket, but for 'being moved' from A to B or for attending a concert/stage performance. Those services of 'being moved' or 'concert performance' are the actual values bought, and these will never be delivered via any technical infrastructure (at least not within the limits of current imagination). Therefore, a ticket, even if bought and – with regard to the specific piece of paper – delivered over the Web does not represent unbundled, stand-alone value of content. It does not belong to ODC as understood in this chapter. (For simplicity reasons, this illustration leaves out the possibility of reselling a ticket and thus giving it a monetary function.)

ONLINE DELIVERED CONTENT – CHARACTERISTICS AND CLASSIFICATION

In general, ODC is characterized by three fundamental attributes (Choi *et al.*, 1997; Goldfinger, 1997):

1. *Indestructibility/non-subtractivity.* The same ODC can be consumed repetitively either by the same consumer or by a different one. Consumption by one person does not reduce anyone else's consumption.
2. *Transmutability.* ODC is easy to modify, thus leading to enormous product differentiation and customization.
3. *Reproducibility.* Fast and cheap reproducibility raises – among other aspects – issues of copyright protection and economies of scale.

As a consequence of these characteristics, exclusivity of ODC may be difficult to durably maintain. Sharing may be simultaneous or sequential and affects the allocation of property rights. While sellers of physical goods lose their property right, a seller of ODC may continue to hold it. Even 'illegally sharing' ODC often causes positive network externalities, which may even exceed the cost of sharing if caught. Once ODC has positive network externalities, control over reproduction and sharing is the primary objective of copyright protection.

Related to the issue of externalities is the issue of value generation. Often there is no direct link between a transaction and the generation of value. Furthermore, ODC value can hardly be measured solely in monetary terms. For instance, the appreciation of free television broadcasts could be measured in terms of viewing time and viewer numbers, while appreciation of academic papers (increasingly provided as ODC) may be measured in terms of the number of citations. Indirect value creation and the related problem of ODC value measurement lead to the problem of adequately pricing ODC (discussed later in this chapter).

A next step is to *classify* ODC products, i.e. to look at different criteria for further distinguishing homogeneous kinds of products *within* the still rather broad category of ODC. Five dimensions for classifying general digital products are outlined by Choi *et al.* (1997): 'transfer mode', 'timeliness', 'intensity in use', 'operational usage' and 'externalities'. These are analysed below for their relevance to ODC.

Transfer mode: delivered versus interactive products

ODC is, by definition, delivered. However, the differentiation between delivered and interactive transfer modes is becoming increasingly difficult. Notwithstanding, as long as content consumption is initiated based on a 'pull approach', this implies a certain degree of interactivity. Therefore, this chapter prefers to distinguish between ODC based on push and pull approaches. Further, those ODC products delivered via a pull approach can be further differentiated based on the degree of customization resulting from interactive communication. Clearly, these two dimensions are highly interdependent: push-based delivery excludes strong customization based on interactive communication; pull-based delivery allows for all degrees of customization.

Timeliness: time dependence versus time independence

ODC may be very time dependent (e.g. stock market information), rather time independent (e.g. dictionary information) or somewhere in the middle, e.g. street maps for drivers, hotel information and phone numbers. The criterion of 'timeliness' will be important for identifying homogeneous packages of ODC to be traded based on consistent business models.

Intensity in use: single-use versus multiple-use products

Similar to the previous criterion, 'intensity in use' is an important aspect for further classifying ODC. There is a significant overlap between 'timeliness' and 'intensity in use' – only rather time-independent ODC will be used more frequently, i.e. more intensively. However, the two criteria have different implications for trading.

Operational usage: executable program versus fixed document

Fixed documents delivered electronically are ODC. Executable programs are only counted as ODC if their focus is on the content execution provides. It may well be that a certain form of delivering content includes executable components. For instance, whenever users can determine the search function, the content includes some operational features in addition to the content in the narrow sense of the word.

Externalities: positive versus negative

Externalities refer to economic consequences that are not fully accounted for by the price or market system. Different kinds of externalities are a valid criterion for further classifying ODC. For example, positive network externalities imply that the value of the product increases the more people use it (e.g. academic papers or awareness-raising content about medical innovations). Negative externalities occur when the use of ODC is a zero-sum game. This means that whenever someone gains (from consuming ODC), someone else loses. Examples include all kinds of competitive content, e.g. for information related to research and development (R&D).

ONLINE DELIVERED CONTENT – ISSUES OF PRICING

Conventional pricing and transaction mechanisms are barely suitable for capturing the economic value of ODC. The price of a product normally consists of three elements: production (and logistics) costs, coordination costs and the profit margin (Benjamin and Wigand, 1995). Coordination costs include the transaction (or governance) costs of all the information processing necessary to coordinate the work of people and machines that perform the primary processes (Malone *et al.*, 1987). It is now becoming clear that – with variable production (and logistics) costs near zero, drastically reduced transactions costs due to information and communication technology (ICT) usage, and eroding profit margins in current business models – new concepts have to be put in place for determining ODC prices (Johnston and Mak, 2000).

Production costs cannot be used as a guideline for pricing since there is no link between input and output. Mass consumption does not require mass production. Economies of scale are determined by consumption, not by production. Economies of scale in ODC production are limited, but economies of scale in ODC distribution can be significant due to a combination of high fixed costs of creating the necessary infrastructure and low variable costs of using it. Economies of scale in distribution are accentuated by consumption characteristics: consumers tend to use the supplier with the largest variety even though they typically take advantage of less than 5 per cent of the choice (Goldfinger, 1994).

Traditionally the pricing of content has been based on the delivery medium – mostly measured in convenience – rather than on actual quality (Goldfinger, 1997). For instance, the price of a book depends heavily on print quality and the number of pages, while the price for an excellent book is often the same as for a poor one. Electronic trading in ODC implies unbundling: content can be priced separately from the medium allowing for price differentiation based on the estimated value of the content. The unbundling, however, also raises problems. Administration becomes more complex, and cross-subsidies between profitable and non-profitable (but nonetheless desirable) content on offer diminish.

A consumer's willingness to pay is often influenced by consumption or non-consumption of other consumers. Accordingly, it is not an adequate approach to assess the value of ODC, given the ease of replication/sharing and associated externalities. Further, it is often difficult for the customer to determine whether it is worthwhile to obtain a given 'piece of ODC' without knowing its content (Schlee, 1996).

Furthermore, the pricing of ODC raises the fundamental issue of inherent volatility of valuation when the value of ODC is highly time sensitive. For example, stock market information may be worth millions in the morning and have little value in the afternoon.

The range of ODC pricing schemes has broadened and become more sophisticated since the early days of the Internet. The Internet provides a variety of possibilities for selling, sharing and giving away. Moreover, consumers can be charged based on the actual 'use of ODC' or based on fixed access charges. In addition, there are pricing models that imply giving actual goods away for free and then charging for complementary services, updates, and so on.

Offering ODC over an extended period of time has led to the establishment of electronic communities. Following Armstrong and Hagel (1996), value from electronic communities can be created in five different ways: usage fees, content fees, transactions (commissions), advertising and synergies with other parts of the business. Translating these opportunities for income to the narrower defined area of ODC, *usage fees* models subsume 'fixed subscriptions', 'paying per page' or 'paying per time period' independent of the quality of the content. *Content fees* are often based on 'fixed amounts per page', but should tackle the issue of valuing the content (particularly for quality or relevance). *Commissions and advertising income* are triggered by attractive ODC on display. Strictly speaking, however, the subsequent income does not stem from ODC, but from either attracting customers to a page regardless of its content or from offering some 'empty space' for third party advertising in addition to the actual ODC offered (Loebbecke *et al.*, 1998).

Economists have been developing theoretical solutions to the problem areas mentioned. However, some of the mechanisms developed (e.g. MacKie-Mason and Varian, 1995) demand an enormous amount of data, thus questioning the trade-off between allocative efficiency and operational cost effectiveness (Mitchell and Vogelsang, 1991).

ONLINE DELIVERED CONTENT – IMPACTS OF ABUNDANCE

While conventional logic of economics is concerned with scarcity, the dematerialization logic inherent in ODC is concerned with abundance (Goldfinger, 1997). ODC is extremely cheap to replicate and is not eliminated through consumption (i.e. it has non-subtractivity). The resulting abundance of production is followed by the abundance of accumulation leading to a dramatically expanding imbalance between supply and demand. Efficient management of ODC overload requires yet more information/content. Information about information has become a growing business – as examples of search engine business models illustrate.

Abundance and resulting ODC overload – the huge variety of ODC available to almost everybody – confront consumers with a dilemma. Customers want to take advantage of the increased choice of ODC, and at the same time they seek to minimize the costs of searching. In order to respond to the first objective, new modes of consumption have emerged: 'zapping', 'browsing' or 'surfing'. These are characterized by a short attention span, latency, high frequency of switching and capriciousness. The distinction between consumption and non-consumption becomes difficult, rendering pricing problems even more intractable. The expanded choice of content makes consumer choice more difficult, thus continuously raising the cost of acquiring information about the content. To minimize these costs, choice is increasingly determined by criteria other than product characteristics, e.g. brand familiarity or fashion (Goldfinger, 1997).

The traditional rationale for the existence of companies, as articulated by Coase and others, is the minimization of transaction costs (Coase, 1974; Williamson and Winter, 1993). This analysis is no longer generally valid. Not only has ICT dramatically reduced transaction costs, but the growing volume and importance of ICT-based intangible assets and artefacts has changed the nature of markets (Peterson *et al.*, 1997).

While traditional interfirm linkages may be modelled by input/output analyses to measure the economic impact of each player in an interorganizational value chain or network, the intangible economy has introduced another linkage among companies – the 'monitoring' linkage (Goldfinger, 1997). Low transaction costs lead to an excessive volume of transactions that generate 'noise' rather than useful content. An abundance of products and services stimulates the development of activities whose purpose is to monitor, evaluate and explain their characteristics and performance.

CASE STUDY: FALK

The following case study analyses the transition of a German cartography specialist that has changed its focus from only providing traditional goods to a combination of traditional goods and ODC. Looking at the completed transition helps to put the theoretical contribution discussed above into perspective. Further, the case delivers implications on how to apply the ODC concept in practical terms.

The roots of Falk

In 1945, the company's founder, Gerhard Falk, combined two ideas to satisfy the need for orientation support in the emerging large cities of the twentieth century. First, he noticed that the display of traditional cartographic techniques was not well suited for large cities where the display of every detail in the centre of the city was more important than the similar display of the outskirts. He developed a progressive scale that allowed the display of the centre of the city to be larger and in much more detail than the outskirts. Second, Gerhard Falk noticed that using a map in the city required easy handling of the map. Unfolding the entire map was not appropriate. He developed and patented a folding technique that allowed the user to skip through the map like a book, only unfolding a single area of interest.

Based on those two ideas, Falk expanded his company quickly from offering its first map illustrating the city of Hamburg in 1946 to other German cities. In 1950, Falk published its first foreign map, the map of Rome. In the 1990s, Falk became the largest city map publisher in the world.

In 1994, Falk started a new venture called GeoData (or Geographic Databases) focusing on publishing roadmaps. GeoData provided Falk's entry ticket into the later emerging navigation market. In 1998, Falk was bought by 'Mairs Geographischer Verlag' (Mairs Geographic Publishing) which, as of 2005, operates as MairDumont and ranks 11th in size (by revenue) among German book publishers.

Falk's ODC offerings

By the first half of the 1990s, cartographic raw data was recognized as a major asset. Falk started to digitize most of its maps, but did not shift all of its efforts into electronic maps. Instead, it maintained the traditional brands and map products. In parallel, it started Falk Marco Polo Interactive (FM-I), a subsidiary which concentrated on the exploitation of cartographic data in electronic products. Recently, FM-I has developed a broad portfolio of electronic products – a few are still bundled to storage or display media while others fit the ODC definition.

Falk Marco Polo Interactive licenses raw cartographic data to corporate customers for their respective applications. In this case, Falk's role in the value chain is restricted to content creation and – depending on specific requests – to parts of content packaging (see Figure 2.4). Similarly targeted at corporate customers, Falk Marco Polo Interactive offers the 'Falk Filialfinder' (Falk store locater) and the 'Falk Anfahrtsplaner' (Falk route planner), for corporate customers to integrate into their websites. The 'Filialfinder' allows companies to have all

Figure 2.4
Falk's value chain for raw cartographic data offering (source: after European Commission, 1996)

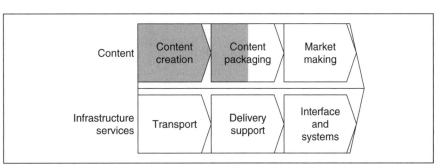

their outlets displayed in maps on their Web site. The 'Anfahrtsplaner' offers the opportunity to enter an address and subsequently receive the directions from that address to the corporate headquarters or any pre-specified company outlet. Concerning both products, additional address information of corporate customers is added to the cartographic data and then delivered online. Both products are prime examples of ODC offerings.

Falk Marco Polo Interactive also offers electronic products to end consumers. The 'Falk Navigator' series comprises of small GPS equipped handheld navigation devices. As physical handheld devices, the Navigator series cannot be classed as ODC though. However, software similar to that deployed in the navigator devices is combined with cartographic data and then offered for notebooks, mobile phones and personal digital assistants (PDAs). As Falk Marco Polo Interactive in this case sells the cartographic raw data together with the intelligent appliance – unattached from any physical device – it may be regarded as ODC.

Finally, Falk Marco Polo Interactive operates the Falk.de Web site with online route planning (http://www.falk.de). Users enter a starting point and a destination and the website displays the fastest or the shortest way to the destination along with a written description of the route. Users do not pay for this product; instead advertising customers pay for exposure to the users of Falk.de. With this offering, Falk covers the entire value chain from content creation to system and interface operation (see Figure 2.5).

Falk Marco Polo Interactive continues to acquire advertising customers for its product portfolio. It integrates the location information of advertising customers into the products. For example, car rental companies or hotel chains pay for having all their branches displayed in the maps.

In 2007, Falk Marco Polo Interactive does not plan to restrict its future navigation offerings. Future plans include those to expand services for travel preparations and for travel expense reports.

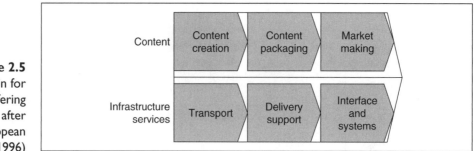

Figure 2.5
Falk's value chain for Falk.de offering (source: after European Commission, 1996)

Financial impact of offering ODC

Following an increase of 68 per cent in 2003, Falk Marco Polo Interactive reported a revenue increase of almost 150 per cent from €4.1 million to €10.2 million in 2004 and a further rise to €26 million in 2005. This comes only nine years after launching the first experimental ODC services. However, this also includes revenues from the Navigator handheld device series. Overall, adding ODC products to its portfolio has proven to be successful for Falk. In 2005, its total sales increased by 23 per cent from €123 million to €160 million.

Lessons learned from Falk's ODC experience

Traditionally, cartographic information and maps were sold to individuals that pay a price per good. On the Internet, free usage of content offerings has become very popular and introducing fees for content has been painful for several companies. The challenge for companies offering ODC lies in the acquisition of new revenue sources. Falk Marco Polo Interactive has selected fields to create revenue from:

- ODC is offered directly to corporate customers who can use, repackage and resell the content. Corporate customers pay directly; in B2B markets, no such for-free mentality exists.
- ODC is offered to individual users for free. Corporate advertising customers serve as a financing source. The success of such financing depends on the capability of integrating the advertising into the free content.

CONCLUSIONS

This chapter makes the point that within the wide field of e-commerce there are many fundamentally different products – both physical and digital – traded via various business models. One type of product defined here – online delivered content (ODC) – is particularly interesting. ODC is a good that is manufactured, delivered, supported and consumed via the Internet or similar networks. Typical examples of ODC are music, information and expert knowledge.

Traditional economic models based on scarcity and uniqueness leading to a market based on demand and supply do not apply to these types of products. Once created, ODC is extremely easy/cheap to replicate. Furthermore, distribution costs are almost zero, and most other transaction costs – except perhaps marketing and sales – barely exist.

ODC characteristics and classification criteria have been discussed in some detail in this chapter. The purpose is to warrant a careful investigation of the nature of ODC. Such an investigation is important either for preparing a business plan for a new offering or for researching the nature of a particular ODC.

The free offering of ODC has become extremely popular in the Internet arena and a multitude of traditional bricks-and-mortar companies and emerging start-up companies have started trading. The solutions offered by the company Falk have been briefly discussed in this chapter. Falk has taken advantage of its existing content archives and has been successful in offering customers (new as well as established) the possibilities of buying ODC. Questions still exist concerning pricing mechanisms, security, protection of intellectual property rights, and so on, for which solutions still have to be found in order to make ODC a viable business proposition. Answers to those questions promise significant theoretical advancement and attractive business opportunities. With the steadily increasing volume of material on the Web – information, content and knowledge – it seems an economic waste not to profitably exploit these untapped resources.

REFERENCES

Armstrong, A. and Hagel, J. (1996). The real value of online communities. *Harvard Business Review*, May–June, 134–141.

Benjamin, R. and Wigand, B. (1995). Electronic markets and the virtual value chains on the Information Superhighway. *Sloan Management Review*, Winter, 62–72.

Choi, S.-Y., Stahl, D. and Whinston, A. (1997). *The Economics of Electronic Commerce*. Macmillan Technical Publishing.

Coase, R. (1974). The market for goods and the market for ideas. *American Economic Review*, 64, 384–391.

Dewan, R., Freimer, M. and Seidman, A. (2000). Organizing distribution channels for information goods on the Internet. *Management Science*, 46 (4), 483–495.

European Commission (1996). *Strategic Developments for the European Publishing Industry towards the Year 2000 – Europe's Multimedia Challenge*. DG XIII/E. European Commission.

Gelfand, J. (2004). The ubiquity of grey literature in a connected content context. *Publishing Research Quarterly*, 20 (1), 54–61.

Goldfinger, C. (1994). *L'utile et le futile, l'economie de l'immateriél.* Editions Odile Jacob.

Goldfinger, C. (1997). Intangible economy and its implications for statistics and statisticians. *International Statistical Review*, 65, 191–220.

Goldfinger, C. (1998). Trading intangible goods. *Workshop on Electronic Commerce of Intangible Goods.* European Commission.

Johnston, R. and Mak, H. (2000). An emerging vision of Internet-enabled supply chain electronic commerce. *International Journal of Electronic Commerce*, 4 (4), 43–59.

Kalakota, R. and Whinston, A. (1996). *Electronic commerce: a manager's guide.* Addison-Wesley.

Levitt, T. (1981). Marketing intangible products and product intangibles. *Harvard Business Review*, May–June, 95–102.

Loebbecke, C. (1999a). A case study at the reference frontier. *Journal of Electronic Publishing*, 4, 4. www.press.umich.edu/jep/04-04/loebbecke.html

Loebbecke, C. (1999b). Electronic trading in online delivered content. *Proceedings of the Thirty-Second Hawaii International Conference on Systems Sciences*, Maui, Hawaii.

Loebbecke, C. (2003). E-business trust concepts based on seals and insurance solutions. *Information Systems and e-Business Management*, 1 (1), 55–72.

Loebbecke, C. and Powell, P. (1999). Electronic publishing: assessing opportunities and risks. *International Journal of Information Management*, 19, 293–303.

Loebbecke, C., Powell, P. and Trilling, S. (1998). Investigating the worth of Internet advertising. *International Journal of Information Management*, 18, 181–193.

MacKie-Mason, J. and Varian, H. (1995). Pricing the Internet. In *Public Access to the Internet* (B. Kahn and J. Keller, eds), Prentice Hall.

Malone, T., Yates, J. and Benjamin, R. (1987). The logic of electronic markets. *Harvard Business Review*, May–June, 166–172.

Meinkoehn, F. (1998). Electronic trade of intangible commodities: a technological and legal challenge. In *Electronic Commerce: Opening up New Opportunities for Business* (P. Timmers, B. Stanford-Smith and P. Kidd, eds), pp. 81–86, Cheshire-Hensbury.

Meisel, J. and Sullivan, T. (2002). The impact of the Internet on the law and economics of the music industry. *Info – The Journal of Policy, Regulation and Strategy for Telecommunications*, 4 (2), 16–22.

Mitchell, B. and Vogelsang, I. (1991). *Telecommunications Pricing.* Cambridge University Press.

Pachet, F. (2003). Content management for electronic music distribution. *Communications of the ACM*, 46 (4), 71–75.

Peterson, R., Balasubramanian, S. and Bronnenberg, B. (1997). Exploring the implications of the Internet for marketing. *Journal of the Academy of Marketing Science*, 25, 329–346.

Schlee, E. (1996). The value of information about product quality. *RAND Journal of Economics*, 27, 803–815.

Waller, A., Jones, G., Whitley, T., Edwards, J., Kaleshi, D., Munro, A., MacFarlane, B. and Wood, A. (2002). Securing the delivery of digital content over the Internet. *Electronics & Communication Engineering Journal*, 14 (5), 239–248.

Wang, R., Lee, Y., Pipino, L. and Strong, D. (1998). Manage your information as a product. *Sloan Management Review*, Summer, 95–105.

Werbach, K. (2000). Syndication: the emerging model for business in the Internet era. *Harvard Business Review*, 78 (3), 84–93.

Williamson, O. and Winter, S. (1993). *The Nature of the Firm*. Oxford University Press.

CHAPTER 3

Beyond the 'eBay of blank': next stage digital intermediation in electronic commerce

Alina M. Chircu, Robert J. Kauffman and Bin Wang

INTRODUCTION

Interactions between buyers and sellers in a market normally reflect the existence of a *transaction process*, in which goods or services are exchanged between customers and suppliers (Bakos, 1991). This process may involve none, one or several intermediaries, depending on the kind of the goods or services that are involved in the transaction, and other situational factors (Spulber, 1999) (see Figure 3.1).

Since the middle of the 1990s, new technologies for electronic commerce on the Internet have dramatically changed the spectrum of

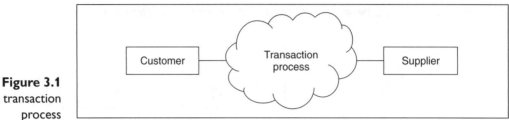

Figure 3.1
The transaction
process

possibilities for making transactions in the marketplace. Such technologies have also changed the manner in which the various players are able to interact (Benjamin and Wigand, 1995; Rayport and Sviokla, 1994; Whinston *et al.*, 1997), and the present value of growth opportunities that market-transforming technology companies create (Dehning *et al.*, 2003). Consider such well-known players in electronic commerce as Hotwire, Orbitz, Amazon and eBay. (See Appendix 3.1 at the end of this chapter for background information on all organizations mentioned in this chapter.) Hotwire has been highly successful in providing a buyer-driven marketplace for leisure travel services, putting some control back into the hands of the consumer, similar to the market pioneer, Priceline.com. Orbitz, meanwhile, emphasizes greater transparency on prices and travel itineraries for its customers, and has recently led the way towards reductions in the informational biases of online markets. Amazon, over the years, has embedded collaborative filtering technology that enables the appropriate book and movie titles to be shown to the right kinds of customers, in effect digitizing the expertise the firm has with respect to the market for books and DVDs, and the related consumer demand. And LetsBuyIt.com has created a group-buying auction market that permits consumers to engage in intermediated 'power buying', which results in lower prices as more buyers participate (Kauffman and Wang, 2002). eBay, as the title of this chapter suggests, has been highly successful over the years since it was founded in improving market liquidity for all kinds of goods. These include collectible goods, which do not always transact as easily as other commodity goods such as books, CDs and new cars. Today, they also include the stale inventories of major corporations, such as Best Buy in the United States, whose senior managers decide at some point that the time of sale becomes more important than the price of the sale. Such decisions warrant the use of an unbranded 'fire sale' auction channel, which eBay is able to supply.

Investors, observing the continuing digital industrial revolution, have also recognized the long-term value of the related stocks, especially for those companies which have been able to operate in *breakthrough markets*. Day *et al.* (2003) coined this term and contrasted it with *reformed markets*. The former is possible when the technologies of the Internet and e-commerce fundamentally change the basis for competition, lead to the creation of new products and services, and completely alter business processes. When more modest changes occur – for example, the rehosting of a business process with a similar design overall, or the use of similar selling mechanisms as in traditional stores, only in the online channel – reformed markets are more likely to be seen. These are less likely to win extraordinary value in the equity markets, though they may be critical to support a strong and effective multi-channel strategy. Some examples that come to mind are the large American retailers Wal-Mart, Target, the Home Depot and Best Buy, which collectively operate hundreds of physical stores, but also operate in the Internet channel with Walmart.com, Target.com, HomeDepot.com and BestBuy.com.

The reality of the late 1990s capital markets for e-commerce and dot.com firm equity, however, was well understood by David Baltaxe, an industry analyst for the Web-based e-journal *Current Analysis*. He noted the 'irrational exuberance' and inappropriate willingness to take risks of e-commerce sector investors, in spite of the sometimes sketchy and poorly thought out business plans that were offered:

> You have no idea how many companies come in with a five-minute pitch: 'We want to be the *eBay of blank*.' Just fill in the blank for a country. That's the entire business plan. (Baltaxe, 1999)

Today, the truth of Baltaxe's words continue to ring in our ears – as well as in the ears of venture capital investors, who lost a historically large amount of wealth during the 'dot.com crash' of 2000 and 2001. During that period of time, many of the market indicators had pointed towards high value for the new forms of digital intermediation that Internet firms were expected to be able to achieve in the financial markets.

We recognized some of the potential problems in this market when we wrote an earlier version of this chapter a number of years ago. The high market capitalizations of some of the best known dot.com firms of the time may not have had a rational basis in terms that an investment banker might understand in the markets we have today. Table 3.1 reports on the stock prices and market capitalizations of some of these dot.com firms in 1999, with updates for 2006. It is easy to see that both stock prices and market capitalizations are now more in line with those of traditional firms, and that a number of dot.com firms are no longer

Table 3.1

Stock price ranges, market capitalizations and acquisitions of leading e-commerce and related firms

Firm	1999 figures					2006 figures				
	52-wk low	52-wk high	Market price	# shares (mm)	Market cap ($mm)	52-wk low	52-wk high	Market price	# shares (mm)	Market cap ($mm)
● *Booksellers*										
Amazon	$13.37	$221.25	$115.25	163.122	$18 799.80	$34.41	$52.50	$26.78	418.942	$11 219.28
BN.com	$14.12	$26.62	$20.82	25.000	$520.50	40% owned by Barnes & Noble's Bookstore and 40% by Bertelsmann AG, 1999. Acquired: Barnes & Noble's bought back in early 2004 at $3 per share.				
Barnes & Noble's	$18.50	$40.25	$24.50	69.005	$1690.62	$32.64	$48.41	$26.41	84 180 000	$2223.19
● *E-auctions*										
eBay	$8.43	$234.00	$169.75	127 185 979	$21 589.82	$22.83	$47.86	$24.12	1415.394	$34 139.31
OnSale	$10.62	$108.00	$17.50	19 188 571	$335.80	Acquisition and name change: Egghead.com in November 1999.				
Priceline	$58.00	$165.00	$109.13	142 809 072	$15 584.04	$18.20	$32.66	$26.41	42.425	$1120.44
Sotheby's	$15.00	$47.00	$35.44	57 352 804	$2032.44	$15.01	$33.84	$28.43	63.657	$1681.17
uBid	$30.00	$189.00	$35.06	8 909 804	$312.40	$4.50	$7.20	$5.30	20.333	$107.77

● *E-brokers*										
Ameritrade	$5.62	$188.37	$85.31	58 570 901	$4996.83	$13.30	$26.37	$17.77	631.382	$11 219.66
DLJ Direct	$28.25	$45.62	$38.25	85 000 000	$3251.25	Acquired: Credit Suisse First Boston, 2000.				
E-Trade	$2.50	$72.25	$42.28	233 233 880	$9861.42	$14.70	$27.76	$23.42	425.924	$9975.14
Schwab	$18.50	$155.00	$104.44	406 352 986	$42 438.49	$12.75	$18.53	$15.97	1392.092	$22 231.70
● *Miscellaneous*										
AutoByTel	$15.50	$58.00	$21.69	17 858 674	$387.31	$2.80	$6.00	$3.20	42.332	$135.46
CDNow	$7.00	$39.25	$17.06	29 483 956	$503.07	Acquired: Amazon.com, 2002.				
Doubleclick	$6.75	$176.00	$87.50	39 580 000	$3463.25	Acquired: Click Holdings, Hellman & Friedman, and JMI Equity, 2005.				
MarketWatch	$45.50	$130.00	$50.00	11 750 000	$587.50	Acquired by Dow Jones and Co., 2005.				
Net Perceptions	$18.50	$35.00	$16.50	21 321 212	$351.80	$0.53	$0.90	$0.64	29.113	$18.63

Notes: 1999 data are as of 27 May 1999; 2006 data are as of 7 August 2006. Certain low and high prices do not reflect a 52-week period due to stock offerings. The initial public offering (IPO) of DLJDirect.com occurred on Wednesday, 25 May 1999. Net Perceptions' IPO occurred on Friday, April 23, 1999. BN.com completed its IPO offering on May 25, 1999. The traditional basis for evaluating equity prices fails in the case of Internet stocks. Equity values are typically computed using two bases: discounted current and future earnings and the present value of growth opportunities (PVGO). Since future growth opportunities are so uncertain for the companies listed, one expects to see large variances in Internet firm asset prices over time. The price ranges that are observed indicate the extent to which variations in value are observed, driven to a large extent by under-informed (but certainly interested) investors with 'great expectations' of performance. For additional information on equity evaluation in this area, the interested reader should see Burnham (1999), which did a good job to guide many individual investors during the dot.com bubble in the stock markets. Sources: Castonguay (1999), PR Newswire (1999), Quicken Excite (1999), Marketwatch.com (2006), Reuters.com (2006), and annual reports of firms.

operating on their own, as a result of successful sell-out strategies, acquisitions under market pressure and bankruptcies.

In this rapidly changing environment of innovation, there are many products and services that could not be offered in the way they are offered today without these technologies. Along with eBay, FirstAuction.com, Onsale.com and uBid.com, among others – the new electronic consumer auction markets of the Internet – come to mind. These digital intermediaries were among the first to create opportunities for transactions to occur that simply did not previously exist in the marketplace (Bailey and Bakos, 1997). They also offered – and sometimes required – new roles that intermediaries had not taken on before. Furthermore, the traditional processes associated with transacting may have been fundamentally changed. As a result, some intermediaries saw their roles threatened by new competitors that appeared in the market in the late 1990s. This led to new opportunities for IT-focused middlemen (Bakos, 1998).

Most digital intermediaries support the interaction of buyers and sellers on the Internet. As a result, we have seen the emergence of a new organizational form that moves in to fill a gap in the existing organization of various industries: the *digital intermediary* or *cybermediary* (Sarkar *et al.*, 1995). This digital support role – emphasizing *buyer/seller intermediation* – generally is not assumed by traditional players right away and, as a result, we have often seen new entrants to the market acting in this capacity.

ANALYSING DIGITAL INTERMEDIATION

According to the Gartner Group, there were about 300 electronic marketplaces operating on the Internet in 1999. Laseter *et al.* (2001), in a Booz Allen Hamilton study, documented 2233 announced e-markets; however, fewer – about 1802 – could be identified with Web sites on the Internet. What kinds of benefits were these digital procurement intermediaries intending to create along the way? These include: matching buyers with suppliers; providing a level of trust that no other party to the transaction could deliver; offering product-related and transactional expertise and informational support; and supplying assurance that transactions can be successfully completed (Bakos, 1998; Dai and Kauffman, 2002).

However, a number of interesting questions relate to digital intermediaries on the Internet. Have they been able to successfully compete with more established players in the marketplace? What kinds of strategies have made them most successful? Is the role of the cybermediary a defensible and sustainable role in most marketplaces? If so, then what theories, frameworks and perspectives are appropriate to help senior managers develop useful ways to think about the issues that their companies must confront in this arena?

Digital intermediaries, in their roles as Internet-focused competitors, have been able to apply various approaches to achieve short-run competitive advantage and maintain long-run competitive parity. However, there are very few strategies that will provide sustainable competitive advantage. Unfortunately for many firms, long-run competitive advantage is likely to be based more on how well these Internet intermediaries leverage their *first-mover advantage,* by 'stealing the march', while established market leaders are still only dimly aware of the competitive threats. This creates a foundation for longer-term gains, though it certainly does not ensure success.

We next will formulate a basis for analysing the strategies of digital intermediaries. We present a framework that describes the context of competition among traditional and digital intermediaries. We begin by laying out the core terminology we will use in the remainder of this chapter.

Intermediation 101

Intermediation is the process by which a firm, acting as the agent of an individual or another firm (a buyer or a seller), creates value by leveraging its middleman position to foster communication with other agents in the marketplace that will lead to transactions and exchange that create economic value. There are a number of roles that an intermediary can play that lead to the creation of value in the marketplace. They include: *aggregation of information* on buyers, suppliers and products; *facilitation of search* for appropriate products; *reduction of information asymmetries* through the provision of product and transactional expertise; *matching buyers and sellers* for transactions; and *trust provision* to the marketplace to enhance transactability (Bakos, 1998; Chircu and Kauffman, 2000b).

Traditional and digital intermediaries

It is useful to distinguish between two different kinds of intermediaries. *Traditional intermediaries,* for instance, tend to rely upon their capabilities to efficiently deliver products to customers and foster close interactions and communications with the customer. In contrast, *digital intermediaries* tend to rely upon the communication-enhancing capabilities of the Internet, and through it are able to project aggregation, expertise, search, facilitation, matching and settlement capabilities into the virtual space of the Internet marketplace.

Linking intermediaries and information intermediaries

When technology enhances intermediation, it typically creates impacts on two somewhat different functions. The first is a *linking function*, which enables new relationships between buyers and suppliers to be created, and existing relationships to be expanded, in support of transactions involving physical goods and services. The second is an *information function*, which enhances the movement of information between counterparties in a transaction, provides a basis for greater product and price transparency, creates trust, and increases the likelihood that a transaction can be completed to the satisfaction of the buyer and the seller.

These different functions give rise to two distinctly different kinds of digital intermediaries that one can observe in the marketplace. A *digital linking intermediary* typically profits by reducing the transaction costs associated with the lifecycle of a transaction that involves the exchange of goods or services. Insight Inc. (www.insight.com) is an example of such an intermediary. Insight advertises in such well-known computer industry periodicals as *Computer Shopper* and *PC Week*, among others, but in addition, it makes all its listings of computer hardware, software and peripherals available via the World Wide Web.

Another interesting example of a digital linking intermediary is the New York Stock Exchange (NYSE) Group's Arca (the former Archipelago electronic communication network or ECN). It is now fully integrated into the NYSE, extending the operations of the traditional stock exchange in New York to the hours of 4:00am to 8:00pm. The Arca infrastructure also provides a 'National Order Book' mechanism that is designed to maximize liquidity, and rewards best price execution and competition among dealers. The innovative capabilities of NYSE, in combination with ARCA's technological infrastructure, have the potential to create value in the national financial marketplace by linking buyers and sellers of stocks, cutting transaction costs to the minimum through electronic transaction-making and increasing the transparency of electronic financial market operations (see Figure 3.2).

In contrast, a *digital information intermediary* profits by controlling or enhancing the flow of information presented via the Internet. In the real estate industry in the US, for years real estate brokers have profited as information aggregators for homebuyers, controlling the latter's access to residential multiple listing service (MLS) information. However, in the past decade, we have seen the emergence of digital substitutes,

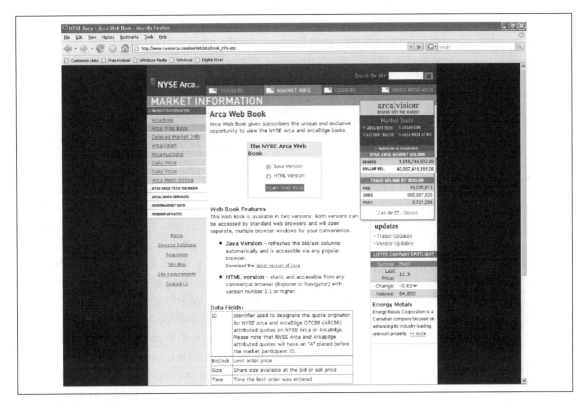

Figure 3.2
New York Stock Exchange's Arcatechnology infrastructure (from the Archipelago electronic communication network) uses the Internet to provide investors with national electronic market trading opportunities with extended hours of operation to maximize liquidity via a range of tools, including ArcaBook, ArcaWebBook and ArcaVision

especially MLS.com, which makes the multiple listing service information directly available to consumers, and also available to other real estate agents whose business processes have changed in the presence of the Internet. Now it is common for real estate agents to share this information directly with prospective homebuyers, who can do 'assisted' browsing and pre-screening, as well as 'in-the-car' comparisons of different properties in real time.

In addition, new digital intermediaries, including Owners.com and FSBO.com, are chipping away at the traditional realtors' control of information. FSBO.com is especially interesting: the value proposition it has promoted is to create a place on the Internet so that potential sellers can make 'for sale by owner' (FSBO) listings, enabling the bypass of realtors entirely, saving commission expenses for the seller.

The same kind of digital information intermediation has occurred in the segments of the financial markets that, heretofore, had been the most resistant to digital intermediation and the freeing up of control on market information for buyers and sellers: fixed income securities and related derivatives, especially government Treasury bonds, corporate fixed income securities, bond futures and foreign exchange trading. Over the past ten years, many new digital intermediaries have come into the market to create information sharing and market exchange solutions that permit much greater transparency and access than we have seen in the past (Economides, 2001; Granados *et al.*, 2005).

For example, Cantor Fitzgerald created eSpeed, which operates a number of different e-marketplaces that are primarily offered to market dealers. Cantor Fitzgerald and eSpeed were famous for their 105th floor location in the World Trade Center, which was destroyed in September 2001 by a terrorist attack. eSpeed offers digital markets for: United States government agency bonds and Treasury bills; government bonds for European governments, as well as Canada and Japan; and very large-scale foreign exchange trading. In addition, MarketAxess provides a multi-dealer system that is aimed at improving trading efficiency, liquidity and market transparency for high-grade corporate bonds, European bonds and emerging markets fixed income securities.

Other players have a somewhat different emphasis in the market. An example is the New York-based MuniCenter, which focuses on the range of financial instruments involved in municipal and government fixed income securities, and certificates of deposit. Another similar and influential issuance-focused player which facilitates electronic bond market operations is the Grant Street Group of Pittsburgh, Pennsylvania, which reported that it had conducted nearly 50 000 auctions involving more than a trillion US dollars as of August 2006. All of these firms have developed the capacity to technologically *bypass* existing traditional intermediaries (e.g. Wall Street's interdealer brokers, municipal bond advisors and investment banks), who have historically exerted significant control over the mechanism for trading such financial instruments. They enhance the flow of information in marketplaces where best bid and best offer prices have been difficult for institutional investors, retirement plan representatives and individual investors to discover.

Disintermediation

Disintermediation occurs when a middleman gets pushed out by other firms or when the services it provides become irrelevant, particularly as other ways to perform transactions become available. Ten years ago, senior managers at well-known securities industry firms such as Merrill

Lynch and American Express Financial Advisors would have been hard-pressed to predict that a large portion of the retail stock trading business would rapidly move to the Internet. However, since then, traditional brokerage and financial advisory intermediaries have been challenged by the new business models that emerged in the e-commerce sector. Moreover, efforts to disintermediate traditional middlemen have occurred everywhere: in the travel industry, diminishing the value of travel agents (Chircu *et al.*, 2001); in the home financing business, as mortgage lending specialists' offerings are eclipsed by Internet-based loan rate listings (Wigand *et al.*, 2005); and in the jewellery and precious gems industry, where sites like BlueNile.com create new demand among less experienced buyers (similar to the home mortgage industry), by supplying 'how to purchase a diamond' information and related decision support tools.

Current theory predicts that there will be considerable movement to market transactions in the presence of electronic communication technologies. Nearly two decades ago, in what has come to be recognized as a seminal article, Malone *et al.* (1987) wrote that such technologies would create the basis for an *electronic brokerage effect*. This effect is important because it predicts that *non-specific assets* and *commodity-like products* will transact more easily in *electronic marketplaces*. Their insights from 20 years ago, it turns out, enable us to explain a range of intermediation and market-related phenomena as they emerge and capture the attention of the marketplace. As search costs in the presence of IT fall, intermediaries are no longer needed. Only those middlemen with enough market power will manage to remain in the value-added chain (Hess and Kemerer, 1994). Others will be disintermediated unless they find new ways to compete. Granados *et al.* (2006a; 2006b), for example, report on new market mechanisms in air travel ticket reservation making that manipulate the transparency of intermediation mechanisms used to display prices, quantities available and travel product descriptions. (The interested reader should visit the Web sites of Booking Buddy, FlySpy, Hotwire, Kayak and Orbitz to see some of the new developments with respect to transparency.)

The financial services industry is a hotbed of innovation in this respect, providing an apt demonstration of the theory. In fact, technology-led *Darwinian competition* seems to have overtaken the more traditional *sports competition* of similarly configured players in what once was a highly regulated marketplace (Wunsch, 1997). For example, as long ago as 1969, Instinet created agent brokerage services to support institutional block trading, supplementing the 'upstairs' trading practices of the major Wall Street firms. After its acquisition by Reuters in 1987, Instinet's capabilities later developed into a full-blown electronic communication network (ECN) for financial market trading, with the automation to support direct buyer/seller trade matches. In 2005, Instinet was acquired by NASDAQ, and now operates as a global agency broker, linking NASDAQ to more than 40 equity markets around the world, again transforming the marketplace (Waller, 2005).

Other examples include Steve Wunsch's Single Price Auction Works (SPAWorks) in support of the move to decimalized pricing (e.g. $10.10, not $10\frac{1}{16}$ or $10\frac{1}{8}$) and the Arizona Stock Exchange (AZX) for after-exchange closing supply-and-demand crossing. Unfortunately, both are now defunct, as Wall Street proved its ability to move in the appropriate direction of more accessible and transparent markets. In the early 1990s, J. P. Morgan's electronic bond issuance market, Capitalink, tipped off observers that the more complex fixed income securities market would eventually move to embrace electronic issuance.

Shortly after that in the mid-1990s, New York City-based Spring Street Brewery made its own move to raise capital via the Internet to expand its business. The efforts of lawyer and Spring Street CEO Andrew Klein resulted in a real world 'eBay of blank': the Wit Capital Group, the first Internet-based investment bank (Klein, 1998). The company sought to reduce fees and make the issues process for small company stocks cheaper and faster, further democratizing the financial markets of Wall Street. Nevertheless, even here, the excitement was short-lived. Wit Capital acquired the Soundview Technology Group in 2000, which operated for a time as Wit Soundview, until it was acquired several years later by Charles Schwab, which created a new capital markets group around it.

Reintermediation

In spite of the picture we have painted about the forces that support disintermediation, we do not mean to imply that this is the only outcome that traditional intermediaries are subject to. In fact, in our view, over time we have seen many instances of reintermediation occurring in the e-commerce marketplace. *Reintermediation* is a process by which a competitor that has once been disintermediated, or pushed out of a profitable market niche as an intermediary, is able to re-establish itself – typically by exploiting the capabilities of technology to become an *electronic commerce-able intermediary*. Looking through the lens of Malone *et al.*'s theory, we would expect to see *biased and personalized electronic markets*, operated by large firms with significant standing in their industries, subject to their continuing strategic commitment to a given marketplace. In practice though, there has been some movement towards less biased markets (Granados *et al.*, 2006a; 2006b).

The emergence of *Internet-only intermediaries* in the travel industry – for example, Priceline.com, Internet Travel Network (which later changed its name to GetThere.com and is now a part of Sabre Holdings) and Preview Travel in the late 1990s – led to the creation of new ways to make reservations on the World Wide Web (Internet Travel Network, 1999). Nevertheless, we expected to see – and have actually witnessed in the past ten years – major industry players, such as American Airlines, Northwest Airlines and American Express Travel Related Services, creating biased and personalized electronic markets of their own. In 1997, Cathay Pacific Airlines, for example, was first to use the Internet to conduct a 'fire sale' of excess airline ticket inventory. In addition, many of the major competitors in the airline industry followed up with their own direct reservation and ticketing Web sites (e.g. Northwest Airlines' NWA.com and United Airlines' UAL.com) for business and leisure travellers. Such direct supplier links affect the traditional intermediary, the travel agent and the Internet-only intermediary. In addition, building on the success of its Sabre computerized reservation system (CRS) subsidiary, American Airlines has been highly successful with Travelocity. com, one of the most used reservation-making sites on the Internet.

UNDERSTANDING THE IDR CYCLE

In tackling the above issues, a number of important questions arise. When are we likely to see disintermediation and reintermediation occurring – changing the structure of competition in an industry? How do Internet-only intermediaries formulate successful strategies? What situational factors can be used to predict the occurrence of digital intermediation and disintermediation? Further, once they succeed, how can traditionally powerful firms recapture the high ground, leveraging the opportunity to reintermediate and effectively compete with new market entrants? The following analysis sheds some light on these issues.

The IDR cycle

Our view is that the evolution of firm strategy in the presence of electronic innovations occurs in three distinct, but related, phases. We called this the *intermediation-disintermedation-reintermediation cycle* (or IDR cycle) in research that we did in the late 1990s (Chircu and Kauffman, 1999; 2000a). We will next describe the three phases in terms of the strategies and value propositions that we have observed in the marketplace.

The intermediation phase

Firms in this phase typically pursue pure electronic intermediation strategies. They identify a product, service or information flow gap that no traditional provider currently occupies. Then, through technological innovation, they become an Internet-only intermediary, and thus create value in the marketplace by delivering something that has not been available there before. eBay has exemplified this kind of intermediation. Never before was there such a large-scale solution for trading non-commodity collectible items other than through occasional and fragmented, physical regional markets. *The value proposition that eBay brought to its marketplace was to give life and liquidity for non-commodity items – whether they were used cars, stamp collections, boating equipment or porcelain dolls.* Indeed, eBay's play in the market was to fill in a 'blank' for intermediation, a remarkable entrepreneurial insight, but one that was only possible with the technological innovations associated with the World Wide Web.

The disintermediation phase

In this phase, as Internet-only intermediaries attract customers, their next logical strategic step is to disintermediate traditional middlemen, if they exist, and capture broader market share. By unbundling the financial advice from the trade execution, e-brokers such as E*Trade put tremendous pressure on full-service brokers, effectively disintermediating them in various segments of the market. *The value proposition that E*Trade brought to the marketplace with its Internet-based retail trading solutions was to reduce the commission costs for trading stocks by nearly an order of magnitude for the typical retail brokerage customer.*

We also have observed Internet-only players who choose voluntarily to disintermediate themselves. This occurred when Internet-only intermediaries realized that they could become IT providers to their industries. They recognized that they could earn higher profits as providers of a technological solution or an emerging IT standard than if they were to continue to compete head to head with traditional players who invested in IT to make themselves Internet-able.

The reintermediation phase

In the final phase, the focus shifts to firms whose interests have been harmed by digital intermediaries entering the marketplace. The broad expectation in the marketplace in the early years of e-commerce was to see traditional intermediaries fighting back, making themselves

Internet-able. An example of this occurred when the large traditional bookseller Barnes & Noble's Bookstores was beaten to the Internet market by the bold business strategies of Amazon.com. The former launched BN.com, an Internet-only company, in May 1997, in association with an equal investment from Bertelsmann AG. *The value proposition that BN.com, in combination with the traditional bricks-and-mortar Barnes & Noble's Bookstores, delivered to the marketplace was to interact with customers through the new channel of the Internet, speeding product distribution through regional inventory maintenance, while maintaining the immediacy of the physical shopping experience in local stores.*

However, as the market capitalizations in Table 3.1 show (as of 27 May 1999), Amazon.com's first-mover advantage was considerable, enabling the firm to amass a market value over 35 times that of BN.com. At the time, the market's perception of Amazon.com was that it had potential beyond just being a bookseller; it was viewed as a market mechanism for the digital sale of a variety of goods, such as CDs and other commodity-like products, whereas BN.com was merely an extension of Barnes & Noble's Bookstores' physical bookselling operations. Interestingly, in the ensuing years, the market capitalization gap between the two firms would grow dramatically. The value of BN.com's stock fell below $0.50 a share in late 2002, and the independent firm BN.com was later bought by Barnes & Noble's Bookstores' physical bookselling company in the first and second quarters of 2004 for around $3.00 per share. The total market capitalization of BN.com and Barnes & Noble's Bookstores was worth $2.211 billion in 1999 ($520.40 million for BN.com plus $1690.62 million for the traditional firm). So, with about $18.8 billion in market capitalization in 1999, Amazon.com was still worth more than 10.5 times that of Barnes & Noble's Internet and physical stores. By mid-2006, the market capitalization gap between Amazon.com (at $11.219 billion) and the combined Barnes & Noble's Bookstores (at $2.223 billion) narrowed considerably to 5.1 times, as Amazon.com's stock price fell, and Barnes & Noble's received renewed market interest. Clearly, Amazon.com continues to have a much higher market capitalization in absolute terms, based on the span of its business beyond bookselling towards more of an Internet-based selling intermediary. Its success is in part explained by its ability to combine the best steps of online and offline transactions, thus creating value for its customers by replacing offline experiences such as browsing through a book or inspecting a product with online photos, virtual tours and advanced searches, and adding offline conveniences such as picking up products in stores such as Circuit City (Chircu and Mahajan, 2007). Barnes & Noble's has not been able to achieve this, in spite of its earlier start in the bookselling business and its Internet capabilities. In view of its profitability and the present value of its future growth opportunities, our sense is that Barnes & Noble's Bookstore will continue to experience challenges in becoming a bookselling-focused reintermediator and regaining its former place in the sector.

Of course, the developments have not stopped here. Recent past changes and other changes that are under way – such as in the electronic bond markets that we discussed earlier and the Internet-based bookselling sector – suggest that future changes in the market structure of industries will be impacted by the Internet-only strategies of new entrants and the Internet-enabling strategies of incumbents.

Conditions for reintermediation in the IDR cycle

Among the three phases of the IDR cycle, the reintermediation phase is the one that is least well understood by academic researchers and senior managers. In previous research (Chircu and Kauffman, 1999), we proposed that there were three conditions for reintermediation: *ownership of co-specialized assets* for both market intermediation and electronic commerce innovations; *weak appropriability* of electronic commerce innovations; and *economies of scale*. Let us consider each in turn once again.

Ownership of co-specialized assets

Reintermediation occurs when electronic innovations are imitable by competitors. *Firm-specific assets*, including IT, reputational, relational and other assets, are likely to play a major role in determining a digital intermediary's competitive position. These are things that actually can create disadvantages for most newly entering Internet-only intermediaries, because they start out with little more than a Web page and an entrepreneurial vision. To be successful in creating sustainable competitive advantage, technological innovations require *complementary assets* to be put in place as well. However, Internet-only intermediaries have sometimes found it hard to acquire the necessary complementary assets. For example, as long as profitability is uncertain, suppliers will tend to stay with traditional intermediaries for distribution due to the risks involved (Clemons *et al.*, 1993). Oracle's 1999 purchase of E-Travel.com is a case in point. In lieu of building expertise in e-commerce application development, Oracle chose to shortcut the *path dependencies* (Teece, 1992) associated with creating their own solution for the travel industry.

If traditional intermediaries exist in the value chain, they often already have significant *complementary assets*: their expertise, customer base and relationships with suppliers (Teece, 1987). They also may not have the appropriate expertise to rapidly succeed in e-commerce. However, traditional intermediaries often have the resources to buy into appropriate solutions. The Bank of New York, a major international commercial banking player in the fixed income securities market, obtained an important complementary asset through an alliance with BondNet, when the latter was an independent electronic trading software solution innovator operating out of Connecticut. The bank had the fixed income securities market operational expertise but, prior to its purchase of BondNet, did not have e-commerce application development expertise. Although the bank could not sustain the value of its investment in BondNet as pressure grew from other significant competitors and the industry structure for fixed income securities trading changed, the strategy that the Bank of New York used is a classic example.

Traditional intermediaries, as we have seen in the past six or seven years, cannot afford to rely too much on their pre-existing assets and *not* adopt e-commerce innovations. We have seen that if they want to stay in the competition, they have needed to start the reintermediation process as quickly as possible to prevent Internet-only intermediaries from acquiring or building their own co-specialized assets. Even if a traditional intermediary has all the necessary co-specialized assets for market intermediation, it still may lack those related to the development of e-commerce applications. Here, technology investments become a strategic necessity. To prepare for reintermediation, a firm can either develop the requisite technologies by itself or acquire them from existing providers. In both cases, the idea is to acquire co-specialized complementary assets necessary to appropriate benefits from technological innovations in an electronic marketplace.

Another good example is the strategy that American Express Travel Related Services used in the late 1990s. The firm possessed many well-established corporate travel management relationships (its complementary assets), but still chose to rely upon Microsoft's capability with software development for e-commerce applications to create American Express Interactive (AXI). This Web-based reservations system for business travellers initially benefited from a number of co-specialized complementary assets, including the IT development experience of Microsoft, and American Express's travel industry experience. Although the exclusive access to Microsoft's technology that American Express negotiated lasted only two years (McNulty, 1999), this kind of asset was still hard for competitors to imitate, since it relied so heavily on Microsoft's experience with developing its Internet Explorer browser and, later, its own Web-based reservation system, Expedia.com. American Express also tapped into the expertise of GetThere.com (formerly Internet Travel Network, now a part of Sabre Holdings) to provide Internet-based travel reservation services for its clients after the exclusive agreement with Microsoft ended. It has only recently developed its own Internet-based travel reservation system. Clearly, even for a company at the top of its industry, leveraging co-specialized assets and obtaining the requisite technical expertise for successfully launching an e-commerce operation is not trivial.

More broadly, co-specialized complementary assets may consist of industry-specific expertise and transaction data, in addition to customer and supplier relationships. Another related example makes this point well. In the 1980s, strong airlines were able to successfully capture the benefits of airline computer reservation systems by offering these systems to travel agencies (the co-specialized complementary assets). Travel agents, in turn, made the CRSs an integral part of their business process, transforming the operational mechanics of the industry (Duliba *et al.*, 2001).

Economies of scale

Internet-only intermediaries will not succeed if they cannot achieve economies of scale. However, many traditional intermediaries will have achieved economies of scale in traditional markets, and can use this advantage to leverage their attempts to reintermediate. Thus, the problem that senior management often faces is in effectively implementing an e-commerce solution.

The perspective that we recommend emphasizes that an important way for an Internet-only intermediary to maintain its first mover competitive advantage is to become a technology provider. For example, it can become a technology provider for traditional intermediaries, if they exist and encroach upon the Internet-only intermediary's competitive space, or for suppliers and customers, if the traditional market structure does not contain intermediaries. For example, GetThere.com has positioned itself not only as an Internet-only corporate travel reservation system, but as a technology provider for travel agencies such as Carlson Wagonlit Travel and Navigant International and meeting management providers like HelmsBriscoe. Thus, Internet-only intermediaries may welcome reintermediation, but only if they can benefit from it and not be pushed out of the marketplace. Here, broad agreement in the marketplace about whether a technology provider's solutions will reach critical mass or become a *de facto* standard is critical.

Weak appropriability

An innovation's weak appropriability (Teece, 1987) is amplified by the independence of an e-commerce application from the customers' installed software and hardware base. As long as the application resides on the intermediary's Web site, switching costs are almost zero. Since the same browser software can be used to access any Web site, customers can easily switch to a competitor, without being required to make extensive investments in proprietary hardware and software. Therefore, relying solely on their technological innovation cannot be a source of sustained competitive advantage for firms doing business on the Internet. This seems true for first movers, such as Amazon.com, which implemented e-commerce innovations but had limited industry expertise when it was founded. Established players, such as Barnes & Noble's Bookstores and Borders Books, were able to quickly imitate the first mover's innovations and provide similar services on their own Web sites. Moreover, firms that control *co-specialized complementary assets* – in other words, those that only have value in association with other assets – are in a better position to appropriate benefits where dependence on the technological innovation exists (Teece, 1987).

Relevant competitive strategies

There are four characteristic competitive strategies that firms are observed to use in the IDR cycle (see Table 3.2). They include *partnering for access, technology licensing, partnering for content,* and *partnering for application development.* Each strategy varies in the extent to which it confers upon the firm that employs it the ability to achieve sustainable competitive advantage.

Partnering for access

This strategy has often been used by Internet-only intermediaries, but traditional competitors have also used it to become more effective in the Internet-based channel. This approach sometimes involves contracting for exclusivity agreements with high-traffic Web sites, such as search engines, browser providers and Internet service providers (ISPs). Since this strategy is readily available to other intermediaries, however, its success depends on the success of the chosen partners. Consider Google's (www.google.com) partnerships with a variety of authors, including Richard Lowry and Susan Foote, booksellers, including DRC, Arcadia Publishing, Upper Access Inc. and Idea Group Inc. The latter three firms pay for access to Google's Web site and its highly valuable user base (see Figure 3.3).

Table 3.2
Four strategies for sustainable competitive advantage for Internet middlemen (source: after Chircu and Kauffman, 1999)

Strategy	Description	Conditions for sustainable competitive advantage	Environmental conditions under which the strategy is appropriate
Partnering for content	The intermediary becomes an aggregator for products and services.	The digital intermediary can customize and brand the content, as well as retain control over customers' transactions.	Market niches are not yet stable; market search costs are too high; and insufficient value is available for firms to be able to appropriate it with individual offerings via the Internet; opportunities to create value through product or content aggregation still exist.
Partnering for access	The digital intermediary becomes the provider of services for other agents involved in electronic commerce (e.g. search engine and Internet service providers).	The partner is a leading online service provider with whom the digital intermediary has an exclusivity agreement.	Cost pressures begin to favour rationalization of Internet-focused software development; some Internet services begin to achieve dominance or become de facto standards; but service provision may be incompletely covered.
Partnering for application development	The digital intermediary forms alliances and service relationships with established industry participants.	The right combination of assets (e.g. technological and industry-specific expertise) is obtained by the digital intermediary through partnering.	No technology standards have been established yet; establishing them confers significant value upon participants in the coalition of organizations promulgating the standard.
Technology licensing	The digital intermediary becomes a technology provider for other Web sites, either by selling them the technology or by sharing the profits resulting from transactions referred by other Web sites.	The digital intermediary is continuously innovating and licensing, moving value to the marketplace as rapidly as possible.	The profits from providing products or services online are lower than the profits from being a technology provider for other Internet-only and Internet-able intermediaries.

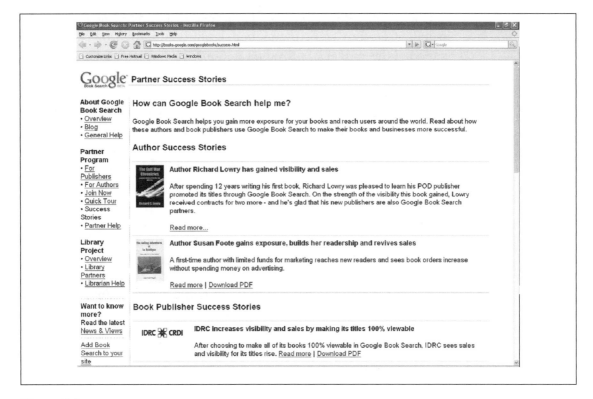

Figure 3.3
Several authors and booksellers take advantage of Google's partnering for access strategy (source: Google's Web site, 22 March 2007)

By placing their logos and links on Google, the booksellers maximize the likelihood of being able to take advantage of Google's clear and commanding market share in the United States of 48 per cent of all Internet searches as of June 2006 (Vise, 2006). Yahoo! (www.yahoo.com) is another potential access partner, although it now only has a market share of 22 per cent of Internet searches in the USA. In the absence of key partners like these, a partnering for access strategy is probably not a means to achieve meaningful competitive advantage.

Technology licensing

Technology licensing is an effective strategy used by Internet-only intermediaries where the benefits from intermediating individual transactions are lower than the benefits from providing the technology for other industry players. However, licensing software and various hardware technologies cannot alone create a basis for sustainable competitive advantage. When licensing is used in combination with a continuous innovation strategy, it is possible for the innovating firm to become a supplier to other firms that would otherwise disintermediate it. Examples include GetThere.com, mentioned earlier, and Amazon.com, which extended this model by providing not only e-commerce technology, but also order fulfilment and guest services operations for the Web sites of retailers such as Target.

Technology licensing occurs in the emerging electronic bill payments (EBPP) segment of the financial services industry. Checkfree, the largest EBPP services provider in the USA, works with several strategic partners to create capabilities that the firm would be unable to muster on its own. One example is BillMatrix Corporation, whose technology makes it possible for Checkfree to automate paper-based interfaces to increase the straight-through processing of remittances on behalf of its clients. In addition, Checkfree works with Intuit Inc., which provides personal and small business investment management and accounting software products and services. Checkfree also works with Yahoo!, which offers access to the exceptional installed user base of Yahoo! Bill Pay, further increasing the span of Checkfree's online financial management solutions (Checkfree, 2006).

A second example of technology licensing in e-commerce is the approach that ITA Software has pursued in the travel industry. ITA Software, a technology start-up founded at MIT in the late 1990s (Robinson, 2002), has prospered in a context where the role of computational complexity in the construction of flight itineraries, price choices and distribution solutions is only beginning to be well understood. If ITA Software were to have focused on disintermediating traditional travel firms, then it would eventually have been subject to the threat of an industry-wide response, diminishing its likelihood of success. However, ITA Software chose the approach of licensing its technology to major travel services and travel solutions providers (including Delta and some travel agents; see Robinson, 2002). This created a basis for getting potential competitors to 'buy in' to a set of solutions that has increasingly become recognized as a standard distribution solution for airline ticket prices in the industry.

Of course, this approach is not new in the marketplace among technology firms. For example, Clemons (1991) reported that Merrill Lynch made a similar play with its investment in Bloomberg Financial in the pre-Internet marketplace of the 1980s. Merrill initially held back from making its financial information delivery capabilities available marketwide, but later maximized the value of its Bloomberg investment by licensing the use of the information to competitors. This strategy paid off well both for Merrill Lynch and market leader Bloomberg during the time it was employed.

Partnering for content

This approach involves product and information aggregation, another widely used strategy by Internet-only intermediaries. This strategy is likely to work best for first movers. However, sustainable competitive advantage cannot be achieved through this strategy: other players can imitate it quite easily. Instead, what is required is an amalgam of service capabilities, definitive content and operational prowess that makes it difficult for other firms to compete. We see this in the electronic brokerage industry, for example.

In the late 1990s when e-brokers such as Charles Schwab and E*Trade began to compete, they chose to provide no specific financial advisory services. Instead, they decided to partner for content with other well-known providers, simultaneously avoiding the legal responsibility for financial advice that full-service firms must bear. Today, however, the competition is much keener, and many firms in the online brokerage community, including Scottrade and E*Trade, have made efforts to create branch networks and locate investment management kiosks in public places to increase the accessibility of their services. Such firms also now do more to provide advisory services for individual investors.

Figure 3.4 shows a current example of partnering for content involving the business intelligence information provider, Factiva, and

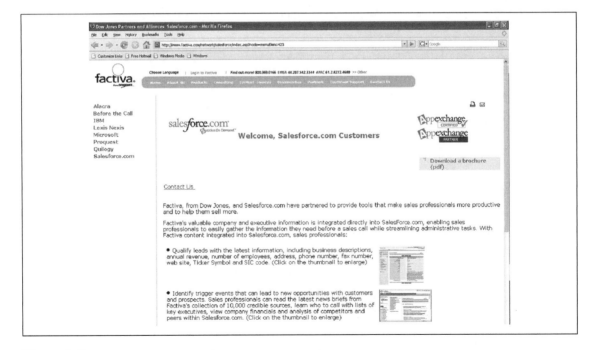

Figure 3.4
Factiva partners for content with SalesForce.com to support effective selling through business intelligence (source: Factiva's Web site information on content partners, 22 March 2007)

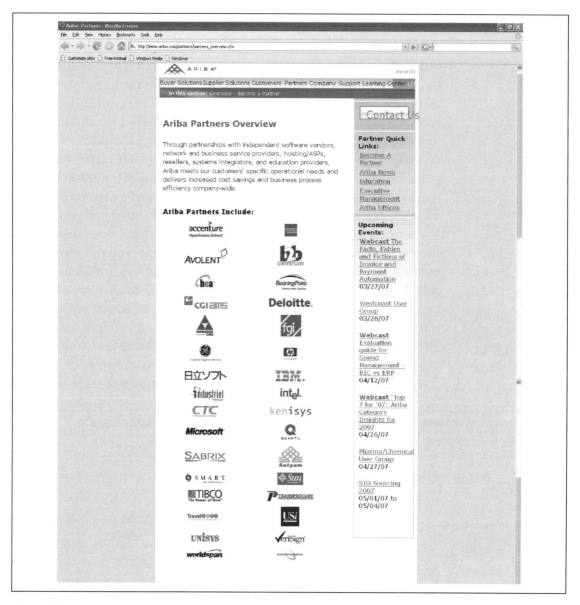

Figure 3.5
Ariba's licensing partnerships with software providers, system integrators, network and business services providers and others (Ariba Web site, 22 March 2007)

SalesForce.com, a customer relationship management solution that supports the identification of market events that act as triggers for firms to initiate new or increased ongoing sales activities. Factiva's role is to provide the market content that permits SalesForce.com to present a compelling package of information services to potential clients to enhance their efforts to sell products to effectively generate revenue.

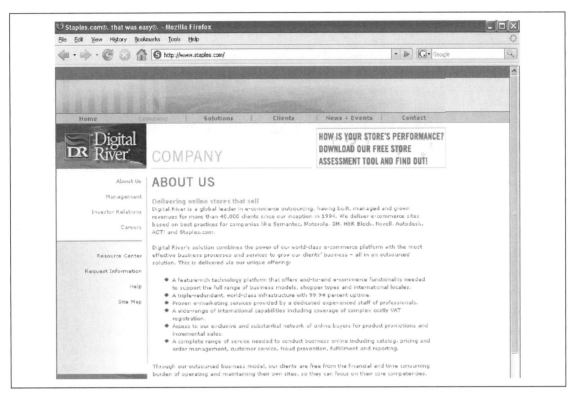

Figure 3.6
Digital River Inc. partners for application development with Motorola, 3 M, H&R Block and Staples
(Digital River Inc. Web site, 22 March 2007)

Partnering for application development

Finally, *partnering for application development* involves an alliance between a technology provider and a well-established industry participant. This strategy is more likely to be used for new services where no traditional intermediaries have been present. This strategy can also be used for managing the risk of developing large and very complex applications for the Internet. If the right combination of technology and industry expertise is achieved, this strategy has the potential to generate sustainable competitive advantage, as we discussed earlier in the case of Microsoft and American Express Travel Related Services with AXI. Other examples include Ariba, which developed licensing partnerships with software providers, system integrators, network and business services providers and others (Figure 3.5), and Staples Inc. (Figure 3.6), who have partnered with Minneapolis, Minnesota-based Digital River Inc. (Figure 3.7) for development and operation of its Web site, www.staples.com.

Figure 3.7
Staples Inc.'s Web site was built with the partnership of Ariba Inc. (Staples Inc.'s Web site, 22 March 2007)

CONCLUSIONS

Today, much is known about competition between traditional and electronic market players (Bailey and Bakos, 1997; Bakos, 1991; 1998; Bakos and Brynjolfsson, 1993; Clemons *et al.*, 1993; Hess and Kemerer, 1994; Sarkar *et al.*, 1995; Steinfield *et al.*, 1995). Among the things that we have learned from this and related work by Mata *et al.* (1995) is that IT alone is rarely a source of sustainable competitive advantage. To become an 'eBay of blank' – in other words, to find a unique niche for intermediation in the digital marketplace – takes far more in the way of business vision, entrepreneurial marketing skills and operational and corporate finance capabilities (combined with the luck of doing things in the right place and at the right time).

However, IT can help to leverage critical firm resources, such as the expertise of specific human capital, experience in a market niche, and an understanding of how to fine-tune manufacturing and services business processes to create sustainable competitive advantage (Clemons, 1991; Clemons and Row, 1991). We expect that this same view should apply in the arena of digital intermediation, so that the current and future 'eBays' of the electronic commerce world will be subject to all the same forces that most market leaders in traditional business have been.

Another important thing that senior managers must keep in mind is that their firm must *either* create or control relevant complementary assets to their e-commerce technology innovations. We have argued that this is a crucial element, and that it is as important for Internet-only intermediaries who seek to sustain their position in the marketplace as it is for traditional intermediaries who wish to reintermediate and reinvigorate their business strategy in the emerging marketplace. The four strategies that we discussed – partnering for access, technology licensing, partnering for content and partnering for application development – each, in their own way, provide a foundation for creating complementary assets.

Finally, apart from securing ownership of necessary co-specialized assets, digital intermediaries need to renew organizational skills, resources and functional competencies to sustain the advantages that they build (Teece *et al.*, 1997). As a result, current innovation must be the wellspring for further innovation, as new technology replaces the old. Eventually, this must become systemic for the firm, but it requires more tightly coupled business processes (Chesbrough and Teece, 1996). In this context, Teece (1992) has pointed out the importance of *strategic alliances for interorganizational process coupling* in sustaining competitive advantage. This is likely to be true among various kinds of intermediaries (digital linking and information intermediaries, and Internet-only and Internet-able intermediaries) that we have discussed in this chapter (Dai and Kauffman, 2004).

FURTHER READING

For additional background on the topics and research areas discussed in this chapter, the interested reader should see Kauffman and Walden (2001) for a general survey, Spulber (1999) for coverage of the theory of intermediation, Kauffman *et al.* (2002; 2006) for assessments of strategic morphing and business model changes in e-commerce, Chircu and Mahajan (2007) for understanding e-commerce retailer strategies for minimizing transaction costs and maximizing customer value, and finally Bockstedt *et al.* (2006) for coverage of the transformation of music industry structure in the wake of digital music technology innovations.

REFERENCES

Bailey, J. P. and Bakos, J. Y. (1997). An exploratory study of the emerging role of electronic intermediaries. *International Journal of Electronic Commerce*, 1, 7–20.

Bakos, J. Y. (1991). A strategic analysis of electronic marketplaces. *MIS Quarterly*, 15, 295–310.

Bakos, J. Y. (1998). The emerging role of electronic marketplaces on the Internet. *Communications of the ACM*, 41, 35–42.

Bakos, J. Y. and Brynjolfsson, E. (1993). From vendors to partners: information technology and incomplete contracts in buyer-supplier relationships. *Journal of Organizational Computing*, 3, 301–328.

Baltaxe, D. (1999). Industry Analysis. *Current Analysis*, March.

Benjamin, R. and Wigand, R. (1995). Electronic markets and virtual value chains on the information superhighway. *Sloan Management Review*, 36, 62–72.

Bockstedt, J., Kauffman, R. J. and Riggins, F. J. (2006). The move to artist-led music distribution: explaining market structure changes in the digital music market. *International Journal of Electronic Commerce*, 10, 7–38.

Burnham, B. (1999). *How to Invest in E-Commerce Stocks*. McGraw-Hill.

Castonguay, G. (1999). Focus: DLJ sets $320 million online unit offering. *Reuters/Quicken Excite*, 25 May. http://quicken.excite.com/investments/news/story/rtr/?story=/news/stories/rtr/18/n25238818.htm&symbol=amtd

Checkfree (2006). Strategic partners, 13 November. http://www.checkfreecorp.com/cda/corp/L5.jsp?layoutId=50034&contentId=270& menuId=50064&pId=50064

Chesbrough, H. W. and Teece, D. J. (1996). Organizing for innovation. *Harvard Business Review*, 74, 65–73.

Chircu, A. M. and Kauffman, R. J. (1999). Tactics and strategies for Internet middlemen in the intermediation-disintermediation-reintermediation cycle. *Electronic Markets – The International Journal of Electronic Commerce and Business Media*, 9, 109–117.

Chircu, A. M. and Kauffman, R. J. (2000a). Reintermediation strategies in business-to-business electronic commerce. *International Journal of Electronic Commerce*, 4, 7–42.

Chircu, A. M. and Kauffman, R. J. (2000b). Limits to value in electronic commerce-related IT investments. *Journal of Management Information Systems*, 17, 59–80.

Chircu, A. M., Kauffman, R. J. and Keskey, D. (2001). Maximizing the value of Internet-based corporate travel reservation systems. *Communications of the ACM*, 44, 57–63.

Chircu, A. M. and Mahajan, V. (2007). Managing electronic commerce transaction costs for customer value. *Decision Support Systems*, 42, 898–914.

Clemons, E. K. (1991). Evaluation of strategic investments in information technology. *Communications of the ACM*, 34, 22–36.

Clemons, E. K., Reddi, S. P. and Row, M. C. (1993). The impact of information technology on the organization of economic activity: the 'move to the middle' hypothesis. *Journal of Management Information Systems*, 10, 9–35.

Clemons, E. K. and Row, M. C. (1991). Information technology at Rosenbluth Travel: competitive advantage in a rapidly growing global service company. *Journal of Management Information Systems*, 8, 53–79.

Dai, Q. and Kauffman, R. J. (2002). Business models for Internet-based B2B electronic markets. *International Journal of Electronic Commerce*, 6 (4), 41–72.

Dai, Q. and Kauffman, R. J. (2004). Partnering for perfection: an economics perspective on B2B electronic market strategic alliances. In *Economics, IS and E-Commerce* (K. Tomak, ed.) pp. 43–79, Idea Group Publishing.

Day, G., Fein, A. J. and Ruppersberger, G. (2003). Shakeouts in digital markets: lessons from B2B exchanges. *California Management Review*, 45, 131–150.

Dehning, B., Richardson, V. and Zmud, R. (2003). The value relevance of announcements of transformational information technology investments. *MIS Quarterly*, 27, 637–656.

Duliba, K., Kauffman, R. J. and Lucas, H. C. Jr. (2001). Appropriating value from CRS ownership in the airline industry. *Organization Science*, 12, 702–728.

Economides, N. (2001). The impact of the Internet on financial markets. *Journal of Financial Transformation*, 1, 8–13.

Granados, N., Gupta, A. and Kauffman, R. J. (2005). Transparency strategy in Internet-based selling. In *Advances in the Economics of Information Systems* (K. Tomak, ed.) pp. 80–112, Idea Group Publishing.

Granados, N., Gupta, A. and Kauffman, R. J. (2006a). The impact of IT on market information and transparency: a unified theoretical framework. *Journal of the Association for Information Systems*, 7, 148–178.

Granados, N., Gupta, A. and Kauffman, R. J. (2006b). IT-enabled transparent electronic markets: the case of the air travel industry. *Information Systems and E-Business Management*, 5, 65–91.

Hess, C. M. and Kemerer, C. F. (1994). Computerized loan origination systems: an industry case study of the electronic markets hypothesis. *MIS Quarterly*, 18, 251–275.

Internet Travel Network (1999). ITN's portfolio: online travel excellence, 28 May. http://www.itn.com/cgi/get?portfolio:JPgQlw_Kl8u*itn/ord=927 901554.13696,itn/agencies/itnpublic

Kauffman, R. J. and Walden, E. A. (2001). Economics and electronic commerce: survey and directions for research. *International Journal of Electronic Commerce*, 5, 4–115.

Kauffman, R. J. and Wang, B. (2002). Bid together, buy together: on the efficacy of group-buying models in Internet-based selling. In *Handbook of Electronic Commerce in Business and Society* (P. B. Lowry, J. O. Cherrington and R. R. Watson, eds) pp. 99–137, CRC Press.

Kauffman, R. J., Miller, T. and Wang, B. (2002). When Internet companies morph: understanding organizational strategy changes in the 'new' new economy. *First Monday – The Peer Reviewed Journal on the Internet*, 7 (7). http://www.firstmonday.org/issues/issue7_7/kauffman/index.html

Kauffman, R. J., Miller, T. and Wang, B. (2006). Understanding the survival of Internet firms. *First Monday – The Peer-Reviewed Journal on the Internet*, 11 (7). http://www.firstmonday.org/issues/special11_7/kauffman/index.html

Klein, A. (1998). *WallStreet.com: Fat Cat Investing at the Click of a Mouse.* Henry Holt and Company.

Laseter, T., Long, B. and Capers, C. (2001). B2B benchmark: the state of electronic exchanges. *Strategy + Business*, 25, 33–42.

Malone, T. W., Yates, J. and Benjamin, R. I. (1987). Electronic markets and electronic hierarchies. *Communications of the ACM*, 30, 484–497.

Marketwatch.com (2006). Dow-Jones financial news and information service, with stock quote lookup and investment information. *Marketwatch.com*, 7 August. http://www.marketwatch.com.

Mata, F. J., Fuerst, W. L. and Barney, J. B. (1995). Information technology and sustained competitive advantage: a resource-based analysis. *MIS Quarterly*, 19, 487–505.

McNulty, M. A. (1999). AXI hits open market. *BTN Online*, 7 June. http://www.btnonline.com/db_area/archives/1999/06/99060725.htm

PR Newswire (1999). NetPerceptions announces initial public offering. *Quicken Excite*, 23 April. http://quicken.excite.com/investments/news/story/pr/?story=/news/stories/pr/19990423/hsf036.htm&symbol=netp

Quicken Excite (1999). Investment quotes. 27 May. http://quicken.excite.com/investments/quotes/

Rayport, J. F. and Sviokla, J. J. (1994). Managing in the marketspace. *Harvard Business Review*, 72, 141–150.

Reuters.com (2006). Financial markets news and information, stock quotes and financial statements repository. *Reuters.com*, 7 August. http://today.reuters.com/news/home.aspx

Robinson, S. (2002). Computer scientists find unexpected depths in airfare search problem, *SIAM News* 35, 1–3.

Sarkar, M. B., Butler, B. and Steinfield, C. (1995). Intermediaries and cybermediaries: a continuing role for mediating players in the electronic marketplace. *Journal of Computer-Mediated Communication*, 1. http://jcmc.huji.ac.il/vol1/issue3/sarkar.html

Spulber, D. F. (1999). *Market Microstructure: Intermediaries and the Theory of the Firm.* Cambridge University Press.

Steinfield, C., Kraut, R. and Plummer, A. (1995). The impact of electronic commerce on buyer-seller relationships. *Journal of Computer-Mediated Communication*, 1. http://jcmc.huji.ac.il/vol1/issue3/steinfld.html

Teece, D. J. (1987). Profiting from technological innovation: implications for integration, collaboration, licensing and public policy. In *The Competitive Challenge* (D. J. Teece, ed.) pp. 185–219, Harper & Row.

Teece, D. J. (1992). Competition, co-operation, and innovation: organizational arrangements for regimes of rapid technological progress. *Journal of Economic Behavior and Organizations*, 18, 1–25.

Teece, D. J., Pisano, G. and Shuen, A. (1997). Dynamic capabilities and strategic management. *Strategic Management Journal*, 18, 509–553.

Vise, D. (2006). Think again: Google. *Foreign Policy*, May–June. http://www.foreignpolicy.com/users/login.php?story_id=3425&URL=http://www.foreignpolicy.com/story/cms.php?story_id=3425

Waller, P. (2005). Reuters sells Instinet to NASDAQ. *Manchester Online*, 25 April. http://www.manchesteronline.co.uk/business/media/s/156/156059_reuters_ sells_instinet_to_nasdaq.html

Whinston, A. B., Stahl, D. O. and Choi, S. Y. (1997). *The Economics of Electronic Commerce*. Macmillan.

Wigand, R. T., Steinfield, C. W. and Markus, M. L. (2005). Information technology standards choices and industry structure outcomes: the case of the U.S. home mortgage industry. *Journal of Management Information Systems*, 22, 165–192.

Wunsch, S. (1997). Letter to Jonathan G. Katz, Secretary, United States Securities and Exchange Commission. *Arizona Stock Exchange*, 15 September. http://www.azx.com/pub/katzwuns.html

Appendix 3.1

An overview of leading firms in electronic commerce

Firm name (URL)	Business description
Amazon.com (www.amazon.com)	First mover in the online market for books; has used its strong brand name to expand online sales of a variety of products, such as CDs and electronics.
AA.com (www.aa.com)	Direct booking Web site for airline tickets deployed by American Airlines, which also founded Travelocity.com.
American Express Travel Related Services (www.americanexpress.com)	Major corporate travel firm that partnered with Microsoft in the late 1990s to create American Express Interactive (AXI), a predecessor of Expedia, and later on with GetThere.com, before developing its own proprietary travel reservation system, the TravelBahn^{SM} network.
America Online (www.aol.com)	Leading Internet service provider (ISP) in the United States.
Arizona Stock Exchange (www.azx.com)	Low cost, single price auction crossing market for US equities that aimed to disintermediate the major stock exchanges, but failed in 2002 due to a lack of trading volume.
AutoByTel (www.autobytel.com)	First highly successful Internet-based referral service for retail purchases of new and used motor vehicles.
Best Buy (www.bestbuy.com)	US-based national retailer of music and DVDs, consumer electronics, software and appliances, with a well-developed brick-and-clicks strategy that integrates Web-based ordering with store location-based delivery.
Bill Matrix Corporation (www.billmatrix.com)	Outsourcing services provider in the electronic billing space, founded in 1994, but with connectivity via automated telephone systems and Web sites.
Bloomberg (www.bloomberg.com)	A leading provider of news and information for financial markets operations.
BlueNile.com (www.bluenile.com)	Established in 1999, and now recognized as the largest Internet-based seller of diamonds and fine jewellery; offers decision support tools for gem purchases.
BN.com (www.bn.com)	Leading traditional bookseller's brand name extension to electronic commerce; late to market; set up as a separate entity from Barnes & Noble's Bookstores.
BondNet (www.bony.com)	Entrepreneurially-developed live, screen-based electronic market for corporate fixed income securities, later purchased by the large money centre bank, Bank of New York, which formed a division for online bond trading.
Bond Express (www.bondexpress.com)	A provider of electronic trading systems for bonds and of a database with information about bond trading.

Firm name (URL)	Business description
BookingBuddy (www.bookingbuddy.com)	A travel search tool operated by SmartTravel.com (www.smarttravel.com), a consumer membership and discounting firm, associated with SmarterLiving.com (www.smarterliving.com). SmartTravel offers unbiased travel advice, and does not act as an intermediary for airline ticket purchases.
Cantor Fitzgerald (www.cantor.com)	The first provider of an electronic single-price auction system for the US Treasury futures market, eSpeed (www.espeed.com), and now operating foreign exchange and other government agency security electronic auctions.
Capitalink	First electronic issuance market for high-grade corporate bonds. Developed with J.P. Morgan, which later killed it when bank got bond underwriting authority under SEC Shelf Registration Rule 415 in the early 1990s.
Cathay Pacific Corporation (www.cathaypacific.com)	The first airline to provide electronic ticket auctions on its Web site.
CDNow	Internet-only distributor of popular and classical music compact discs; merged with Music Boulevard; acquired by Bertelsmann e-Commerce Group in September 2000.
Charles Schwab (www.schwab.com)	Discount stockbroker from the 1980s that recently transformed its strategy to emphasize the Internet.
Cheap Tickets (www.cheaptickets.com)	Founded in 1986 by Cendant Corporation, and currently offered through its Travel Distribution Services Division, to supply the leisure travel services marketplace with comprehensive access to low fare and vacation packages.
Checkfree (www.checkfree.com)	One of the first companies to provide electronic bill payment and bill presentment services in the USA.
CNN (www.cnn.com)	The online news service of Cable News Network (CNN), a leading news provider.
Digital River (www.digitalriver.com)	Founded in 1994, Digital River is a leading provider of store platforms for Internet-based selling.
eBay (www.ebay.com)	Early and highly successful digital intermediary for Internet-based auction market for collectible items.
E*Trade (www.etrade.com)	The fastest growing Internet-only electronic brokerage in the USA during the 1990s, now matured into a relatively full service player, emphasizing Internet.
E-Travel	Another early leader in the provision of Web-based reservation systems for business travel, merged into Oracle Corporation which made its booking solution a part of a larger suite of travel and transportation enterprise systems.
Expedia (www.expedia.com)	Microsoft-founded, but now independently operated, booking engine and travel service firm for airline tickets, hotel rooms and rental cars.

(continued)

Appendix 3.1

(continued)

Firm name (URL)	Business description
Factiva (www.factiva.com)	A Dow-Jones and Reuters-owned company specializing in business news, content delivery and business intelligence.
FirstAuction.com	Created by the Internet Shopping Network in the late 1990s as one of the first Web sites to offer instant, two-hour auctions, but no longer operating.
FlySpy (www.flyspy.com)	A Minneapolis, Minnesota-based Internet start-up that provides comparative information on the market for airfares in the United States in a visual format.
FSBO.Com (www.fsbo.com)	For Sale By Owner, for Internet-based sales of real estate without the involvement of real estate agents, and early innovator for disintermediation.
Galileo International (www.galileo.com)	Founded by United Airlines in 1971 in conjunction with the creation of the computerized reservation system Apollo. Now a leading global electronic travel information distribution services provider, associated through an acquisition with Cendant Corporation's family of travel services solutions.
GetThere.com (www.getthere.com)	See *Internet Travel Network*.
Grant Street Group (www.grantstreet.com)	Founded in 1997 as MuniAuction.com, with patented approaches to electronic market operations and technology support for the issuance of public debt, and now expanded to include a range of fixed-income securities.
Hotwire.com (www.hotwire.com)	Launched in 2000, Hotwire is the leisure travel 'outlet' on the Internet for Expedia.com, which offers consumers prices from competing airline, hotel and other participating travel-related suppliers.
Insight Inc. (www.insight.com)	Traditional reseller of computer hardware and software, with a major presence on the Internet.
Instinet Corporation (www.instinet.com)	A leading agency brokerage company that provides electronic trading systems for its clients; now affiliated with NASDAQ.
Internet Travel Network *(ITN)* (www.itn.com)	An early leader in the online travel agency market, unable to sustain its competitiveness as a consumer travel reservation engine in the face of Expedia, Travelocity and other better funded players. Founded in 1995, ITN was renamed GetThere.com in the late 1990s and was acquired by Sabre Holdings (the owner of the Sabre global distribution system and of the Travelocity Internet-based travel reservation system) in 2000. Over the years, it has transformed itself into a technology provider for travel agencies and corporations and a leader in establishing direct connections between travel providers and their customers.
Kayak.com (www.kayak.com)	A travel and airfares search engine with a Google-based business model that gives consumers maximum control over pricing and product comparisons, and emphasizes high transparency.

Firm name (URL)	Business description
LetsBuyIt.com (www.letsbuyit.com)	A Netherlands Internet-based seller; offers group buying for consumer electronics and high liquidity products; early user of this business model.
Market Axess (www.marketaxess.com)	An electronic bond trading marketplace on the Internet for institutional investors established in 2000, now emphasizing high grade corporate bonds, emerging markets and Eurobonds.
MuniCenter (www.municenter.com)	An Internet-based municipal bond and other fixed income securities electronic marketplace, founded by a consortium of broker/dealers in 1999 in New York.
NASDAQ (www.nasdaq.com)	A New York-based securities market well known for its technological innovations and the trade of technology stocks.
NWA.com (www.nwa.com)	Northwest Airlines was an early adopter of the Internet for direct air ticket sales through NWA.com.
Onsale.Com (www.onsale.com)	Internet-only wholesaler and auction Web site for computer peripherals.
Optimark Technologies (www.optimark.com)	A provider of confidential electronic markets that has introduced the concept of optimal matching using its patented 'three-dimensional trading' technology.
Orbitz.com (www.orbitz.com)	Online travel agency owned by a consortium of major American airlines, and known for its use of product and price transparency to compete with Priceline.com and other direct supplier Web sites in the airline industry.
Owners.com (www.owners.com)	Residential real estate listing service for 'for sale by owner' properties.
Priceline.com (www.priceline.com)	Buyer-driven marketplace for leisure travel ticket, hotel and rental car purchases, among other services.
Preview Travel (www.previewtravel.com)	One of the early movers in the online travel agency business in the USA; now absorbed into Travelocity.com.
Reuters (www.reuters.com)	News and financial market quote vendor with global coverage.
SalesForce.com (www.salesforce.com)	Leading provider of on-demand customer relationship management services; originally founded by an ex-Oracle executive in 1999.
Scottrade (www.scottrade.com)	Discount online broker founded as Scottsdale Securities in the 1970s, now with national bricks-and-clicks coverage in the US market, and recent efforts made to create a beachhead in the market for discount brokerage services in China.
SpaWorks	Single-price crossing auction market to permit stock trading after the normal hours of the New York-based stock exchanges; failed in the wake of market structure changes due to the electronic communication networks (ECNs), including Instanet and Archipelago in the 1990s.

(continued)

Appendix 3.1

(continued)

Firm name (URL)	Business description
Spring Street Brewery	First American company to raise capital with an initial public offering of stock via the Internet.
Staples (www.staples.com)	Large American national retailer of office supplies, back-to-school items and computer-related equipment, with Internet-based selling capabilities.
Target (www.target.com)	Large American national retailer which operates in multiple channels, including traditional retail stores and on the Internet via Target.com
Trading Edge Bond Express (www.bondexpress.com)	An early Internet-only electronic screen-based trading mechanism for fixed income securities for retail investors.
Transpoint	Early joint venture of Microsoft and First Data Corporation for electronic bill payment and presentment services, later purchased by Checkfree.
Travelocity (www.travelocity.com)	A leading Web-based reservation system for leisure travel, developed by SABRE, a computerized reservation system (CRS) that was initially affiliated with American Airlines.
UAL.com (www.ual.com)	Direct booking Web site of United Airlines.
UBid Inc. (www.ubid.com)	An Internet-based auction house for computers, jewellery, travel, collectibles and other sale items with live-action bidding.
Wal-Mart (www.walmart.com)	Large American retailing chain, with physical stores and Internet channel operations via Walmart.com, also known for its unique use of '2', '4' and '8' price endings (e.g., $234.48 or $24.82), unlike other stores which use '9' (e.g., $29.99 or $99) to signal best prices.
Wit Capital (www.witcapital.com)	The first Internet-based investment bank in the United States, famous for bringing the equity of Spring Street Brewery to market in a Web-based IPO. Subsequently purchased by the Soundview Technology Group to form Wit Soundview.
Yahoo! (www.yahoo.com)	Second largest search services provider in the USA, with a significant global presence.

CHAPTER 4

E-business and the intermediary role of virtual communities

P. K. Kannan, Ai-Mei Chang and Andrew B. Whinston

INTRODUCTION

Online or virtual communities have become very popular recently with the rapid use of the World Wide Web for social computing applications. Words such as 'blogging', 'wikis', MySpace, Facebook and ITToolBox as used in the context of virtual or online communities did not exist five years ago. These new concepts and words may suggest that virtual communities are a very recent phenomenon. However, the notion of a virtual community existed even in the early days of e-mail when researchers used the online medium to exchange ideas and information and to collaborate on research projects. For example, the Unix operating system and its derivatives, Sendmail software and other similar products, were developed collaboratively as 'open source software' on the online medium (e.g. e-mail and Usenet discussion boards) by researchers and programmers who hardly interacted with each other face-to-face. Many online services also provided local bulletin boards for special interest groups (SIGs) to exchange content. Later, as the World Wide Web environment started growing, many offline communities (for example, those centred around magazines) started gravitating towards the Internet to take advantage of its connectivity and reach to help the communities grow. In addition, many unique communities started forming on the Internet itself. The early communities on the Internet were centred mainly on non-commercial interests and activities. However, as commercial use of the Web increased, many communities have been formed on the Internet to cater to members' or organizers' commercial interests. Thus, there are communities on the Web that are formed, organized and maintained by members themselves (with or without any commercial focus); some that are organized and controlled by marketers; and some that are organized and maintained by third parties who act, on the one hand, as intermediaries between the members, and on the other, as marketers and advertisers. Given the empirical evidence and trends, it is clear that these communities will be playing a very important role in the growth of electronic commerce. The focus of this chapter is to explore this potential of virtual communities – to complement e-business – viewing them as important intermediaries. We describe how virtual communities organized for business motives differ from other types of communities and explore conditions under which such business-oriented virtual communities can evolve successfully. We argue that, in order to ensure healthy growth, virtual communities should increasingly take on the role of an intermediary in:

1. Exchange relationships between community members; and
2. Exchange relationships between community members, marketers and advertisers.

Drawing parallels from extant research in financial intermediation and drawing upon social exchange theory, we postulate conditions and market mechanisms under which virtual communities could provide great impetus for the growth of electronic commerce on the Web. Wherever possible, we provide empirical examples to support our argument.

In the next section we provide a brief introduction to virtual communities and discuss how value is created within a business-oriented community. We follow this up in the third section with a discussion on how virtual communities can act as intermediaries and provide services to both community members and corporate clients. In the fourth section, we present a model for an intermediary and our postulates regarding the conditions under which virtual communities can evolve and thrive. Finally, we round off the chapter with some concluding comments on the future of virtual communities.

VIRTUAL COMMUNITIES AND VALUE CREATION

Types of virtual communities

In their narrowest form, virtual communities can be defined as:

> *social* aggregations of a *critical mass* of people on the Internet who engage in public discussions, *interactions* in chat rooms, and information exchanges with sufficient *human feeling* on matters of common interest to form webs of *personal relationships* (Rheingold, 1993).

According to this definition, virtual communities are made up of individuals who aggregate into a critical mass driven by common needs, which are mainly social in nature. This common bonding is strengthened by personal relationships that ensure some degree of loyalty of the members to the community. However, commercial interests are a part of individual level needs, and it is not uncommon to find communities for business transactions focused on individual and organizational needs – communities of buyers and sellers, such as eBay, uBid and AucNet. These individual- and business-oriented communities consist of a critical mass of members whose needs are mainly *commercial* in nature and who use the communities principally for *networking* and/or building *business relationships*. While these communities may lack the human feeling element and social interactions, there is such significant informational exchange and communication that we consider these communities as virtual communities.

Extending our analysis, we find that there are essentially four types of virtual communities in existence on the Web – each depending on the types of consumer needs they meet (Armstrong and Hagel, 1995; 1996). Thus, communities could be transaction oriented, interest oriented, fantasy oriented, or relationship oriented. It is also possible that some virtual communities meet several of the above needs. Let us consider each category in turn.

Transaction-oriented communities primarily facilitate the buying and selling of products and services and deliver information that is related to fulfilling those transactions. These communities do not address the members' social needs in any manner; the focus is on interaction between members either to transact business or provide informational leads or consultations about other possible participants in transactions. Examples of communities of transactions include: BestBuy.com or CircuitCity.com, where consumers get information tips from the vendor and buy products at the Web site; Amazon.com, where visitors can get reviews about books from other readers; and business communities such as DigitalMediaNet.com, which meet members' transactional and/or informational needs. Although communities of transactions could be organized by anyone, the organizers are usually the vendors themselves.

The second type of community is a community of interest. Here, members have significantly higher degrees of interactions than in a community of transactions and the interactions are usually on topics of their common interest. Examples include: MySpace, LiveJournal, YouTube and FaceBook, which are rapidly emerging as communities for social interactions – allowing members to share content and interact through blogging, chats and so on; Motley Fool, a community for financial investors; the Well, one of the oldest communities; BioMedNet, a professional community for physicians; and ITToolBox, a community for IT professionals. These communities usually have chat rooms, message boards and discussion groups for extensive member interaction. Thus, they are characterized by a significant amount of user-generated content.

The third type of community is a fantasy-oriented community where users create new environments, personalities, stories and role-play. For example, some online applications create fantasy environments in which groups of users can interact by typing special commands and messages (often referred to as Multi-User Dungeons or MUDs). The popular fictional works of writers such as J.R.R. Tolkien (e.g. *The Hobbit* and *Lord of the Rings*) and William Gibson (e.g. *Neuromancer*) often influence such environments. Examples include ESPNet, Sony.com, and many of the fantasy and gaming communities such Runescape.com, Tricksteronline.com and Worldof WarCraft.com.

The fourth and final type of community is the community of relationships built around certain life experiences that are usually very intense and lead to personal bonding between members. Examples include the Cancer Forum, a community for cancer patients and their close friends and family, as well as communities that focus on religion, divorce and other topics.

Many virtual communities have an overlap of several of the above orientations. For example, communities such as Geocities, MySpace and others have allocated 'concept spaces' where members with similar interests can put up Web sites, transact business with each other, play out their fantasies, and build relationships through interactions. These are meta-communities or 'portals' which organize several smaller, focused, virtual communities centred on common interests and relationships. Similarly, in the business-to-business realm, vertical mega-portals organize a number of tightly focused virtual communities in vertical industries. In this sense, the concept of a virtual community is still evolving. In the discussions that follow we use the term virtual community to encompass all of the above interpretations. All of the different types of virtual communities that we have discussed – transaction, interest, fantasy and relationship communities – can be organized for profit. Non-profit communities generally tend to be less transaction oriented.

Value creation

Figure 4.1 provides a snapshot of how value is created in a community, based on the work of Kannan *et al.* (1998). Members' input to the community consists of information content in the form of comments, feedback, elaborating their attitudes and beliefs, and informational needs. Members may provide such content unsolicited, or in response to

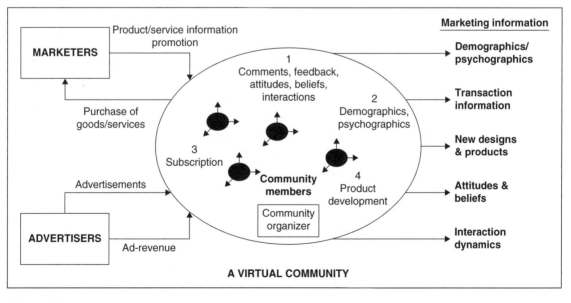

Figure 4.1
Value creation in electronic communities (source: Kannan *et al.*, 1998)

queries by other members or the organizer of the community. Thus, members provide useful information that is retrieved and used by other members of the community. The community organizers may also put in their own content which members may find very valuable. For example, the organizers of BioMedNet provide content in the form of information on the latest medical research and techniques, which the physician members would find very useful. In such communities, the members would also be willing to pay *subscription fees* to become members of the community since they may highly value the information they receive from the community. People pay subscription fees in order to become members of communities such as AOL. Such subscription fees may be viewed as a charge that members need to bear to be part of an exclusive community or for accessing content in the communities that they value.

Another possibility for value creation in virtual communities arises from the fact that a community brings together consumers of specific demographics and interests. This presents opportunities for transacting business and communicating messages about products and services that are of interest to consumers – an activity which marketers and advertisers value and are consequently willing to pay for. In as much as business transactions take place in communities, value is created. In addition, virtual communities can attract ad revenues from advertisers eager to communicate their messages to community members (which is currently a significant source of revenue for virtual communities). In addition to business transactions and ad revenues, there are also other opportunities for value creation. These arise from the marketing information that is generated within communities, which the environment (marketers and advertisers among others) would find valuable. Such information includes the demographics and psychographics of members, their attitudes and beliefs about products, services and issues, their behaviour data with regard to business transactions within communities, and information on their interactions and interaction dynamics. If members do not object, such information could be sold to marketers and advertisers. The value of such opportunities can be very significant – as the recent moves to acquire communities such as Facebook by Microsoft can attest to (Delaney *et al.*, 2006).

Research communities working on software projects such as Linux OS kernel, Apache server software and Perl also add value by designing and creating new software products and extensions. Although none of these communities are formed with for-profit motives, members derive value from each other's contribution and work towards the common good of the researcher and user communities.

The exact manner in which value is created in virtual communities also depends on who organizes the community and who owns it. Transaction-oriented communities are generally organized, controlled and run by marketers. In such virtual communities, value is created mainly though transactions rather than through ad revenues. The marketing information generated in the communities may also reside with the marketers who may or may not sell such information. In many cases, marketers who own virtual communities can use such information to derive synergies for other related business functions, such as better customer service, mass customization in service and delivery, marketing research feedback, and so on. If the community is controlled and owned by members themselves, the main focus of such communities is to derive sole benefits for the members and value is created in content exchange and/or through subscription fees. If the community organizers and those who run it are not marketers, advertisers or members but unrelated third parties, such communities are in a better position to leverage the full range of possibilities for value creation. This intermediary role of virtual communities is a key focus of this chapter.

VIRTUAL COMMUNITIES AS INTERMEDIARIES

One of the main reasons for focusing on the intermediary role of virtual communities is that they are increasingly called upon to play that role in order to achieve healthy growth. As an illustration consider Parentsplace.com (now part of iVillage.com). This was a community started by a Californian couple interested in bringing together parents in cyberspace to discuss issues of mutual interest. The community was started with the objective of selling children-related products to the community members, particularly as they ventured out of the chat rooms and into the retail sections of the community. As the community grew in the chat rooms and discussion rooms, members were more interested in their common interests, getting tips and information on child-rearing, rather than on transacting business. The organizers quickly realized this, and in order to keep the community growing, they adopted the business model of an ad revenue supported community rather than a transaction revenue supported community. This was achieved by selling ad space to advertisers and removing the retail section of the community, thereby pushing the community into more of an intermediary role than a marketer's role.

In addition to the above example illustrating role changes within virtual communities, many analysts, manufacturers and community members are increasingly questioning the idea that businesses can easily 'build' a community to sell their products or services. While some marketers with strong brand presence may be able to sow the seeds for forming a community and encouraging its growth, it is not possible for them to control and manipulate what happens in the community in the manner that they may envision. This increasingly supports the notion that communities grow essentially through members' initiatives and through mutual trust and respect between community organizers and members. If members start questioning the motives of organizers or perceive a pushy agenda from marketers, it may adversely affect the community. These arguments lend credence to the following proposition.

Proposition 1:
Electronic communities will have to increasingly adopt the role of intermediary between marketers and members to ensure healthy community growth.

In order to understand the specific issues involved in performing the above role, it will be useful to list the services that virtual communities provide to members on the one hand and marketers and advertisers on the other. Let us consider each in turn.

First, consider the members of communities. Typically, members enrol in a community for one or more of the following reasons:

1. To extract or download content from communities with the assurance that the content is of 'good' quality and not 'junk'. This could be, for example: input from other community members such as opinions and experiences with products or services; input from community organizers which could be investment advice, or tips on health, and so on; and input from marketers and advertisers such as product and service information, information about loyalty programmes, and so on.

2. To provide content of their own that could be of use to other members. This could be, for example, their own opinions and experiences with respect to products, services and other issues.

3. To forge 'useful' relationships with other members of the community and/or with marketers and advertisers without compromising their privacy. We define 'useful' in terms of meeting social or commercial needs without the problems of 'spamming' or 'stalking' on the Web.

Second, we turn to corporate clients. Typically, these could consider virtual communities useful for the following reasons:

1. To gain access to consumers of a specific demographic and psychographic profile on the Web in order to communicate messages such as advertisements, product or service information, and so on.
2. To transact business with community members and provide personalized offerings using information on their demographics and psychographics. To forge long-term relationships with them and to earn their loyalty.
3. To buy information from virtual communities on members' attitudes and preferences, their interactions with other members, their transaction information, and demographics and psychographics for marketing research purposes.

This creates a number of implications. Specifically, given the above needs of members and corporate clients, virtual communities must maintain the following two conditions to be an effective intermediary:

1. Ensure that the content input by community members, advertisers and marketers is of 'good' quality.
2. Ensure that members' privacy is protected even as appropriate relationships are forged between community members and marketers.

This leads us on to several issues involved in ensuring the above conditions – the absence of which could lead to the meltdown of a virtual community.

Content quality

If members join virtual communities for their content – whether member, organizer or marketer generated – then one of the major tasks of virtual communities must be to ensure that all content made available meets some quality standards. This could be an easy or difficult task depending on the content made available within communities. For example, if content is generated by community organizers (as in ITToolBox) then editorial staff are responsible for maintaining quality. However, if content is member-generated then maintaining quality may not be an easy task. Such member input could vary from opinions to experiences and reviews where it may be difficult to judge quality. Similarly, if the members put up videos as content (as in YouTube or

Google Video) the appropriateness of content for general viewing may be questionable. There is nothing preventing a community member from inputting deliberate lies or misrepresentations about their experiences with products or services, thereby misleading other community members. In most cases, virtual communities can put up a disclaimer regarding the member-generated content. Typically, disclaimers state that communities cannot fully vouch for the quality or appropriateness of content, suggesting that they are the opinions of individuals. Notwithstanding, unless there is some intervention to assure quality, the community can easily disintegrate, as serious community members will start looking elsewhere. The intervention can be in the form of moderators in chat rooms or editors who will continuously monitor the nature and quality of input and interactions and take action against members who continuously disrupt the community. Ensuring the quality of information from advertisers and marketers may also be difficult, but in most cases the virtual community can rely on their corporate image and reputation as proxies for their information quality. Virtual communities can thus ensure that their community members are not subject to the manipulations of 'fly-by-night' operators and schemes.

Free-riding members

For a community that relies on members' input for value generation, members who 'free-ride' can be a problem. For example, consider a virtual community devoted to vacation travelling. Members can access useful information from travel agents and other marketers of vacation packages, but can also refer to other members' reviews of and experiences with different packages – which can be much more useful. If community members participate only as 'lurkers' and do not actually contribute any useful information (i.e. by trying out a package or service themselves), then the community can suffer (Choi *et al.*, 1997). Over time, such free-riding can lead to a paucity of useful content within the community. Thus, as an intermediary, virtual communities have to ensure active participation of members. In some cases, this may come through economic incentives.

Members' privacy

Members who join virtual communities usually provide demographic, lifestyle and interest information to the community organizers. This information is usually required to better meet member needs of social and commercial interactions, e.g. a senior citizen may like to interact with other senior citizens who have similar interests and concerns, and they may be interested in learning about new medical insurance plans that they may want to enrol in. The community organizers also need information to maintain the relative homogeneity of the community in terms of interests and/or demographics. In addition, a virtual community can also generate significant information regarding members' interests through chat rooms and discussion groups where they interact with other members. Virtual communities can also track members' transaction information. While all such information has value for marketers and advertisers, most members expect virtual communities to respect their privacy and safeguard their personal information and not to let advertisers and marketers use the information indiscriminately to 'spam' members. Members also expect similar privacy in dealing with other members. Thus, virtual communities may choose to use *aggregated* personal information to provide to marketers and not to divulge individual-level information. Any serious breach of privacy can lead to litigation, negative publicity and ultimately to the disintegration of the community. A recent case involving Facebook.com, which started providing highly personal information about its members (such as the status of their relationships) to other members, created serious backlash among its members (of mostly college students). This led Facebook.com to withdraw such features in deference to its members' wishes and to add new privacy options (Vauhini, 2006), thus proving that community organizers may have to continue to tread lightly when it comes to users' privacy rights (Rust *et al.*, 2002).

Corporate clients' needs

Advertisers and marketers expect value for the revenue that they provide to virtual communities by way of ad fees and commissions. They derive such value through communicating their messages to the right target segment, forging long-term relationships with members and getting information on how best to meet their needs. This implies that corporate clients expect to get 'good' quality demographic and interest information from virtual communities that do not contain deliberate falsifications and misrepresentations. In addition, they would like to focus on individual consumers and their specific needs to take advantage of the one-on-one marketing opportunities that the Web facilitates. This implies that corporate clients may demand individual-level data from virtual communities – even though virtual communities are concerned about protecting members' privacy. If virtual communities cannot deliver significant value to corporate clients, advertising and commission revenue may dry up quickly, thus adversely affecting their financial status.

Maintaining critical mass

For any community to thrive it needs to achieve a critical mass. If the chat rooms and discussion rooms are empty or do not have new content, membership dwindles quickly. Business-to-business communities are also similar in this respect. For example, Industry.Net was never able to attain the necessary critical mass in time for the community to thrive. Since many businesses adopted a 'wait-and-see' approach, the community never took off. Critical mass is necessary for membership growth and for healthy revenues from corporate clients. As intermediaries virtual communities have a special role to play in maintaining a critical mass.

In the next section, we focus on a model of intermediation, and the economic and incentive mechanisms that are needed to maintain a healthy virtual community while considering the various trade-offs among the issues identified above.

A MODEL OF INTERMEDIATION

We use the principal/agent framework to model intermediation (see, for example, Diamond, 1984; 1996). Consider a cybermarket with two groups of players – consumers who are risk averse and marketers who are risk neutral. Assume that consumers possess demographic and psychographic information about themselves that is of significant value to the marketer. This information has value for marketers as it can help them design products and services tailored to consumer needs, thereby increasing the chances of significant earnings. We also assume that consumers value their personal information – either because they know marketers value it and/or because they value their privacy. If their personal information becomes easily available it could potentially be costly for them in trying to avoid or stop unnecessary 'spamming'. Thus, consumer information has value for consumers, just as monetary assets have value. While monetary assets have value that is practically homogeneous across consumers, the valuation, v, of consumer information can vary across the consumer population. For example, marketers may value demographic and psychographic information about certain consumers more than others. For now, let us assume that each consumer's information, prior to being obtained, is valued at the distribution's mean, $E(v)$. Without any loss of generality, let us assume that $E(v) = 1$.

In the absence of intermediaries, marketers have to go directly to consumers in search of appropriate consumer information. Also, they will need personal information from a significant number of consumers, say m. Using information from the m consumers, the marketer would be able realize a return which could include increased profits through personalization of their products or services, increasing customer loyalty, and so on. The marketer could then share this profit with consumers as a return on their information. When consumers provide information to marketers in exchange for some future return as just explained, they would like to monitor what the marketer does with the information and ensure that the marketer uses the information properly to generate a return for their investment of personal information. There is a cost involved in monitoring, denoted by K. Realistically, there is no available mechanism on the Internet for consumers to monitor what marketers do with their personal information, other than through their experience and interactions with the marketer over time (say, through loyalty programmes or through finding product offerings tailored to their interest, all of which may provide indications as to how their personal information is being used; or via indications of misuse if they are subject to spamming). Thus, the cost of monitoring can be assumed to be prohibitively high, that is, $K \geqslant 1$, which is the expected valuation of information. There are also savings, S, associated with monitoring. These savings could be interpreted as the benefits arising from the information remaining private.

Let us assume that a marketer enters into contracts with consumers for obtaining their personal information. If there is no monitoring by consumers of what the marketer does with the personal information, then the nature of the optimal contract will depend on the actual realization (or perception) of profits through the use of personal information. Let the profits earned be $Prf = m*1*f(m)$ where $f(m)$ is a function of m that takes a value of zero for values of m less than some critical mass, and takes on a value greater than 1 beyond the critical mass, increasing at a diminishing rate. That is, the marketer cannot make a profit from the information if less than the critical mass of consumers sign up, and the exact profit level depends on the number of customers beyond the critical mass. One could specify the function form of $f(m)$ and the probability distribution of m, but for now, let us assume a discrete distribution for Prf: $Prf = m(1.6)$ with a probability $p = 0.6$, *while Prf* = 0 with *p* = 0.4. Assume that this information is common knowledge for the marketer as well as for consumers. What does this information imply for the consumers? The probabilities indicate that consumers give the marketer a 60 per cent chance of succeeding in getting a return on their personal information (in whatever form – better products, longer-term relationships, lower prices, better services, and so on). On average, if they are expecting a 10 per cent return on their information invested, valued at 1, then the optimal contract payment, *Cp*, that the marketer needs to offer can be calculated from the equation $0.6 * Cp = 1.1$, which results in a *Cp* of 1.833, a 83.3 per cent return. (In fact, since we have assumed consumers are risk averse, the value of *Cp* will be even higher.)

Thus, based on the uncertainty that the consumer faces regarding the success of any venture that requires their personal information, the marketer will have to promise a significant return for the consumers in exchange for their personal information. If the marketer fails to generate the return that the consumer expects or fails to share the realized profit with the consumers, then the consumers can blacklist the marketer and refuse to deal with the marketer in the future. This ensures that if the marketer profits then there is an incentive to honour the contract. How do concerns about privacy impact the contract? At present there is no mechanism to stop the marketer from reselling the personal information to others to make a profit. This is an added impediment for consumers to share their personal information. It is to be noted that even with a contract with an optimal *Cp*, there will be some consumers who will not enter into such a contract. These are the consumers who have valuations in the upper tail of the distribution of *v* (i.e. those who value their privacy and information much more than the average consumer). Since *Cp* is designed with respect to the average consumer's valuation *E*(*v*), these consumers will not find *Cp* attractive enough to exchange their information. On the basis of the above modelling framework, the following proposition can be made:

Proposition 2:
Marketers will incur a significant cost in obtaining personal information directly from consumers in cyberspace. This cost will be higher: (1) for marketers with lower reputation; (2) as the return for information is less concrete; and (3) as the percentage of consumers in the target population who already share information with other marketers is lower.

This proposition follows by noting the effects of the above factors on the variables that determine the optimal *Cp*. When a marketer's reputation is low, consumers' perception of overall success of the marketer's project will also be low. This effect will be felt through a lower mean of the distribution of m, that is, consumers perceive that the marketer cannot gather information from a significant number of consumers. Here, the probability of success decreases and the optimal contract Cp increases, sometimes even so far beyond the level of believability that marketers cannot approach the consumers. If the return for information is in an abstract form – such as better service and better quality that cannot be easily perceived – then, given the risk-averse nature of consumers, they may seek higher returns (say, more than the 10 per cent assumed in the model). By the same token, if consumers already share their information with other marketers, the marginal return they may seek from sharing the same information might be much lower than otherwise (that is, their marginal costs of sharing their private information are much lower now).

The above proposition has many implications for a community of transactions. It implies that marketers with established reputation in other channels have an advantage over Internet start-ups with lower reputation in building a transaction-based community. At the same time, start-ups have a better chance of collecting information from consumers who are already cyberspace savvy and have shared information with other firms, and by providing concrete monetary rewards – such as discounts, coupons and cash – for information sharing.

What can marketers do to reduce the costs of acquiring consumer information without the intervention of any intermediary? One way to reduce costs is to increase the probability of a larger community membership base, m, through several value-added measures. They can provide chat rooms and discussion groups, which can meet consumers' social needs and increase the chances of a larger community base. These may lower the return consumers would seek for exchange of information as they are already obtaining some value in the social dimension. Value-added content on marketers' Web sites also has the same effect. In order to lower costs further the marketer may have to take on the role of an intermediary. The impact of intermediaries in the value chain is discussed below.

Impact of intermediaries

In financial intermediary theory (see Bhattacharya and Thakor, 1993), intermediation is often justified on the basis of avoiding duplication of monitoring efforts. Using the notation introduced earlier, if m consumers spend K (the cost of monitoring), then the total cost of direct monitoring is mK. S is the total savings from monitoring (that is, keeping all information private), and if there is no monitoring, S is also the cost without monitoring. If the total cost of monitoring an intermediary is less than the minimum of mK and S, then intermediaries create value in the transaction. With the intermediary, the total cost of monitoring is K plus a cost of monitoring the intermediary, T. Thus, if $K + T <$ min (S, mK), then having an intermediary is cost effective (Diamond, 1996: 54). In the context of our application, if T – the cost of monitoring the intermediary – is as high as mK, that is, if the intermediary is just like another marketer to the consumers, then intermediation will not create any value. Thus, T has to be much less than mK. Under what conditions can T be small? T can be small if: (1) the community that is providing the monitoring function is controlled by the members themselves; and (2) if the community is run by a third party who has a vested interest in keeping the community alive, i.e. the third party has no ulterior motive in running the community. We explain below the intuition behind this result in the context of our application.

When consumers provide their private information to the intermediary, the intermediary has a conflict of interest with the members. To be precise, the intermediary can do whatever they want with the information. How can consumers avoid having to monitor the intermediary? This can be done through the intermediary entering into contracts with the consumers, providing an attractive return in exchange for their information. If the intermediary fails to do so, the intermediary will face the disintegration of the community. This threat of disintegration is enough incentive for the intermediary to honour the contracts, since not doing so will threaten its well-being.

Proposition 3:
Electronic communities taking on the role of intermediaries can significantly lower the costs of obtaining consumer personal information and access for marketers.

The impact of intermediaries on the costs of obtaining consumer information can be gauged through an understanding of how the different variables – such as consumers' expected return on investment of information, the distribution of expected profits, the membership base and consumers' perception of the probability of success – are affected.

The first advantage that intermediaries can provide is diversification. In other words, consumer information is provided to multiple marketers and, therefore, the probability of an eventual success increases significantly. This can be viewed as a reduction of uncertainty through the law of large numbers. This increase in the probability of successful returns reduces the magnitude of Cp, the optimal cost of the contract.

The second impact is through protection of privacy. Intermediaries, as third parties with no connection to marketers, are in a good position to provide mechanisms and assurance for consumer information protection. By crafting clever mechanisms for consumer privacy and securing members' trust, intermediaries can lower the expected return that consumers expect for their private information (say, from the 10 per cent that we had assumed earlier in this section to 5 per cent).

Third, given the different relationships that the intermediary can forge with multiple marketers, they would be in a much better position than with individual marketers to provide value to their members in terms of product or service information content and varied choice. This also enables them to secure members' trust in less time than would be possible for an individual marketer – as they would not be hindered by an agenda of pushing a specific product or service at members. For the same reason, intermediaries can better fulfil the social needs of members through chat rooms, discussion rooms and content as compared to marketers. As intermediaries can effectively provide a variety of services to members of a virtual community, they are also in a better position to maintain the critical mass of members and help grow the community. Meeting members' needs in multiple ways also impacts the probability distribution of m positively (i.e. consumers will be more certain about the ability of the community to attract members) and this leads to a perception of higher profits and thus the return promised in the contract is more believable.

The net effect is that those consumers who prefer to remain on the sidelines when a marketer approaches them for private information are more likely to join a virtual community because of the increased probability of success with their information. The protection of privacy also increases their likelihood of joining the virtual community.

The preceding discussion provides a clear understanding of how even though intermediaries incur a significant cost in monitoring marketers (K), the overall cost of obtaining consumer information can be much lower. Intermediaries can incur additional costs in monitoring the quality of content that enters the community, whether from members or marketers. The costs of monitoring quality from members could be significant – moderating chat rooms, discussions forums, and so on. If there are still serious problems, then the intermediary could even charge subscription fees from members to weed out unwanted input, keep membership exclusive and to sustain a high quality of input. Some virtual communities charge a nominal fee for members to post their messages in the discussion forums to prevent frivolous postings. If members derive significant value from the content generated in the virtual community (like, for example, in BioMedNet), then subscription fees act as a mechanism to maintain the quality of content and contribute towards a healthy virtual community.

Subscription fees can also help in reducing the enrolment of purely 'free-riding' members as they incur a cost in enrolling. Such fees can be set high for initial enrolment and as members remain for a longer period of time the fees could be gradually reduced. It is to be noted that such charges are possible only if members value content significantly enough to enrol. However, revenue from marketers and advertisers could be used to subsidize these fees significantly, with those members who have been loyal for a longer time reaping the benefits.

We have seen that maintaining the privacy of consumers can bring the costs down appreciably (see also Rust *et al.*, 2002). At the same time, however, intermediaries have to meet the needs of marketers to keep revenue flowing into the virtual communities. Such a trade-off can be accomplished by clever mechanisms such as loyalty programmes. These programmes allow the collection of demographic and psychographic information over a period of time from those consumers who apply for the programme. The programmes then offer consumers full control over their personal information as to what could be shared and what not, who to share with and who not to, and so on. The marketer uses this information to personalize the service and product offering to members, to develop a relationship with the customer, to direct customers to their own communities of like-minded members, and so on.

CONCLUDING COMMENTS

In this chapter we have focused our attention on virtual communities from the perspective of how they can contribute to electronic commerce rather than viewing them as a pure social phenomenon from a social computing perspective. We have made arguments as to why virtual communities need to take on an intermediary role to keep the communities healthy. Obviously, this argument is valid only when we view virtual communities from a commercial perspective. It is not necessary for a relationship-oriented community to take on this role if revenue generation is not one of the objectives of the community. What we have shown is that virtual communities can offer a win/win situation for both members and marketers. Based on our exploratory work it could be hypothesized that for virtual communities to thrive as a part of a digital economy, they need to transform themselves as intermediaries. Communities run by marketers will have their limitations in terms of offering members variety. Such communities may not be able to take criticism from members easily. Further, controlling a community will not be easy. These are not issues when virtual communities are in the hands of intermediaries. In addition, as we have shown, there are strong economic arguments for community existence based on the value they create. Notwithstanding, there are many interesting issues that require exploration. How do virtual communities diffuse in cyberspace? What are the mechanisms – social, economic, cultural or otherwise – that lead to their formation? What is the future scenario for virtual communities? What mechanisms will allow the value from social-oriented communities to be harnessed effectively? We hope that the thoughts expressed in this chapter will contribute in some way to this exploration.

REFERENCES

Armstrong, A. and Hagel, J. (1995). Real profits from virtual communities. *The McKinsey Quarterly*, 3, 127–141.

Armstrong, A. and Hagel, J. (1996). The real value of online communities. *Harvard Business Review*, 74, 134–140.

Bhattacharya, S. and Thakor, A. V. (1993). Contemporary banking theory. *Journal of Financial Intermediation*, 3, 2–50.

Choi, S.-Y., Stahl, D. and Whinston, A. B. (1997). *The Economics of Electronic Commerce*. Macmillan Technical Publishing.

Delaney, K. J., Buckman, R. and Guth, R. (2006). Facebook: riding a Web trend flirts with a big-money deal. *Wall Street Journal*, 21 September, A1.

Diamond, D. (1984). Financial intermediation and delegated monitoring. *Review of Economic Studies*, 51, 393–414.

Diamond, D. (1996). Financial intermediation as delegated monitoring: a simple example. *Federal Reserve Bank of Richmond Economic Quarterly*, 82, 51–66.

Kannan, P. K., Chang, A. and Whinston, A. B. (1998). Marketing information on the I-way. *Communications of the ACM*, 41, 35–43.

Rheingold, H. (1993). *The Virtual Community: Homesteading on the Electronic Frontier*. Harper Perennial Publishers.

Rust, R. T., Kannan, P. K. and Peng, N. (2002). The customer economics of privacy in e-service. *Journal of Academy of Marketing Science*, 30 (4), 455–464.

Vauhini, V. (2006). Facebook adds privacy option after new features draw backlash. *Wall Street Journal*, 8 September, B3.

CHAPTER 5

Assessing e-commerce quality

Stuart Barnes, Eduard Cristóbal, Frederic Marimon and Richard Vidgen

INTRODUCTION

The Internet allows organizations to reach new markets and new consumers. Notwithstanding, it is also necessary to retain new customers and to build loyalty. However, not all companies with an online presence recognize the importance of Web site quality. The Healey & Baker consultancy (2000) affirmed that a large percentage of attempts to purchase over the Internet fail – 46 per cent of transactions are cancelled and, in some countries such as Spain, this figure is as high as 75 per cent. It is possible that these failed attempts to purchase result from technical problems, such as deficiencies in communication networks or connection problems, or due to a lack of experience in the use of the Internet by consumers. What is more likely is that the failed attempts to purchase are due to other factors: errors in the transaction, a lack of required information to complete the purchase, difficulty in the use of the Web site, and so on.

The retention of an online consumer is difficult and expensive (Van Riel *et al.*, 2001). Consumers can easily evaluate and compare the services offered by different online providers and, therefore, companies must provide a quality online service if they are to retain customers and generate loyalty. Numerous early studies showed that the higher that quality is perceived in the Web site, the higher the levels of yield are for the provider (Hoffman *et al.*, 1995; Lohse and Spiller, 1998; 1999; Swaminathan *et al.*, 1999; *inter alia*). An important strand of the emergent literature in business-to-consumer electronic commerce tries to identify the attributes and the dimensions that define online quality from the perspective of the consumer or user and the impact on his or her future behavioural intentions. Most of the measures used in these studies assess perception scores or levels of performance. Quality is typically defined as the discrepancy between the awaited or expected level of performance and the actual perceived level of performance (Parasuraman *et al.*, 1988; Parasuraman, 1995). However, the literature has defended and empirically demonstrated the greater capacity of measures of perception alone, as compared to measures of difference (that is, performance expectation), to predict the perceived global quality and behavioural intentions of the consumer (Babakus and Boller, 1992; Brown *et al.*, 1993; Cronin and Taylor, 1992).

A large portion of the relevant literature in this area is generally focused on elements of graphical design and usability as perceived from a Web site (Aladwani and Palvia, 2002; Li *et al.*, 1999; Mandel and Johnson, 1999; Menon and Khan, 1997; Yang *et al.*, 2003; 2005; Yoo and Donthu, 2001). Therefore, it is necessary to complement these contributions by examining what aspects of the service given by a Web site – beyond an attractive interface and usability – determine the perceived quality of the consumer and therefore their behaviour. This latter research stream has grown in significance in the last five years as researchers have sought to apply the ideas of service quality to electronic commerce (e.g. see Barnes and Vidgen, 2002; Kim and Stoel, 2004; Long and McMellon, 2004; Madu and Madu, 2002; Negash *et al.*, 2002; Parasuraman *et al.*, 2005; Wolfinbarger and Gilly, 2003; Zeithaml *et al.*, 2001).

This chapter focuses on the evaluation of perceived Web site quality from a broad customer perspective, integrating a variety of theoretical strands including usability, Web site design, information quality, trust and service quality. To set the scene, the next section provides a general discussion of the variety of Web quality instruments available. This is followed by an example of the application of one specific instrument – eQual – in the domain of online bookshops. The penultimate section examines the implications for e-commerce quality. Finally the chapter rounds off with a summary and conclusions.

WEB QUALITY INSTRUMENTS

With the ever-increasing use of e-commerce, the need to appraise service has rapidly moved to the virtual world. To this end, a number of different studies have been carried out, the majority of which being aimed at developing measurement scales adapted to this new medium (see Table 5.1 for a list of these – which was up to date at the time of writing). For the purpose of simplifying the review of the literature, the different studies of online service quality can be split into two principal categories according to their focus: Web site design quality and e-commerce quality. Let us discuss each of these in turn.

Web site design quality

Instruments in this research grouping tend to focus more on the Web site itself, how it is designed and how it interacts, more than the commercial and service aspects *per se*. Typically, investigators approach the research from an information systems perspective.

Yoo and Donthu (2001) developed the SITEQUAL scale to measure the perceived quality of an online shop. This led to a nine-item scale of four dimensions: ease of use, aesthetic design, processing speed and security. For their part, Barnes and Vidgen (2002) developed the WebQual 4.0 scale (now called eQual), made up of 22 items divided into five dimensions: usability, design, information, trust and empathy. It is interesting to note that this instrument also incorporates measures of importance to the perception measures. Liu and Arnett (2000) highlight the presence of four factors: information and service quality, system use, playfulness and system design quality. Lastly, Loiacono *et al.* (2002) created the WebQual™ scale, composed of 36 items and 12 dimensions: informational fit-to-task; interactivity; trust; response time; design appeal; intuitiveness; visual appeal; innovativeness; flow (emotional appeal); integrated communication; business process; and substitutability.

In spite of these efforts made to measure the quality construct perceived in Internet service distribution, it is clear that research in this area is still at an early phase (Van Riel *et al.*, 2001). In fact, we may observe some general deficiencies in the work in this group:

■ Many of the studies are found to focus on technical aspects. Thus, it would seem reasonable to study additional aspects in depth, such as those that allow us to explain the relationships between online service quality and satisfaction or the customer's intention to purchase again.

Table 5.1
Web quality instruments

Authors	Target/dependent variable	Dimensions identified/independent variables		Web sites analysed
Liu and Arnett (2000)	Website success	1. Quality of Information 2. Service 3. System use	4. Playfulness perceived by consumers 5. Design of the Web site	Webmasters for Fortune 1000 companies
Loiacono et al. (2000) 'WEBQUAL™'	Intention to purchase/ intention to revisit	1. Informational fit to task 2. Interactivity 3. Trust 4. Response time 5. Design appeal 6. Intuitiveness	7. Visual appeal 8. Innovativeness 9. Flow (emotional appeal) 10. Integrated communication 11. Business process 12. Substitutability	Web sites selling books, music, airline tickets and hotel reservations
Cox and Dale (2001)	E-commerce operating environment	1. Accessibility 2. Communication 3. Credibility	4. Understanding 5. Appearance 6. Availability	Online shopping sites
Van Riel et al. (2001)	Overall satisfaction, intentions to continue using the site in the future and perceived value of the service	1. Core service 2. Supporting services	3. User interface	Medical information portal
Yoo and Donthu (2001) 'SITEQUAL'	Overall site quality, attitude toward site, online purchase intention, site loyalty and site equity	1. Ease of use 2. Aesthetic design	3. Processing speed 4. Security	Online shopping sites
Zeithaml et al. (2001) 'E-SERVQUAL'	Quality	1. Reliability 2. Responsibility 3. Access 4. Flexibility 5. Ease of navigation 6. Efficiency	7. Assurance/trust 8. Security 9. Price knowledge 10. Site aesthetics 11. Customization/ personalization	Online shopping sites

Study	Focus	Dimensions		Context
Aladwania and Palvia (2002)	Web site quality	1. Specific content 2. Content quality	3. Appearance 4. Technical adequacy	Different sites, including a bank, bookshop, car manufacturer and electronic retailer
Barnes and Vidgen (2002) 'WEBQUAL 4.0' (now eQual 4.0)	User satisfaction	1. Web site usability 2. Web site design 3. Information quality	4. Empathy 5. Trust	Internet bookstores
Madu and Madu (2002)	Quality of products, service and virtual operations	1. Performance 2. Features 3. Structure 4. Aesthetics 5. Reliability 6. Storage capacity 7. Serviceability 8. Security and system integrity 9. Trust	10. Responsiveness 11. Product/service differentiation and customization 12. Web store policies 13. Reputation 14. Assurance 15. Empathy	Online shopping sites
Negash et al. (2002)	User satisfaction	1. Informativeness 2. Entertainment 3. Interactivity 4. Access	5. Tangible reliability 6. Responsiveness 7. Assurance 8. Empathy	Customer support systems
Yang and Jun (2002)	Online retailing service quality	1. Reliability 2. Access 3. Ease of use	4. Personalization 5. Security 6. Credibility	Online shopping sites
Trocchia and Janda (2003)	Internet service quality	1. Performance 2. Access 3. Security	4. Sensation 5. Information	Online shopping sites
Wolfinbarger and Gilly (2001; 2002; 2003) 'ECOMQ/ETAILQ'	Global quality, satisfaction, attitude toward the Web site, loyalty intentions	1. Web site design 2. Reliability	3. Privacy/security 4. Customer service	Online shopping sites

(continued)

Table 5.1
(continued)

Authors	Target/dependent variable	Dimensions identified/independent variables	Web sites analysed
Yang et al. (2003)	Satisfaction/ dissatisfaction	1. Responsiveness 2. Credibility 3. Ease of use 4. Reliability 5. Convenience 6. Communication 7. Access 8. Competence 9. Courtesy 10. Personalization 11. Continuous improvement 12. Collaboration 13. Security/privacy 14. Aesthetics	Online shopping sites
Kim and Stoel (2004)	Consumer satisfaction	1. Web appearance 2. Entertainment 3. Informational fit-to-task 4. Transaction capability 5. Response time 6. Trust	Online apparel shops
Long and McMellon (2004)	Overall quality and intention to recommend the Web site	1. Tangibility 2. Assurance 3. Reliability 4. Responsiveness 5. Purchasing process	Online shopping sites
Flavian et al. (2006)	Loyalty	1. Usability 2. Trust (honesty, benevolence, competence) 3. User satisfaction	User selected site (previous experience required)
Parasuraman et al. (2005) 'E-S-QUAL/ E-RecS-QUAL'	Quality	Seven dimensions form a core and a recovery service scale. *Core e-SQ* 1. Efficiency 2. System availability 3. Fulfilment 4. Privacy *Recovery e-SQ* 1. Responsiveness 2. Compensation 3. Contact	Online shopping sites
Yang et al. (2005)	Overall service quality	1. Usability 2. Usefulness 3. Adequacy of information 4. Accessibility 5. Interaction	Web portals

■ Many empirical studies use online surveys, which restrict the results in different ways (e.g. by creating an Internet-user influenced sample, via voluntary questionnaires, and so on). In fact, online service quality studies using personal interviews are few and far between (Yang and Fang, 2004). Moreover, the use of personal interviews is usually subordinated by the presence of a limited number of participants, which prevents the identification of sufficiently explanatory dimensions (Van Riel *et al.*, 2001).

E-commerce quality

Instruments in this research grouping are less focused on the Web site and more on how interaction with the consumer provides quality of service in an e-commerce environment. Researchers in this area are often influenced by ideas from marketing and operations, as well as from information systems.

In keeping with earlier research on service quality in conventional distribution channels, Zeithaml *et al.* (2000; 2001; 2002) and Parasuraman *et al.* (2005) carried out a study on Internet service quality, from which they developed the e-SQ scale. This scale is defined as the degree to which a Web site facilitates effective and efficient purchasing. From the onset, the e-SQ scale comprised of 11 dimensions (Zeithaml *et al.*, 2001). However, later studies reduced this figure to seven dimensions (Parasuraman *et al.*, 2005).

Gefen (2002) maintains that service quality dimensions may be divided into three categories: tangibles; a combined dimension of responsiveness, reliability and assurance; and empathy. In keeping with this is the .comQ scale by Wolfinbarger and Gilly (2002). This scale is made up of 14 items divided into four factors: Web site design; reliability; privacy/security; and customer service. Further, Cox and Dale (2001) show which traditional dimensions of service quality, e.g. competence, courtesy, clarity, comfort and friendliness, were not relevant to online sales; other factors, e.g. accessibility, communication, credibility and appearance, were very important to being successful in an online environment. Madu and Madu (2002) identify 15 dimensions: performance; features; structure; aesthetics; reliability; storage capacity; serviceability; security and system integrity; trust; responsiveness; product/service differentiation and customization; Web store policies; reputation; assurance; and empathy. Finally, Vázquez and Trespalacios (2006) propose a more general model, in which they also include a dimension on the product in itself, composed of three items – price, range and quality of the product. The other two dimensions are 'experience in the purchase' and 'service to the client'.

In this section we have examined some of the most important contributions in the study of online service quality. The emphasis of these studies is on the processes that the consumer faces in order to finish an online purchase. In this field, Zeithaml *et al.* (2002) indicate the necessity to investigate questions about the importance of different dimensions and perceptual attributes to overall electronic service quality and its consequences. In this way, these authors point to a number of different aspects: the necessity to understand the effects of informational attributes of Web sites on perceptions of e-service quality (i.e. the way in which the information is organized on Web sites); the impact of different types of information on e-service quality; the effect of personalization/customization on e-service quality; and how the consumers judge the privacy of a Web site (e.g. trust symbols, company reputation and appearance of the site).

By the same token, some instruments in this group start from dimensions derived from the traditional service quality literature (Van Riel *et al.*, 2001). Van Riel *et al.* argue that the scale items must be reformulated to adapt to an e-service context. For example, 'tangibility' could be replaced with 'user interface' or 'assurance' could refer to the safety of online transactions and general trustworthiness, which has been considered as one of the most important factors of e-service satisfaction (Urban *et al.*, 2000). Unfortunately, little research has integrated models from traditional service quality and information systems quality, and consequently the unique quality aspects of online services (particularly those from service-intensive industries) cannot be fully reflected (Yang and Fang, 2004). In addition, the very few exploratory studies on online service quality that exist have utilized focus groups and personal interviews. These research methods usually have very limited numbers of participants, which prevents them from uncovering more comprehensive dimensions and subdimensions (Van Riel *et al.*, 2001).

Finally, research in this group has typically not studied demographic, behavioural and experiential aspects related to e-service quality in any depth (Zeithaml *et al.*, 2002). Does the age, gender or income of customers affect their perceptions of online service quality? Are there other behavioural aspects that influence perceptions? All of these questions remain unanswered.

The next section focuses on the application of one specific research instrument – eQual – in an e-commerce environment. The instrument has been developed by two of the authors over a number of years and is applied in this chapter in the context of online bookshops.

E-COMMERCE QUALITY ASSESSMENT IN ACTION: eQual

The provenance of eQual

The first version of the eQual instrument was developed in the domain of UK business schools (Barnes and Vidgen, 2000). The development methodology for the instrument was to use quality function deployment (QFD), which is a 'structured and disciplined process that provides a means to identify and carry the voice of the customer through each stage of product and or service development and implementation' (Slabey, 1990). Using raw qualities collected in workshops a pilot questionnaire was developed and refined using the literature on information quality, particularly Bailey and Pearson (1983), DeLone and McLean (1992) and Strong *et al.* (1997).

In applying eQual to business-to-consumer (B2C) Web sites it became clear that the interaction perspective of quality was largely missing from eQual 1.0. Bitner (1990: 72) adopts Shostack's (1985) definition of a service encounter as 'a period of time during which a consumer directly interacts with a service' and notes that these interactions need not be interpersonal – a service encounter can occur without a human interaction element (Bitner *et al.*, 2000). Bitner (1990) also recognizes that 'many times that interaction is the service from the customer's point of view' (p. 71). In eQual 2.0 the interaction aspects were developed further by adapting and applying the work on service quality, chiefly SERVQUAL (Parasuraman, 1995; Parasuraman *et al.*, 1988; 1991; Zeithaml *et al.*, 1990; 1993) and IS SERVQUAL (Kettinger and Lee, 1997; Pitt *et al.*, 1995; 1997; Van Dyke *et al.*, 1997). The eQual 2.0 instrument was applied to online bookshops (see Barnes and Vidgen, 2001a, for a full account).

While eQual 1.0 was strong on information quality, it was less strong on service interaction. Similarly, where eQual 2.0 emphasized interaction quality it lost some of the information quality richness of eQual 1.0. Both instruments contained a range of qualities concerned with the Web site as a software artefact. In reviewing the instruments we found that all of the qualities could be categorized into three distinct areas: site quality, information quality and service interaction quality. This new version of eQual (3.0) was tested in the domain of online auctions (Barnes and Vidgen, 2001b).

Analysis of the results of eQual 3.0 led to the identification of three dimensions of e-commerce Web site quality: usability, information quality

Table 5.2
eQual 4.0 instrument

Category	Questions
Usability	1. I find the site easy to learn to operate
	2. My interaction with the site is clear and understandable
	3. I find the site easy to navigate
	4. I find the site easy to use
	5. The site has an attractive appearance
	6. The design is appropriate to the type of site
	7. The site conveys a sense of competency
	8. The site creates a positive experience for me
Information quality	9. Provides accurate information
	10. Provides believable information
	11. Provides timely information
	12. Provides relevant information
	13. Provides easy to understand information
	14. Provides information at the right level of detail
	15. Presents the information in an appropriate format
Service interaction	16. Has a good reputation
	17. It feels safe to complete transactions
	18. My personal information feels secure
	19. Creates a sense of personalization
	20. Conveys a sense of community
	21. Makes it easy to communicate with the organization
	22. I feel confident that goods/services will be delivered as promised
OVERALL	23. Overall view of the Web site

and service interaction quality. The resulting eQual 4.0 instrument is shown in Table 5.2. This instrument has been applied in a number of studies and domains (e.g. see Barnes and Vidgen, 2002; 2003a; 2003b; 2006).

Assessing Internet bookshop quality

Using eQual 4.0 three bookshops were evaluated: Amazon, Bertelsmann Online (BOL) and the Internet Bookshop (IBS). At the time these were the largest players in the UK Internet bookstore market (Mintel, 2000). Amazon.com was launched in July 1995. However, although Amazon.com is accessible from all over the world, in the last few years the company has also established a localized presence in other international markets – including the UK, Germany, France and Japan – to comply with publishers' territorial rights while minimizing shipping costs. Amazon established a UK presence in 1998, Amazon.co.uk, with headquarters in Slough, a town 25 miles west of London. BOL (Bertelsmann Online) is owned by the media conglomerate Bertelsmann AG, and launched in 1999. The launch of BOL followed Bertelsmann's acquisition of a 50 per cent share in US-based Barnes and Noble's online book retailing subsidiary BarnesandNoble.com for $200 million in October 1998 (Mintel, 2000). Barnes and Noble is one of the world's largest physical booksellers with around 1000 bookstores. The Internet Bookshop (IBS) was established in 1993, making it one of the UK's longest-established Internet bookstores. The owner of the IBS Web site, WH Smith, is a traditional UK high-street business, selling newspapers, books, music and stationery.

There are a number of ways of evaluating the quality of a Web site, including competitive analysis, scenarios, inspection, log analysis and online questionnaires (Cunliffe, 2000). The eQual approach is to use an online questionnaire targeted at real users of an e-commerce offering. The use of students as experimental subjects can lead to results that are artificial, particularly where students are asked to perform a task of which they have little experience. However, in the case of Internet bookstores the students and staff of a university make excellent subjects given that both groups buy books as a matter of course and have considerable experience of this area of e-commerce. We were therefore comfortable that the target population would be representative of online bookstore customers and constitute a valuable market segment for book retailers.

To ensure a deeper level of commitment to the evaluation of the site the respondents were asked to find a book on the site that they would like as a prize. Respondents were asked to supply the title, price and delivery cost. Using the terminology of Spool *et al.* (1999), these are 'facts' that the respondent is asked to determine, which made it more likely that a respondent would engage in searching and navigating the site. Further, in setting a task we aimed to maintain a more 'natural' and representative flow of interaction between the user and the Web site.

Respondents were asked to evaluate each of the sites using a Likert scale. For eQual 4.0, a seven-point scale was used (as in SERVQUAL; see Zeithaml *et al.*, 1990) where the anchors are 1 = 'strongly disagree' and 7 = 'strongly agree'. The importance scale was anchored with

1 = 'least important' and 7 = 'most important' (as recommended in the QFD literature; see King, 1989). In the eQual 4.0 survey we received 376 usable responses. The survey involved a first prize of £250, in addition to the four book prizes. In this study we tried to address the possibility of ordering or comparison bias and each respondent evaluated only one site (selected randomly). Overall, we received 143 responses for Amazon, 117 for BOL and 116 for the Internet Bookshop.

We collected data on the book buying habits of the respondents. The majority of the sample was experienced in online book purchasing. The sample was also very experienced in Internet use with a high intensity of use; more than three-quarters of the sample had used the Internet in excess of two years with two-thirds using it more than once per day. Of the different bookstores evaluated, the market leader – Amazon.co.uk – was the most familiar for previous purchases and the tendency to buy while evaluating was greater for Amazon. In order to verify that book buying did not bias the responses, we conducted Levene's test for equality of variances and a t-test for means. No significant effects were found.

The importance rankings suggested that there are a number of priorities demanded from online bookshops by Web site users. In particular, customers are most concerned with ease of site use, finding accurate information, and being able to reliably transact and receive goods. Intuitively, these are the features one would expect as critical to an e-commerce Web site. In relative terms, there seems to be much less emphasis placed upon technical issues, which appears to be a general trend (Dutta and Segev, 2001). Interestingly though, softer qualities such as community, personalization and site experience rate quite low in importance. This is likely to be due, in part, to slow adoption and acceptance of some of these ideas in this commercial domain (Chang *et al.*, 1998).

There were some differences in the standard deviations of ratings for particular questions and sites, although overall, the patterns were quite similar. For example, the respondents appeared more certain about harder service interaction qualities (questions 1 to 4 in eQual 4.0) and information qualities (questions 9 to 10 and 12 to 15 in eQual 4.0) than about softer qualities such as reputation (question 16 in eQual 4.0) and empathy (questions 19 to 21 in eQual 4.0). The standard deviations and errors for the Amazon site appear lower overall than for the other sites.

To obtain weighted scores, each respondent's site rating for a question was multiplied by the importance attached to it by the individual. Table 5.3 displays the average of weighted scores for each site for eQual 4.0. In each case, Amazon appears to rank highest, with some competition among the other players. The total weighted scores give some indication of this.

Table 5.3

Weighted scores and the eQual index ($n = 376$)

No.	Description	Max. score	Amazon Wgt. score	Amazon EQI	BOL Wgt. score	BOL EQI	IBS Wgt. score	IBS EQI
1	I find the site easy to learn to operate	41.74	35.57	0.85	32.44	0.78	33.84	0.81
2	My interaction with the site is clear and understandable	40.73	33.29	0.82	30.62	0.75	31.99	0.79
3	I find the site easy to navigate	42.45	35.10	0.83	32.53	0.77	33.25	0.78
4	I find the site easy to use	42.22	36.20	0.86	33.27	0.79	33.61	0.80
5	The site has an attractive appearance	31.85	23.08	0.72	20.85	0.65	21.85	0.69
6	The design is appropriate to the type of site	33.21	27.31	0.82	24.67	0.74	23.08	0.69
7	The site conveys a sense of competency	37.42	32.39	0.87	27.95	0.75	28.03	0.75
8	The site creates a positive experience for me	32.08	25.15	0.78	21.32	0.66	21.02	0.66
9	Provides accurate information	43.49	36.62	0.84	31.41	0.72	33.73	0.78
10	Provides believable information	39.97	35.30	0.88	30.07	0.75	31.28	0.78
11	Provides timely information	36.30	30.38	0.84	23.78	0.65	27.77	0.76
12	Provides relevant information	40.12	33.46	0.83	29.06	0.72	31.29	0.78
13	Provides easy to understand information	40.44	34.17	0.84	31.59	0.78	33.29	0.82
14	Provides information at the right level of detail	39.64	31.16	0.79	25.84	0.65	28.95	0.73
15	Presents the information in a appropriate format	38.33	30.74	0.80	28.68	0.75	29.13	0.76
16	Has a good reputation	36.88	36.73	1.00	17.16	0.47	15.19	0.41
17	It feels safe to complete transactions	43.47	36.47	0.84	23.63	0.54	23.07	0.53
18	My personal information feels secure	42.93	34.28	0.80	22.54	0.52	23.86	0.56
19	Creates a sense of personalization	29.79	23.64	0.79	16.10	0.54	16.59	0.56
20	Conveys a sense of community	22.04	13.17	0.60	12.17	0.55	10.27	0.47
21	Makes it easy to communicate with the organization	34.59	23.88	0.69	20.33	0.59	23.28	0.67
22	I feel confident that goods/services will be delivered as promised	43.21	37.24	0.86	28.98	0.67	29.82	0.69
	Totals	**832.91**	**685.32**	**0.82**	**565.00**	**0.68**	**584.21**	**0.70**

However, the raw weighted scores make it difficult to give an overall benchmark for the sites. One way to achieve this is to index the total weighted score for a site against the total possible score. The highest possible score that a site can achieve is the mean importance multiplied by 7, the maximum rating for a question (the maximum score column in Table 5.3). In Table 5.3, BOL, for example, achieves a score of 565.00 out of a maximum possible 832.91, giving it an eQual Index (EQI) of 0.68, or 68 per cent. Table 5.3 also shows the EQI for the individual questions. Overall, Amazon is benchmarked well above the other two cyber-bookstores, with an overall EQI of 0.82; IBS follows with an EQI of 0.70, while BOL is close behind at 0.68.

Perhaps more interesting is some conceptual assessment of how the Web sites differ in quality. For this, we need to move beyond the scores and indices of individual questions towards a set of meaningful and reliable subgroupings. To this end, we need to derive a set of subcategories that can be applied to the analysis.

To better facilitate comparison between the Web sites, the research attempted to establish a number of question subgroupings. In this sense, the generation of subcategories is relatively similar to the work associated with SERVQUAL (Zeithaml *et al.*, 1990). As a starting point, and to establish that the qualities can be disentangled and are not part of a single scale, a factor analysis was conducted on the data. In particular, we were interested in testing the construct validity of the usability, information quality and service interaction quality groupings from earlier studies.

Factor analysis was conducted on the set of 376 cases. The Varimax factor rotation converged in eight iterations and a relatively simple factor structure emerged. Five factors are shown quite clearly in the principal components analysis – as given in Table 5.4. Factor loadings in excess of 0.7 can be considered 'excellent' (Comrey, 1973). The eQual groupings from Table 5.2 are confirmed in the data and demonstrate nomological and discriminant validity. Specifically, all the information qualities load as a single factor, while usability and service interaction qualities both load as two sets of factors. The usability quality consists of 'usability' (questions 1 to 4) and 'design' (questions 5 to 8). Service interaction quality is made up of 'trust' (questions 16, 17, 18 and 22) and 'empathy' (questions 19 to 21). The usability and service interaction constructs each miss one quality – questions 7 and 16 have factor loadings less than the 0.55 cut-off point. However, the factor loadings for both questions can be considered near misses (and still significant at the 5 per cent level) and consequently we have retained them in the analysis and presentation of results. These questions have loaded in other tests of eQual.

Table 5.4

Exploratory factor analysis (principal components method with varimax rotation; loadings $\geqslant 0.55^{*}$)

	Component				
	1	**2**	**3**	**4**	**5**
Q1		.780			
Q2		.789			
Q3		.794			
Q4		.777			
Q5				.713	
Q6				.726	
Q7					
Q8				.576	
Q9	.702				
Q10	.711				
Q11	.756				
Q12	.706				
Q13	.599				
Q14	.608				
Q15	.594				
Q16			.607		
Q17			.887		
Q18			.862		
Q19					.688
Q20					.882
Q21					
Q22			.684		

[*] The cut-off point for loadings is .01 significance, which is determined by calculating $2.58/\sqrt{n}$, where n is the number of items in the questionnaire (Pitt et al., 1995)

Based on the emerging factor structure, Cronbach's Alpha (Cronbach, 1970) was computed to assess reliabilities of all scales and subscales. Table 5.5 shows the alpha reliability statistics for each scale as computed from the data, both for each site and as a mean of site scores. All of the alpha scores for the three constructs are in the range of acceptability

Table 5.5

Reliability analysis for constructs

Scale	Questions	Amazon α	BOL α	IBS α	Average α
Usability	*1 to 8*	*0.88*	*0.88*	*0.87*	*0.88*
Usability	1 to 4	0.88	0.89	0.93	0.90
Design	5 to 8	0.78	0.76	0.72	0.75
Information quality	*9 to 15*	*0.89*	*0.88*	*0.90*	*0.89*
Information	9 to 15	0.89	0.88	0.90	0.89
Service interaction quality	*16 to 22*	*0.82*	*0.85*	*0.76*	*0.81*
Trust	16 to 18 and 22	0.83	0.83	0.75	0.80
Empathy	19 to 21	0.72	0.74	0.64	0.70
OVERALL	*1 to 22*	*0.93*	*0.93*	*0.92*	*0.93*

(Nunnally, 1978). Moreover, the alpha scores of all subcategories are also acceptable – with one exception; 'empathy' falls below the 0.7 mark on the IBS data set.

To summarize, there appear to be five factors in the eQual instrument. These factors can be grouped into three main components that confirm earlier research:

- *Usability.* Qualities associated with 'site design' and 'usability'; for example, appearance, ease of use and navigation and the image conveyed to the user.
- *Information quality.* The quality of the content of the site: the suitability of the information for the user's purposes, e.g. accuracy, format and relevancy.
- *Service interaction quality.* The quality of the service interaction experienced by users as they delve deeper into the site, embodied by 'trust' and 'empathy'; for example, issues of transaction and information security, product delivery, personalization and communication with the site owner.

By utilizing a framework of categories, we are able to build a profile of the qualities of an individual Web site that makes it easy to compare with its rivals. Thus, we may examine why some sites fared better than others on the eQual Index. Accordingly, we may use the categories from the factor analysis on the eQual 4.0 data.

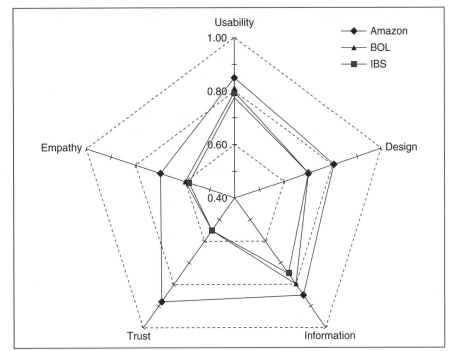

Figure 5.1
Radar chart of eQual 4.0 subcategories for the three Web sites

As a starting point, the data were summarized around the five questionnaire subcategories for eQual 4.0. Then, and similarly to the eQual Index in Table 5.3, the total score for each category was indexed against the maximum score (based on the importance ratings for questions multiplied by 7). Figure 5.1 is the result, which rates the three Web sites using these criteria. Note that the scale has been restricted to values between 0.4 and 1.0 to allow for clearer comparison.

Figure 5.1 demonstrates very clearly that the Amazon UK site stands 'head and shoulders' above its two rivals. The indices for the Amazon subcategories make a clear circle around the other two sites. Trust rates particularly well – more than 30 points in excess of the two competitors. Other areas are less strong, in relative terms, although still 4 to 12 points ahead of the nearest rival. Empathy had the lowest EQI for Amazon (although still 12 points above IBS), with other categories somewhere in between. Some explanations for these results are discussed in the next section.

The scores of the two other bookshops for eQual 4.0 are very close, with IBS edging only slightly ahead of BOL for three of the subcategories. Information quality presents the largest discrepancy – a lead of 5 points for IBS – with empathy and usability both 2 points ahead. The remaining categories contain almost equal scores.

IMPLICATIONS FOR E-COMMERCE QUALITY

The eQual survey indicates that the differences in usability between the three sites are relatively small, suggesting that once a basic level of usability is achieved then the design of the Web site is unlikely to be a differentiating competitive factor. Dutta and Segev (2001) argue that, generally, less emphasis is being placed on the technical aspects of Web sites. With regard to design, the difference is more marked, indicating that the design of the Amazon site is preferred, although this may be due in part to respondents being more likely to be familiar with the Amazon site. It is a relatively straightforward task for an organization to benchmark the usability of its Web site, for example by holding a usability workshop (Nielsen, 1993; Spool *et al.*, 1999). Indeed, Nielsen (2000) goes as far as to argue that five users are enough to evaluate the usability of a site.

Respondents rated 'accurate information' as the most important item in the eQual instrument. This suggests that e-commerce businesses need to pay attention to the content of their Web sites. Lack of control over content is evident when, for example, organizations do not remove special offers that have expired (a Web content management system should remove documents automatically based on an expiry date). However, managing information quality is likely to be rather more difficult than improving Web usability. Web content management is becoming a major issue for organizations; Ovum (2000) predicted that the market for Web content management tools grew from the 1999 level of $475 million to $5.3 billion in 2004. Web content management is concerned with the lifecycle of Web documents, from creation through Web publishing to destruction. Whereas usability can be evaluated quickly, information quality is likely to require an enterprise-wide approach that addresses all the sources of content, encompassing authors, existing systems and databases.

Whereas usability and information quality might be addressed largely through internal changes, service interaction quality requires a stronger external perspective. The greatest differentiator of the sites is 'trust', where Amazon is a long way ahead of its competitors. Indeed, 'trust' appears to be a key aspect of competition in e-commerce (Clarke, 1999; Cranor, 1999; Gefen, 2000; Gefen *et al.*, 2003; Gefen and Straub, 2004; Jarvenpaa *et al.*, 2000; McKnight *et al.*, 1998; 2002; van der Heijden *et al.*, 2003). Notwithstanding, the concept of 'trust' has a degree of ambiguity; research has discovered a variety of definitions of trust, including those related to benevolence, integrity, competence and predictability, among others (Manchala, 2000; McKnight and Chervany, 2001; McKnight *et al.*,

2002). However, these ideas surface comfortably through the questionnaire items. Interestingly, of the four questions that comprise 'trust', three of the questions were rated as second, third and fourth most important by respondents (only 'accurate information' rated more highly in terms of customer importance).

It is unlikely that excellent Web site design and judicious use of new technology will increase the perception of trust by customers, since trust is affected by external factors, such as the strength of the brand, the customer's previous experiences, and the whole range of communications generated by the brand-owner, the media and word of mouth (Aaker and Joachimsthaler, 2000; Briggs and Hollis, 1997; Gilmore and Pine, 2000; McKenna, 2000). There are Web site design implications for 'trust', such as making sure that the privacy policy is visible, and displaying the logo of a third party for accreditation of security mechanisms (Benassi, 1999; Hoffman *et al.*, 1999). However, given Amazon's first-mover advantage and the switching costs incurred by customers in moving to a competitor, BOL and the Internet Bookshop need to go further than Web site design considerations and offer something that distinguishes them from Amazon. In the case of the Internet Bookshop this might involve integration of online activity with the physical high-street network of its owner, WH Smith, and for BOL with its partner Barnes and Noble (Chircu and Kauffman, 2001).

To improve service interaction quality an organization will need to integrate both its front office operations – Web-based or otherwise – with its back office systems (Zeithaml *et al.*, 1988) and integrate e-marketing with traditional marketing and customer relationship management activities. Consequently, established organizations with successful e-commerce offerings may tend to be mature users who have embraced the Internet wholeheartedly rather than as a bolt-on to their current organizational form, i.e. they pursue advanced levels of process integration. For example, the loss of traditional interpersonal elements in the move to cyberspace has implications for the removal of physical surroundings (Bitner, 1990) and service employees (Hartline and Ferrell, 1996), while virtual environments, avatars and intelligent agents can present interesting alternatives (Maes *et al.*, 1999).

SUMMARY AND CONCLUSIONS

The business world's preoccupation with quality management has experienced different phases over time. The first steps, at the beginning of the last century, went towards inspection in manufacturing processes (James, 1996). Another stage was centred in the control of quality, later the emphasis fell into quality assurance and finally to total quality management (TQM). Many years were spent before the first contributions towards services management arrived (Parasuraman *et al.*, 1988). More recently, with e-commerce's growth, several attempts have been made to evaluate quality in this new domain. We appear to be in the initial phases of the 'curve life' for e-commerce: innovation (Vázquez and Trespalacios, 2006). In this phase, sales grow quickly, although they are not always reflected in benefits due to a great variety of problems. In addition, it is necessary to consider that in this phase, the profile and ability of purchasing over the Internet is typical of a developing market. The profile of the buyer coincides largely with the habitual user of the network, which differs remarkably from the normal distribution of the population.

As classic authors in quality management for the manufacture of physical goods advised, it is worthwhile considering Deming's cycle (i.e. Plan-Do-Check-Act). The contributions analysed at the beginning of this chapter – on the quality measures applied to e-commerce – provide us with a review of salient knowledge in this area. We have demonstrated the value of one of these instruments, eQual, as applied to the domain of online bookshops in the UK.

As we see in the Amazon case, its success lies in its innovating character and its orientation towards the client. In fact, where Amazon differs more from its competitors is in the 'trust' dimension: one of the keys to the success of e-commerce. Another issue is the value of the quality of the information. This aspect is essential to compete online. It is a condition *sine qua non*. It is not possible to operate in the market without offering detailed, well-organized and well-managed information. There is no doubt that evaluating the quality of Web site information is a complex process, since it requires the analysis of numerous aspects; it is necessary to evaluate not only the contents, but also the format, order, amount of information, level of detail, and so on. Overall, as a company begins to grapple with Web content issues, it has to create clear rules for how to balance which information is needed by buyers and which information may be peripheral. Whatever a company can do to improve 'trust' will increase overall perceptions; a company that transmits a greater sensation of veracity and security in a transaction is one that will obtain greater benefits. On the other hand, this research demonstrates that, by comparison, less attention might be paid to merely technical or design issues.

REFERENCES

Aaker, D. A. and Joachimsthaler, E. (2000). *Brand Leadership*. Harvard Business School Press.

Aladwania, A. M. and Palvia, P. C. (2002). Developing and validating an instrument for measuring user-perceived Web quality. *Information and Management*, 39 (6), 467–476.

Babakus, E. and Boller, G. W. (1992). An empirical assessment of the SERVQUAL scale. *Journal of Business Research*, 24, 253–268.

Bailey, J. E. and Pearson, S. W. (1983). Development of a tool measuring and analyzing computer user satisfaction. *Management Science*, 29 (5), 530–544.

Barnes, S. J. and Vidgen, R. T. (2000). WebQual: an exploration of Web site quality. *Proceedings of the Eighth European Conference on Information Systems*, Vienna, July.

Barnes, S. J. and Vidgen, R. T. (2001a). An evaluation of cyber-bookshops: the WebQual method. *International Journal of Electronic Commerce*, 6, 6–25.

Barnes, S. J. and Vidgen, R. T. (2001b). Assessing the quality of auction Web sites. *Proceedings of the Hawaii International Conference on Systems Sciences*, Maui, Hawaii, January.

Barnes, S. J. and Vidgen, R. T. (2002). An integrative approach to the assessment of e-commerce quality. *Journal of Electronic Commerce Research*, 3 (3), 114–127.

Barnes, S. J. and Vidgen, R. T. (2003a). Measuring Web site quality improvements: a case study of the Forum on Strategic Management Knowledge Exchange. *Industrial Management and Data Systems*, 103 (5), 297–309.

Barnes, S. J. and Vidgen, R. T. (2003b). Interactive e-government: evaluating the Web site of the UK Inland Revenue. *Journal of Electronic Commerce in Organizations*, 2 (1), 42–63.

Barnes, S. J. and Vidgen, R. T. (2006). Data triangulation and Web quality metrics: a case study in e-government. *Information and Management*, 43 (6), 767–777.

Benassi, P. (1999). TRUSTe: an online privacy seal program. *Communications of the ACM*, 42 (2), 56–59.

Bitner, M. (1990). Evaluating service encounters: the effects of physical surroundings and employee responses. *Journal of Marketing*, 54 (2), 69–82.

Bitner, M. J., Brown, S. W. and Meuter, M. L. (2000). Technology infusion in service encounters. *Academy of Marketing Science*, 28 (1), 138–149.

Briggs, R. and Hollis, N. (1997). Advertising on the Web: is there response before click-through? *Journal of Advertising Research*, 37 (2), 33–45.

Brown, T. J., Churchill, G. A. and Peter, J. P. (1993). Research note: improving the measurement of service quality. *Journal of Retailing*, 69 (1), 127–139.

Chang, A. M., Kannan, P. K. and Whinston, A. B. (1998). Marketing information on the i-way. *Communications of the ACM*, 41, 35–43.

Chircu, A. M. and Kauffman, R. J. (2001). Digital intermediation in electronic commerce – the eBay model. In *E-Commerce and V-Business* (S. J. Barnes and B. Hunt, eds) pp. 43–66, Butterworth-Heinemann.

119

Clarke, R. (1999). Internet privacy concerns confirm the case for intervention. *Communications of the ACM*, 42 (2), 60–68.

Comrey, A. (1973). *A First Course in Factor Analysis*. Academic Press.

Cox, J. and Dale, B. G. (2001). Service quality and e-commerce: an exploratory analysis. *Managing Service Quality*, 11 (2), 121–131.

Cranor, L. F. (1999). Internet privacy. *Communications of the ACM*, 42 (2), 28–31.

Cronbach, L. (1970). *Essentials of Psychology Testing*. Harper and Row.

Cronin, J. J. and Taylor, S. A. (1992). Measuring service quality: a re-examination and extension. *Journal of Marketing*, 56, 55–68.

Cunliffe, D. (2000). Developing usable Web sites – a review and model. *Internet Research*, 10, 295–308.

DeLone, W. H. and McLean, E. R. (1992). Information systems success: the quest for the dependent variable. *Information Systems Research*, 3 (1), 60–95.

Dutta, S. and Segev, A. (2001). Business transformation on the Internet. In *E-Commerce and V-Business* (S. J. Barnes and B. Hunt, eds) pp. 5–22, Butterworth-Heinemann.

Flavian, C., Guinaliu, M. and Gurrea, R. (2006). The role played by perceived usability, satisfaction and consumer trust on website loyalty. *Information and Management*, 43, 1–14.

Gefen, D. (2000). E-commerce: the role of familiarity and trust. *Omega*, 28 (6), 725–737.

Gefen, D. (2002). Customer loyalty in e-commerce. *Journal of the Association for Information Systems*, 3, 27–51.

Gefen, D., Karahanna, E. and Straub, D. W. (2003). Trust and TAM in online shopping: an integrated model. *MIS Quarterly*, 27 (1), 51–90.

Gefen, D. and Straub, D. W. (2004). Consumer trust in B2C e-commerce and the importance of social presence: experiments in e-products and e-services. *Omega*, 32, 407–424.

Gilmore, J. H. and Pine, B. J. (2000). The four faces of mass customization. In *Markets of One* (J. H. Gilmore and B. J. Pine, eds), Free Press.

Hartline, M. and Ferrell, O. (1996). The management of customer-contact service employees: an empirical investigation. *Journal of Marketing*, 60, 52–70.

Healey & Baker (2000). *Global E-Tailing 2000*. Healey & Baker.

Hoffman, D. L., Novak, T. P. and Chatterjee, P. (1995). Commercial scenarios for the Web: opportunities and challenges. *Journal of Computer Mediated Communication*, 1 (3), 23–45.

Hoffman, D. L., Novak, T. P. and Peralta, M. (1999). Building consumer trust online. *Communications of the ACM*, 42 (4), 80–84.

James, P. (1996). *Total Quality Management: An Introductory Text*. Prentice Hall.

Jarvenpaa, S. L., Tractinsky, N. and Vitale, M. (2000). Consumer trust in an internet store. *Information Technology and Management*, 1 (1), 45–71.

Kettinger, W. and Lee, C. (1997). Pragmatic perspectives on the measurement of information systems service quality. *MIS Quarterly*, 21 (2), 223–240.

Kim, S. and Stoel, L. (2004). Dimensional hierarchy of retail website quality. *Information and Management*, 41(5), 619–633.

King, R. (1989). *Better Designs in Half the Time: Implementing QFD*. GOAL/QPC.

Li, H., Kuo, C. and Russell, M. G. (1999). The impact of perceived channel utilities, shopping orientations, and demographics on the consumer's online buying behaviour. *Journal of Computer Mediated Communication*, 5 (2). http://jcmc.indiana.edu/vol5/issue2/hairong.html

Liu, C. and Arnett, K. (2000). Exploring the factors associated with Web site success in the context of electronic commerce. *Information and Management*, 38 (1), 23–33.

Lohse, G. L. and Spiller, P. (1998). Electronic shopping: the effect of customer interfaces on traffic and sales. *Communications of the ACM*, 41 (7), 81–87.

Lohse, G. L. and Spiller, P. (1999). Internet retail store design: how the user interface influences traffic and sales. *Journal of Computer Mediated Communication*, 5 (2). http://jcmc.indiana.edu/vol5/issue2/lohse.htm

Loiacono, E. T., Watson, R. T. and Goodhue, D. L. (2000). *WebQual: A Web Site Quality Instrument*. Working Paper 2000-126-0, University of Georgia.

Loiacono, E. T., Watson, R. T. and Goodhue, D. L. (2002). WebQual: a measure of Web site quality. *Proceedings of the AMA Winter Educators' Conference*, American Marketing Association, Chicago.

Long, M. and McMellon, C. (2004). Exploring the determinants of retail service quality on the Internet. *Journal of Services Marketing*, 18 (1), 78–90.

Madu, C. N. and Madu, A. A. (2002). Dimensions of e-quality. *International Journal of Quality and Reliability Management*, 19 (3), 246–258.

Maes, P., Guttman, R. and Moukas, A. (1999). Agents that buy and sell. *Communications of the ACM*, 42 (3), 81–91.

Manchala, D. W. (2000). E-commerce trust metrics and models. *IEEE Internet Computing*, 4 (2), 36–44.

Mandel, N. and Johnson, E. (1999). *Constructing Preferences Online: Can Web Pages Change What You Want?* Working Paper, University of Pennsylvania.

McKenna, R. (2000). Marketing in an age of diversity. In *Markets of One* (J. H. Gilmore and B. J. Pine, eds), Free Press.

McKnight, D. H., Cummings, L. L. and Chervany, N. L. (1998). Initial trust formation in new organizational relationships. *Academy of Management Review*, 23, 473–490.

McKnight, D. H. and Chervany, N. L. (2001). Conceptualizing trust: a typology and e-commerce customer relationships model. *Proceedings of the Hawaii International Conference on System Sciences*, Maui, Hawaii, January.

McKnight, D. H., Chervany, N. L. and Kacmar, C. (2002). Developing and validating trust measures for e-commerce. *Information Systems Research*, 13 (3), 344–359.

Menon, S. and Kahn, B. (1997). *Cross-Category Effect of Stimulation on the Shopping Experience: An Application to Internet Shopping*. Working Paper 97-006, The Wharton School, University of Pennsylvania.

Mintel (2000). *Internet Retailers*. Mintel International Group Limited.

Negash, S., Ryan, T. and Igbaria, M. (2002). Quality and effectiveness in Web-based customer support systems. *Information and Management*, 40, 757–768.

Nielsen, J. (1993). *Usability Engineering*. Morgan Kaufmann.

Nielsen, J. (2000). Why you only need to test with five users. *Useit.com*, 19 March. http://www.useit.com/alertbox/20000319.html

Nunnally, G. (1978). *Psychometric Theory*. McGraw-Hill.

Ovum (2000). *Web Content Management*. Ovum.

Parasuraman, A. (1995). Measuring and monitoring service quality. In *Understanding Services Management* (W. Glynn and J. Barnes, eds), Wiley.

Parasuraman, A., Zeithaml, V. A. and Berry, L. (1988). SERVQUAL: a multiple-item scale for measuring consumer perceptions of service quality. *Journal of Retailing*, 64 (1), 12–40.

Parasuraman, A., Zeithaml, V. A. and Berry, L. (1991). Refinement and reassessment of the SERVQUAL scale. *Journal of Retailing*, 67 (4), 420–450.

Parasuraman, A., Zeithaml, V.A. and Malhotra, A. (2005). E-S-Qual: a multiple-item scale for assessing electronic service quality. *Journal of Service Research*, 7 (3), 213–233.

Pitt, L., Watson, R. and Kavan, C. (1995). Service quality: a measure of information systems effectiveness. *MIS Quarterly*, 19 (2), 173–187.

Pitt, L., Watson, R. and Kavan, C. (1997). Measuring information systems service quality: concerns for a complete canvas. *MIS Quarterly*, 21 (2), 209–221.

Shostack, G. (1985). Planning the service encounter. In *The Service Encounter* (J. Czepiel, M. Solomon and C. Surprenant, eds), Lexington Books.

Slabey, R. (1990). QFD: a basic primer. Excerpts from the implementation manual for the three day QFD workshop. *Transactions from the Second Symposium on Quality Function Deployment*, Novi, Michigan.

Spool, J., Scanlon, T., Schroeder, W., Snyder, C. and DeAngelo, T. (1999). *Web Site Usability: A Designer's Guide*. Morgan Kaufmann.

Strong, R., Lee, Y. and Wang, R. (1997). Data quality in context. *Communications of the ACM*, 40 (5), 103–110.

Swaminathan, V., Lepkowska-White, E. and Rao, B. P. (1999). Browsers or buyers in cyberspace? An investigation of factors influencing electronic exchange. *Journal of Computer Mediated Communication*, 5 (2). http://jcmc.indiana.edu/vol5/issue2/swaminathan.htm

Trocchia, P. J. and Janda, S. (2003). How do consumers evaluate Internet retail service quality? *Journal of Services Marketing*, 17 (3), 243–253.

Urban, G. I., Sultan, F. and Qualls, W. (2000). Placing trust at the center of your Internet strategy. *Sloan Management Review*, 42 (1), 39–48.

van der Heijden, H., Verhagen, T. and Creemers, M. (2003). Understanding online purchase intentions: contributions from technology and trust perspectives. *European Journal of Information Systems*, 12, 41–48.

Van Dyke, T., Kappelman, L. and Prybutok, V. (1997). Measuring information systems service quality: concerns on the use of the SERVQUAL questionnaire. *MIS Quarterly*, 21 (2), 195–208.

Van Riel, A. C. R., Liljander, V. and Jurriëns, P. (2001). Exploring consumer evaluations of e-services: a portal site. *International Journal of Service Industry Management*, 12 (4), 359–377.

Vázquez, R. and Trespalacios, J. A. (2006). *Estrategias de Distribución Comercial*. Thomson.

Wolfinbarger, M. and Gilly, M. C. (2001). Shopping online for freedom, control and fun. *California Management Review*, 43 (2), 34–55.

Wolfinbarger, M. and Gilly, M. C. (2002). *Comq: Dimensionalizing, Measuring and Predicting Quality of the E-tailing Experience*. Working Paper No. 02–100, Marketing Science Institute.

Wolfinbarger, M. and Gilly, M. C. (2003). Etailq: dimensionalizing, measuring and predicting etail quality. *Journal of Retailing*, 79, 183–198.

Yang, Z., Peterson, R. T. and Cai, S. (2003). Services quality dimensions of Internet retailing: an exploratory analysis. *Journal of Services Marketing*, 17 (7), 685–700.

Yang, Z., Cai, S., Zhou, Z. and Zhou, N. (2005). Development and validation of an instrument to measure user perceived service quality of information presenting web portals. *Information and Management*, 42, 575–589.

Yang, Z. and Fang, X. (2004). Online service quality dimensions and their relationships with satisfaction. *International Journal of Service Industry Management*, 15 (3), 302–326.

Yang, Z. and Jun, M. (2002). Consumer perception of e-service quality: from Internet purchaser and non-purchaser perspectives. *Journal of Business Strategies*, 19 (1), 19–41.

Yoo, B. and Donthu, N. (2001). Developing a scale to measure the perceived service quality of Internet shopping sites (SiteQual). *Quarterly Journal of Electronic Commerce*, 2 (1), 31–47.

Zeithaml, V. A., Berry, L. and Parasuraman, A. (1988). Communication and control processes in the delivery of service quality. *Journal of Marketing*, 52, 35–48.

Zeithaml, V. A., Parasuraman, A. and Berry, L. (1990). *Delivering Quality Service: Balancing Customer Perceptions and Expectations*. The Free Press.

Zeithaml, V. A., Berry, L. and Parasuraman, A. (1993). The nature and determinants of customer expectations of service. *Journal of the Academy of Marketing Science*, 21 (1), 1–12.

Zeithaml, V. A., Parasuraman, A. and Malhotra, A. (2000). *E-Service Quality: Definition, Dimensions and Conceptual Model*. Working Paper, Marketing Science Institute.

Zeithaml, V. A., Parasuraman, A. and Malhotra, A. (2001). *A Conceptual Framework for Understanding E-Service Quality: Implications for Future Research and Managerial Practice*. Working Paper No. 00–115, Marketing Science Institute.

Zeithaml, V. A., Parasuraman, A. and Malhotra, A. (2002). *An Empirical Examination of the Service Quality-Value-Loyalty Chain in an Electronic Channel*. Working Paper, University of North Carolina.

CHAPTER 6

The value of Internet technologies and e-business solutions to micro-enterprises in Atlantic Canada

Charles H. Davis and Florin Vladica

INTRODUCTION

A key contemporary business management issue is how to create value from the networked interactivity made possible by advances in ICTs (Amit and Zott, 2001; Porter, 2001). The Internet and associated information and communication technologies offer unprecedented opportunities for business innovation. Firms can use the Internet and associated technologies extensively as a 'global and cost-effective platform to communicate and conduct commerce' (Rao *et al.*, 2003), opening up new possibilities for interacting with customers, suppliers and partners, and making possible new value propositions and new business models. Small and medium enterprises (SMEs) would seem particularly apt to benefit from Internet technologies and e-business solutions, and many observers have suggested the Internet and e-business can provide major advantages to SMEs, including micro-enterprises, by 'levelling the playing field' and allowing these firms to compete against much larger firms. The development potential of micro-enterprises seems to be huge, but these firms face numerous obstacles to growth. Numerous studies have demonstrated that, in the aggregate, larger firms are the most rapid adopters, and the smallest firms the slowest adopters, of Internet technologies and e-business solutions (Burke, 2005; CEBI, 2004; Davis and Vladica, 2006).

Do Internet technologies and e-business solutions provide significant value-creation opportunities to micro-enterprises? This chapter is about the use of Internet technologies and e-business solutions to create business value by micro-enterprises (firms with fewer than five employees) in Atlantic Canada. Micro-enterprises make up the majority of firms in most countries. Canada has more than half a million employer micro-enterprises, representing 77 per cent of all firms (Industry Canada, 2001). If firms without employees (i.e. owner-operated firms) are included, the number of micro-enterprises is much larger.

Atlantic Canada has a larger than average population of micro-enterprises, with higher than average rates of entry and exit (ACOA, 2005). Comprised of the provinces of New Brunswick, Newfoundland and Labrador, Nova Scotia and Prince Edward Island, Atlantic Canada is a relatively poor region of Canada, and e-business promises to create new and better growth and development opportunities for the region. Atlantic Canada faces significant challenges in the knowledge-based economy. It lacks large urban centres and significant financial centres; its economy is overly specialized in low value-added resource industries; its air and road transportation system is inadequate; and it is located relatively far from major markets (Desjardins, 2005; Ruggieri, 2003). The region suffers from demographic stagnation that is exacerbated by out-migration and low attractiveness to immigrants. Atlantic Canada has an impressive number of institutions of higher education, but they are small and dispersed. On most indicators of science, technology and innovation, Atlantic Canada lags well behind the rest of the country (Bourgeois and LeBlanc, 2003; Locke *et al.*, 2004). Among Atlantic Canada's strengths are its educated labour pool, energy resources, a growing capability in health sciences, marine and bio-resource innovation, and an emerging generation of export-oriented entrepreneurs (MacMillan, 2001). The Atlantic Canadian regional market of around 2.3 million people, by its size and location, imposes limits to the growth of firms. Growth-oriented Atlantic SMEs need to seize opportunities to reach new markets. Harnessing e-business in order to catch up and overcome the disadvantages of their peripheral location may be more important to SMEs in Atlantic Canada than in other parts of the country. However, lack of awareness, lack of qualified staff and costs of implementing e-business solutions are obstacles that prevented many Atlantic Canadian SMEs from establishing an e-business presence in the late 1990s (Innova Quest, 2000) (see below for definitions of e-commerce, e-business, Internet technologies, e-business solutions and micro-enterprises).

Most research on the e-business activities of SMEs has focused on SMEs in general. Little has been published specifically about the technological behaviour of micro-enterprises. Moreover, much of the research on SMEs' use of e-commerce focuses on adoption patterns and barriers to adoption, rather than on business outcomes. In the present chapter we build on these lines of research to describe and analyse micro-enterprises' patterns of use and value creation with Internet technologies and e-business solutions. Most research on the technological behaviour of micro-enterprises is qualitative. We complement this work by using data from two recent online surveys of SME e-commerce users in Atlantic Canada. Since the firms were reached via e-mail and data were collected via an online survey, our sample represents 'adopter' firms – ones with at least modest online capabilities. We analyse their survey responses to the following questions:

1. How do micro-enterprises differ from larger online SMEs regarding age, rate of growth, competitive pressure, market orientation and perceived barriers to business expansion?
2. In what ways do micro-enterprises lag larger SMEs in use of Internet technologies and e-business solutions?
3. How do micro-enterprises differ from larger SMEs in creating value with Internet technologies and e-business solutions?
4. What are structural sources of e-business value creation in micro-enterprises?

The chapter is organized as follows. We first discuss micro-enterprises in terms of their organizational characteristics and growth challenges, showing that micro-enterprises form a heterogeneous group of firms with significant differences of purpose, motivation and capabilities. We then review the small existing literature on e-business and IT use among micro-enterprises and discuss the question of value creation and strategic use of IT capabilities, focusing on a class of models that can help to explain e-business outcomes among micro-enterprises. After providing methodological and definitional details, we address the four questions outlined above. In the concluding section we summarize our findings and outline the theoretical and practical implications of our work.

CHARACTERISTICS AND GROWTH CHALLENGES OF MICRO-ENTERPRISES

Definitions of micro-enterprise vary from country to country. In Europe, micro-enterprises are firms with fewer than ten employees. The Association for Enterprise Opportunity, a membership-based micro-enterprise trade association in the United States, defines a micro-enterprise as a firm with five or fewer employees and less than $35 000 in start-up capital. In Canada, micro-enterprises are defined as firms with fewer than five employees. This is the definition we use here (for a review of definitions of micro-enterprises see: González, 2005; OECD, 2004).

In every case, micro-enterprises are owner-operated businesses with limited capital, technology and human resources. By definition no micro-enterprise dominates its market segment although micro-enterprises are numerically preponderant in many industries. Micro-enterprises 'typically serve as a self-employment option', i.e. as an alternative to working for someone else (Cook and Belliveau, 2004). Micro-enterprises provide important sources of personal income and employment. In about three-quarters of Canadian micro-enterprises, the firm is the sole or most important source of income for its owner. Nearly half of Canadian micro-enterprises are located in homes (Papadaki and Chami, 2002). Usually start-up costs are very low. In northern countries, micro-enterprises tend to concentrate on untraded services, while in less-developed southern countries, they are also active in manufacturing (Woller and Schreiner, 2003). Our discussion focuses on micro-enterprises in the Canadian and North American contexts.

The micro-enterprise population is heterogeneous, reflecting the variety of motivations and capabilities among entrepreneurs. In industrial northern countries, drivers of micro-enterprise formation include the erosion of secure middle class jobs, corporate downsizing and the recourse to contingent and temporary workers, immigration, decline in rural and inner city communities, the need for parents (especially women) to reconcile income generation with parenting and care giving responsibilities, and an ageing population (persons over 50 have a higher rate of self-employment) that seeks to supplement its income or engage in post-employment career activities (Edgcomb and Klein, 2005).

Entrepreneurial goals can be grouped as extrinsic (involving wealth generation), intrinsic (personal accomplishments), independence and autonomy, and family security (Kuratko *et al.*, 1997). These motivations give rise to several types of micro-enterprise. Among the micro-enterprises described by Industry Canada (2001) and Papadaki and Chami (2002), around one-third are 'growth oriented'. Growth-oriented micro-enterprises include high-growth ventures, i.e. firms established by entrepreneurs with growth as a primary objective. High-growth micro-enterprise ventures are identifiable by entrepreneurial intent (i.e. growth objectives) as well as by characteristics of the entrepreneurs and their business plans (Friar and Meyer, 2003). Certain characteristics of Canadian micro-enterprises or their owners are positively related to firm growth: educational level of the entrepreneur, entrepreneurial intensity of the firm, informal networking with customers and suppliers, business partnering activities, product innovation, adoption of e-business technologies, managerial delegation, focus on the local market, age and size (since younger, smaller firms grow faster) (Papadaki and Chami, 2002; Perren, 1999).

However, in general, Canadian employer micro-enterprises are not noticeably growth oriented. Two-thirds have no expansion plans. The rate of graduation to the next size category of SMEs is about 1 per cent over ten years (Industry Canada, 2001). Firm longevity is impressive – 83 per cent of micro-enterprises are over seven years old (*ibid.*). The owner-manager performs most of the business operations. Surveys of Canadian employer micro-enterprises show that more than three-quarters are owned by males, and over 80 per cent of micro-enterprise owners are 40 years of age or older (Industry Canada, 2001; Papadaki and Chami, 2002). However, surveys that include owner-operated micro-enterprises (i.e. firms without employees) show a much higher degree of participation by females and younger persons (Robichaud and McGraw, 2004).

It is useful to explore the range of reasons for weak growth orientation among micro-enterprises. These firms have various origins and purposes: they may be lifestyle firms, firms with few resources and weak capabilities, unregistered owner-operator firms, family firms, firms established in distressed environments as vehicles to escape from poverty, or firms operated on a part-time basis to generate supplementary income. Self-employment does not necessarily imply strongly enterprising behaviour. For example, in many cultural industries, self-employment is commonplace, but firm-building, growth-oriented ('enterprising') behaviour is not (Baines and Robson, 2001). Lifestyle firms, such as small husband-and-wife tourism operations, seek business profitability within the larger context of lifestyle and family goals (Getz and Carlsen, 2000). Many micro-enterprises are located in households, where they are embedded in family relationships that can extend to the use of family members' paid or unpaid labour (Bains and Wheelock, 1998). Family relationships impact on micro-businesses outside the household as well. Marginal firms often survive by relying on the labour of family and kin. Family resources can represent assets, as when transnational kinship relationships are activated for purposes of input sourcing or product distribution, and they can represent liabilities, as when conflict occurs over decisions, distribution of rewards or succession (Edwards and Ram, 2006).

Home-based telework is often associated with micro-enterprises. Home-based telework is hailed as the wave of the future by those who see it as friendly to families and the environment. Some governments, motivated by the desire to keep up with corporate employers and alleviate commuter congestion, are mandating their agencies to provide IT support services for workers who may work from home (Joice, 2002). ICT enablement of the home for purposes of work performance makes possible a variety of telework and home-based work behaviours, including moonlighting, family members' use of infrastructure for work purposes and freelancing in retirement. Teleworking conditions, autonomy and degree of discretion in work tasks vary considerably from one occupation to another. Executive, management and technical telework tends to be performed by males under conditions of greater autonomy than translation, word processing and secretarial work, which tends to be performed by females (Tremblay, 2003). Teleworking is associated with micro-enterprise formation and development in a number of ways, including via precarious contractual employment relationships that may deliberately or inadvertently serve to incubate a micro-enterprise. However, telework does not necessarily lead to the formation of micro-enterprises, much less to growth-oriented micro-enterprises.

A large 'micro-enterprise industry' has grown up in the past two decades to service the technical, training and financial needs of micro-enterprises (Edgcomb and Klein, 2005). There are more than 600 such programmes in the US alone. The effectiveness of micro-enterprise programmes in assisting the poorest and most disadvantaged individuals to move from welfare to self-employment appears to be modest, and the micro-entrepreneurs who most successfully benefit from micro-enterprise development programmes are the ones with 'the most assets, the most years of school, the most skills and experience, the strongest support networks, and one or more wage jobs' (Schreiner, 1999). As a poverty alleviation strategy 'micro-enterprise is not a panacea' (Servon and Bates, 1998). It is fair to say that micro-enterprise promotion as a strategy to alleviate deep poverty and micro-enterprise promotion as a broader economic adjustment strategy are not entirely compatible since the needs and capabilities of their target clients are so dissimilar.

It is an important challenge to develop coherent and effective enterprise support programmes (Henry *et al.*, 2003). In many respects, heterogeneity among micro-enterprises in terms of capabilities, assets, goals and motivations trumps the commonality of firm size when it comes to requirements for externally supplied financial, educational and technical support services. Micro-enterprise development programmes display considerable diversity in terms of target population and type of services offered. Micro-enterprise support programmes usually offer credit, training, technical support, networking and mentoring services. IT-related technical support is also occasionally offered but information technology or e-business is not a major focus of most micro-enterprise programmes, which are not likely to have strong technological capabilities.

Only a small empirical literature is available regarding support services for e-business innovation among SMEs. The heterogeneity of the small business sector requires a differentiated approach to the delivery of e-business support services, not a one-size-fits-all, 'blanket' approach (Martin and Matlay, 2001). Good practices for e-commerce awareness creation encompass general awareness activities, action via intermediaries and focused support to SMEs (Papazafeiropoulou *et al.*, 2002). Simpson and Docherty (2004) judge public sector e-business advisory services in the UK to be poor and potentially dangerous. Muske *et al.* (2004) identify training and advisory roles for extension services in support of ICT use among micro-enterprises. Martin and Halstead (2004) show that parental interest in children and their school, rather than a concern for business performance, motivates participation in ICT training among certain micro-entrepreneurs. Davis and Vladica (2005b) analyse six possible sets of drivers of demand for nine e-business support services among SMEs in New Brunswick, finding that personalized expert services are the most highly desired support service. Problem solving, extent of prior use of e-business technologies, and strategic development of business capabilities are associated with the strongest demand for services. Firm size, growth orientation and intensity of competition are not associated with strong demand for e-business support services. Since SMEs are not a homogeneous group when it comes to adoption of e-commerce, service providers need to segment them according to motivation, desired capabilities, pain points, and so on (Davis and Vladica, 2005b; Martin and Matlay, 2001; Stockdale and Standing, 2006).

To summarize this section, micro-enterprises are heterogeneous small organizations with a range of purposes, not all of which imply growth. Micro-enterprises' perceived barriers to growth and performance are influenced by the characteristics, capabilities, interests, preferences, social networks, resources and motivations of the owner(s), who typically manage the firm and also predominate in the firm's day-to-day operations (Devins *et al.*, 2005). Because micro-enterprises obey a variety of economic and social logics, management knowledge developed for and about larger firms does not scale down well to micro-businesses.

ADOPTION AND USE OF INTERNET TECHNOLOGIES AND E-BUSINESS SOLUTIONS: WHAT ARE SOURCES OF BUSINESS VALUE?

Are the processes of technology adoption in micro-enterprises similar to the processes in larger firms, except on a smaller scale? The evidence suggests not. It is clear that firm size makes a significant difference in the firm's technological behaviour:

> [S]maller sized firms are less likely to report Internet use, Web site use, and non-Internet-related computer use than even incrementally larger businesses. Additionally, [...] size accounts for significantly more predictive power in [small business information system] adoption than CEO or industry factors. (Burke, 2005)

Growth requires that a firm lower its operating costs, improve its productivity and quality, and 'respond to the increased requirements of their customers and other business partners' (Raymond *et al.*, 2005). Smaller firms by definition have limited internal resources and capabilities with respect to production, finance, management, marketing and information technology. Fillis and Wagner (2005) identify three size-related differences between larger and smaller firms. First, there is a higher degree of uncertainty in their operations because of 'limited customer base, product line and owner/firm's objectives'. Second, small firms are more likely to introduce new products or services. Third, smaller firms are more flexible and agile, able to react, change, grow or evolve faster. Premkumar (2003) summarizes differences between larger and smaller firms from an organizational behaviour perspective: in small firms 'decision making is centralized in one or two persons, bureaucracies are minimal', the firms are organizationally flat without long-term planning or standard practices, and there is 'greater dependence on external expertise and services for information systems (IS) operations'. De Berranger *et al.* (2001) and Fillis *et al.* (2004) emphasize the importance of the competencies and orientation of the micro-enterprise owner-manager, the perception of opportunity and value, and the implications of risk aversion for small firm engagement in e-business.

In Atlantic Canada, SMEs believe that they would improve their business performance if they could improve the quality of their products or services, deliver these products and services more effectively and efficiently to customers, attract new domestic customers, formulate and communicate their marketing messages more effectively, and develop specialized niches in the domestic market (Davis *et al.*, 2006). Firms that have more than five employees consider staff recruitment, retention, managing and communicating with staff and productivity to be more significant than other barriers to growth. Once firms grow to more than 50 employees, they face a different set of growth challenges that reflect the transition to a larger organization with more formal management and business routines. Finally, older companies consider equipment costs, attracting and retaining key staff, increasing staff productivity, and managing and reporting financial and tax information as the most important barriers to growth (*ibid.*).

How should the use of IT to create business value be conceptualized? Value creation from IT assets is an unsettled area in IS/IT research and is characterized by considerable conceptual and methodological diversity (Amit and Zott, 2001; Cronk and Fitzgerald, 2002; Kim *et al.*, 2004; Kwon *et al.*, 2002; Pflughoeft *et al.*, 2003; Porter, 2001). The literature contains an impressive array of models of IT adoption and value creation by firms. Stage or 'ladder' models are used in policy and some scholarly literature on e-commerce adoption by SMEs. Stage models refer to increments of maturity, steps of engagement in increasing technological complexity or process integration, or degrees of capability (see, for example: Daniel and Grimshaw, 2002; Ihlstrom and Nilsson, 2003; Rao *et al.*, 2003). Because they introduce concepts of evolution, technological trajectories and technology packages (bundles of interconnected technologies), stage models provide a potentially valuable framework for understanding the dynamics of technological change in firms. However, the stage model seems not to accurately describe the technological behaviour of small firms (Levy and Powell, 2003; Zheng *et al.*, 2004); empirical research suggests patterns of adoption in specific functional areas of the firm, often in response to perceived opportunities or threats represented by customers, suppliers or competitors (Levy and Powell, 2003).

When asking 'whether e-business delivers value to firm performance, and if so, what factors contribute to e-business value' (Zhu *et al.*, 2003), we need to look at the firm's competitive environment, the characteristics of the firm and of its senior management, the firm's 'pain points' or problems that it is attempting to resolve, its technological capabilities, the nature of its products or services, and its performance ambitions. Much e-commerce and IT adoption research conceptualizes adoption and business outcomes in terms of technological, organizational and environmental variables, based on Tornatzky and Fleischer's (1990) technology-organization-environment (TOE) framework (for a review of this literature see Windrum and de Berranger, 2002). Technological context describes both the internal and external technologies relevant to the firm, such as existing technologies inside the firm and technologies in the market. Organizational context considers firm size and scope, the centralization, formalization and complexity of its managerial structure, the quality of its human resources and the internal availability of resources. Finally, environmental context is the arena in which a firm conducts its business – its industry, competitors, access to resources supplied by others and dealings with government (Zhu *et al.*, 2003). These three groups of factors affect the capability of the firm to innovate and create value.

We will call these models TOE (technology-organization-environment) models after Zhu *et al.* (2003). In TOE models, the dependent variable can be adoption, business performance or business value, and many combinations of independent variables have been used (*cf.* Van der Veen, 2004). We assembled a composite list of possible outcomes of the use of Internet technologies and e-business solutions from the scholarly literature and from statistical agency survey questionnaires, and we streamlined this list to the following 15 business outcomes as indicators of value creation:

- increased productivity;
- increased profitability;
- decreased cost of production;
- increased quality of goods and services;

- improved rate of new product development;
- development of a unique expertise or market;
- increased speed of delivery;
- increased adaptability;
- increased domestic market share;
- increased international market share;
- increased customer service;
- improved relationships with existing customers;
- an ability to keep up with competitors;
- improved coordination with partners or suppliers; and
- improved brand or image.

Respondents in our surveys estimated the effects of using Internet technologies and e-business solutions for each of these fifteen possible business outcomes on a five-point Likert scale from 'no impact' to 'very great impact'. We also posed questions regarding the socio-demographic characteristics of the firm, its connectivity, Web site functionality, use of various Internet technologies and e-business solutions, extent of engagement in online transactions, geographical market orientation, perceived barriers to business expansion, and perceived facilitators of the adoption of e-business solutions (Davis and Vladica, 2004).

DEFINITIONS AND DATA SOURCES

Small business Internet commerce is broadly defined as 'the use of Internet technology and applications to support business activities of a small firm' (Poon and Swatman, 1999). The terms 'e-business' and 'e-commerce' are often used interchangeably, blurring their distinctiveness (Fillis and Wagner, 2005). We restrict the term e-commerce to 'transactions carried out over computer-mediated channels that comprise the transfer of ownership or the entitlement to use tangible or intangible assets' (Statistics Canada, 1999). The concept of electronic (e-)business, on the other hand, can be defined broadly as 'the sharing of business information, maintaining business relationships, and conducting business transactions by means of Internet-based technology' (Poon and Swatman, 1999). E-business encompasses all Internet-based business-to-business and business-to-consumer transactions, as well as non-transactional electronic interactions throughout the customer transaction cycle (Davis and Vladica, 2005a). With this definition, 'e-business' includes e-commerce, so that a firm can be engaged in e-business without conducting online transactions (i.e. e-commerce). For example, e-business includes non-transactional steps in the customer transaction cycle, such as online marketing or post-sale service delivery. It also includes the internal use of information and communication technologies for purposes of coordination and business support, such as intranets.

We use the term Internet technologies as shorthand to refer to the inter-networkable technological components or solutions that firms can deploy, including hardware and software, protocols and ways of combining them. For example, Internet technology can refer to the Internet itself, to a specific method of connection (e.g. dial-up), application hosting, data storage, or to a Web site. Hardware includes computing and data storage or transfer equipment, electronic circuitry, wires and cables. Software and protocols make the hardware and circuitry function meaningfully. When Internet-related technologies are assembled within organizations and deployed to support business functions, tasks or processes, we refer to them as e-business solutions. The examples are numerous: online catalogues, shopping carts, online payment systems, order tracking, customer relationship management, e-mail, chat, and so on. Internet technologies and e-business solutions support business activities along the transaction cycle and throughout the value chain for purposes of internal process integration and coordination, coordination and integration with partners, interaction and communication with customers, and for decision support.

We also distinguish between the adoption and the use of various Internet technologies and e-business solutions. Adoption refers to whether or not a small firm has implemented particular Internet technologies or e-business solutions. Use refers to patterns of deployment, to the breadth and depth of integration into the business activities of firms.

We conducted an online survey of the use of Internet technologies and e-business solutions among SMEs in the four provinces of Atlantic Canada in June and July 2005. Responses were solicited by e-mail regarding technology use, the economic and social characteristics of the firm, perceived constraints to and facilitators of adoption of Internet technologies and e-business solutions, desired support services, and perceived impacts or benefits of adoption of these technologies. Respondents could complete the questionnaire in English or in French. Invitations were e-mailed to 8520 Atlantic SMEs that we identified from a variety of mailing lists and business directories. The survey questionnaire was available online, on a secure password-controlled Web site, linked from the e-mail sent to participants. With 776 usable responses, the response rate was 9.1 per cent. Although we made every attempt to ensure geographical representativeness in our mailing list, firms from Prince Edward Island are over-represented among respondents in proportion to the population of the province, firms from New Brunswick and Nova Scotia are more or less proportionately represented, and firms from Newfoundland and Labrador are under-represented among respondents. It is not possible to determine how closely our sample of firms replicates the sectoral distribution of Atlantic Canadian SMEs. Around two-thirds of the respondents are in the following sectors: professional and business services, tourism, IT and telecommunications, and commerce. For further details see Davis *et al.* (2006). Data from this survey are used in the analysis presented in the sections below.

A largely identical questionnaire was used in an earlier survey of SMEs in New Brunswick in March and April 2004. With 280 usable responses the response rate was about 12 per cent. Around half of the respondents are in tourism, arts and crafts, consulting and professional services, IT services, and other services. For further details see Davis and Vladica (2004). Data from this survey are used below to estimate a structural model of the sources of business value among New Brunswick micro-enterprises.

The main drawback of online surveys is that they exclude possible respondents who do not have online capabilities (Evans and Mathur, 2005). Since our research focuses only on current e-business users, exclusion of non-users is not an issue. In other words, our research refers only to the users of Internet technologies and e-business solutions. It does not refer to non-users or potential users.

RESULTS

How do micro-enterprises differ from larger SMEs in terms of age, rate of growth, market orientation, competitive pressure, online sales, online exports and perceived barriers to business expansion?

Table 6.1 provides basic descriptive information, by size class, about the population of firms in our survey. Our sample consists of 483 micro-enterprises and 293 larger SMEs from Atlantic Canada. The firms that participated in this survey have an estimated 16 410 employees and conduct an estimated CAD$1.27 billion in sales. Micro-enterprises represent 62.4 per cent of the firms in the population, but only 7.4 per cent of all employees and 2.4 per cent of all sales. They report an annual revenue growth rate of 18.9 per cent.

Table 6.1

Main characteristics of firms in the survey

	Micro (<5)	Very small (5–19)	Small (20–49)	Medium (50–499)	Total
No. of firms in the survey	483	195	54	44	776
Percentage of total respondents	62.24%	25.12%	6.95%	5.67%	100.0%
No. of total employees	1207.5	2340	1863	11 000	16 410.5
Percentage of total employees	7.4%	14.3%	11.4%	67.0%	100.0%
Average estimated 2004 gross sales ($000)	$468	$2044	$5505	$11 822	$1948.4
Total estimated 2004 gross sales ($000)	$181 925	$357 625	$269 725	$461 050	$1 270 325
Percentage of all estimated 2004 gross sales for all respondents	2.4%	10.3%	27.7%	59.6%	100.0%
Estimated annual growth rate past 3 years	18.9%	15.8%	18.5%	17.6%	18.0%
Average age (in years)	11.1	19.0	24.3	27.2	14.9
Percentage of 2004 revenue earned in Atlantic Canada	60.9%	69.0%	56.6%	62.4%	62.8%
Percentage of 2004 revenue earned internationally (USA and other)	14.9%	10.7%	18.7%	20.8%	16.7%
Percentage of 2004 revenue earned online	34.0%	24.6%	19.6%	16.2%	20.8%
Perceived intensity of competition (1 = low, 2 = medium, 3 = high)					
■ Regionally	2.15	2.29	2.28	2.28	2.20
■ Canada	2.26	2.39	2.47	2.33	2.31
■ Internationally	2.23	2.29	2.49	2.13	2.26

We tested for significant differences between micro-enterprises and all other SMEs in the respondent population. For all tests of significance involving a dichotomous variable and an ordinal or interval variable, we do not assume normal distribution of data and so use the Mann-Whitney U test for two independent samples. In the case of two dichotomous variables, statistics indicate asymptotic significance (2-tailed) of the Pearson chi-square statistic.

■ Micro-enterprises are significantly younger than larger SMEs (average age is 11.1 years vs 21.2 years, $p = 0.000$).

- Micro-enterprises do not grow more rapidly than larger SMEs (18.9 per cent vs 16.6 per cent average annual growth over the past three years, $p = 0.657$).
- Micro-enterprises are not significantly more oriented toward the regional market or toward international markets than larger SMEs (60.9 per cent vs 65.7 per cent of revenue earned in Atlantic Canada, $p = 0.130$; 14.9 per cent vs 13.7 per cent of revenue earned in international markets, $p = 0.567$).
- Micro-enterprises report significantly lower intensity of competition in regional and national markets than larger SMEs, but similar intensity in international markets (regional 2.15 vs 2.3 on a three-point scale, $p = 0.009$; national 2.26 vs 2.40, $p = 0.007$; international 2.23 vs 2.30, $p = 0.315$).
- Micro-enterprises earn significantly more revenue online than larger SMEs (34.0 per cent vs 22.4 per cent, $p = 0.001$).
- Micro-enterprises do not earn significantly more online revenue from international customers than larger SMEs (18.7 per cent vs 18.1 per cent, $p = 0.749$).

Table 6.2 compares micro-enterprises' and larger SMEs' assessment of the importance of 17 possible barriers to business expansion. Micro-enterprises' scores differ significantly from those of larger SMEs in 11 cases. In each of these 11 cases, micro-enterprises' assessment of importance of the barrier to business expansion is *lower* than that of the larger SMEs. This finding is congruent with micro-enterprises' reports of lower levels of competition in regional and national markets and with our earlier literature review indicating that growth is not always a primary goal of micro-enterprises.

In what ways do micro-enterprises lag larger SMEs in use of Internet technologies and e-business solutions?

We assessed Atlantic Canadian SMEs' engagement with Internet technologies and e-business solutions by measuring four groups of variables: degree of connectivity, performance of online transactions, use of e-business technologies and solutions, and extent of Web site functionality (for firms with their own Web site). Table 6.3 compares micro-enterprises with larger SMEs across each group of variables. In terms of connection to the Internet, no significant differences exist between micro-enterprises and larger SMEs (Table 6.3a). Most firms of all sizes enjoy high speed access to the Internet. Regarding performance of

Table 6.2
Perceived barriers to business expansion

	Less than 5 employees	5 or more employees	Mann–Whitney asymp. 2-tailed
Attracting new domestic customers	4.27	4.21	0.228
Getting marketing message out	4.24	4.18	0.199
Improving the quality of products/services	4.20	4.35	**0.058**
Developing niche, specialized markets	4.18	4.15	0.385
Delivery of products/services to customers	4.17	4.40	**0.017**
Keeping overhead costs down (i.e. office space, consumables)	4.00	4.32	**0.001**
Managing customer information	3.85	4.11	**.000**
Implementing new information and communication technologies	3.76	3.91	0.224
Managing office information technology	3.66	3.98	**.000**
Managing and reporting financial and tax information	3.60	3.80	**0.073**
Equipment costs	3.50	3.99	**.000**
Increase staff productivity	3.23	4.27	**.000**
Attracting and retaining key staff	3.22	4.40	**.000**
Geographical distance from clients and suppliers	3.15	3.45	**0.004**
Finding customers abroad	3.08	2.91	0.105
Purchasing supplies and raw materials	3.00	3.52	**.000**
Managing and communicating with mobile staff	2.64	3.48	**.000**

Notes: Scale items: 5 = Very important, 4 = Important, 3 = Neutral, 2 = Little importance, 1 = No importance. Significant differences are highlighted in bold.

online transactions (Table 6.3b), over 80 per cent of respondents use the Internet for purchasing. Micro-enterprises are not significantly different from larger SMEs in this regard. However, more micro-enterprises than larger SMEs use the Internet for selling (49 per cent vs 40 per cent) – a significant difference.

Regarding use of e-business solutions, Table 6.3c shows that the simplest solutions (e-mail, personal computers and use of the Internet for information collection) are widespread among SMEs regardless of size. Micro-enterprises also use videoconferencing and solutions for secure transactions with businesses, government and consumers as frequently

Table 6.3
Use of Internet technologies and e-business solutions among Atlantic Canadian micro-enterprises and larger SMEs

	Less than 5 employees (n = 483)	5 or more employees (n = 293)	Asymp. sig. (2-tail.)
(a) Connectivity of Atlantic Canadian SMEs			
Regular dial-up telephone line with a standard modem	32.3%	27.6%	0.172
Cable modem	20.7%	21.2%	0.879
High speed (ISDN/DSL line)	63.6%	61.8%	0.618
T1 line or greater (1.544 Mbps or greater)	7.4%	5.8%	0.377
Wireless connection	27.1%	27.3%	0.956

Notes: Columns 1 and 2 indicate the percentage of firms in each size class that use each method of connecting to the Internet (multiple methods allowed). Column 3 shows the results of Pearson's chi-square test of significance.

	Less than 5 employees	5 or more employees	Asymp. sig.
(b) Use of online transactions by Atlantic Canadian SMEs			
Uses the Internet for purchasing	84.8%	88.5%	0.154
Uses the Internet for selling	48.9%	40.0%	**0.016**

Notes: Column 3 shows results of Pearson's chi-square test of significance. Significant differences are highlighted in bold.

	Less than 5 employees	5 or more employees	Asymp. sig.
(c) Use of e-business solutions among Atlantic Canadian SMEs			
E-mail (electronic mail)	93.3%	93.0%	0.876
Personal computer, workstation or terminals	92.3%	92.7%	0.837
Internet; surfing the Internet, visiting Web sites, etc.	91.6%	92.0%	0.863
Network/information security technology (e.g. firewall, anti-virus software, access control)	77.8%	82.9%	**0.091**
Functional software packages (e.g. accounting, human resources, marketing)	69.1%	85.3%	**.000**
Presenting own Web site (on the Internet)	61.8%	70.8%	**0.012**
Wireless communications	56.5%	68.8%	**0.001**
Conducting secure business transactions with other businesses or government	42.2%	44.7%	0.502
Shared file folders	39.7%	75.4%	**.000**
Conducting secure transactions with consumers	30.7%	34.2%	0.325
Remote data storage	18.4%	26.1%	**0.013**

(continued)

Table 6.3 (continued)

	Less than 5 employees (n = 483)	5 or more employees (n = 293)	Asymp. sig. (2-tail.)
(c) Use of e-business solutions among Atlantic Canadian SMEs (continued)			
Hosted software solutions	16.9%	22.7%	**0.053**
Internal company Web site and communications (intranet)	16.3%	31.8%	**.000**
Meetings over the network (e.g. videoconferencing)	15.8%	18.7%	0.312
Remote help desk assistance for employees	7.9%	15.8%	**0.001**
Extranet	7.4%	13.7%	**0.005**
Radio Frequency Identification (RFID)	2.0%	6.9%	**0.001**
Biometrics	0.7%	1.4%	0.296

Notes: Column 3 shows results of Pearson's chi-square test of significance. Significant differences are highlighted in bold.

(d) Web site functionality among Atlantic Canadian SMEs			
Online payment (complete transactions and payment online)	14.1%	12.5%	0.599
Two-way communication (e.g. feedback forms)	34.4%	40.6%	**0.081**
Interactivity (two-way communication in real time, e.g. online chat)	8.1%	1.8%	**0.001**
Digital products or services (e.g. music, software or business services)	13.4%	12.5%	0.749
Secure Web site	20.6%	23.2%	0.471
Privacy policy statement	20.6%	17.9%	0.422
Access via wireless mobile devices	7.2%	5.8%	0.523
Information about products or services	77.8%	86.2%	**0.014**
Information about the business	78.4%	86.2%	**0.022**

Notes: Column 3 shows results of Pearson's chi-square test of significance. Significant differences are highlighted in bold.

as larger SMEs do. The adoption lag between micro-enterprises and larger SMEs occurs mainly with respect to use of network security, functional software packages, presentation of a Web site, wireless, shared file folders, remote data storage, hosted software solutions, intranets, extranets, remote helpdesks and radio frequency ID tags. Several of these solutions serve to support coordination with staff, customers and suppliers, and imply greater organizational complexity than is present in micro-enterprises. Therefore, it is not surprising to find a lower intensity of use among micro-enterprises. However, hosted software solutions, remote data storage and especially presentation of a Web site are solutions that would seem to be accessible and valuable to micro-enterprises.

Regarding Web site functionality, Table 6.3d shows that among SMEs with a Web site, micro-enterprises do not significantly differ from larger SMEs with respect to transaction enablement, security and privacy statements. However, micro-enterprises' Web sites are relatively less informative than larger SMEs' Web sites, and they are used more for synchronous and less for asynchronous communication than larger SMEs' Web sites.

To summarize this section, micro-enterprises' lower rates of adoption of Internet technologies and e-business solutions are partly explained by the fact that technologies supporting internal organizational coordination and external logistics are less relevant to micro-enterprises than to larger firms. Micro-enterprises use the Internet more intensively for selling than larger SMEs do. Furthermore, micro-enterprises do not lag larger SMEs in the use of technologies for transaction security. However, micro-enterprises do lag larger SMEs in the use of Web services such as hosted software solutions or remote data storage. Micro-enterprises also lag larger SMEs in the use of specialized or more recently available ICTs such as radio frequency identification (RFID) or functional software packages. Finally, micro-enterprises lag larger SMEs in the use of Web sites for purposes of communicating written information. Micro-enterprises practically never lead larger firms in the adoption of particular Internet technologies and e-business solutions. Although certain Internet technologies and e-business solutions may be scale neutral, none are biased in favour of adoption by the smallest firms.

How do micro-enterprises differ from larger SMEs in creating value with Internet technologies and e-business solutions?

Table 6.4 compares micro-enterprises' and larger SMEs' reported business outcomes of using Internet technologies and e-business solutions. Of the 15 outcomes that we measured, micro-enterprises differ significantly from larger SMEs regarding only one outcome – increase in business profitability; micro-enterprises attribute significantly greater profitability to the use of Internet technologies and e-business solutions than larger SMEs

Table 6.4

Business impacts of using Internet technologies and e-business solutions

	Less than 5 employees	5 or more employees	Mann–Whitney asymp. sig. (2-tail.)
Increased business productivity	2.97	2.92	0.562
Increased business profitability	2.94	2.68	**0.015**
Increased speed of supplying and/or delivering services or goods	3.00	2.90	0.366
Increased ability to adapt to different client demands	2.97	2.94	0.739
Increased business domestic market share	2.48	2.45	0.997
Increased business international market share	2.11	2.03	0.679
Increased level of customer service and satisfaction	3.12	3.10	0.703
Building and enhancing relationships with existing customers	3.19	3.05	0.139
Allowed the business to keep up with its competitors	3.14	3.17	0.947
Decreased the cost of producing goods or services	2.25	2.20	0.885
Improved the quality of goods or services	2.73	2.57	0.164
Improved coordination with partners or suppliers	2.78	2.93	0.206
Improved the rate of development and introduction of new products/services	2.62	2.58	0.885
Developing unique expertise or a unique market	2.66	2.50	0.194
Improved the brand and image of the business and its product/service	3.22	3.19	0.652

Notes: Columns 1 and 2 show the mean score for each business outcome and size class of firm. Business outcomes were estimated on a five-point Likert scale as follows: 1 = No impact; 2 = Low impact; 3 = Medium impact; 4 = High impact; 5 = Very high impact. Difference in scores was measured using the Mann–Whitney U statistic; significant differences are highlighted in bold.

do. Although micro-enterprises use Internet technologies and e-business solutions less extensively than larger firms, they have experienced similar patterns of value creation as larger SMEs, with the exception of greater reported profitability gains among micro-enterprises.

What are structural sources of e-business value creation in micro-enterprises?

This section is based on a previous study reported in Davis and Vladica (2006). Our structural model is a TOE model of technology adoption,

Table 6.5

Variables originally in the structural model

Business value: increased productivity, increased profitability, decreased cost of production, increased quality of goods and services, improved rate of new product development, developed unique expertise or market, increased speed of delivery, increased adaptability, increased domestic market share, increased international market share, increased customer service, improved relationships with existing customers, kept up with competitors, improved coordination with partners or suppliers, improved brand or image, average annual rate of growth in past three years.
Internal factors: nature of goods or services sold, skilful employees, business processes that support learning, capability of managing technological change, management effectiveness, management commitment, leadership quality, strategic objectives, internal business culture, attitude toward risk, entrepreneurship, focus, keeping overhead costs down, improving the quality of products and services, improving staff productivity, attracting and retaining staff, managing customer information, managing and communicating with mobile staff, managing office information technology, implementing new information and communication technologies, managing and reporting financial and tax information.
External factors: purchasing supplies and raw materials, costs of equipment, developing niche or specialized markets, delivery of products and services to customers, attracting new domestic customers, find customers abroad, getting marketing message out, geographical distance from customers and suppliers, possibility to access new markets, competitive threats, demanding customers or suppliers, access to specialized suppliers, access to financial resources, favourable regulatory environment, intensity of competition.
Index of connectivity: use of dial-up, cable modem, high speed, T1 or greater, wireless.
Index of e-business use: use of e-mail; personal computer, workstation or terminals; Internet, surfing the Internet, visiting Web sites, etc.; network/information security technology (e.g. firewall, anti-virus software, access control); functional software packages (e.g. accounting, HR, marketing); presenting own Web site (on the Internet); wireless communications; shared file folders; conducting secure business transactions with other businesses or government; conducting secure transactions with consumers; internal company Web site and communications (intranet); remote data storage; hosted software solutions; meeting over the network (e.g. videoconferencing); remote help desk assistance for your employees; extranet; Radio Frequency Identification (RFID).
Index of transactions: use of Internet to buy, to sell; per cent of gross sales conducted over the Internet.
Index of Web site functionality: organization has a Web site, online payment, asynchronous two-way communication, synchronous two-way communication, digital products or services delivered via the Web site, secure Web site, privacy policy statement, wireless access, information about products, information about the business.

and our measurement model uses an index of business outcomes as the dependent variable. We test a range of internal and external enabling and constraining factors as exogenous variables that respondents rated in importance on a five-point Likert scale. Since the purpose of this research is to identify sources of business value, Internet technologies and e-business solutions are exogenous variables in our model (i.e. we do not seek to identify the factors that explain their adoption).

The model contains seven composite variables (as described in Table 6.5). Indicators measuring the use of Internet technologies and e-business solutions are grouped into four composite variables: connectivity, Web site functionality, e-business use and transactions. Indicators measuring internal and external enabling and constraining factors are grouped into two composite variables: internal and external factors. The composite dependent variable, business value, is comprised of 16 outcome indicators as described in Table 6.5. Most of the business value variables measure the respondent's perception of the impact of ICT use on business outcomes on a five-point Likert scale, as previously discussed. We included the rate of revenue growth as an object-ive measure among the business value variables.

This model is estimated with data from 181 micro-enterprises in New Brunswick collected in our 2004 survey. We modelled the data using the technique of partial least squares (PLS) in PLS Graph 03.00. All of the measurement relationships between indicators and constructs in our model are specified as formative. In other words, the latent constructs are conceived as being formed by the indicators that measure them, rather than the reverse. Constructs created with formative indicators are linear composites of the indicators, and are conventionally called composite variables or indices. Reflective indicators must be uni-dimensional and correlated, while formative indicators need not be (Chin, 1998; Gefen *et al.*, 2000). The literature does not contain tested constructs or validated scales that are suitable for use as reflective indicators for measuring use or perceived impacts of Internet technologies and e-business solutions. Although formative indicators are less robust than reflective indicators, the current state of theory obliges us to use formative indicators and composite variables.

The structural model is shown in Figure 6.1. The composite variables 'external factors' and 'internal factors' are hypothesized to moderate the effects of the use of Internet technologies and e-business solutions on firm performance. We also hypothesize that these e-commerce technologies have direct effects on firm performance.

The significance levels of variables were measured using PLS's bootstrap re-sampling procedures. Exogenous variables with significant negative weights were eliminated from the model in several iterations, but variables with non-significant weights were not removed from the model.

Significant exogenous variables in the model are shown in Table 6.6, along with their path weights and levels of significance. Table 6.7 shows the levels of significance of hypothesized pathways and Figure 6.1 shows path coefficients. As seen in Table 6.6, the model has modest predictive power for two of the dependent variables (external factors and internal factors), and good predictive power for the composite variable

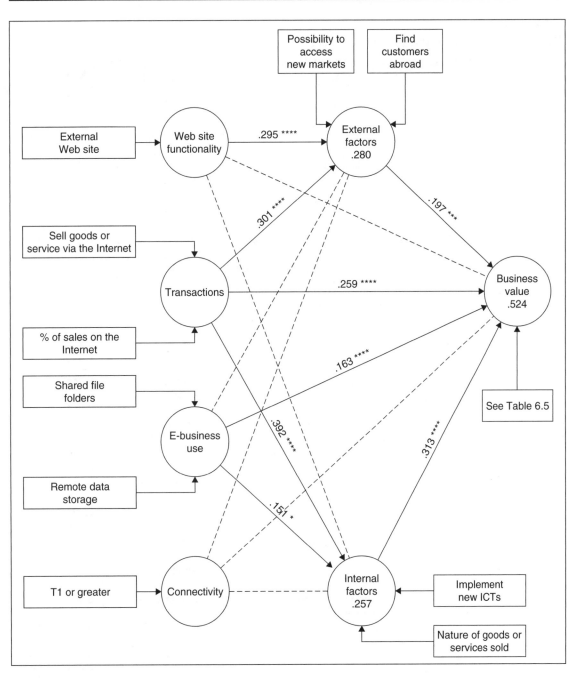

Figure 6.1

Structural model of sources of business value among 181 New Brunswick micro-enterprise users of Internet technologies and e-business solutions (source: after Davis and Vladica, 2006)

Notes: Significance levels denoted are $p < 0.001$ (****); $p < 0.01$ (***); $p < 0.05$ (**); and $p < 0.1$ (*). Non-significant pathways are denoted by dotted lines. Non-significant variables are not shown.

Table 6.6

Significant indicators in the structural model

Construct	Code	Explanation	Metric	Wgt.	Sig.
Connectivity	Q35_4	T1 line or greater	don't use/plan to use/use now	0.461	**
E-business use	Q40	shared file folders	don't use/plan to use/use now	0.515	***
	Q47	remote data storage	don't use/plan to use/use now	0.46	**
Web site functionality	Q42	external Web site	don't use/plan to use/use now	0.67	***
Transactions	Q56	goods or services sold via Internet	don't use/plan to use/use now	0.842	****
	Q57i	per cent of gross sales conducted on the Internet	Continuous	0.505	***
External factors	Q26r	find customers abroad	5-point scale	0.326	**
	Q76r	possibility to access new markets	5-point scale	0.445	***
Internal factors	Q32r	implementing new ICTs	5-point scale	0.261	*
	Q75r	nature of goods or services sold	5-point scale	0.586	***
Business value	Q59r	increased productivity	5-point scale	0.086	****
	Q60r	increased profitability	5-point scale	0.084	****
	Q61r	increased speed of delivery	5-point scale	0.081	****
	Q62r	increased adaptability	5-point scale	0.088	****
	Q63r	increased domestic market share	5-point scale	0.09	****
	Q64r	increased international market share	5-point scale	0.091	****
	Q65r	increased customer service	5-point scale	0.086	****
	Q66r	improved relationships with existing customers	5-point scale	0.086	****
	Q67r	kept up with competitors	5-point scale	0.092	****
	Q68r	decreased cost of production	5-point scale	0.076	****
	Q69r	increased quality of goods and services	5-point scale	0.084	****
	Q70r	improved coordination with partners or suppliers	5-point scale	0.075	****
	Q71r	improved rate of new product development	5-point scale	0.084	****
	Q72r	developed unique expertise or market	5-point scale	0.088	****
	Q73r	improved brand image	5-point scale	0.1	****
	Growth	average annual rate of growth in past three years	Continuous	0.042	****

Notes: Significance levels denoted are $p < 0.001$ (****); $p < 0.01$ (***); $p < 0.05$ (**); $p < 0.1$ (*). Non-significant variables are not shown.

Table 6.7
Significance of pathways in the structural model

	External factors	Internal factors	Connectivity	Transactions	E-business use	Web site functionality
External factors			n.s.	****	n.s.	****
Internal factors			n.s.	****	*	n.s.
Business value	***	****	n.s.	****	****	n.s.

Notes: Significance levels denoted are $p < 0.001$ (****); $p < 0.01$ (***); $p < 0.05$ (**); and $p < 0.1$ (*).

for business value ($R^2 = 0.524$). All dependent variable R^2s are significant at $p < 0.001$.

The meaning of the model can be summarized as follows:

- Micro-enterprises report greatest business value from market development, information sharing with customers and undertaking online transactions. Market development and recruitment of distant customers are significant external moderating factors, while ICT implementation capabilities and strategic choice of products and services that lend themselves to Internet commerce are significant internal moderating factors.

- Web site functionality has a strong indirect effect on business value via external factors (as defined by exogenous variables measuring market development) if the firm has an external Web site.

- E-business use (as defined by the exogenous variables measuring use of shared file folders and remote data storage) has a strong direct effect on business value.

- Transactions (as defined by exogenous variables measuring online presence and intensity of online commercial activity) have strong direct effects on business value as well as strong indirect effects via internal and external factors.

- Connectivity (i.e. speed, mode or combination of connections to the Internet) has no measurable direct or indirect effects on business value. More generally, connectivity, Web site functionality and interactivity *per se* are not important sources of business value for micro-enterprises.

■ In micro-enterprises, the production of value from e-business appears to be lumpy. Increased profitability, increased productivity, increased adaptability and increased market share tend to appear together – improvements in one area seem to bring improvements in other areas.

Our model portrays micro-enterprises that grow by adopting Web-based commerce and developing new markets for products and services, especially products and services that lend themselves to Internet commerce. The firms create business value that includes top-line and bottom-line benefits. This business model does not characterize the average member of the community of New Brunswick micro-enterprises. It seems, instead, to characterize micro-enterprises that are actively exploiting Internet technologies and e-business solutions for purposes of business development and export growth. The fact that this business model emerges clearly from the survey data suggests that evolutionary pressures and learning processes are at work on some members of the micro-enterprise community, inducing them to use Internet technologies and e-business solutions to undertake business activities that produce value in new ways. However, many of the micro-enterprises in our survey are in segments of the service industry, and with the exception of tourism the market for these services is primarily local. Enablement of global reach is of little interest to these firms, but affordable and reliable Internet technologies and e-business solutions that provide local visibility, security, interactivity, data sharing and mobility should be of interest.

SUMMARY AND CONCLUSIONS

This chapter focuses on creation of the business value by micro-enterprises that are users of Internet technologies and e-business solutions. SMEs and, within this group, micro-enterprises have a prominent role in local and national economies, but for a variety of reasons many micro-enterprises are actively looking for growth or are capable of growing. This chapter describes the barriers to growth and the reported benefits of using Internet technologies and e-business solutions by micro-enterprises. We compare micro-enterprises with larger SMEs and show how patterns of use and value creation differ between those two groups. Micro-enterprises practically never lead larger firms in the adoption of particular Internet technologies and e-business solutions. Moreover, micro-enterprises do not use the more complex and newer Internet technologies and e-business solutions as intensively as larger SMEs do, especially the solutions and technologies that support internal and external coordination and logistics. However, micro-enterprises are more likely to sell online than larger SMEs. Consistent with previous findings, micro-enterprises also report lower levels of competition in regional and national markets. Micro-enterprises assess the barriers to business expansion to be *lower* than larger SMEs' assessment. Our structural model, using a TOE conceptual framework, clearly identifies a high value creation micro-enterprise business model involving the use of advanced Web-based services and export-oriented commercialization of products and services that lend themselves to Internet commerce. Although enablement of global reach is of little interest to most micro-enterprises, affordable and reliable Internet technologies and e-business solutions that provide local visibility, security, interactivity, data sharing and mobility should be of concern.

More research is needed on a number of areas of interest. In particular, future research should focus on the relationships between entrepreneurial motivation, capabilities, technology use, learning, value creation and growth in micro-enterprises and very small firms.

A few policy directions can be provided on the basis of the material presented. Educators, policymakers, associations, economic development agencies and service providers can all contribute to 'facilitating a community of providers' that is responsive to SMEs' development objectives and e-business targets and to their needs for reliable and affordable expert advice (Davis and Vladica, 2005b). For example, initiatives could promote programmes that encourage hiring and matching small firms with professionals and other skilled workers (Papadaki and Chami, 2002). We agree that a 'blanket' policy orientation needs to be corrected by a consideration of the particular characteristics of the business owner. In particular, micro-enterprises that 'want to grow' (Papadaki and Chami, 2002) and that 'have a learning orientation' are better suited to adopt and exploit Internet technologies and e-business solutions than other micro-enterprises are (Davis and Vladica, 2005b).

ACKNOWLEDGEMENTS

The research reported here was supported by a project funded by the Social Sciences and Humanities Research Council (SSHRC) for research in Atlantic Canada on *Innovation Systems and Economic*

Development: The Role of Local and Regional Clusters in Canada and by a contract to the Electronic Commerce Centre of the University of New Brunswick in Saint John from the Atlantic Canada Opportunities Agency (ACOA) to develop e-business training and awareness services for SMEs in New Brunswick. This support is gratefully acknowledged.

REFERENCES

ACOA (2005). *The State of Small Business in Atlantic Canada 2005*. Policy and Programs Branch, Atlantic Canada Opportunities Agency.

Amit, R. and Zott, C. (2001). Value creation in e-business. *Strategic Management Journal*, 22, 493–520.

Bains, S. and Robson, L. (2001). Being self-employed or being enterprising? The case of creative work for the media industries. *Journal of Small Business and Enterprise Development*, 8 (4), 349–362.

Bains, S. and Wheelock, J. (1998). Re-inventing traditional solutions: job creation, gender, and the micro-business household. *Work, Employment & Society*, 12 (4), 579–601.

Bourgeois, Y. and LeBlanc, S. (2003). *Innovation in Atlantic Canada*. Canadian Institute for Research on Regional Development, Université de Moncton.

Burke, K. (2005). The impact of firm size on internet use in small business. *Electronic Markets*, 15 (2), 79–93.

CEBI (2004). *Net Impact Study Canada: Strategies for Increasing SME Engagement in the e-Economy*. Final Report, Canadian e-Business Initiative, September.

Chin, W. (1998). The partial least squares approach to structural equation modelling. In *Modern Business Research Methods* (G.A. Marcoulides, ed.) pp. 295–336, Lawrence Erlbaum.

Cook, R. G. and Belliveau, P. (2004). The influence of human capital attributes in micro-enterprise training. *Journal of Small Business and Enterprise Development*, 11 (4), 467–473.

Cronk, M. C. and Fitzgerald, E. P. (2002). Constructing a theory of 'IS business value' from the literature. *Electronic Journal of Business Research Methods*, 1 (1), 11–17.

Daniel, E. and Grimshaw, D. J. (2002). An exploratory comparison of electronic commerce adoption in large and small enterprises. *Journal of Information Technology*, 17, 133–147.

Davis, C. H. and Vladica, F. (2004). *Adoption of Internet Technologies and e-Business Solutions by Small and Medium Enterprises (SMEs) in New Brunswick*. Working Paper, Electronic Commerce Centre, University of New Brunswick-Saint John.

Davis, C. H. and Vladica, F. (2005a). Adoption and use of Internet technologies and e-business solutions by Canadian micro-enterprises. *Proceedings of* the Annual Conference of the International Association for Management of Technology [IAMOT], Vienna, May.

Davis, C. H. and Vladica, F. (2005b). Demand for e-business support services among New Brunswick SMEs. *Proceedings of the Atlantic Schools of Business Conference*, Halifax, September.

Davis, C. H. and Vladica, F. (2006). Micro-enterprises' use of Internet technologies and e-business solutions: a structural model of sources of business value. *Proceedings of the Hawaii International Conference on Systems Science* (HICSS 39), Hawaii, January.

Davis, C. H., Lin, C. and Vladica, F. (2006). Internet technologies and e-business solutions among small and medium-sized enterprises (SMEs) in Atlantic Canada – patterns of use, business impacts, and demand for support services. *Proceedings of the 7th World Congress on Management of e-Business*, Halifax, July.

De Berranger, P., Tucker, D. and Jones, L. (2001). Internet diffusion in creative micro-businesses: identifying change agent characteristics as critical success factors. *Journal of Organizational Computing and Electronic Commerce*, 11 (3), 197–214.

Desjardins, P.-M. (2005). *A Socio-Economic Profile of Atlantic Canada*. Canadian Institute for Research on Regional Development, Université de Moncton.

Devins, D., Gold, J., Johnson, S. and Holden, R. (2005). A conceptual model of management learning in micro businesses. *Education and Training*, 47 (8–9), 540–551.

Edgcomb, E. L. and Klein, J. A. (2005). *Opening Opportunities, Building Ownership: Fulfilling the Promise of Micro-Enterprise in the United States*. FIELD, Apen Institute.

Edwards, P. and Ram, M. (2006). Surviving on the margins of the economy: working relationships in small, low-wage firms. *Journal of Management Studies*, 43 (4), 895–916.

Evans, J. R. and Mathur, A. (2005). The value of online surveys. *Internet Research*, 15 (2), 195–219.

Fillis, I., Johansson, U. and Wagner, B. (2004). Factors impacting on e-business adoption and development in the smaller firm. *International Journal of Entrepreneurial Behaviour and Research*, 10 (3), 178–191.

Fillis, I. and Wagner, B. (2005). E-business development: an exploratory investigation of the small firm. *International Small Business Journal*, 23 (6), 604–634.

Friar, J. H. and Meyer, M. H. (2003). Entrepreneurship and start-ups in the Boston region: factors differentiating high-growth ventures from micro-ventures. *Small Business Economics*, 21, 145–152.

Gefen, D., Straub, D. W. and Boudreau, M.-C. (2000). Structural equation modeling and regression: guidelines for research practice. *Communications of the Association for Information Systems*, 4 (7). http://cais.isworld.org/articles/default.asp?vol=4&art=7

Getz, D. and Carlsen, J. (2000). Characteristics and goals of family and owner-operated businesses in the rural tourism and hospitality sectors. *Tourism Management*, 21, 547–560.

González, T. E. (2005). Problemas en la definición de microempresa. *Revista Venezolana de Gerencia*, 10 (31), 408–423.

Henry, C., Hill, F. and Leitch, C. (2003). Developing coherent enterprise support policy. *Environment and Planning C: Government and Policy*, 21, 3–19.

Ihlstrom, C. and Nilsson, M. (2003). E-business adoption by SMEs – prerequisites and attitudes of SMEs in a Swedish network. *Journal of Organisational Computing and Electronic Commerce*, 13 (3/4), 211–223.

Industry Canada (2001). *Micro-Enterprises Survey 2000: A Progress Report*. Small Business Policy Branch, Industry Canada.

Innova Quest (2000). *The State of Electronic Commerce in Atlantic Canada*. Atlantic Canada Opportunities Agency. http://dsp-psd.pwgsc.gc.ca/Collection/C89-4-64-2000E.pdf

Joice, W. (2002). The road not traveled: mainstreaming telework. *The Journal of Public Inquiry*, Spring/Summer, 17–19.

Kim, E., Nam, D. and Stimpert, J. L. (2004). The applicability of Porter's generic strategies in the digital age: assumptions, conjectures, and suggestions. *Journal of Management*, 30 (5), 569–589.

Kuratko, D. D., Hornsby, J. S. and Naffziger, D.W. (1997). An examination of owners' goals in sustaining entrepreneurship. *Journal of Small Business Management*, 35 (1), 24–33.

Kwon, D., Watts-Sussman, S. and Collopy, F. (2002). *Value Frame, Paradox and Change: The Constructive Nature of Information Technology Business Value*. Sprouts Working Papers on Information Environments, Systems and Organizations.

Levy, M. and Powell, P. (2003). Exploring SME Internet adoption: towards a contingent model. *Electronic Markets*, 13 (2), 173–181.

Locke, W., Davis, C. H., Freedman, R., Godin, B. and Holbrook, A. (2004). *Indicators for Benchmarking Innovation in Atlantic Canada*. Canadian Science and Innovation Indicators Consortium.

MacMillan, C. (2001). *Focusing on the Future: Atlantic Canada's Quiet Revolution*. Council of Atlantic Provinces Premiers.

Martin, L. H. and Halstead, A. (2004). Attracting micro-enterprises to learning: community initiatives or growth incentives? *Community, Work and Family*, 7 (1), 29–42.

Martin, L. H. and Matlay, H. (2001). 'Blanket' approaches to promoting ICT in small firms: lessons from the DTI ladder adoption model in the UK. *Internet Research*, 11 (5), 399–410.

Muske, G., Stanforth, N. and Woods, M. D. (2004). Micro business use of technology and extension's role. *Journal of Extension*, 42 (1). http://www.joe.org/joe/2004february/a4.shtml

OECD (2004). *Promoting Entrepreneurship and Innovative SMEs in a Global Economy. Towards a More Responsive and Inclusive Globalisation.* Organisation for Economic Cooperation and Development.

Papadaki, E. and Chami, B. (2002). *Growth Determinants of Micro-Businesses in Canada.* Small Business Policy Branch, Industry Canada.

Papazafeiropoulou, A., Pouloudi, A. and Doukidis, G. (2002). A framework for best practices in electronic commerce awareness creation. *Business Process Management Journal,* 8 (3), 233–244.

Perren, L. (1999). Factors in the growth of micro-enterprises. Part 1: developing a framework. *Journal of Small Business and Enterprise Development,* 64, 366–385.

Pflughoeft, K., Ramamurthy, A. K., Soofi, E. S., Yasai-Ardekani, M. and Zahedi, F. (2003). Multiple conceptualizations of small business web use and benefit. *Decision Sciences,* 34 (3), 467–512.

Poon, S. and Swatman, P. M. C. (1999). An exploratory study of small business Internet commerce issues. *Information & Management,* 35, 9–18.

Porter, M. E. (2001). Strategy and the Internet. *Harvard Business Review,* 79 (3), 63–78.

Premkumar, G. (2003). A meta-analysis of research on information technology implementation in small business. *Journal of Organizational Computing and Electronic Commerce,* 13 (2), 91–121.

Rao, S. S., Metts, G. and Monge, M. C. A. (2003). Electronic commerce development in small and medium sized enterprises: a stage model and its implications. *Business Process Management Journal,* 9 (1), 11–32.

Raymond, L., Bergeron, F. and Blili, S. (2005). The assimilation of e-business in manufacturing SMEs: determinants and effects on growth and internationalization. *Electronic Markets,* 15 (2), 106–118.

Robichaud, Y. and McGraw, E. (2004). Les objectifs entrepreneuriaux comme facteur explicatif de la taille des entreprises. *Proceedings of the 7ème Congrès International Francophone en Entrepreneuriat et PME,* Montpellier, October.

Ruggieri, J. (2003). *Atlantic Canada in the Knowledge-Based Age.* Policy Studies Centre, University of New Brunswick.

Schreiner, M. (1999). Self-employment, micro-enterprise and the poorest Americans. *The Social Service Review,* 73 (4), 496–523.

Servon, L. and Bates, T. (1998). *Micro-Enterprise as an Exit Route from Poverty: Recommendations for Programs and Policy Makers.* Discussion Paper 98–17, Center for Economic Studies, US Bureau of the Census.

Simpson, M. and Docherty, A. J. (2004). E-commerce adoption support and advice for UK SMEs. *Journal of Small Business and Enterprise Development,* 11 (3), 315–328.

Statistics Canada (1999). *A Reality Check to Defining E-Commerce.* Science, Innovation and Electronic Information Division Working Papers, Statistics Canada.

Stockdale, R. and Standing, C. (2006). A classification model to support e-commerce adoption initiatives. *Journal of Small Business and Enterprise Development,* 13 (3), 381–394.

Tornatzky, L. G. and Fleischer, M. (1990). *The Processes of Technological Innovation.* Lexington Books.

Tremblay, D.-G. (2003). Telework: a new mode of gendered segmentation? *Canadian Journal of Communication,* 28 (4), 461.

Van der Veen, M. (2004). Measuring e-business adoption in SMEs. In *New Technology-Based Firms in the New Millennium* (W. During, R. Oakey and S. Kauser, eds) pp. 31–53, Elsevier.

Windrum, P. and de Berranger, P. (2002). *The Adoption of e-Business Technology by SMEs.* Paper No. 2002–023, MERIT-Infonomics Research Memorandum Series.

Woller, M. and Schreiner, G. (2003). Micro-enterprise development programs in the United States and in the developing world. *World Development,* 31 (9), 1567–1580.

Zheng, J., Caldwell, N., Harland, C., Powell, P., Woerndl, M. and Xu, S. (2004). Small firms and e-business: cautiousness, contingency, and cost-benefit. *Journal of Purchasing and Supply Chain Management,* 10, 27–39.

Zhu, K., Xu, S. and Dedrick, J. (2003). Assessing drivers of e-business value: results of a cross-country study. *Proceedings of the 24th International Conference on Information Systems,* Seattle, December.

CHAPTER 7

The emergence of mobile commerce

Stuart Barnes and Eusebio Scornavacca

INTRODUCTION

The number of mobile phone users worldwide has increased rapidly over the last five years; from an estimated 1.87 billion in 2004 to 2.5 billion in September 2006 (InfoSync World, 2004; Usability News, 2006). In Japan, already seven out of 10 people have cell-phone accounts, and in countries such as Italy, Norway, Sweden and the United Kingdom, the market penetration of mobile phones has already exceeded 100% (Sultan and Rohm, 2005). Undoubtedly the mobile phone has been one of the fastest adopted consumer products of all time (Kalakota and Robinson, 2002; Scornavacca *et al.*, 2006). In addition, according to Forrester Research (2005), some 90 per cent of all phones in use will be mobile Internet-capable this year.

The proliferation of Internet-enabled mobile devices has created an extraordinary opportunity for e-commerce to leverage the benefits of mobility (Barnes and Huff, 2003; Clarke, 2001; Durlacher Research, 2002). The conduit for this is mobile e-commerce, commonly known as m-commerce, which refers to the ability to conduct financial transactions (including, but not exclusively, the ability to purchase goods or services) through a wireless Internet-enabled device (Barnes, 2002a; Scornavacca and Barnes, 2006).

M-commerce allows e-commerce businesses to expand beyond the traditional limitations of the fixed-line personal computer, increasing the overall market for e-commerce. Traditional e-commerce models are generally poor at representing m-commerce features. M-commerce has a unique value proposition that provides easily personalized access to goods and services anytime and anywhere (Durlacher Research, 2002; Newell and Lemon, 2001). Due to current technological limitations, some problems – such as uniform standards, ease of operation, security for transactions, minimum screen size, display type and the relatively impoverished Web sites – are yet to be overcome (Barnes, 2002a; Clarke, 2001; Scornavacca and Hoehle, 2006).

This chapter explores the emergence of m-commerce. The next section discusses the fundamental differences between e-commerce and m-commerce. This is followed by an examination of m-commerce value propositions as well as the possible effects of m-commerce in the business-to-consumer value chain. Subsequently, several case studies explore the business models being employed, and analyse the strategic implications of these models for different m-commerce markets. The penultimate section examines the growth of mobility in business markets – m-business. Finally, the chapter concludes with a discussion about the future of mobile commerce.

DIFFERENCES BETWEEN E-COMMERCE AND M-COMMERCE

M-commerce should not be viewed as e-commerce with limitations, but rather as a unique form of e-commerce with its own unique benefits (Scornavacca and Barnes, 2006; Zhang *et al.*, 2003). Additionally, m-commerce is not a substitute for PCs. Rather, it is a new and a much more powerful way to communicate with customers. Zhang *et al.* (2003) indicate that there are some fundamental differences between m-commerce and e-commerce in terms of their origin, technology and the nature of the services:

- *Origin.* Due to widely expanding networks and nearly free access to the Internet, e-commerce bridges distances and enables companies to display and sell goods and services cheaply to consumers and businesses around the world. In the Internet world, much is given away free or at a discount in the hope that a way will eventually be found (presumably through advertising income) to turn traffic into profits. Contrarily, m-commerce is rooted in paid-for services in the private mobile phone industry where business competition is stiff. In the telecommunications world, users pay for airtime, by the size of the data packet transmitted, and by the services used. Therefore, due to their different origins, the customer bases of m-commerce and e-commerce are quite different.

- *Technology.* The fundamental infrastructure of e-commerce is the Internet. It has a well-established protocol, TCP/IP (Transmission Control Protocol/Internet Protocol), which solves the global internetworking problem and ensures that computers communicate with one another in a reliable fashion. In contrast, m-commerce services are constrained by a variety of wireless media communication standards ranging from global (e.g. via satellite), to regional (e.g. third generation (3G) network standards, wireless fidelity (WiFi) (the IEEE 802.11 family of standards), and i-mode network standards), to short distance (e.g. Bluetooth and Ultra Wideband). Cellular carriers use different systems and standards such as GSM (Global System for Mobile), TDMA (Time Division Multiple Access), and CDMA (Code Division Multiple Access) to compete with each other. As a consequence, m-commerce applications tend to be device and carrier dependent. The boom in e-commerce applications is actually due to the widespread use of PCs, which have complete text input keyboards, large screens, substantial memory and high processing power. Contrarily, mobile devices such as cell phones and PDAs (Personal Digital Assistants – such as the iPAQ and Palmpilot) still present some obstacles, including uniform standards, ease of operation, security for transactions, minimum screen size and display type.

- *Nature of services.* The Web is widely accessible enabling search and delivery of rich information. Sophisticated electronic transaction processes can be integrated easily with back-end enterprise information systems. In contrast, the delivery of m-commerce applications relies on private wireless communications carriers. These services are usually delivered to a specific region, and are rather simple, more personalized, location-specific and time-sensitive. Moreover, the rapid growth of e-commerce began with the boom of dot.com companies aimed at online shopping and customer services. Gradually, the emphasis shifted to business-to-business (B2B), and more recently to e-business, to take advantage of the real business value of the Internet. In contrast, mobile commerce started with

Table 7.1
Major differences between m-commerce and e-commerce (source: adapted from Zhang *et al.*, 2003)

	E-commerce	M-commerce
Origin		
Sponsorship	Government-sponsored Internet	Private mobile phone industry
Business entry cost	Low	High
Access cost	Free or low-cost Internet access	High mobile service charge
Technology		
Message transmission	Packet-switched data transmission	Circuit switched for streamlined voice communication
Protocol	TCP/IP, HTTP	GSM, TDMA, CDMA, 3G
Standardization	Highly standardized	Multiple incompatible standards
Connectivity	Global	Mainly regional
Bandwidth	High	Medium
Identity	URL with IP and domain name	Phone number
Application development	General computer applications	Device-specific applications
Interface device	Personal computers	Cell phones and PDAs
Mobility	Fixed location	Mobile
Display	Big screen	Small screen
Main input mode	Keyboard for full text input	Voice with small key pad
Main output mode	Text, sound and graphics	Sound and small display
Local processing power	Powerful CPU with large memory and disk space	Limited processing power with small memory chip
Software and programming	Support a variety of programming languages	Java or specific script languages
Trend	Towards sophistication	Towards minimization
Services		
Service range	Global	Regional
Delivery destination	PC connected to the Internet	Person with a mobile device
Transaction complexity	Complete and complex transactions	Simple transactions
Information provided	Rich information	Simple and short messages
Timing	Less time critical	Time critical
Geographic location	No	Yes
Target mobility	Service to a fixed point	Service to a moving target
Back-end business connection	Strong connection to back-end business information systems	Weak connection to back-end business information systems

person-to-person communication, and developed as more services were introduced through interactions between people and systems, e.g. local weather information, finding a local restaurant, and so on. The authors suggest that rather than apply B2C and B2B classifications to m-commerce, P2P (person-to-person) and P2S (person-to-system) would be more appropriate to address the nature and trend of m-commerce applications.

Table 7.1 summarizes some of the major differences described above.

From a different perspective, Junglas and Watson (2003) point out that compared to e-commerce, m-commerce has the following characteristics that make it distinct: reachability, accessibility, localization, identification and portability. Let us examine each of these in turn.

Reachability covers the idea that a person can be in touch and reached by other people 24 hours a day, seven days a week – assuming that the mobile network coverage is sufficient and the mobile device is switched on. On the other hand, as opposed to reachability, *accessibility* describes the fact that a user can access the mobile network at any time and from any location – again assuming adequate mobile network coverage. *Localization* describes the ability to locate the position of a mobile user. As such, localization is key to providing geographically-specific value-added services (so-called location-based services or LBS) and is expected to be the most distinct characteristic of m-commerce compared to e-commerce. *Identification* is enabled by technological capability and personal usage. Mobile devices can be used as the virtual substitute for an individual's identity, containing not only personal information, but also billing information. Finally, *portability* comprises the physical aspects of mobile devices – one is able to readily carry them.

In summary, the principal difference between e-business and m-business revolves mostly around the nature of the medium for supporting exchanges between parties. The following section explores the value propositions of m-commerce.

M-COMMERCE VALUE PROPOSITIONS

Value propositions define the relationship between supplier offerings and consumer purchases by identifying how the supplier fulfils the customer's needs across different consumer roles (Porter, 1998). The value proposition furthermore solidifies the relationship between the user and various dimensions of product value.

Clarke (2001) presented one of the first approaches towards this problem. The author understood that m-commerce differs from e-commerce in terms of the following value proposition attributes:

- *Ubiquity.* Mobile devices offer users the ability to receive information and perform transactions from virtually any location on a real-time basis. M-commerce users are everywhere, or in many places simultaneously, with a similar level of access available through fixed-line technology. Communication can take place independently of the user's location. The advantages presented by the omnipresence of information and continual access to commerce will be exceptionally important to time-critical applications.

- *Convenience.* The agility and accessibility provided by wireless devices allow m-commerce to differentiate its abilities from e-commerce. People are no longer constrained by time or place in accessing e-commerce activities. Consumers may recognize a special convenience, which can translate into an improved quality of life. M-commerce also offers tremendous opportunities to expand a client-base by providing value-added services to customers that may be difficult to reach.

- *Localization.* Knowing the location of the Internet user creates a significant advantage for m-commerce over wired e-commerce. Location-based technologies such as variants of the Global Positioning System (GPS) can accurately identify the location of the user. Utilizing this technology, m-commerce providers are able to receive and send information relative to a specific location. Location-specific information leverages the key value proposition of m-commerce over traditional e-commerce by supplying information relevant to the current geographic position of the user.

- *Personalization.* Since mobile devices are typically used by one individual, they are ideal for individual-based target information. Mobile technology offers the opportunity to personalize messages to various segments, based upon time and location, by altering both sight and sound. Mobile databases become a primary factor of m-commerce success by compiling personalized information and providing personalized services. A value proposition is developed as superior consumer value is created through an increasingly targeted Internet experience for mobile users.

In a slightly different view, Zhang and Yuan (2002) analysed key differences between m-commerce and e-commerce business models. They concluded that the differentiation between m-commerce and

Table 7.2
Differences between e-commerce and m-commerce value propositions
(source: adapted from Zhang *et al.,* 2003)

Value proposition	E-commerce	M-commerce
Mobility	Low	High
Location dependence	High	Low
Personalization	Low	High
Cost of communication	Low	High
Device capabilities	High	Low

e-commerce value propositions derives from differences in terms of mobility, location dependence, personalization, cost of communication and device capabilities (see Table 7.2).

Zhang and Yuan (2002) focused on a consumer perspective, suggesting that what attracts customers to enter the e-commerce world is the very low cost and unlimited Internet access. On the other hand, they point out that mobile person-to-person communication is what initially brings consumers to m-commerce, followed by the possibility of accessing several services anywhere at anytime. Based on a similar argument used by Clarke (2001), they also highlighted the idea that location awareness creates significant value for m-commerce. In theory that is correct, but in practice, due to technological limitations of the mobile devices, very few mobile/wireless systems have leveraged this value proposition.

M-COMMERCE AND THE VALUE CHAIN

Moving beyond an understanding of traditional Internet-based commercial activities to the area of m-commerce, Barnes (2002a) presented a systematic analysis of the potential opportunities of wireless and mobile technologies in a value chain (Porter and Millar, 1985). Figure 7.1 presents the m-commerce value chain (Barnes, 2002a).

The basic model consists of six core processes in two main areas: (a) content; and (b) infrastructure and services. In m-commerce these are interpreted as:

Content

■ *Content creation.* The focus in this value space is on creating digital material such as audio, video and textual information.

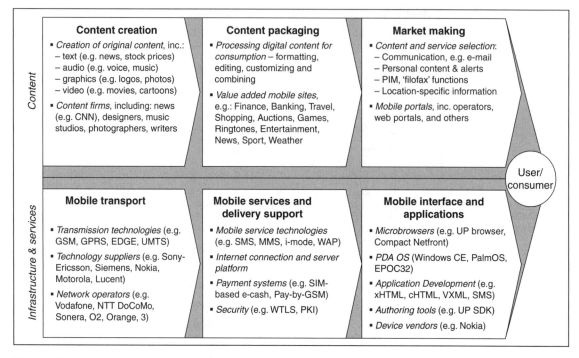

Figure 7.1
The m-commerce value chain (source: Barnes, 2002)

For example, digital news feeds and real-time stock information are available from Reuters.

■ *Content packaging*. Formatting, editing, customizing and the use of software to combine and package content. This can include, for example, packaging Reuters' stock information for FT.com, the online version of the business and financial newspaper. The information on this site is also customizable for individual users who may, for example, only be interested in certain financial markets.

■ *Market making*. Marketing and selling content is the primary role of mobile portals. This includes programme development, service delivery and customer care. For example, the Yahoo! Mobile Web portal provides a one-stop shop for a large number of services.

Infrastructure and services

■ *Mobile transport*. This is the basic network involved in communications, including transportation, transmission and switching for voice and data. This includes major telecommunications players such as NTT DoCoMo and Vodafone, and high-speed transmission technologies such as the Universal Mobile Telecommunications System (UMTS).

■ *Mobile services and delivery support.* This involves, for example, the infrastructure in connecting to the Internet, security, the server platform and payment systems. Standards such as the wireless application protocol (WAP) and i-mode are key building blocks towards enabling the delivery of Internet services via mobile handsets. Key standards for payment and security have yet to be developed.

■ *Mobile interface and applications.* This process centres on integrating the infrastructure and systems with users – hardware, software and communications. This includes the user interface, navigation and application/middleware development, as well as the authoring tools.

Up to now, we have focused on providing a solid foundation for understanding the concept of m-commerce. The following section explores a number of cases studies of m-commerce applications. This should help to put some flesh on the bones of the conceptual discussion above.

CASE STUDIES OF MOBILE COMMERCE

In this section, we examine three specific sets of m-commerce applications offered to consumers around the world – mobile advertising, mobile banking and mobile games. We have focused on exemplars of existing applications that are being offered to and used by consumers in distinct markets such as Japan, New Zealand and the United Kingdom. Let us consider each of these in turn.

Mobile advertising

Mobile marketing or wireless marketing is a subset of electronic marketing and is defined by Dickinger *et al.* (2005) as '… using a wireless medium to provide consumers with time-and-location-sensitive, personalized information that promotes goods, services and ideas, thereby benefiting all stakeholders'. Mobile marketing can also be seen as: 'All activities required to communicate with customers through the use of mobile devices in order to promote the selling of products or services and the provision of information about these products and services' (Ververidis and Polyzos, 2002).

Mobile advertising has typically been categorized into push- and pull-models (Barnes, 2002b). In the pull-model campaign, the marketer sends the information requested by the consumer; whereas in the push-model campaign, the marketer takes the initiative to send messages to the consumer. The latter model includes much of SMS advertising and raises the issue of consumers' permission, since it is the marketer that initiates contact and communication. Permission marketing refers to the asking of consumers' consent to receive commercial messages while giving the individual an opportunity to stop receiving them at any time (Tezinde et al., 2002). This approach can considerably reduce individuals' privacy concerns and build trust (Sheehan and Hoy, 2000). Unfortunately, some marketers manipulate consumers' inattention and cognitive laziness to get their consent. Bellman et al. (2001) affirm that: 'Using the right combination of question framing and default answer, an online organization can almost guarantee it will get the consent of nearly every visitor to its sites'.

The most prevalent mode of mobile advertising is via SMS (Short Message Service) to handheld devices, notably mobile phones. SMS, known as text messaging, is a store-and-forward communication system for the mobile phone. Recent variants, such as MMS (Multimedia Message Service), have added multimedia capabilities. According to the GSM Association, cell-phone users send more than 10 billion SMS messages each month, making SMS the most popular mobile data service (Dickinger et al., 2004).

Barwise and Strong (2002) identify six ways of using SMS for advertising: brand building, special offers, timely media 'teasers', competitions, polls/voting, products, services and information requests. Text message ads have been found to boost consumers' inclination to purchase by 36 per cent, which partly explains their growing popularity among marketers (Enpocket, 2005b). According to Enpocket (2005a), text message campaigns also deliver a 15 per cent response rate, which they estimate is twice as much as direct mail or e-mail campaigns; apparently, text messages are 50 per cent more successful at building brand awareness than TV and 130 per cent more successful than radio (Enpocket, 2005b).

The push-model campaigns involve unsolicited messages, usually via SMS alerts, while pull-model campaigns promote information requested by the consumer (Dickinger et al., 2004). A third type of campaign, as suggested by Jelassi and Enders (2006), revolves around the mobile dialogue model, where the marketer tries to build a long lasting relationship with the consumer over a series of interactions.

The wireless channel benefits from the potential for detailed user information and personalization; the message can be tailored for each customer to enable better targeting. Since mobile phones are personal objects marketers can specifically address the person targeted, as well as recognizing their social context, individual preferences, time and location. Context-sensitive systems such as Ad-me (advertising mobile e-commerce) provide examples of the potential of this channel – equipping consumers with tailored, relevant information according to the context where they are (Hristova and O'Hare, 2004). SMS location-based services are likely to become increasingly valued as a marketing tool (Ververidis and Polyzos, 2002). Via the mobile channel, the response can be nearly immediate, interactive and the consumer can be reached everywhere at anytime because the service is typically ubiquitous (Jelassi and Enders, 2006).

The acceptance of SMS advertising has been examined by Bauer *et al.* (2005). Using a large sample and structural equation modelling they find that the most important factors that affect attitudes toward mobile marketing are: consumers' attitudes toward advertising in general; perceived utility (in terms of information, entertainment and social aspects); perceived risk (in terms of privacy and data security); consumers' knowledge about the technology; and social norms that impact on consumers' behaviour.

One of the core issues in SMS advertising is privacy: an individual's control over information held about them by third parties. Dickinger *et al.* (2005) observed that: 'The mobile phone cannot distinguish between spam and genuine communication automatically'. They also found that consumers fear registration on SMS-based information services because of privacy concerns. Permission-based mobile advertising (PBMA) is considered to be the easiest way to tackle the privacy issue (Godin, 1999). In a study of 16- to 30-year-olds in the USA, evidence suggests that 51 per cent of respondents were 'very satisfied' and 42 per cent were 'fairly satisfied' by PBMA. Some 72 per cent agreed that PBMA was relevant to them and 84 per cent were willing to recommend it (Barwise and Strong, 2002). On the other hand, there is a negative relationship between the volume of ads received and the attitude towards direct marketing (Phelps *et al.*, 2000). If the consumer is interrupted during his or her daily activities this can severely damage brand image (Hoyer and MacInnis, 2004). Petty (2000) describes this cost as an involuntary cost borne by the consumer who faces an unselected exposure.

The major privacy violations in term of information capture are demographics and purchase data disclosure without consumers' consent, click stream patterns and browsing history, and physical location and purchase context (for example, via GPS). For this reason, the notion of control over the wireless service provider is pertinent (Barnes and Scornavacca, 2004; Carroll *et al.*, 2007). In the UK, under Privacy and Electronic Communication Regulations, permission is a requirement of SMS ads, as is opt-out and data protection from misuse and inaccuracy. Similar legislation is found in other parts of the EU; for example, in the Nordic countries you cannot approach clientele with SMS in any way before obtaining permission and so other media must be used to attract attention.

The principal way of obtaining permission is by signing a contract. Bamba and Barnes (2007) found that the preferred form of receiving such a contract is mainly divided between online and SMS-based (both 41.8 per cent) versions. Bamba and Barnes also found that freedom of opting out (95.2 per cent), message frequency (89.2 per cent) and control over third parties (95 per cent) were the most important aspects of the contract. Time and location are less important although still notable.

Most importantly, Bamba and Barnes (2007) found that permission to receive SMS ads only tends to occur when consumers have a high control over opt-in conditions, when the SMS ad is relevant and when the brand is familiar. Moreover, using a scenario-based analysis they discovered that brand familiarity is significantly less important than either ad relevance or control over opt-in conditions, which share similar importance. This supports earlier research by Carroll *et al.* (2007). Thus, even big brand names need to be wary of the way advertising campaigns are approached.

This new channel of advertising clearly has potential. However, it is not without problems. To appeal to consumers, marketers must adapt their ads to individual use of text messaging and to areas of interest. Marketers should try to find a single point that regroups all of the permission threads for ads from different sources so that consumers will not have to repetitively answer whether or not they wish to give permission for every ad they receive. Companies that launch an opt-in SMS advertising campaign should register with cell-phone operators or specialized SMS information services to reach the maximum number of consumers. These companies can act as a filter for unsolicited SMS ads.

Mobile banking

One of the first commercial applications of mobile commerce was mobile banking (m-banking) (Barnes and Corbitt, 2003). M-banking is a further development over earlier customer channel extensions such as phone banking and online banking (Barnes and Corbitt, 2003; Kumar, 2004; Laukkanen and Lauronen, 2005; Laukkanen, 2006; Pousttchi and Schurig, 2004). M-banking can be simply defined as a channel whereby a customer interacts with a bank through data communications via a mobile device (e.g. a cell phone or PDA) (Scornavacca and Barnes, 2004).

The two most popular platforms used to deliver m-banking are SMS banking and WAP banking. SMS banking services are based on the idea of customers generating SMS messages (usually in combination with a personal identification number or PIN) sending them to customer service centres and receiving personal account and other information via their phones (Barnes and Corbitt, 2003; Laukkanen and Lauronen, 2005). WAP banking, on the other hand, enables users to communicate via a browser (Barnes and Corbitt, 2003). WAP banking users authenticate via a PIN and authorize each transaction via transaction numbers (TANs) (Laukkanen and Lauronen, 2005; Pousttchi and Schurig, 2004). This concept has become common in electronic banking but restricts users to carrying around a TAN list to execute transactions (Laukkanen and Lauronen, 2005; Pousttchi and Schurig, 2004).

Table 7.3 compares the mobile banking services available on SMS and WAP platforms.

Table 7.3

Typical mobile banking services

Services	SMS	WAP
Checking the account balance	Yes	Yes
Transaction enquiry	Limited	Yes
Viewing the last transactions made	Yes	Yes
Checking the status of a cheque number	No	Yes
Transferring funds from one account to another	Limited	Yes
Requesting a transaction statement	Yes	Yes
Requesting a cheque book	Yes	Yes
Cancelling a service request	Limited	Yes
Checking the status of service requests	No	Yes
Changing a password	Yes	Yes
Check credit card information	No	Yes
Account maintenance and administration	No	Yes

Surprisingly, despite the high penetration of SMS services, very few European banks offer m-banking services (Barnes and Corbitt, 2003). Barnes and Corbitt (2003) point out that the acceptance of WAP phones and the usage of Internet services through mobile phones have been slow to take off.

The success of mobile banking is likely to vary considerably from country to country (Scornavacca and Hoehle, 2006). In countries in which neither PC penetration nor mobile device saturation is achieved it is most likely that banking consumers rely on traditional banking services (Barnes, 2003a). However, in many developed markets, banks have already adopted a multiple distribution channel approach.

Recent studies by Scornavacca and Barnes (2004), Scornavacca and Cairns (2005) and Scornavacca and Hoehle (2006) explored the state-of-the-art of mobile banking in Japan, New Zealand and Germany. The New Zealand and German m-banking markets are still at a stage of relative infancy (Scornavacca and Cairns, 2005; Scornavacca and Hoehle, 2006). In comparison with Scornavacca and Barnes' (2004) study, the German and New Zealand m-banking portfolio is far less developed than its Japanese counterparts. For example, in Germany, only 14 out of 100 banks studied offer m-banking to their customers. These 14 banks all have a very distinct strategy and present a diverse range of services. These services are provided to customers independently of wireless service providers (Scornavacca and Hoehle, 2006).

The high level of mobile penetration can be seen as the foundation for a more comprehensive m-banking market. It is therefore likely that m-banking will develop at a more rapid pace in future years. As m-banking continues to develop, and with the strength of online banking, it is likely that m-banking will become a part of a multi-channel strategy. New mobile plans with a 'flat rate' for unlimited data transmission will offer good opportunities for customers as well as for banks (E-Plus, 2006). So far banking transactions conducted on mobile devices have been expensive for customers. The emergence of low-cost Internet flat rates in combination with high PC penetration rates in Europe encouraged banking customers to use the online channel (Barnes, 2003a). Perhaps the same trend may happen with the mobile channel.

The next three years will provide important evidence regarding the future of m-banking. Besides the recent introduction of 3G devices, there is considerable speculation regarding future integration between wireless service providers and financial institutions. Based on the lessons learned from the initial 'mobile hype', the mobile banking industry may soon develop a much stronger and sustainable m-banking channel for its customers.

Mobile games

Mobile devices possess advantages over other digital gaming media; most notably, mobile phones are multifunctional as opposed to a specialist device such as a radio and thus consumers habitually possess them wherever they go – they are both ubiquitous and networked. By working around limitations and utilizing advantages, mobile games have the potential to deliver a revolutionary gaming experience. For the purposes of this chapter, mobile games are defined as games played on mobile phones that are either embedded or at some stage require the use of wireless connectivity, excluding any games that are reliant upon cartridges.

Beyond simply allowing gaming at anytime and anywhere, mobile games can be massively multiplayer and can exploit information gathered – such as players' location and proximity to one another – to create a new concept in mobile entertainment (Datacomm, 2002). The use of location-based services has created an ability to play virtual games in a 'real-world' context. An article featured in *BusinessWeek* (Kharif, 2001), discussing an increasingly popular game known as BotFighters, epitomizes this phenomenon.

BotFighters allows players to create a robot that is housed in their mobile phone, by choosing the robot's armour, shield and eyes, which they then set upon other robots by sending text 'attack messages' to the central game server. Those messages are then relayed to their local game opponents in the form of beeps. The game has become so addictive that players have been known to play for many hours in order to defeat opponents (Kharif, 2001). An involved player, who plays on average 30 minutes a day, will pay somewhere between US$5 and US$10 per month in addition to regular mobile phone charges.

An important component of combat games, such as BotFighters, is that they consist of provisions which prevent players interacting within a proximity close enough to reveal real identities. BotFighters is just one illustration of the pioneering location-based games starting to appear around the world (It's Alive, 2000).

One other notable example that helps illustrate the current diversity of location-dependent gaming is TreasureMachine (Unwiredfactory, 2001). Developed by Unwiredfactory, TreasureMachine releases clues to guide players to a predefined location. Whenever a player believes that they physically stand on the right spot, they 'dig' for the treasure using their mobile phone. The first player to 'dig' for the treasure at the predefined location wins. Players are charged a small fee for each clue they receive and for each digging attempt (Unwiredfactory, 2004).

BotFighters, released in November 2001, and TreasureMachine, not long after, were the world's earliest location-based games (It's Alive, 2004; Unwiredfactory, 2004). Partly due to their release being at a time when WAP-capable handsets were not widespread these games were made available over both short message service and WAP platforms to increase circulation. Both messaging and WAP platforms offer distinctive capabilities for mobile games.

SMS, together with multimedia message service applications, form a gaming category that can be classified as messaging mobile games. The means of interaction among these games is analogous to other data communications. To initiate game-play an SMS or MMS message is sent to a game server. The player then receives a reply message consisting of instructions. From this point onwards, messages are sent back and forth consisting of commands from the player as well as status and directions from the game server until the game is concluded. Games that are particularly well suited for this medium include trivia, combat and strategy. Messaging games can be played either as single or multiplayer, and are able to feature location-sensitive game-play.

WAP games are always played through a sustained connection to the mobile Internet. Thus, along with constraints created by devices, the limitations in mobile networks restrict the dynamics and interactivity of WAP games. However, WAP is designed to accommodate these limitations by bridging the gap between wired and wireless environments. Originally termed WAP 1.0 and written in the WML programming language, the latest version, WAP 2.0, has now progressed to employ the more advanced extensible HTML (xHTML) and has adopted more recent Internet standards. WAP 2.0 attempts to optimize the usage of higher bandwidths, packet-based connections and improved device capability, while at the same time providing backward compatibility to pre-existing WAP content (WAP Forum, 2002). The most significant advancement for games based on this platform is that WAP 2.0 recognizes the capabilities of users' devices, such as screen size and colour, in order to maximize performance potential and bring increased consumer satisfaction. Furthermore, WAP games are easily customizable to user preferences and profile. Genres suited to this medium include role player, casino and trivia games. These games are typically of a 'start-stop' nature.

In addition to WAP, the Japanese mobile service i-mode also provides a form of online games. I-mode originally differentiated itself from WAP 1.0 by being based on compact HTML (cHTML), a subset of HTML. However, the release of WAP 2.0 has signalled the unification of cHTML and xHTML. Unique to i-mode is that it has been able to provide a form of online gaming not previously seen with older versions of WAP. For example, one i-mode service links mobile phones to video arcade games. This i-mode service complements the video games by allowing a number of functions to be played over handsets. The arcade game Virtual Fighter 4 allows players to check their fighting match history, national rankings, customize their characters, search for arcades with Virtual Fighter 4, and communicate with other players nationwide (NTT DoCoMo, 2001).

The forecasted growth among each of the various mobile game formats displays some disparity. Messaging and WAP games lie heavily out of favour, perhaps even fading away towards the year 2008. At the same time, downloadable games are destined to offer the greatest potential for growth.

Downloadable games – which are made possible by way of technologies such as Java, BREW (binary runtime environment for wireless) and Symbian – are downloaded into devices and can be played repeatedly without the need for any further network interactivity. Embedded mobile phone games are essentially also included in this category. At present, due to mobile network limitations and sophistication of downloadable games, synchronous multiplayer capability is restricted to short-ranged embedded technologies such as Bluetooth, while asynchronous multiplayer functions such as the uploading of high scores is facilitated by mobile networks. Already there exists a comprehensive range of branded downloadable games, including The Lord of the Rings, Tiger Woods PGA Tour and Pacman. Downloadable games are arcade styled and sufficiently advanced to contribute to the ubiquitous network of gaming. In Japan, consumers are able to play portions of Sony PlayStation console games over Java-enabled i-mode mobile phones (NTT DoCoMo, 2001); i-mode phones plug into a PlayStation console permitting games to be played later while on the move.

The advancement of mobile devices, networks and applications and the ability to provide an innovative form of gaming previously unattainable are suggestive of the future direction of mobile gaming. These advances will undoubtedly enhance integral game elements such as media richness and responsiveness.

FROM M-COMMERCE TO M-BUSINESS

The focus of this chapter is on mobile commerce. However, more broadly speaking, mobile (m-)business is likely to have a tremendous impact on organizations, as wireless technologies and applications begin to challenge the existing processes, strategies, structures, roles of individuals and even cultures of organizations. Here, m-business is defined as the use of the wireless Internet and other mobile information technologies for organizational communication and coordination, and the management of the firm. This is briefly touched upon in some chapters in the next section of the book, but interested readers are encouraged to look at Barnes (2003b) and Barnes and Scornavacca (2005a, b).

Wireless data communications can provide significant business benefits for corporate infrastructure and a large number of corporate solutions have been developed to this end. In the business space, applications include sales force automation, navigation, tracking, field force automation, wireless telemetry and the mobile office.

Messaging is one key area of application. For example, advances in wireless messaging allow mobile workers to direct specific incoming messages to specific devices; such control helps mobile workers direct urgent emails to handheld devices or cell phones, and less urgent matters to secondary devices such as desktop personal computers. Other mobile office tools are also available – linking to fax, databases, schedules and file transfer.

On a much broader level, wireless networks and devices can help to strongly integrate remote, disparate or roaming employees into the corporate infrastructure. These include functionally disparate or mobile employees, such as salespersons, and remote workers, such as integrating geographically dispersed units. Thinking more generally about the mobile workforce, employees are enabled to work in their virtual office at any time, in any place and anywhere. Mobile devices and data connections can provide important links to company networks and systems that are key to the effective performance of work. This is demonstrated in Figure 7.2.

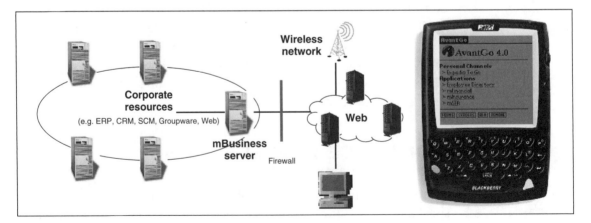

Figure 7.2
Enterprise mobility – accessing the corporate resources (source: Barnes, 2003)

In the example, the Blackberry is an additional channel for data communication, but it provides access to a variety of corporate systems such as customer relationship management (CRM), sales force automation (SFA), groupware, the Web, and even some supply chain management (SCM) and enterprise resource planning (ERP) functions.

SUMMARY AND CONCLUSIONS

The convergence of wireless telecommunications and the Internet provides many exciting possibilities and predictions for the growth of mobile e-commerce. This chapter has attempted to examine how value is added in this new era of mobile Internet, using both concept and some examples. Without doubt, the emergence of new standards such as xHTML, i-mode, 3G and 4G will drive the wireless Internet forward. However, in many cases the technologies and services currently on offer to consumers do not reflect well on the possibilities achievable in the mobile medium. A fresh, creative look at the needs of the wireless consumer will shed new light on this issue and possibly break some of the technological constraints that are holding m-commerce back. Location-specific technologies could present some important pieces of this puzzle and enable LBS applications that get to the heart of adding value in a mobile environment. Similarly, short-range wireless technologies will allow a new era of localized wireless interactivity for mobile data appliances. The next few years will be very important in the development of technologies and services that provide truly mobile commerce.

REFERENCES

Bamba, F. and Barnes, S. J. (2007). SMS advertising, permission and the consumer: a study. *Business Process Management Journal*, in press.

Barnes, S. J. (2002a). The mobile commerce value chain: analysis and future developments. *International Journal of Information Management*, 22 (2), 91–108.

Barnes, S. J. (2002b). Wireless digital advertising: nature and implications. *International Journal of Advertising*, 21 (3), 399–420.

Barnes, S. J. (2003a). Pocket money: banking on mobile devices. *E-business Strategy Management*, 4 (4), 263–271.

Barnes, S. J. (2003b). *Mbusiness: The Strategic Implications of Wireless Communications*. Butterworth-Heinemann.

Barnes, S. J. and Corbitt, B. (2003). Mobile banking: concept and potential. *International Journal of Mobile Communications*, 1 (3), 273–288.

Barnes, S. J. and Huff, S. L. (2003). Rising sun: iMode and the wireless Internet. *Communications of the ACM*, 46 (11), 78–84.

Barnes, S. J. and Scornavacca, E. (2004). Mobile marketing: the role of permission and acceptance. *International Journal of Mobile Communications*, 2 (2), 128–139.

Barnes, S. J. and Scornavacca, E. (2005a). *Cases in mBusiness*. Idea Group Publishing.

Barnes, S. J. and Scornavacca, E. (2005b). The strategic impact of wireless applications in NZ business. *Proceedings of the Hong Kong Mobility Roundtable*, Hong Kong, May.

Barwise, P. and Strong, C. (2002). Permission-based mobile advertising. *Journal of Interactive Marketing*, 16 (1), 14–24.

Bauer, H., Barnes, S. J., Neumann, M. and Reichardt, T. (2005). Driving consumer acceptance of mobile marketing: a theoretical framework and empirical study. *Journal of Electronic Commerce Research*, 6 (4), 181–192.

Bellman, S., Johnson, J. and Lohse, G. L. (2001). To opt-in or opt-out? It depends on the question. *Communications of the ACM*, 44 (2), 25–27.

Carroll, A., Barnes, S. J., Scornavacca, E. and Fletcher, K. (2007). Consumer perceptions and attitudes toward SMS advertising: recent evidence from New Zealand. *International Journal of Advertising*, 26, 79–98.

Clarke, I. (2001). Emerging value propositions for m-commerce. *Journal of Business Strategies*, 18 (2), 133–148.

Datacomm (2002). *Winning Business Strategies for Mobile Games*. Datacomm Research.

Dickinger, A., Haghirian, P., Murphy, J. and Scharl, A. (2004). An investigation and conceptual model of SMS marketing. *Proceedings of the 37th Hawaii International Conference on System Sciences*, Hawaii, January.

Dickinger, A., Scharl, A. and Murphy, J. (2005). Diffusion and success factors of mobile marketing. *Electronic Commerce Research and Applications*, 4 (2), 159–173.

Durlacher Research (2002). *Mobile Commerce Report*. July. www.durlacher.com

Enpocket (2005a). *Direct Response Report*. http://www.enpocket.co.uk

Enpocket (2005b). *Brand Performance of SMS Advertising*. http://www.enpocket.co.uk

E-Plus (2006). *E-plus: Online flat!* 1 February. http://www.eplus.de/frame.asp?go=/tarife/0/0_0/0_0.asp

Forrester (2005). *European Mobile Forecast: 2005 to 2010*. Forrester Research.

Godin, S. (1999). *Permission Marketing: Turning Strangers into Friends and Friends into Customers*. Simon and Schuster.

Hoyer, W. D. and MacInnis, D. J. (2004). *Consumer Behaviour*. Houghton Mifflin.

Hristova, N. and O'Hare, G. (2004). Ad-me: wireless advertising adapted to the user location, device and emotions. *Proceedings of the 37th Hawaii International Conference on System Sciences*, Hawaii, January.

InfoSync World (2004). *1.87 Billion Mobile Users by 2007.* 17 June. http://www.infosyncworld.com/news/n/5048.html

It's Alive (2000). It's Alive launches world's first location-based mobile game. *Itsalive.com,* January. http://www.itsalive.com/page.asp?t=pressandid=61

It's Alive (2004). *BotFighters.* 26 January. http://www.botfighters.com/

Jelassi, T. and Enders, A. (2006). Mobile advertising: a European perspective. In *Unwired Business: Cases in Mobile Business* (S. J. Barnes and E. Scornavacca, eds) pp. 82–95, IRM Press.

Junglas, I. A. and Watson, R. T. (2003). U-commerce: a conceptual extension of e-commerce and m-commerce. *Proceedings of the Twenty-Fourth International Conference on Information Systems,* Seattle, December.

Kalakota, R. and Robinson, M. (2002). *M-Business: The Race to Mobility.* McGraw-Hill.

Kharif, O. (2001). Excuse me I've got to take this game. *BusinessWeek Online,* 2 July. http://www.businessweek.com/bwdaily/dnflash/jul2001/nf2001072_760.htm

Kumar, S. (2004). Mobile communications: global trends in the 21st century. *International Journal of Mobile Communications,* 2 (1), 67–86.

Laukkanen, T. (2006). Customer perceived value of e-financial services: a means-end approach. *International Journal of Electronic Finance,* 1 (1), 5–17.

Laukkanen, T. and Lauronen, J. (2005). Consumer value creation in mobile banking services. *International Journal of Mobile Communications,* 3 (4), 325–338.

Newell, F. and Lemon, K. N. (2001). *Wireless Rules: New Marketing Strategies for Customer Relationship Management Anytime, Anywhere.* McGraw-Hill.

NTT DoCoMo (2001). *DoCoMo iMode Service Information.* NTT DoCoMo.

Petty, R. D. (2000). Marketing without consent: consumer choice and cost, privacy and public policy. *Journal of Public Policy and Marketing,* 19 (1), 42–53.

Phelps, J., Wowak, G. and Ferrell, E. (2000). Privacy concerns and consumer willingness to provide personal information. *Journal of Public Policy and Marketing,* 19 (1), 27–41.

Porter M. (1998). *The Competitive Advantage of Nations.* Free Press.

Porter, M. and Millar, V. E. (1985). How information gives you competitive advantage. *Harvard Business Review,* 63 (4), 149–160.

Pousttchi, K. and Schurig, M. (2004). Assessment of today's mobile banking applications from the view of customer requirements. *Proceedings of the 37th Hawaii International Conference on System Sciences,* Hawaii, January.

Scornavacca, E. and Barnes, S. J. (2004). M-banking services in Japan: a strategic perspective. *International Journal of Mobile Communications,* 2 (1), 51–66.

Scornavacca, E. and Barnes, S. J. (2006). Barcode enabled m-commerce: strategic implications and business models. *International Journal of Mobile Communications,* 4 (2), 163–177.

Scornavacca, E. and Cairns, J. (2005). Mobile banking in New Zealand: a strategic perspective. *Proceedings of the Hong Kong Mobility Roundtable*, Hong Kong, May.

Scornavacca, E. and Hoehle, H. (2006). Mobile banking in Germany. *Proceedings of the Helsinki Mobility Roundtable*, Helsinki, June.

Scornavacca, E., Barnes, S. J. and Huff, S. (2006). Mobile business research published in 2000–2004: emergence, current status, and future opportunities. *Communications of the Association for Information Systems*, 17, 635–646.

Sheehan, K. B. and Hoy, M. G. (2000). Dimensions of privacy concerns among online consumers. *Journal of Public Policy and Marketing*, 19 (1), 62–73.

Sultan, F. and Rohm, A. (2005). The coming era of 'brand in the hand' marketing. *Sloan Management Review*, 47 (1), 83–90.

Tezinde, T., Smith, B. and Murphy, J. (2002). Getting permission: exploring factors affecting permission marketing. *Journal of Interactive Marketing*, 16 (4), 28–36.

Unwiredfactory (2001). The launch of the world's first location-based competition. *Unwiredfactory.com*, 22 January. http://www.unwiredfactory.com/

Unwiredfactory (2004). *TreasureMachine*. January. http://www.unwiredfactory.com/pdf_documents/TreasureMachine.pdf

Usability News (2006). Mobile phones hit 2.5 billion mark. *Usability News*, 12 December. http://www.usabilitynews.com/news/article3394.asp

Ververidis, C. and Polyzos, G. (2002). Mobile marketing using location-based services. *Proceedings of the First International Conference on Mobile Business*, Athens, Greece.

WAP Forum (2002). *Wireless Application Protocol 2.0*, December. http://www.wapforum.org/

Zhang, J. and Yuan, Y. (2002). M-commerce vs. Internet-based e-commerce: the key differences. *Proceedings of the American Conference on Information Systems*, August.

Zhang, J., Yuan, Y. and Archer, N. (2003). Driving forces for m-commerce success. *Journal of Internet Commerce*, 1 (3), 81–106.

Section Two

Shaping the Virtual Organization

CHAPTER 8

Defining the virtual organization

Lucas D. Introna and Dimitra Petrakaki

INTRODUCTION

> ... the only constant in today's world is exponentially increasing change.
> (Huey, 1994)

Never before in the history of business have organizations been subjected to as much change – or so some argue. According to du Gay (2003: 664) change has become an imperative in contemporary society – so much so that those who fail to thrive in ongoing conditions of radical transformation become 'history'. The conditions of this change are both complex and various. Stewart (1993) suggests that there are four, large, unruly forces that condition change: the globalization of markets; the spread of information technology (IT); the birth of the information economy; and the dismantling of hierarchy. These forces are simultaneous and inter-reactive. Not only have these forces threatened the very survival of many great corporations such as IBM (Chesbrough and Teece, 1996) and General Motors (Drucker, 1994), but they may have caused the disintegration of traditional organizations and their once seemingly untroubled environment:

> Global competition wrecked stable markets and whole industries. Information technology created ad hoc networks of power within corporations. Lightning-fast, innovative entrepreneurs blew past snoozing corporate giants. Middle managers disappeared, along with corporate loyalty. (Huey, 1994)

In response to this challenge, a wide range of management approaches and techniques emerged. Outsourcing, business process re-engineering (BPR), downsizing, employee empowerment, total quality management (TQM), core competence and decentralization have all been used, with varying degrees of success, to reshape and redefine organizations – not only in for-profit organizations but more recently also in governmental and volunteer organizations (Ashkenas, 1995; Drucker, 1994; Gallivan, 2001). Each approach – some might use the word 'fad' – became a powerful metaphor that fired the imaginations of large numbers of academics, futurists, consultants and managers. Nevertheless, it could be argued that they all seem to capture only part of the picture. Even when successfully implemented, these techniques for driving organizational change seem to bring only marginal or short-term returns. In a business environment that is increasingly volatile such techniques seem incapable of sustaining organizational survival – let alone longevity.

From this bleak picture emerged the concept of the *virtual organization*. Davidow and Malone (1992) – in their book *The Virtual Corporation* – are credited as the first to articulate this idea explicitly and coherently. The virtual organization now seems to represent a new corporate model to structure and revitalize organizations for the twenty-first century. Grenier and Metes (1995) argue that unlike earlier management change metaphors which were conceived as a means of resolving specific ends, the virtual organization is now perceived as the *end* in itself. Davidow and Malone (1992) support this view with the bold claim that the virtual organization can 'for the first time tie all of these diverse innovations together into a single cohesive vision of the corporation in the twenty-first century'. If true, then this must be a concept in need of serious consideration. If false, then it needs to be made explicit why the promise of the virtual organization may indeed remain 'virtual'.

SOME DEFINITIONS

For its many proponents, the concept of virtual organization seems to emerge as a logical answer for today's fast moving organizational environment where markets are global, competition is fierce and market opportunities are transitory. Hence, the evolving virtual organization ought to contain the characteristics of *speed, flexibility* and *fluidity* (Byrne, 1993b; Coates, 1993). Nevertheless, these are perceived in different forms by different authors, defining the virtual organization as:

- '... an *enterprise* that uses *collaborations* both inside and outside its boundary to marshal more resources than it currently has on its own' (Byrne, 1993a).
- '... the use of *technology* to execute a wide array of temporary alliances in order to seize specific market opportunities' (Byrne, 1993a). Of particular import is the potential of information technology to facilitate communication across temporal and geographical boundaries (see Ariss *et al.*, 2002).
- '... a collection of *management theories* ranging from JIT [just-in-time] production, lean manufacturing, and trust' (Davidow and Malone, 1992).
- A *network* or loose coalition of manufacturing and administrative services uniting for a specific *business purpose*, disassembling when the purpose has been met (Anonymous, 1994; Clases *et al.*, 2004; Kasper-Fuehrer and Ashkanasy, 2001; Nohria and Eccles, 1992; Snow *et al.*, 1992).
- A certain *rationality* encapsulated in the notion of 'meta-management', which allows for 'switching' between various ephemeral contractors that provide the necessary means for the satisfaction of various ends (Mowschowitz, 1994; 1997).
- A convincing 'imagery' that presents the virtual organization as a platform that exists in space, possesses bits, represents a community and is organized in a network form (Schultze and Orlikowski, 2001).

For some, the virtual organization is essentially the creative use of technology. For others, it is a framework of one or more alliances, a particular managerial rationality or an imaginary concept. The salient literature is diverse, and there is evidently a lack of a generally agreed definition of the virtual organization. This is arguably because the concept of the virtual organization is still – in spite of being around for a while – rather tentative and immature, and the fact that the idea is also surrounded by a fair degree of managerial 'hype'. The following definition by Byrne is perhaps the most representative idea of what may be implied by a virtual organization:

> A virtual corporation is a temporary network of independent companies – suppliers, customers, even erstwhile rivals – linked by information technology to share skills, costs, and access to one another's markets. It will have neither central office nor an organization chart. It will have no hierarchy and no vertical integration. (Byrne, 1993b)

Byrne's definition suggests that a virtual organization is a coalition between different – essentially independent – groups of people or organizations. However, for Byrne, the term 'virtual organization' also implies, at its centre, the use of information technology in some way. The reasons for this link with IT may be related to the way in which the term 'virtual' evolved from computing technology.

The 'virtual' in virtual organizations

According to the *Cambridge Dictionary*, the word 'virtual' is defined as 'almost, even if not exactly or in every way'. In recent years, 'virtual' has successfully become the metaphor for technology. The computer industry has popularized such neologisms as 'virtual memory', 'virtual computer', 'virtual reality' and 'virtual space' (i.e. the space provided by the Internet). In each of these instances, the word 'virtual' connotes information technology that possesses the ability to: (1) provide a way of making a computer act as if it holds more (storage capacity) than it really possesses (Byrne, 1993a); (2) give users the illusion to exist at any time and in any place needed (Davidow and Malone, 1992); or (3) create something that *looks real in effect but is not in fact* (Sotto, 1996). Similarly, Bloomfield and McLean (2003: 55) defined virtual as 'virtual by way of what it lacks' and in line with the above views Mantovani (1995) compared virtual to a 'hallucination'.

The term 'virtual organization' has caused the technology-inspired idea of virtuality to enter the domain of organizations. A current example of this is the appearance of the term 'the virtual state' (Fountain, 2001), which implies the organization of various agents (not exclusively governmental) into networks for the delivery of public services. Virtuality may not solely imply technology but rather the ability to summon vast capabilities as a result of various collaborations assembled *only as required* (Byrne, 1993a). Based upon this, virtuality is thought to enable the ordering of people by positioning them 'in the right place at the right time' (Bloomfield, 2001), to provide the means for a liberating communication (Watt *et al.*, 2002), to assist in solidarity by bringing together those with common interests that have previously been distanced (Nettleton *et al.*, 2002), and to help in bridging spatial and temporal gaps that excluded people from various opportunities such as educational opportunities (Crook and Light, 2002). Unlike the earlier examples of 'virtual', the above examples imply that the existence of a virtual organization is not wholly dependent on IT – though some IT may still be required. This can also be concluded by the sort of language that is used in speaking about virtuality, i.e. IT is thought to *enable*, to *provide* the means for achieving an end, to *assist* in a target, and so on. Many proponents argue that IT now plays a secondary role. They suggest that IT is merely an enabler, or a messenger, with the task of disseminating the timely and local information which is critical to a virtual organization (DeSanctis and Monge, 2004; Grenier and Metes, 1995). As Knights *et al.* (2002) argued 'it is important to distinguish hype from reality … it is not clear that the new technologies actually possess the capacities and effects attributed to them …'. This brings us onto another important facet of our definition – the nature of 'organization' in virtual organizations.

The 'organization' in virtual organizations

An organization can be defined as 'a group of people who work together in a structured way for a shared purpose'. Here, 'together' does not necessarily mean that an organization must be in the form of a physical entity (bound in the unity of time/space) such as the traditional organization of enterprise. Conversely, Scott Morton (1991) has advocated that an organization comprises 'five sets of forces in dynamic equilibrium among themselves even as the organization is subjected to influences from an external environment'. These forces are: structure, strategy, technology, roles (positions held by individuals) and a management process. By advocating such a view, Scott Morton recognizes that the organization, being made up of the five forces, must be able to maintain its coherence as it *moves through time* in order to accomplish its objectives.

Framing the organization in this way has prompted business managers to realize the importance for the organization to transform itself to meet the needs of the time. Some argue that central to such ongoing transformations are two essential conditions. These conditions are: (1) the creation of a vision which must be clearly understood and supported by everyone in the organization; and (2) the need to align infrastructures (such as IT, work structures and processes) with the organization's business goals. The most important of these, so it is argued, is a commonly shared vision. This is necessary so that 'virtual employees' know and comply with that which is expected from them (Wilson, 1999). Vision is often used in religious terms. It implies a change towards a better state of affairs. In the organizational vocabulary vision is thought to give 'a clear sense of where an organization is going and what its core activities are' (Du Gay, 2000). Indicative of vision's importance in virtual organizations is Markus *et al.*'s (2000: 13) suggestion that individuals in them should be treated as if they were 'unpaid volunteers, tied to the organization by commitment to its aims and purposes'. It is suggested that these conditions must remain true no matter what form or structures the organization takes – even for the virtual organization.

From this perspective, virtual organizing can be conceptualized as an essential part of the ongoing process of organizational transformation (Scott Morton, 1991). Hence, the virtual organization is postulated as a mutable – almost protean – organization in which resource allocation remains flexible to meet the changing business environment and customer needs (Ashkenas, 1995; Coates, 1993). In such a perspective the virtual organization must challenge formerly well-delineated structures so as to regenerate itself continually. As Davidow and Malone (1992) suggest:

> To the outside observer, the virtual corporation will appear almost edgeless, with permeable and continuously changing interfaces between company, supplier, and customers. From inside the firm the view will be no less amorphous, with traditional offices, departments, and operating divisions constantly reforming according to need. Job responsibilities will regularly shift, as will lines of authority – even the very definition of employee will change, as some customers and suppliers begin to spend more time in the company than will some of the firm's own workers.

It is our view that in the long run it might be better to speak about *virtual organizing* rather than virtual organizations. It seems clear that most contemporary organizations will increasingly be more or less hybrids of physical and electronically mediated organizing processes. In other words virtuality will be a matter of degree rather than an absolute state.

ELEMENTS OF THE VIRTUAL ORGANIZATION

From the above, it seems evident that the virtual organization is almost the perfect antithesis of the traditional bureaucratic organization whose efficiency is built on principles such as: a clear division of labour that indicates clearly demarcated jurisdictional areas, well-defined hierarchical structures, impersonality in dealing with a variety of cases, general rules for the execution of work processes, professional expertise, and so on (Weber, 1947; 1948). However, what does this mean? How will this entity (if we can call it this) operate? To answer these questions we need to introduce some other notions central to the idea of virtual organizing.

Strategic alliance

John Sculley, the Chairman of Apple Computer Inc., is quoted as saying:

> When we talk about virtual corporations today, we're mainly talking about alliances and outsourcing agreements. Ten or twenty years from now, you'll see an explosion of entrepreneurial industries and companies that will essentially form the real virtual corporations. Ten or thousands of virtual organizations may come out of this. (Ogilvie, 1994)

For most authors the key attribute of a virtual organization is strategic alliances or partnering (Byrne, 1993b; Ogilvie, 1994). This is a strategy frequently used by organizations to command speed and flexibility so as to: (1) gain access into new markets or technologies; (2) break down market barriers to new products by rallying the required skills and expertise from groups, individuals and even rivals from outside their organizational boundaries; and (3) strengthen their position in the market and thus create entry barriers (Speier *et al.*, 1998). This characteristic of being highly adaptable and opportunistic (Byrne, 1993b) suggests that a strategic alliance is – almost by definition – short term or temporary (Malone and Laubacher, 1998). In turn, this means that, once the original goal has been reached, the companies that made up the virtual organization will disband and proceed to create new partnerships with other companies and people. The three targets that were presented above indicate that strategic alliances are often essentially profit-driven. However, the benefits that can be harnessed through the creation of strategic alliances are multiple and can include, among others, economic benefits, such as cost sharing and resource pooling, intellectual gains, such as opportunities for skills development and knowledge sharing, and social rewards, such as prestige and social recognition (Fountain, 2001; Gallivan, 2001; Parkhe, 1998; Speier *et al.*, 1998).

Strategic alliances have long characterized industries such as movie making and construction – where expert teams collaborate for the duration of a specific project. In the computer industry, the first instance of a successful strategic alliance was in 1981, when IBM partnered with Microsoft and Intel to launch the first ever personal computers (Anonymous, 1993; Byrne, 1993b; Chesbrough and Teece, 1996). It is often argued that the virtual organization will mix and match the finest skills and expertise from partners to create a new organization – the virtual organization – that brings together the 'best-of-everything'.

Notwithstanding, the setting-up of a network of strategic alliances between partners in a virtual organization is not without ramifications. For one, a strategic alliance implies a certain mutual dependency between partners to achieve a specific goal – that is, the launch of the *virtual product*. This means that all partners share a destiny tied towards the creation of that product (Das and Teng, 1998). In many ways the relationship is like a house of cards; when one partner falls, the others may be seriously affected. Should this happen, it could jeopardize the integrity of the virtual organization as a whole. Consequently, it is in the combined interests of all parties to create win/win deals and remain mutually supportive; in this way organizations can ensure optimum benefit from the strategic partnership. James R. Houghton, Chairman of Corning Inc., suggests:

> More companies are waking up to the fact that alliances are critical to the future. [This is because] technologies are changing so fast that nobody can do it all alone anymore. (Byrne, 1993b)

Thus, as far as strategic alliances are concerned, a balance between the pursuit of personal interests and compliance to the alliance's common target is necessary for the successful completion of the virtual organization's mission (Das and Teng, 1998). This, however, cannot be secured, as companies' opportunistic behaviour is part and parcel of their purpose as profit-driven organizations (Parkhe, 1998). To sum up: virtual organizing depends on the development of strategic alliances due to the benefits that can be harnessed through interorganizational networks. However, the extent to which social (i.e. trust and reciprocity) and moral (i.e. avoidance of opportunistic behaviour) issues are dealt with needs careful consideration. These issues are discussed in Chapter 15.

Core competence

In 1990, Prahalad and Hamel popularized the idea of core competencies in their article 'The core competence of the corporation'. In this article, the authors advocate that a company should focus on its key activities or processes and thereby be fully equipped to face any challenges presented by the business environment. Core competencies, the theory suggests, are activities (such as marketing or design) that a company does well; via these core activities the company can gain a competitive edge over rivals (Jones and Bowie, 1998). Ogilvie (1994) describes core competencies as those things an organization does that are difficult for competitors to replicate. In a sense the foundations of the organization are embodied in the core products and core competencies. These will remain more or less stable over time. It is important to realize that the company's core competencies are embodied in human agents, i.e. its employees (Applegate *et al.*, 1988). Core competence is not a recipe that anyone can successfully do but rather is a collective, situated and embodied process in which each part contributes uniquely. Thus, a change in any one of these parts may bring about change in the previously held core competence. In effect, the focus on core competencies has led organizations – such as the UK British Home Stores (BHS) and Continental Bank – to dispose of those activities (in the form of outsourcing) that are considered incapable of giving competitive advantage (Fitzgerald, 1994). Firms such as these argue that their goal is a *lean* organization with a world-class operation.

The concept of core competencies connects closely with the idea of strategic partnerships in the creation of a virtual organization (Rouse, 1999). This is seen in the form of a partnership essentially made up of associates who have, in their turn, 'concentrated only on their core competencies, the things that give them their competitive edge' (Ogilvie, 1994). By transforming their own core competencies into the required end-products, partners thus contribute towards the construction of the final product and harness the synergies that are created (Clases *et al.*, 2004; Gallivan, 2001; Lorenzoni and Baden- Fuller, 1995). Thus, it is appropriate to say that value is created when the virtual organization seizes the advantage of acquiring the best efforts of world-class partners to, for example, bring products to market faster (Anonymous, 1993; Byrne, 1993b). This is, surely, a prime reason for creating a virtual organization in the first place.

Trust

In recent years, the notion of trust has gained increasing importance in the management literature. In the context of virtual environments trust emerges as a core issue. A survey of management journals shows that an increasing number of authors – such as Handy (1995), Baillie (1995), Kasper-Fuehrer and Ashkanasy (2001), Ariss *et al.* (2002) and Clases *et al.* (2004) – now argue that trust is an essential element in managing organizational relations. In the face of delayering, decentralization and empowerment, trust is seen as a central issue. This is particularly the case, it is argued, when combined with the ability of technology to distribute knowledge, information and people.

Handy (1995) argues that the increasing 'virtualization' of organizations has prompted management to address the issue of trust more directly. Handy perceives the virtual organization to be made up of people who 'need not be in one place in order to deliver their service' and 'communicate electronically and telephonically rather than face to face in a room'. Handy believes that trust will be the only way for managers to manage a group of people whom they seldom see, if ever. Similarly, Byrne (1993b) suggests that virtual relationships 'make partners more reliant on each other and require far more trust than ever before'. A more in-depth examination of trust in organizing suggests some important implications. In particular, in virtual organizing, this relationship of trust may imply the following:

1. That the partners of a virtual organization exhibit 'unprecedented levels of trust and commitment in placing the fate of the company in the hands of people who are not even employees of the company' (Davidow and Malone, 1992).
2. That this popularity of alliances and tightening of links between customers and suppliers may mean that firms will have to cooperate with potential competitors without the security of legal ties (Baillie, 1995).
3. That the partners in the strategic alliance will have to trust each other in carrying out their designated roles and responsibilities, and in supplying the correct information critical for creating value in the final product.
4. That the individual workers, when trusted, will be forthcoming with their ideas and information (Lewicki and Bunker, 1996: 121).

When management authors write about trust they often treat it as an element that can be managed, for example through the implementation of ICTs or through the development of normative policies and ethical codes (Kasper-Fuehrer and Ashkanasy, 2001). Trust is a crucial element of virtual organizations, some claim the *Achilles' heel of the virtual realm* (Knights *et al.*, 2001: 319). It is suggested that it may be the only factor that could deal with the uncertainty (Reed, 2001), the complexity (Luhmann, 1979), the vulnerability (Clases *et al.*, 2004: 8; Skinner and Spira, 2003: 30) and the possible opportunistic behaviour (Das and Teng, 1998: 494; Gallivan, 2001: 280) that employees in virtual organizations are likely to face. Therefore, one needs to consider very carefully what the source of trust is, whether it can be managed or not, and how. There are various studies that have examined trust in organizations (Bachmann, 2003; Das and Teng, 1998; Hartog, 2003; Jones and Bowie, 1998; Lane, 1998; Lewicki and Bunker, 1996; Powell, 1996). The conclusions that one can draw from these studies are that the sources of trust can be among others: personal interest, increased knowledge about partners and colleagues, and the social bonds that are created through long-term relations or collaborations. Bearing in mind the common interest that binds partners together in virtual organizations along with the high likelihood of a quick dissolution of their collaboration, trust is likely to be developed through employees' perceptions of the structures, the social positions, and the established values and norms of the virtual organization (Bachmann, 2003). Thus, it is this knowledge that will keep partners together. More specifically, it is the partners' beliefs about the roles that each one has to undertake, faith in their respective expertise or specialization and the authority that derives from such expertise that will condition the development of trust (Giddens, 1990; Jones and Bowie, 1998; Luhmann, 1979; Shapiro, 1987; Zucker, 1986). This impersonal, knowledge-based institutional level trust that is 'exterior to any given situation' (Zucker, 1986) is likely to be fundamental to the virtual organization that consists of individuals with limited or no common history or cultural traditions.

Organization restructuring

The final aspect of the virtual organization is that of organizational restructuring. Like conventional corporations, the virtual organization is also dependent on its ongoing structuring for successful execution of work tasks. Grenier and Metes (1995) point out that this entails meticulous planning of all inherent activities and processes to take advantage of the core competencies and information infrastructures of the collaborating partners. Conversely, it also requires the tailoring of information infrastructures around those designated operations.

Herein lies the problem; restructuring virtual operations is an ongoing concern. The virtual organization, by its very definition, is composed of a disparate combination of organizations, people and infrastructures (in which is embodied the core competencies of the partners). Putting together such configurations, which embody the core competencies of the partners, will require that unique virtual operations are designed and implemented every time a new alliance is formed, that is if such a partnership is to be meaningful. From here, it is a small step to suggest that one prerequisite for an alliance partner of a virtual organization lies in a willingness and propensity for periodic and ongoing restructuring. Only by so doing can the virtual organization create value out of an *integrated* operation, which is built in a unique virtual environment that allows all partners to integrate their core competencies and work together effectively but *apart.*

Aside from the imperative for frequent restructuring, virtual organizing requires speed and flexibility in the way the ongoing restructuring is achieved. As Rouse (1999) suggests, the successful virtual organization needs to continuously monitor the environment in order to look for potential opportunities, to design strategic plans, which presuppose the creation of the appropriate alliance, and of course to execute the plan, while remaining alert and flexible.

In virtual organizations, restructuring is ongoing, multiple and quick; it demands alertness for environmental threats and opportunities, coordination, flexibility and a commitment to the enterprise. Restructuring, however, is easier said than done. Its complexity derives from the fact that organizations are the people who work and follow specific processes, which up to an extent are perceived by them as stable. Thus, ongoing restructuring demands both the continuous redesign of processes and the management of the work to be achieved through these processes.

Before discussing these, however, we should mention that restructuring is not only an element but also a distinctive characteristic of the virtual organization. In other words, restructuring is a prerequisite for naming a virtual organization as such. This is because transforming a traditional organization into a virtual one (assuming that this differentiation is real) implies ongoing structural changes, such as delayering and mediation through IT infrastructures, while maintaining the distinctive core competencies of the partners. Understanding of the virtual operations is crucial in this regard.

Virtual operations

So far, we have discussed the idea that a virtual organization can generate value through the achievement of virtual processes built around virtual teams. This would not be possible without the careful design of the virtual operation. Essentially, the virtual operation is the adhesive that binds together all partners and activities into an intrinsic whole (Rouse, 1999). Similarly, Fountain (2001: 24) suggested that the term virtual 'refers to capacity that appears seamless but that exists through the rapid transfer and sharing of the capacity of several discrete units and agents as their partners'.

Virtual work tasks can be defined as work assignments or project-oriented activities designed for simultaneous electronic information access (Applegate *et al.*, 1988; Grenier and Metes, 1995). Using the computerized network as the main means of communication, the work tasks underpin the sharing of online electronic information between partners who may be scattered in diverse locations. Thus, virtual organizations depend on the opportunities that ICTs offer and particularly the Internet, intranets and the various technologies that allow the collaboration of groups in 'Internet time' and offer time and space flexibility (Davenport and Pearlson, 1998; McGrath and Houlihan, 1998). However, it is not the electronic mediation of the social collaboration that is most important.

Virtual organizations depend upon team working, i.e. virtual teams. Virtual teams are temporary groups of people with very often different cultural and historical backgrounds, who are geographically dispersed, work with autonomy and interact through ICTs (Jarvenpaa and Leidner, 1999; Townsend *et al.*, 1998; Yoo and Alavi, 2004). For a virtual organization to be effective such virtual teams should be able to establish commonly shared work practices, language and norms. Thus, virtual teams must not only develop capabilities to work (often in stressful situations) with electronic information and evolving communication technologies, but they must also work with a variety of partners who have their own competence and who are leaders in their own right. As a result, the competencies needed by virtual teams require 'a variety of personal and collective changes in attitudes and behaviours, not to mention knowledge and skills' (Grenier and Metes, 1995). They also need to be able to construct an identity that is compatible with these working conditions (i.e. being an effective member of a virtual team, being able to switch between teams, to collaborate with various unknown partners and to outperform in various and different projects which the team undertakes).

The impermanent character of virtual teams and the rare or non-personal meetings with each other raise various issues for consideration (Townsend *et al.*, 1998). First of all one should focus on how trust could develop between team members, so that knowledge sharing and collaboration are fostered. As we mentioned previously, trust is likely to emerge in an impersonal way due to awareness of the assigned roles that members are attributed and the faith in each other's expertise. Nevertheless, the impersonal character of virtual teams and the difficulty of having face-to-face and verbal communication may obstruct the normal process of social relationship building (Kasper-Fuehrer and Ashkanasy, 2001). The literature suggests that virtual teams ought to work in a joined-up or seamless way, but how can this ideal type be worked out in practice bearing in mind the lack of personal relations between the team members? The issues raised here are also issues in normal face-to-face organizations; one might suggest that they become much more acute in virtual environments.

According to the proponents, learning in a virtual organization ought to be a deliberate part of the ongoing functioning of the organization. As such, learning must be designed in a collaborative, continuous manner for individuals, teams and organizations (Rouse, 1999). Through this learning process the knowledge, skills, perspectives and experience are acquired to: build a team culture; sustain organizational and cross-organizational operations; and to develop the higher levels of speciality and virtual operations capabilities needed to meet the increasing work demands of the virtual future.

The final element of virtual operations we want to highlight is virtual communication. By communication we mean the exchange of, access to, use, distribution, recording and sharing of information to support all work and learning processes. Due to the importance of communication in a virtual environment, it could be regarded as 'work' and not just an adjunct to work. Further, since it plays a complex and critical role in virtual operations, communication is too critical to be allowed to just happen; it must be explicitly considered and facilitated through the information infrastructures of the partners. Obviously there is also the question of whether communication is something that can be left to the ICT infrastructure, bearing in mind its primarily social character (see Barnatt, 1999; DeSanctis and Monge, 2004; Watt *et al.*, 2002), or whether it should be more or less central to the design and implementation of the virtual work practices. These are not trivial issues. They are discussed further in Chapter 15.

CONCLUSIONS

In recent years, the concept of the virtual organization has gained much popularity. The idea itself has enormous appeal in both academic and popular circles. However, as yet, there is no generally accepted consensus on what actually constitutes a virtual organization. In an attempt to clarify matters, this chapter has explored in some detail the concept of virtual organization. This chapter has represented the notion of a virtual organization through the discourse (and rhetoric) of its proponents. We now have a baseline picture of what a virtual organization is or may be. Thus, this chapter lays the foundation for the chapters that follow, each of which examines a particular case or aspect of the virtual organization.

Notwithstanding, it is worth bearing in mind that although the notion of virtual organization has many proponents, the idea itself is not without its problems. The final chapter in this section of the book develops a critique of the virtual organization that uses the articulation of this chapter as its basis. The purpose of the critique is to point out the contradictions and tensions that underlie current thinking. The ultimate aim of the critique is to develop a more critical appraisal of what has become a highly regarded discourse on organizational development.

REFERENCES

Anonymous (1993). Virtual corporations: fast and focused. *BusinessWeek*, 8 February, p. 134.

Anonymous (1994). Make way for the virtual enterprise. *Purchasing*, 15 December, pp. 18–19.

Applegate, L., Cash, J. I. Jr. and Mills, D. Q. (1988). Information technology and tomorrow's manager. *Harvard Business Review*, 66 (6), 128–136.

Ariss, S., Nykodym, N. and Cole-Laramore, A. A. (2002). Trust and technology in the virtual organization. *SAM Advanced Management Journal*, 67 (4), 22–25.

Ashkenas, R. (1995). Capability: strategic tool for a competitive edge. *Journal of Business Strategy*, 16 (6), 13–18.

Bachmann, R. (2003). Trust and power as means of coordinating the internal relations of the organisation: a conceptual framework. In *The Trust Process in Organisations: Empirical Studies of the Determinants and the Process of Trust Development* (B. B. Nooteboom and F. Six, eds), Edward Elgar.

Baillie, J. (1995). Trust: a new concept in the management of people? *People Management*, 1 (11), 53.

Barnatt, C. (1999). Apple pie thinking for the wired age? *Human Relations*, 4, 521–537.

Bloomfield, B. (2001). In the right place at the right time: electronic tagging and problems of social order/disorder. *The Sociological Review*, 49, 174–201.

Bloomfield, B. and McLean, C. (2003). Beyond the walls of the asylum: information and organization in the provision of community mental health services. *Information and Organization*, 13, 53–84.

Byrne, J. A. (1993a). The futurists who fathered the ideas. *BusinessWeek*, 8 February, 103.

Byrne, J. A. (1993b). The virtual corporation. *BusinessWeek*, 8 February, 98–102.

Chesbrough, H. W. and Teece, D. J. (1996). When is virtual virtuous? Organizing for innovation. *Harvard Business Review*, 74, 65–71.

Clases, C., Bachmann, R. and Wehner, T. (2004). Studying trust in virtual organisations. *International Studies of Business and Organisations*, 33 (3), 7–27.

Coates, J. F. (1993). An edgeless future. *Across the Board*, 30, 58–60.

Crook, C. and Light, P. (2002). Virtual society and the cultural practice of study. In *Virtual Society? Technology, Cyberbole, Reality* (S. Woolgar, ed.) pp. 153–175, Oxford University Press.

Das, T. K. and Teng, B. (1998). Between trust and control: developing confidence in partner cooperation in alliances. *The Academy of Management Review*, 23, 491–512.

Davenport, T. and Pearlson, K. (1998). Two cheers for the virtual office. *Sloan Management Review*, 39, 51–66.

Davidow, W. H. and Malone, M. S. (1992). *The Virtual Corporation*. Harper Business.

DeSanctis, G. and Monge, P. (2004). Introduction to the special issue: communication processes for virtual organisations. *Organization Science*, 10, 693–703.

Drucker, P. F. (1994). The theory of business. *Harvard Business Review*, 72, 95–104.

Du Gay, P. (2000). *In Praise of Bureaucracy: Weber, Organization, Ethics*. Sage Publications.

Du Gay, P. (2003). The tyranny of the epochal: change, epochalism and organizational reform. *Organization*, 10, 663–684.

Fitzgerald, G. (1994). *The Outsourcing of Information Technology: Revenge of the Business Manager or Legitimate Strategic Option*. Technical Report No. 9408, Birkbeck College, University of London.

Fountain, J. (2001). *Building the Virtual State: Information Technology and Institutional Change*. The Brookings Institution.

Gallivan, M. (2001). Striking a balance between trust and control in a virtual organisation: a content analysis of open source software case studies. *Information Systems Journal*, 11, 277–304.

Giddens, A. (1990). *The Consequences of Modernity*. Stanford University Press.

Grenier, R. and Metes, G. (1995). *Going Virtual: Moving Your Organization into the 21st Century.* Prentice Hall.

Handy, C. (1995). Trust and the virtual corporation. *Harvard Business Review,* 73, 40–50.

Hartog, D. (2003). Trusting others in organisations: leaders, management and co-workers. In *The Trust Process in Organisations: Empirical Studies of the Determinants and the Process of Trust Development* (B. B. Nooteboom and F. Six, eds) pp. 125–145, Edward Elgar.

Huey, J. F. (1994). The new post-heroic leadership. *Fortune,* 129, 42–50.

Jarvenpaa, S. and Leidner, D. (1999). Communication and trust in global virtual teams. *Organization Science,* 10, 791–815.

Jones, M. and Bowie, N. (1998). Moral hazards on the road to the virtual corporation. *Business Ethics Quarterly,* 8, 273–292.

Kasper-Fuehrer, E. and Ashkanasy, N. (2001). Communicating trustworthiness and building trust in interorganizational virtual organizations. *Journal of Management,* 27, 235–254.

Knights, D., Noble, F., Vurdubakis, T. and Willmott, H. (2001). Chasing shadows: control, vulnerability and the production of trust. *Organization Studies,* 22, 311–336.

Knights, D., Noble, F., Vurdubakis, T and Willmott, H. (2002). Allegories of creative destruction: technology and organization in narratives of the e-economy. In *Virtual Society? Technology, Cyberbole, Reality* (S. Woolgar, ed.) pp. 99–114, Oxford University Press.

Lane, C. (1998). Introduction: theories and issues in the study of trust. In *Trust Within and Between Organisations: Conceptual Issues and Empirical Applications* (C. Lane and R. Bachmann, eds) pp. 1–30, Oxford University Press.

Lewicki, R. and Bunker, B. (1996). Developing and maintaining trust in work relationships. In *Trust in Organisations: Frontiers of Theory and Research* (R. Kramer and T. Tyler, eds) pp. 114–139, Sage Publications.

Lorenzoni, G. and Baden-Fuller, C. (1995). Creating a strategic centre to manage a web of partners. *California Management Review,* 37, 146–163.

Luhmann, N. (1979). *Trust and Power.* John Wiley and Sons Ltd.

Malone, T. and Laubacher, R. (1998). The dawn of the e-lance economy. *Harvard Business Review,* 76, 145–152.

Mantovani, J. (1995). Virtual environment as a communication environment: consensual hallucination, fiction and possible selves. *Human Relations,* 48, 669–683.

Markus, M., Manville, B. and Agres, C. (2000). What makes a virtual organisation work? *Sloan Management Review,* 42, 13–26.

McGrath, P. and Houlihan, M. (1998). Conceptualising telework. In *Teleworking: International Perspectives from Telecommuting to the Virtual Organisation* (P. Jackson and J. Van Der Wielen, eds), Routledge.

Mowschowitz, A. (1994). Virtual organization: a vision of management in the information age. *The Information Society,* 10, 267–288.

Mowschowitz, A. (1997). Virtual organization. *Communications of the ACM*, 40, 30–38.

Nettleton, S., Burrows, R., Pleace, N., Loader, B. and Muncer, S. (2002). The reality of virtual support. In *Virtual Society? Technology, Cyberbole, Reality* (S. Woolgar, ed.) pp. 176–188, Oxford University Press.

Nohria, N. and Eccles, R. (1992). Face-to-face: making network organisations work. In *Networks and Organisations: Structure, Form and Action* (N. Nohria and R. Eccles, eds) pp. 288–308, Harvard Business School Press.

Ogilvie, H. (1994). At the core, it's the virtual organization. *Journal of Business Strategy*, 15, 26–34.

Parkhe, A. (1998). Understanding trust in international alliances. *Journal of World Business*, 33, 219–240.

Powell, W. (1996). Trust based forms of governance. In *Trust in Organisations: Frontiers of Theory and Research* (R. Kramer and T. Tyler, eds) pp. 51–67, Sage Publications.

Prahalad, C. K. and Hamel, G. (1990). The core competence of the corporation. *Harvard Business Review*, 68 (3), 79–91.

Reed, M. (2001). Organisation, trust and control: a realist analysis. *Organisation Studies*, 22, 201–228.

Rouse, W. B. (1999). Connectivity, creativity and chaos: challenges of loosely-structured organizations. *Information, Knowledge, Systems Management*, 1, 117–131.

Schultze, U. and Orlikowski, W. (2001). Metaphors of virtuality: shaping an emergent reality. *Information and Organization*, 11, 45–77.

Scott Morton, M. (1991). *The Corporation of the 1990s*. Oxford University Press.

Shapiro, S. (1987). The social control of impersonal trust. *The American Journal of Sociology*, 93, 622–658.

Skinner, D. and Spira, L. (2003). Trust and control – a symbiotic relationship? *Corporate Governance*, 3, 28–35.

Snow, C. C., Miles, R. E. and Coleman Jr., H. J. (1992). Managing 21st century network organizations. *Organisation Dynamics*, 20, 5–20.

Sotto, R. (1996). Organizing in cyberspace: the virtual link. *Scandinavian Journal of Management*, 12, 25–40.

Speier, C., Harvey, M. and Palmer, J. (1998). Virtual management of global marketing relationships. *Journal of World Business*, 33, 263–276.

Stewart, T. A. (1993). Welcome to the revolution. *Fortune*, 28, 32–38.

Townsend, A. M., DeMarie, S. M. and Hendrickson, A. R. (1998). Virtual teams: technology and the workplace of the future. *Academy of Management Executive*, 12, 17–29.

Watt, S. E., Lea, M., Spears, R. and Rogers, P. (2002). How social is internet communication? A reappraisal of bandwidth and anonymity effects. In *Virtual Society? Technology, Cyberbole, Reality* (S. Woolgar, ed.) pp. 61–77, Oxford University Press.

Weber, M. (1947). *The Theory of Social and Economic Organization*. Oxford University Press.

Weber, M. (1948). *From Max Weber: Essays in Sociology* (H. H. Gerth and W. Mills, eds), T. J. Press (Padstow) Ltd.

Wilson, F. (1999). Cultural control within the virtual organisation. *The Sociological Review*, 47, 672–694.

Yoo, Y. and Alavi, M. (2004). Emergent leadership in virtual teams: what do emergent leaders do? *Information and Society*, 14, 27–58.

Zucker, L. (1986). Production of trust: institutional sources of economic structure. *Research in Organisational Behaviour*, 8, 53–111.

CHAPTER 9

Interorganizational innovations through interorganizational information systems

Feng Li and Howard Williams

INTRODUCTION

The business environment has been undergoing fundamental changes. On the one hand, the nature of the economy has changed as measured by the informational (intangible) elements of our products, services and production processes; the proportion of the workforce whose primary activities are informational rather than physical, often known as information workers or knowledge workers, has increased substantially. Information (or knowledge, intelligence) has become the most important resource upon which the efficiency and competitiveness of all organizations depend, and the main source of future 'value added'. This is true in not only services or high-tech industries, but also in primary and manufacturing industries – and in both private and public sectors. In other words, all activities, products and production processes have become information intensive – even in traditional industries.

In the meantime, the so-called 'Information and Communication Technologies (ICTs) Revolution' continues to gather pace, providing us with increasingly more powerful, versatile, affordable and convenient tools in the forms of technologies, infrastructure and services. From the users' perspective, the *only* purpose of these technologies is to deal with 'information' – to capture, store and retrieve, manipulate, transmit and present information. As a result of the technological advances we are able to deal with information in ways not even possible only a few years ago.

The combination of these two intertwined processes is extremely powerful. Organizations large and small today can, and should, do things differently in order to survive and thrive in the new economy. Many new strategies and business models have been developed, which are increasingly reflected in the way different activities are structured, linked and coordinated at different levels. These changes are happening not only within but increasingly between organizations, sometimes across the entire supply chain (Li, 2006).

The process of using interorganizational information systems to enable interorganizational innovations is not new, and it has been going on for several decades. Back in the 1970s, some large firms placed computer terminals in their customers' offices and offered these customers direct access to certain information (such as stock availability and price) held on their central computers. These systems facilitated information exchange between suppliers and buyers, reduced costs, improved quality of services and stabilized interorganizational relations. However, until the end of the 1980s the development of such interorganizational information systems and innovations was slow and fragmented both in terms of the sectoral penetration and in the range of applications they supported. Since then, interorganizational systems began to diffuse rapidly in an increasing number of sectors, and new forms of interorganizational collaborations based on such systems also began to emerge. Since the mid-1990s, the rapid diffusion of the Internet and related technologies made it much easier – and cheaper – to establish and maintain new interorganizational systems, which has been leading to a range of interorganizational innovations. In this chapter the evolution of interorganizational systems and the associated changes in interorganizational relations are discussed.

Interorganizational innovations are perhaps the most significant among all organizational innovations in the age of the Internet and e-business. Indeed, after several decades of restructuring and re-engineering, as well as exploring different types of new work organization and new ways of working, most potential internal efficiency gains associated with ICTs have perhaps already been squeezed out of most organizations. In contrast, the rapid development of the Internet and related technologies, infrastructure and services has enabled business partners to explore interorganizational innovations in ways not feasible, or not even imaginable, in the past. This allows organizations to extend their internal gains of computer networking and process and functional integration to business partners across the entire supply chain. Some of these interorganizational innovations are closely linked to emerging strategies and business models discussed earlier in the book, such as the strategic reorientation from products and services to solutions and experience, the Web strategy and virtual or network organizations. They are also closely linked to many emerging e-business models, underpinning the entire e-commerce and e-business phenomenon ranging from B2B and B2C to the integration of internal functions and processes with interorganizational applications.

Furthermore, many other forms of organizational innovations, such as the deconstruction and unbundling of integrated business models and processes, depend critically on robust interorganizational systems to reintegrate the unbundled activities and processes across the newly created organizational boundaries. Interorganizational innovations are also closely linked to a wide range of contemporary business phenomena, such as business process and IT outsourcing and offshoring, the commoditization and standardization of a wide range of business processes, and a number of other emerging trends (Li, 2006).

WHAT ARE INTERORGANIZATIONAL INFORMATION SYSTEMS?

Interorganizational information systems, or interorganizational systems (IOS) for short, refer to the computer and telecommunications infrastructure developed, operated and/or used by two or more organizations for the purpose of exchanging information to support a business application or process. These organizations can be suppliers and customers in the same value chain, strategic partners or even competitors in the same or related markets. Such systems are sometimes called interorganizational networks, or computer-mediated interorganizational systems. These systems can take many different forms, ranging from dedicated, closed group systems to semi-closed group networks based on value added network services (VANS) and some B2B portals to completely open systems based on the Internet, which are sometimes referred to as electronic markets or open e-markets.

Before the commercial applications of the Internet in the 1990s, many interorganizational systems were built with technology and interface proprietary to a particular group of organizations. Many such systems are still being used today among strategic partners or within particular sectors, even though more and more systems have been migrated to the Internet platform. As such, firms wishing to join the business network often need to invest in the special hardware and/or software for the system. The reasons for adopting this type of system were divergent. In some cases, they were intended by some firms to lock in customers and lock out competitors. In most cases, it was simply because common standards were not available, or because available open technical solutions could not provide the sophisticated technologies or the level of confidentiality required by the partners for particular applications. There are many advantages with this type of network, but problems such as high development and maintenance costs, low flexibility and so on were increasingly recognized. It is also interesting to note that some strategic collaboration between organizations (e.g. the joint design and development of new products between firms) was often based on this type of interorganizational system.

The second category of IOS, the most widely used form in the 1980s and 1990s, is based on standard, common purpose computing facilities and communication protocols, very often but not always using VANS. VANS describe the electronic communication services provided, usually by a third party, to two or more trading partners that not only establish an information link between the participants, but also assist and add value to the communication process in some way. One of the most widely used standards for VANS is based on electronic data interchange (EDI). EDI has primarily been used in the subcontracting area along value chains, and it has been proven most effective in supporting operational-level applications, mainly because of its limited technical capabilities and the existence of multiple technical standards both within and between sectors. In order to support more complex and strategically more important applications and processes, some firms have preferred to maintain dedicated data links between their computer systems by themselves, using various interfaces and communication protocols capable of handling more sophisticated forms of information exchange.

The situation has changed considerably by way of the Internet since the mid-1990s, where the existing services have been gradually moved onto the Internet platform, and some VAN providers have evolved into B2B exchanges or portals. Most B2B e-commerce is an adaptation of EDI or is based on EDI principles, and even today EDI is still the method used for most electronic B2B transactions (some estimate as much as three-quarters of all B2B transactions). It is important to note that Internet EDI (also called Web EDI or Open EDI) has not replaced traditional EDI because the cost of disinvestment is high; many large companies have significant investments in the computing infrastructure they use for traditional EDI. Concerns about security issues and the inability to provide audit logs and third party verification of transactions also significantly slowed down the proliferation of Internet EDI. Today, most VAN providers offer Internet EDI but they continue to provide traditional EDI services. However, the situation is changing rapidly as security concerns are increasingly alleviated and the open architecture of the Internet allows trading partners virtually unlimited opportunities for customizing their information exchanges. It also provides inexpensive communication channels that traditional EDI could not, which allows more and more small companies to participate in Internet EDI.

In both of these categories, all parties involved in the systems are predetermined and all participants have agreed to trade or exchange information electronically. These types of interorganizational systems are often referred to as 'electronic alliances'. However, the rapid development of the Internet and related technologies has opened up the opportunity for instant encounter and trade between unpredetermined members. Today, any firm can establish electronic communications with any other firms in the world at very low costs; a firm wishing to offer its products and services can simply store an electronic catalogue on its server (or on a third party hosting server) for the world to look at. Such interorganizational systems are referred to as 'electronic markets'. Clearly it takes more than just the Internet to make such open trading and communications work, and many difficult barriers have to be overcome. For example, most commercial transactions between firms are based on trust, which is currently lacking in the electronic market, but many trade organizations and international bodies have been developing various schemes to overcome these barriers. The reputation of companies also plays a key role in some instances (e.g. it is relatively reliable and safe for anyone to do business with Dell or Cisco electronically). Electronic markets are increasingly used for standard, undifferentiated products and services or for trading excess stocks in many industries. The rapid growth of companies such as eBay has also made trading between small companies and between individuals very straightforward.

INTERORGANIZATIONAL INFORMATION SYSTEMS AND CHANGING INTERORGANIZATIONAL RELATIONS

Until the late 1990s, most applications of interorganizational systems were among business partners that have agreed to do business electronically, and the situation has continued today even though open electronic markets have been developing rapidly for certain products and services in the form of B2B and B2C e-commerce. In fact, many B2B transactions are based on established relations between the trading partners. Interorganizational systems are particularly developed among firms along the same supply chain where various benefits such as lower costs, shorter lead times, lower stock levels and improved cash flows are often achieved. For small firms, the benefits and dangers of being locked in or locked out of such systems are highlighted. Most interorganizational systems were usually initiated by a large firm at the centre of the trading network to interact electronically with regular suppliers and/or buyers. The main purpose was typically to reduce transaction costs, stock levels and lead times. In some cases, these systems have been developed through the natural extension of the centre firm's internal computer and communication systems. The development of such systems often entails the extension of the centre firm's internal gains of computer networking to its suppliers and/or customers, in order to reduce the total cost of the final products and to improve the responsiveness of the supply chain to market changes. Sometimes, such systems are imposed on trading partners by the large firm at the centre. The costs to each firm are normally paid back by productivity gains, increased sales or secured long-term contacts, and sometimes the development is directly subsidized by the centre firm.

The development of such interorganizational systems can often serve to stabilize existing relations between suppliers and buyers, and to raise the entry barriers for potential competitors. This is because setting up and maintaining interorganizational systems requires close cooperation between participating firms, which helps them to foster closer partnerships and encourages the sharing of information. The use of such networks can also contribute to the removal of barriers to cooperation by reducing errors typical of paper-based communications; should any errors happen, these networks can also facilitate problem resolution, because the problems can be more easily traced and be dealt with more quickly and effectively. In addition, introducing interorganizational systems requires both time and money, and their maintenance often requires special skills, and there are also security and reliability concerns. Switching partners (suppliers or buyers) would therefore by definition be costly and time-consuming. All these factors have served to stabilize existing interorganizational relations.

FROM ROUTINE TRANSACTIONS TO STRATEGIC APPLICATIONS

Most interorganizational systems have been developed to support routine, repetitive transactions between business partners, such as electronic ordering and invoicing. However, there have been two important developments in recent years. One is that some business partners use interorganizational systems to support strategic collaborations, such as joint new product development and collaborative designs. This is particularly important in the age of virtual organizations. The other, perhaps a more significant one, is that some leading firms are using electronic transactions with suppliers and buyers to support their new business models, such as Dell, Cisco and Toyota. In fact, even though many of the applications and processes supported by interorganizational systems are routine in nature, without seamless electronic transactions among their business networks, the business models that have brought these companies success would not have been possible.

Interorganizational systems and strategic collaborations between firms

Using interorganizational systems to support strategic applications has been going on for many years (Li and Williams, 1999). Back in the early 1990s, a fashion designer and manufacturer in the UK used EDI to exchange market and design information in addition to electronic ordering and invoicing. By adding special software in both the manufacturer's and the retailer's computers, the two companies only needed to exchange limited data between their information systems to enable the designers in the manufacturer and the purchasing staff in the retailer to exchange ideas about new designs and new market requirements, which translated into more frequent orders and new products more closely linked to market demand.

Equally, in the car manufacturing sector, EDI-based ordering and invoicing systems enabled just-in-time production that reduced costs and improved the responsiveness of the entire supply chain. However, once such routine electronic trading was established, some companies started to explore strategic applications as well. The use of interorganizational systems has enabled real just-in-time production in a leading car manufacturer in the UK; some components (e.g. car seats) are delivered to the car assembly lines by the suppliers – with the right variants and specifications – only 12 to 15 minutes after the car manufacturer issues the order. Apart from the locational proximity between them and the convenience of electronic ordering based on EDI, one key to this application was that the suppliers are granted direct access to production planning and forecasting information stored on the car manufacturer's computers, so the suppliers can plan their own production before receiving orders – without it this application would have not been possible. For suppliers in other parts of the UK and in Europe, the lead time from order to delivery has also been reduced dramatically. By the mid-1990s, the car manufacturer's average inventory and stock holding for European originated parts was reduced to less than one day. Essential to the improvement is the sharing of business information between business partners via interorganizational systems.

Other strategically important applications include the joint development of new products. In the car industry, some component suppliers are technically very competent, and it is in the car manufacturer's interest to tap into this expertise. As a result, since the 1990s, some car manufacturers have decided to work with selected suppliers in new car developments. The car manufacturer provides the supplier detailed computer-aided design (CAD) data on the space the component occupies and its technical specifications; the supplier will then begin to design the component, passing it back to the car manufacturer via interorganizational systems for feedback and modifications (to ensure total compatibility). Such interactive communications enable emerging problems to be resolved quickly. Online simulations between different components could also be conducted before the design is finalized.

While the inbound material flows in most car manufacturers are very efficient today, outbound logistics has not been able to achieve the same level of responsiveness, with high levels of inventory for finished cars, which ties in a huge amount of working capital. The key to improving the inventory level of finished cars is to improve the relations between dealers and manufacturers, enabling the sharing of stock movement and production planning information between the car manufacturer and the dealers and between the dealers themselves through interorganizational systems. Today, when a customer walks into a dealership, the salesperson can check stock availability easily by accessing production planning information and a finished car database for both different branches of the car dealership itself or from the manufacturer's production plan and the stocks of other, sometimes competing dealers.

Interorganizational systems and new business models

In addition to supporting strategically important applications between organizations, it is important to note that interorganizational systems have underpinned, or enabled, the business models of many well-known, successful companies that are based on special relations with their partners and customers. Toyota is one such example, which developed lean production systems among its partners and suppliers. The interorganizational information systems are essential in enabling the sharing of information and the effective integration of their operations. This enables Toyota to use operational excellence as a strategic weapon: it designed cars faster, with more reliability, yet at a competitive cost, making it the third largest car manufacturer in the world after General Motors and Ford and it has been expanding faster than its larger competitors.

According to Jeffrey Liker, the Toyota Production System is Toyota's unique approach to manufacturing (Liker, 2004). It is the basis for much of the lean production movement that has dominated manufacturing trends for many years, and it was heralded as the Japanese secret weapon which has spread rapidly throughout the world (Womack *et al.*, 1990). Lean production welds the activities of everyone into a tightly integrated system that responds quickly to market demands. Liker summarized lean manufacturing as a five-part process that includes defining customer value, defining the value stream, making it flow, pulling from the customer back and striving for excellence. To be a lean manufacturer requires organizations to adopt a way of thinking that focuses on making the product flow through value-adding processes without interruption, a pull system that cascades back from customer demand by replenishing at short intervals only what the next operation takes away, and a culture in which everyone is striving continuously to improve the system. Pull means the ideal state of just-in-time manufacturing: giving the customer what they want, when they want it and in the amount they want. All these processes would not be possible without the support of robust interorganizational information systems that are closely integrated with the internal systems of all parties involved in the entire supply chain, both to support routine transactions and to share strategic and operational information.

Another well-known business model based on integrated interorganizational systems is the Cisco model, which made the company very responsive to market changes and allowed Cisco to close its books in 24 hours throughout the year. Cisco's supply chain consists of a group of contract manufacturers who ship directly to customers on demand. These manufacturers depend on other large manufacturers of components for their supply, and these latter companies in turn depend on a large network of global suppliers. To improve the responsiveness of the supply chain, Cisco developed an eHub with its suppliers that works with its Partner Interface Process system. These systems operate in real time and they significantly increase transparency for orders. The Partner Interface Process system sends demand forecasts to both the contract manufacturers and component makers in the supply chain, and ultimately Cisco is able to automate the whole product fulfilment process, and a customer's online transaction will simultaneously update Cisco's financial database and supply chain. Essential to the business model is a flexible, robust IT system that integrates and coordinates the entire manufacturing, supply chain and logistical systems. Furthermore, to harness the expertise of its customer base, Cisco has extended its links further downstream by creating Cisco Connection Online, which provides a suite of interactive, networked services with quick, open access to Cisco's information, resources and systems. The system enables Cisco customers to engage in dialogue and help solve one another's technical problems.

A further example is Dell's direct sales model. Dell is the largest direct supplier of computer systems, and it sells to both individual and business customers. By using the Internet to sell customized computers directly to customers, Dell eliminated the need for a wholesale and retail network and the costly mark-ups associated with this. In addition, Dell is able to ship customized computers as fast as mail-order companies shipping from inventory at a cost not much higher – or even lower – than their non-customized competitors. However, the model requires Dell's operation to be closely integrated with that of its suppliers, contractors and logistical service providers throughout the supply chain. The support of a robust interorganizational system is essential.

Many other companies are following the lead of these market leaders – a trend sometimes referred to as mass customization. For example, Toyota is able to ship custom-built cars in a week; and the car industry is hoping to save billions of dollars each year from reduced inventories alone by producing cars made to order. Similarly, Nike allows customers to customize shoes; and De Beers allow customers to design their own engagement rings. These innovations would not have been possible without the support of interorganizational information systems which enables the close integration of operations across the entire supply chain, from suppliers all the way to the final consumers. Many of these new business models are based on the effective integration of electronic markets downstream (i.e. customers) with the electronic alliances upstream (i.e. suppliers).

FROM LEAN PRODUCTION TO LEAN SERVICES AND LEAN CONSUMPTION

Lean production has undoubtedly transformed manufacturing, and in recent years the same principles have been successfully applied in some service industries. In her paper published in the *Harvard Business Review*, Cynthia Swank described how Jefferson Pilot Financial, a US life insurance and annuities company, successfully applied the principles of lean production to significantly improve operations and increase revenue (Swank, 2003). Just like the assembly line for cars, an insurance policy goes through a series of processes from application, risk assessment and underwriting to policy insurance. Each step adds value to the final 'product'. The main advantage of implementing a lean production initiative over business process re-engineering, for example, is that the new system can be introduced without significantly disrupting operation. Through this initiative, the company transformed its operations from batch processing to continuous flow processing and applied various lean production principles, which significantly reduced the build-up of work in progress. Although lean production is generally seen as a manufacturing concept, Swank believed that many of its tools were originally developed in service industries like retailing, where customers pulled what they wanted from the shelves, which were then replenished for subsequent customers. The application of lean production principles in services may lead to similar changes – including interorganizational innovations – to those we have witnessed in manufacturing sectors.

More significantly, James Womack and Daniel Jones believed that after the transformation of manufacturing (and services) by lean production, the next step is to apply lean thinking to the process of consumption (Womack and Jones, 2005). This new theory is closely linked to the concept of 'experience' (Pine and Gilmore, 1998; Prahalad and Ramaswamy, 2003). With the unstoppable trend towards deregulation in a growing number of areas, people's freedom has increased dramatically, but with this comes new responsibilities. Today, consumers have access to a growing range of products at lower costs, with higher quality and more variety, but this also means they have a growing range of decisions to make – about what product or service to purchase, from which supplier, through different channels, and so on. In this process, the boundary between production and consumption is blurred by ICTs. Consumers need to do an increasing amount of work – unpaid – on behalf of providers (e.g. entering data into order forms and tracking their own orders):

> … these consumers are spending more and more time and energy to obtain and maintain the computers, printers, PDAs, and other technological tools needed to solve routine problems – for themselves and for providers. (Womack and Jones, 2005: 60)

The situation is further exacerbated by changing characteristics of consumers, such as the growing number of two-wage families or single parent households, and an ageing population, which all mean people have declining energy and time to confront expanding choices.

According to Womack and Jones, lean consumption is not about reducing the amount customers buy, but about providing the full value that customers desire from their goods and services with the greatest efficiency and least pain. By minimizing customers' time and effort and delivering exactly what they want, when and where they want it, companies can benefit from the process. However, for lean consumption to work, a fundamental change needs to happen in the way retailers, service providers, manufacturers and suppliers think about the relationship between provision and consumption and the role their customers play in the process. Customers and providers must collaborate in order to minimize total costs and wasted time and create new value, and the processes of provision and consumption need to be tightly integrated and streamlined.

Like lean production, lean consumption has a series of corresponding principles, including: solving the customer's problem completely by ensuring all the goods and services work and work together; don't waste the customer's time; providing exactly what the customer wants, where and when it is wanted; and continually aggregating solutions to reduce the customer's time burden and hassle. To implement these principles, providers need to work together to perfect the entire consumption process rather than deal with their own individual piece of the solution, and to solve problems at source. Companies should use 'pull' (e.g. Nike can profitably deliver customized bags overnight anywhere in

North America), rather than a large inventory, to satisfy customer needs. For consumers, by sharing your plans with a producer and ordering in advance (e.g. a car), it is possible to obtain a customized product for a reduced price; manufacturers could save significantly in reduced inventory costs. However, the current system of manufacturing and purchasing often penalizes customers for planning ahead.

The real challenge for lean consumption is for the retailers, service providers, manufacturers and suppliers to look at the total costs from the consumer's point of view, and eventually to work with customers to optimize the process of consuming. This requires not only changing mindsets on the parts of all stakeholders involved, but also the underpinning of a robust information system that links together the operations of these stakeholders and enables the effective sharing of information. Lean production has in recent years become the dominant model of production, and the proliferation of lean consumption will lead to new forms of interorganizational relations across the entire supply chain – all the way to the consumers.

THE INTERNET AND B2B ELECTRONIC MARKETPLACES

The rapid development of the Internet since the mid-1990s facilitated the emergence of B2B electronic marketplaces. There are several different types of electronic marketplaces, although some of them are perhaps more precisely described as 'electronic alliances', with predetermined trading partners only. Schneider (2006) briefly illustrated several categories of e-marketplaces:

- *Independent Industry Marketplaces*, which are also known as industry marketplaces (which are focused on a single industry), independent exchanges (which are not controlled by one of the established buyers or sellers) and public marketplaces (which are open to new buyers and sellers). Examples include Chemdex and ChemConnect for bulk chemicals.
- *Private Stores and Customer Portals.* For example, Cisco and Dell each offer private stores for each of their major customers within their selling Web site to ensure that they meet the needs of their key customers better than industry marketplaces would.
- *Private Company Marketplaces*, where a large company purchasing from many vendors can open an e-marketplace for its own procurements, sometimes known as e-procurement.

■ *Industry Consortia-Sponsored Marketplaces.* These are market-places formed by several major companies in an industry, such as: Covisint in the auto industry sponsored by DaimlerChrysler, Ford and General Motors, together with several thousand suppliers; and Avendra in the hotel industry, formed by Marriott, Hyatt and three other major hotel chains.

Today, all these models are being used in various industries. It is not clear which of these models will dominate B2B e-commerce in the future, although so far the Industry Consortia-Sponsored Marketplaces appear to be most successful.

In a similar fashion, Laudon and Traver (2003) classified B2B e-marketplaces into Net Marketplaces and Private Industrial Networks. Net Marketplaces can be further classified into four categories:

■ *E-Distributors*: a single firm version of retail and wholesale stores, such as Grainger.com, FindMRO.com and Staples.com.

■ *E-Procurement*: a single firm creating a digital market where thousands of sellers and buyers transact for indirect inputs, such as Ariba.com and CommerceOne.com.

■ *Exchanges*: independently owned digital marketplaces for indirect inputs, such as IMX.com and eSteel.com.

■ *Industrial Consortia*: industry-owned vertical e-markets open only to selected suppliers, such as Covisint.com and Plasticsnet.com; private industrial networks include single-firm networks to coordinate the supply chain with a limited set of partners (e.g. Wal-Mart and Proctor & Gamble), and industry-wide networks to coordinate supply and logistics for the industry (e.g. Nistevo and Globalnetexchange.com).

Turban *et al.* (2004) also illustrated different types of e-marketplaces, but their discussions included both B2B and B2C e-commerce, from electronic storefronts and malls, to private and public e-marketplaces and information portals. They also discussed the various business models used in these e-marketplaces. Some of these e-marketplaces are perhaps more precisely described as electronic alliances, which are similar to electronic trading networks based on VANS or direct interorganizational systems, although the open standards of the Internet make it easier and cheaper than before to establish and maintain the electronic links. Others are similar to open markets enabled by Internet-based communications. In some cases, these developments have significantly increased the transparency of the market in various contexts, and in all cases the efficiency of trading between organizations is significantly improved. Some of the electronic marketplaces serve to enhance and stabilize interorganizational relations, but in others the systems encourage competition between suppliers of the same products.

Today, B2B e-commerce still captures the lion's share of total e-commerce in terms of transaction value even though B2C e-commerce has been growing steadily and rapidly. In some cases the distinctions between B2B and B2C are becoming blurred. The Internet has made it increasingly easy and affordable for almost anyone to set up electronic links with anyone else, which without doubt will facilitate further growth of electronic trading between organizations, between organizations and individuals, and between individuals themselves. The rapid development of companies such as eBay and various services offered by companies such as Yahoo!, MSN and Amazon allow small companies as well as individuals to set up online shops easily to sell virtually anything to other companies or to final consumers, either through auctions or fixed prices. Price comparison sites, such as Froogle from Google and Kelkoo, enable organizations and individuals to identify the cheapest or most suitable providers easily, significantly increasing the transparency of the market. Companies such as Overstock.com enable organizations to sell excess stocks quickly and easily. Priceline.com enables buyers to name their own price and enables providers to sell their products at suitable prices. Other models of e-commerce and e-marketplaces continue to be invented, and rapid developments are likely to continue in the foreseeable future. This is still a rapidly evolving area and further studies are needed to make sense of the latest developments and to understand their implications for interorganizational relations.

BARRIERS TO INTERORGANIZATIONAL SYSTEMS AND INNOVATIONS

There are many barriers to interorganizational systems and innovations, not only serious technical barriers but also cultural and political barriers which are extremely difficult to overcome. Examples include: sharing sensitive business information with suppliers, customers and even competitors; the integration of business processes between firms; the control of one firm by another; the coexistence of competition and collaboration; the integration of production with consumption; and many other related issues. Many of these barriers have to be overcome before some interorganizational innovations in strategic areas can be developed. In fact, the full potential of interorganizational systems probably cannot be achieved without radical changes in the institutional framework in which most organizations operate, and in the perceptions and assumptions of business leaders about the nature of firms and markets in the networked economy.

The main barriers to the future development of interorganizational systems and innovations exist at three levels. At the bottom level, there are technical barriers that organizations have to overcome, in terms of system reliability, security and in managing incompatible standards and networks. Such technical problems – and the lack of trust in such systems – have prevented some firms from developing new collaborations in strategic areas. Although recent developments in technology, infrastructure and services have significantly relieved these problems, technical barriers will continue to constrain the development of interorganizational systems and new applications based on such systems.

A more difficult barrier exists at a second level, which requires radical changes in the understanding of the nature of firms and markets and the new rules of the game in the information economy. Issues such as sharing sensitive business information (e.g. stock availability, forecasting and production planning data) with suppliers, buyers and even rival companies still worry some business leaders. However, if such issues are not resolved, many strategic interorganizational collaborations are simply impossible to develop, and the full potential of interorganizational systems and innovations cannot be achieved. A study by Dyer and Hatch (2004) highlighted how Toyota achieved sustainable advantage by partnering with suppliers and partners and sharing knowledge with them through organized networks.

Even when firms are prepared to share certain business information with each other, the success of interorganizational innovations is still not guaranteed. Successful collaborations between firms requires more than the exchange of information. Differences between the collaborating organizations in terms of aims, culture, structure, procedures, professional and natural languages, accountabilities, and the sheer amount of time and effort required to manage the logistics of communication often mitigates against success. Of particular importance for effective collaboration between organizations is perhaps the development of 'common knowledge', which is essential to successful collaboration but which is an extremely difficult endeavour between organizations. As such, the success of interorganizational innovation through interorganizational systems is much more difficult than many people have perceived. This to some extent explains why the enormous potential of interorganizational systems has been difficult to materialize so far.

For open electronic marketplaces, there are still serious concerns about security, trust, third party verification, payment, and so on. Many organizations are working hard to address such issues. Most of the barriers are non-technical in nature and their removal will facilitate further growth in e-commerce.

INTERORGANIZATIONAL SYSTEMS AND CHANGING INTERORGANIZATIONAL RELATIONS: WHAT NEXT?

In the age of the Internet and e-business, interorganizational systems and interorganizational innovations will continue to develop rapidly. The Internet has made it increasingly easier, and cheaper, to set up and maintain electronic links between organizations, and between customers and organizations. This has not only facilitated the increasing adoption of interorganizational collaborations in routine and strategic applications, but has also enabled the adoption of new business models which have brought success to an increasing number of companies.

Interorganizational innovations are closely linked to some emerging strategies and business models, and are an essential aspect of e-commerce and e-business. They are also closely linked to many contemporary business phenomena ranging from deconstruction and unbundling of the integrated business model and processes, to outsourcing and offshoring of routine and strategic activities, functions and business processes. Many interorganizational innovations have been implemented to extend the benefits of internal gains through restructuring and re-engineering to business partners, suppliers and customers; increasingly, some organizations are exploiting core competencies based on unique relations and applications between organizations. In fact, it has been argued that in the age of the Internet and e-business, companies are increasingly seen as portfolios of capabilities and relationships positioned within a global network of business processes, and it is the dynamic creation of value within the entire network that frames our thinking (Venkatraman, 2004). The integration of operations across value chains has enabled the adoption of new business models in a growing number of industries, which are further leading to significant restructuring of value chains and value networks, new forms of competition and collaboration between business partners and new relationships between businesses and consumers, including lean consumption and the co-construction of value and experience with business partners and consumers. Continued research is clearly needed in this area.

REFERENCES

Dyer, J. H. and Hatch, N. W. (2004). Using supplier networks to learn faster. *Sloan Management Review*, 45 (3), 57–63.

Laudon, K. C. and Traver, C. G. (2003). *E-Commerce: Business, Technology and Society*. Second edition. Pearson Addison-Wesley.

Li, F. and Williams, H. (1999). Inter-firm collaboration through inter-firm networks. *Information Systems Journal*, 9 (2), 103–117.

Li, F. (2006). *What is e-Business? How the Internet Transforms Organisations*. Blackwell.

Liker, J. (2004). *The Toyota Way: Fourteen Management Principles from the World's Greatest Manufacturer*. McGraw-Hill.

Pine, J. and Gilmore, J. (1998). Welcome to the experiences economy. *Harvard Business Review*, 76, 97–105.

Prahalad, C. K. and Ramaswamy, V. (2003). The new frontier of experience innovation. *Sloan Management Review*, 44 (4), 12–18.

Schneider, G. (2006). *Electronic Commerce*. Sixth edition. Thomson Course Technology.

Swank, C. K. (2003). The lean service machine. *Harvard Business Review*, 81 (10), 123–129.

Turban, E., King, D., Lee, J. and Viehland, D. (2004). *Electronic Commerce: A Managerial Perspective*. Pearson Prentice Hall.

Venkatraman, N. V. (2004). Offshoring without guilt. *Sloan Management Review*, 45 (3), 14–16.

Womack, J. P., Jones, D. T. and Ros, D. (1990). *The Machine that Changed the World*. Rawson Associates.

Womack, J. P. and Jones, D. T. (2005). Lean consumption. *Harvard Business Review*, 83 (3), 59–68.

CHAPTER 10

Structure, strategy and success factors for the virtual organization

Peter Marshall, Judy McKay and Judy Young

INTRODUCTION

In recent years the notion of the virtual organization has continued to attract a great deal of research attention. Over the last decade an extensive and broad range of literature on the subject has become available. While criticisms were made with regard to the earlier literature, these have now largely been addressed. For example, issues such as the meaning of the 'virtual organization' and confusion in the terminologies of 'virtual' and 'virtuality' with 'virtuous' and 'virtuousness' are no longer regarded as problematic. According to Walters (2005: 238): 'The concept [virtual organization] has become commonplace in one form or another and to a greater or lesser extent across a range of industries and markets'. This supports the prediction of Black and Edwards (2000) that rather than being a fad, virtual organizations would be used and developed in the foreseeable future. However, there still remains the issue of empirical evidence for many of the assertions made with respect to virtual organizations (Lin and Lu, 2005). Discussion has continued to be focused at a conceptual and theoretical level. Further, it has been proposed that it is not possible to find any guidelines to support how to actually go through the process of establishing a virtual organization (Thorne, 2005). As a consequence, the question of the relevance and veracity of the debate to business practice continues to be justified. In response, this chapter will represent a bold attempt to redress this concern.

Overall, this chapter aims to provide a clear theoretical framework, evaluated against empirical evidence, to describe the notion of the virtual organization that has come to be acknowledged as a new organizational form (Walker, 2006). The chapter will articulate our view of the virtual organization, and in particular will attempt to identify its defining characteristics. A number of possible models of the virtual organization will be defined and illustrated by way of real-life case studies.

CHARACTERIZING THE ESSENCE OF THE VIRTUAL ORGANIZATION

A careful examination of the literature on the virtual organization reveals three approaches with respect to this particular concept. For some, a virtual organization is essentially an electronic one, an online organization. Proponents of this position offer Amazon.com and eBay.com as examples of organizations that have been created primarily to exist in and exploit the opportunities offered by the Web and cyberspace. This so-called virtual (or electronic) organization is discussed in contradistinction to the traditional 'bricks-and-mortar' retail outlet (Czerniawska and Potter, 1998). In essence this form of organization represents an electronic supply chain, facilitated by developments in information and communications technology; it provides seamless interactions based on agility and flexibility that are not burdened by physical structure, stock inventory and geographical location (Walker, 2006).

An alternative to this first definition presents the virtual organization as an organizational structure based primarily on the notion of collaborating entities. Here, firms come together to share competencies, specialized skills, knowledge and other resources for the purpose of producing a particular service or good, or of taking advantage of a particular opportunity. In so doing, the participating firms share the risks and rewards from undertaking a specific business activity that may often involve an entrepreneurial opportunity (Elliot, 2006; Thorne, 2005). While there is the clear expectation that IT and telecommunications play an important role in coordinating and controlling the activities of disparate components of the virtual organization, IT is merely a key component, as opposed to a distinguishing characteristic *per se* (see, for example, Marshall *et al.*, 1999; Turban *et al.*, 1999).

The third approach, with respect to the virtual organization, is perhaps the most confusing. This approach represents an amalgam of the previous two approaches. Here, authors move almost interchangeably between the virtual organization as an electronic or online organization, and the virtual organization as a somewhat transient network of people, ideas, competencies and resources which come together for a particular purpose (see, for example, Siebel and House, 1999).

The position we adopt in this chapter corresponds to the second approach. As a precursor to more detailed discussion, a virtual organization can be defined as:

> ... composed of several business partners sharing costs and resources for the purpose of producing a product or service. [It] can be temporary ... or it can be permanent. Each partner contributes complementary resources that reflect its strengths, and determines its role in the virtual corporation. (Turban *et al.*, 1999: 142)

This stance suggests a need to more fully discuss the essential and fundamental attributes of the virtual organization.

A key characteristic of the virtual organization is its adaptability and flexibility in the face of turbulent business environments – a condition sometimes described as 'agility' (Dani *et al.*, 2006; Metes *et al.*, 1998). Virtual organizations are capable of rapid and adaptable responses to changing markets – whether these arise as a result of globalization, changing cost structures, changing customer needs and wants, or other similar reasons (Goldman *et al.*, 1995). Virtual organizations use existing structures from one or more firms and combine these in creative ways to forge new capabilities and competencies. This strategy thus averts the need to recruit, train and forge new work teams, buy new equipment and buildings, and work through a period of organizational learning (Magretts, 1998). Allied with its agility, an important attribute of the virtual organization is argued to be its more effective utilization of existing resources. This creates an important source of competitive advantage (Turban *et al.*, 1999).

The formation of business partnerships and alliances is pivotal to the concept of the virtual organization (Elliot, 2006; Grenier and Metes, 1995; Henning, 1998). Acquiring and/or developing all the required resources and competencies in order to avail itself of windows of opportunity can be both too time consuming and too costly to be an appropriate response for an organization acting on its own. In other words, in the brief period of time available to exploit business opportunities, a single organization may not have the time or the financial resources available to obtain and/or develop the needed skills, infrastructure or other resources. It may not even have the time to develop efficient business processes. However, access to the required knowledge, skills, resources and infrastructure may be available through entering into alliances or partnerships with all, or a part only, of other organizations. This notion is captured pictorially in Figure 10.1.

On its own, organization 1 may not have the capability to take advantage of a particular perceived business opportunity. Similarly, organizations 2 and 4 may be disadvantaged for different reasons. Organization 3 may possess the necessary knowledge and skills, but may lack other important resources, e.g. financial muscle. Nevertheless, by working cooperatively and synergistically with others, a virtual organization (depicted by the shaded area) may be formed to exploit the opportunity. By each organization contributing different knowledge, skills and resources, the virtual organization formed by the cooperative leveraging of assets and resources in organizations 1 to 4 may be highly successful in availing itself for a time of the original business opportunity.

Implicit in this description of the formation of business alliances is the notion that various components of the virtual organization may

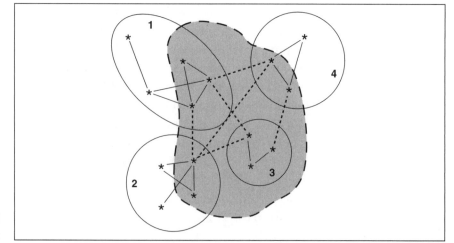

Figure 10.1
Formation of
business alliances

well be geographically dispersed. This gives rise to the challenge of communication and coordination across different time zones, locations, cultures and languages (IMPACT Programme, 1998). This is illustrated in Figure 10.2. Typically, this implies a need for excellent IT to support communication and coordination throughout the virtual organization.

Other key components of the agility ascribed to and required of virtual organizations are its human resources (HR) and its HR management practices (Pfeffer, 1998). The needs and requirements of virtual organizations demand that each employee has the skills to contribute directly to the value chain – contributing directly to the 'bottom line'. For example, this could be in the areas of product and service design, production, marketing or distribution. As each constituent member of the virtual organization contributes core competencies, the resultant collective HR effort would be geared appropriately and directly towards exploiting a particular opportunity. The collective output would thus be expected to surpass any of the individual contributing organizations (Turban *et al.*, 1999).

Ideally, employees must have a number of strong attributes. In addition to a capacity to learn new skills, employees must have a positive attitude towards the need for constant change, and tolerance of ambiguity and uncertainty in their working lives. They should also be sensitive to the possibly changing needs and wants of the organization's customers. For this to be achieved, a noteworthy characteristic of virtual organizations is employee empowerment, whereby decision making, responsibility and accountability are devolved to appropriate component parts of the structure, and are readily accepted as such (IMPACT Programme, 1998). A key issue for employees is to move from a 'me' perspective to a 'we' perspective (Kierzkowski, 2005). Responsiveness and competitiveness

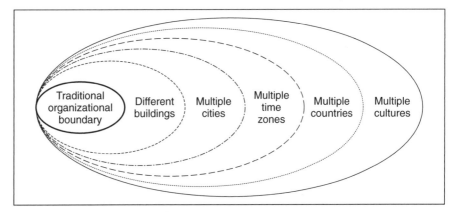

Figure 10.2
Characteristic dispersion of the virtual organization

in global markets imply a need for constancy and excellence in the development of appropriate skills and skill levels. However, it must be recognized that: 'a professional career is the result, only to some degree, of the guarantee of *being employed*, but it is primarily of *being prepared and desired for employment*' (Kierzkowski, 2005: 64). It also requires employees to accommodate their work procedures, skills, skill levels, work times and even working lives to the demands of the organization's customers. However, the virtual organization offers high rewards to skilled and psychologically tough employees. Such rewards can be financial. In addition, many organizations try to give employees as much freedom as possible to structure their workplaces and working hours to fit their own needs and personalities. Outputs and results are carefully monitored and measured, but human inputs are left as much as possible to the individual (Coutu, 1998). Clearly implied is the need for the virtual organization to be rigorous and effective in the management and exploitation of its intellectual capital (i.e. knowledge) while providing a satisfying work experience for its employees (IMPACT Programme, 1998).

Agility and responsiveness also imply a need for administrative processes that are cost-effective and lean. Heavy, clumsy bureaucratic practices have no place in the agile virtual organization. The needs of a centralized administration should impede as little as possible the work of those employees involved in creating value for the organization. Avoided at all costs should be the inertia, heaviness and clumsiness generally associated with the bureaucratic hierarchical organization of the late twentieth century. Unnecessary administrative activities should be minimized or abolished altogether. In the virtual organization, administrative work is done as efficiently as possible by as few staff as possible. Wherever possible, administrative overheads should be attributed to those staff directly involved in value-creating activities. This may be preferable since such staff will only engage in administration that is directly useful. When it becomes necessary to reconsider certain administrative tasks that are no longer viable the administrative activity winds down naturally. This eliminates the difficulties of reducing a central administrative function or reassigning staff to other duties (Benjamin and Wigand, 1995; Goldman *et al.*, 1995). It is essential that the organization retain its ability to respond and adapt to changing conditions. High administrative overhead costs and/or slow, bureaucratic procedures may inhibit this essential characteristic.

Business opportunities are too often fleeting and transient – especially in contemporary business environments. Virtual organizations are opportunistic and avail themselves of profitable business circumstances even if the organization itself is apparently temporary; there is an acceptance of, even an enthusiasm for, change and uncertainty with respect to the organization's products and services, its customer base, its structure and scope, and in its very approach to doing business (IMPACT Programme, 1998). This characteristic means that virtual organizations are at ease with the notion of porous and changing organizational boundaries, and with the use of outsourcing and alliances as effective means of changing and realigning the organization's skills and skill levels. In these ways virtual organizations incorporate the competencies of other organizations so as to adapt quickly to changing business situations. Virtual organizations can thus take advantage of emerging opportunities by changing their skills base to fit different circumstances. Such organizations are adept at coordinating and managing disparate resources and activities throughout the supply chain.

Virtual organizations are information-intensive (Grenier and Metes, 1995), and hence may be heavily reliant on IT. Information and communications technologies underpin and enable their propensity for opportunistic behaviour. IT supports some of the new organizational alliances and forms necessary for designing and producing new goods and services quickly. IT also provides an organization with a fast and convenient channel through which to promote its products and services and to inform potential customers of organizational product and service developments. The same channel can also accept and process sales to customers (Benjamin and Wigand, 1995; Metes *et al.*, 1998). These new technologies provide the information and communications framework necessary for the 'anywhere, anytime' work that takes place in virtual organizations (Upton and McAfee, 1996). However, it must be acknowledged that the virtual organization can exist without heavy reliance on IT (Sor, 1999), although it is generally acknowledged that in most contemporary cases IT will occupy an important position.

In the face of extreme turbulence and uncertainty in the business environment, the virtual organization is put forward as a low-cost, highly responsive and adaptable way to organize and compete. The essential characteristics of the virtual organization have been argued to be:

- Adaptability, flexibility and responsiveness to changing requirements and conditions.
- Effectiveness in utilization of resources.
- Formation of business alliances of varying degrees of permanence.
- Dispersion of component parts.
- Empowerment of staff.

- Stewardship of expertise, know-how and knowledge (intellectual capital).
- Low levels of bureaucracy.
- Opportunistic behaviours, embracing change and uncertainty.
- High infusion of IT to support business processes and knowledge workers.

The practical implications for managers adopting the virtual organization structure and strategy need to be considered further. It is important to note in passing that as soon as one mentions managing in a virtual organization, or of adopting virtual organizing as a deliberate strategy, then there is a sense in which one is almost inevitably talking about interorganizational management. Thus, we refer to the coordinated and cooperative behaviours and endeavours of actors/managers who originate in different organizations and who, after a period of time, may revert to those different organizations.

MANAGING IN THE VIRTUAL ORGANIZATION: SUCCESS FACTORS

On paper, many of the defining characteristics of the virtual organization sound delightfully and seductively simple, indeed obvious. Yet, it would seem that if the virtual organization is to function effectively, a number of important managerial tasks must be accomplished. People in the virtual organization are drawn from diverse sources but, perhaps working in teams, need to find a shared purpose or vision in order to reach successful outcomes and results. A shared purpose or vision serves as the 'glue' of the virtual organization (Hedberg *et al.*, 1994; Wiesenfeld *et al.*, 1998). It also serves as the lifecycle of the virtual organization. This is because the continued existence of the virtual organization depends on the existence of a *raison d'être*: when the desired results have been achieved (and there is no longer glue to hold the structure together), then the virtual organization dissolves. For management and organizational members, therefore, a key function would seem to be quickly identifying and taking ownership of this shared purpose and vision.

However, in order that a purpose may be genuinely shared and for linkages to operate unimpeded, there must exist extraordinary levels of trust. Lipnack and Stamps (1998) suggest that in the virtual organization, trust must function to replace the usual rules, procedures and policies that dictate the behaviours of the more traditional hierarchical and bureaucratic organizations. Without trust among partners the situation needs to revert to the use of bureaucratic or other control mechanisms that are contrary to the concepts of agility and minimal physical resources (Fenwick and De Cieri, 2004). With a trusting relationship in place among virtual organization members, there is also a requirement for the risk(s) associated with the joint initiative (i.e. inherent in the purpose of the virtual organization) to be shared.

Typically, in traditional organizational structures, risk is totally the preserve of a single organization, which alone tends to implement measures to manage exposure to risk. The more interdependent the nature of the virtual organization's activities, the more risk must be seen to be – and accepted as – shared. If risk is to be shared and high levels of trust maintained, then clearly the purpose of the virtual organization must be such that all members benefit in more ways from being within the virtual organization than they would from remaining outside the virtual relationship. Thus, the successful virtual organization relies on the ability of the alliance to offer benefits to individual members in terms of increased productivity, increased revenues, increased profitability, increased market share, and so on (Friedman, 1998).

Fundamental critical success factors for the virtual organization can therefore be posited as a shared purpose, a trusting relationship, a willingness to share risk and a mutual benefit being derived from the virtual organization's existence. This is illustrated in Figure 10.3.

It is thus argued that a successful virtual organization is based very much on the notion that mutual benefit for the parties involved is derived through the timely and appropriate initiation and formation of alliances to take advantage of possibly short-lived business opportunities. However, in order for the alliances to operate effectively and provide benefits to

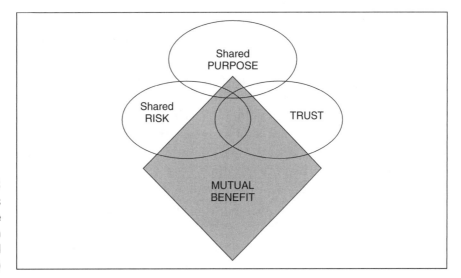

Figure 10.3
Critical success factors for the virtual organization (source: Marshall et al., 1999)

Table 10.1

Inherent tensions in behaviours of the virtual organization (Chesbrough and Teece, 1996)

Strengths	How strengths become weaknesses
Opportunistic, entrepreneurial, risk taking	Personal incentives and rewards for risk taking increase, leading to self-interest in behaviours, etc., making coordination and cooperation among parties more difficult.
Mutual trust, shared risk, opportunistic	When conflicts or misunderstandings do arise, or unforeseen opportunities work to favour some of the parties more than others, there exist few established procedures for negotiation and conflict resolution.
Opportunistic	The spirit that drives parties to collaborate may also cause virtual organizations to fragment if one or more of the parties deliberately act to exploit more benefits for themselves than for the other parties.

all collaborating parties, there is the very important assumption that management activity has achieved the requisite level of shared vision and purpose. Additionally, there needs to be a high degree of trust among virtual organization members, and an acceptance and understanding that risk is to be somehow shared among those standing to benefit.

At this point, some caution needs to be exercised, for the virtual organization and virtual organizing should not be presented as *the* way of the future, almost akin to a business imperative for the successful enterprise in this internetworked era. Many of the characteristics, strategies and claims for the virtual organization are conceptually appealing. However, there seems to be a range of challenges for managers to nurture a successful business within the conceptual framework of virtual organizing. Some commentators would argue that many of the strengths and powerful characteristics of the virtual organization also tend to render it vulnerable. Hence, and paradoxically, its very strengths can be a source of weakness (Chesbrough and Teece, 1996). Chesbrough and Teece (1996) identify a number of such potential tensions in the virtual organization concept. Table 10.1 summarizes some of these.

The type of innovation involved – and the associated information flows and knowledge management strategies – can also enhance or moderate the likely success of the virtual organization. It is argued that, because of the information flows essential for innovation, autonomous innovations (i.e. stand-alone, independent innovations) are more suitable for the

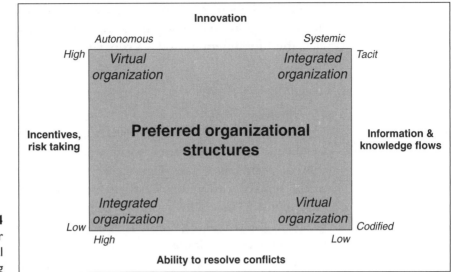

Figure 10.4
A framework for success in virtual organizing

virtual organization than highly interconnected, systemic ones. Codified information (i.e. that which can be easily captured in industry standards and rules, for example) is argued to be as easy to transfer from one party to another in the virtual organization form as it is to transfer within a single organization. On the other hand, tacit knowledge (such as know-how or ingrained perspectives) is not easily transferred or diffused, and is also subject to opportunism by individual parties who can control the extent to which they share it. Thus, autonomous innovation involving codified information and knowledge transfer may be more suitable for exploitation along virtual organizing principles than systemic innovation involving tacit information and knowledge (Chesbrough and Teece, 1996). These notions are captured in Figure 10.4. This framework is a useful predictor of likely success for the virtual organization.

STRUCTURE AND STRATEGIC POSITIONING OF VIRTUAL ORGANIZATIONS

We have so far discussed the fundamentals of virtual organizations and their managerial success factors. It now seems reasonable to conclude that virtual organizations are likely to differ from the structures and behaviours of more conventional organizations in two key areas: by the structures that they adopt and the manner in which they position themselves within their environment. A number of 'models of virtuality' have been articulated previously by Burn *et al.* (1999). Some of these will be further discussed in the remainder of this chapter. This discussion will be supplemented by original case studies to more fully articulate and illustrate the models. The case studies will also serve to further explicate the fundamentals and success factors of the virtual organization outlined above.

Co-alliance model

Co-alliance models are virtual organizations in which there are essentially shared partnerships (see Figure 10.5). Each partner makes approximately equal contribution of resources, competencies, skills and knowledge to the alliance, thus forming a consortium. Given the opportunistic nature of the virtual organization, it would be expected that the composition of the consortium might change to reflect market opportunities or the changing core competencies of each member (Preiss *et al.*, 1998).

Links between co-alliance partners are often premised by mutual convenience on a project-by-project basis. However, provided the co-alliance virtual organization functions effectively and beneficially from the perspective of all concerned, it would be expected to reconvene intermittently on an ongoing basis when suitable opportunities present themselves. This is illustrated in Figure 10.6.

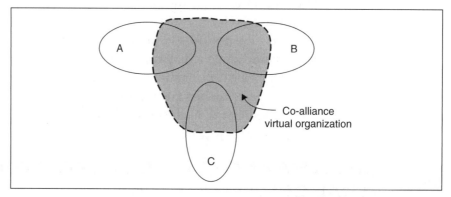

Figure 10.5
Co-alliance model

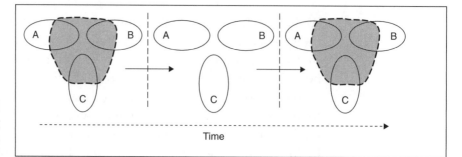

Figure 10.6
The ongoing
operations of the
co-alliance model

The following case study serves to explicate this model.

Case study: Perth Consulting Services (PCS)

Rachel Smith runs Perth Consulting Services (PCS). Rachel is skilled in facilitating strategic IS planning sessions. She guides and coaches groups of managers and professionals from public and private sector organizations in the formulation of corporate visions, missions, strategic plans and strategic IS plans. Rachel can offer very competitive prices for this consulting work since she works from home and has few of the infrastructure costs of the large consulting companies (such as the rent of expensive city office space). However, she cannot offer the broad skill set of the larger consulting companies.

Tony Jones has a very good technical knowledge of IT and offers an IT planning consulting service along with some analysis and programming skills. The analysis and programming services that he offers are limited and are usually restricted to specific small tasks that are identified during his IT planning work. If Tony requires substantial systems development work he contacts the consultancy of Tom and Stephanie More who run a systems development consultancy that offers systems analysis, design and programming services. Tom and Stephanie are skilled systems developers with a wide range of technical IT skills. They can also call on several other highly skilled systems developers to do analysis, design and programming tasks. They contract these systems developers on an 'as needed' project basis.

Together Rachel, Tony, Tom and Stephanie form an agile virtual organization able to respond effectively and inexpensively to a set of needs clustered about strategic planning, IS/IT planning and IS development. All the persons in this virtual organization work from their homes and utilize information technology to keep them in contact with each other and with business and government in Australia and South East Asia. Request for tender documents and templates are downloaded from the Internet and shared between various members as necessary. Business responsiveness and agility is maximized while overhead costs are kept to a minimum.

The structure of this virtual organization is that of the co-alliance. Each of the partners brings approximately equal commitment and effort to this virtual organization. Partners collaborate on an 'as needed' basis and function as a group under the umbrella label of PCS, a consultancy with a reasonably broad set of skills to offer. Provided the parties feel that the co-alliance is operating effectively, Rachel, Tony, Tom and Stephanie reactivate PCS whenever they see business opportunities that require competencies that, individually, none of the partners can fully offer.

However, in the tasks undertaken by PCS, a high degree of collaboration and trust is required in order to carry out an assignment to the satisfaction of the client. In addition, trust has been nurtured over time as – knowing and respecting one another over a long period – none of the individual parties would act opportunistically to the disadvantage of the others. The structure of this virtual organization is shown in Figure 10.7.

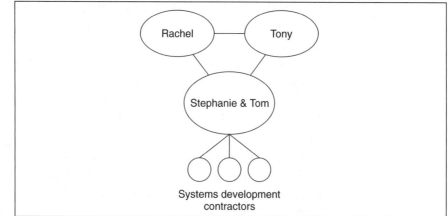

Figure 10.7
Co-alliance model
for business
planning and
systems
development

Star-alliance model

Star-alliance models are coordinated networks of interconnected members made up of a 'core' surrounded by 'satellite' organizations (see Figure 10.8). The core comprises the leader who is the dominant player in the market. The leader tends to dominate and has the power to direct and dictate the supply of competence, expertise, knowledge and resources to members. These alliances are commonly based around similar industry or company types. Typically in the star-alliance model

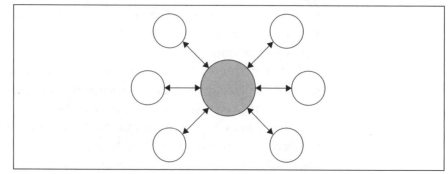

Figure 10.8
The star-alliance
model

there would be an expectation for the fortunes of the entire virtual organization to be closely allied to the fortunes of the dominant central partner.

The following case study explicates this model further.

Case study: Capital City Automobile Association (CCAA)

The Capital City Automobile Association (CCAA) began by offering members an automobile breakdown service in Australian state capital cities. If a member's car broke down, the CCAA would dispatch a qualified mechanic to the location of the breakdown. The CCAA guaranteed to rectify simple causes of vehicle 'breakdown' (such as a flat battery) and enable the motorist to get home or get the car to a garage or vehicle service centre. The CCAA owned a number of specially equipped vans driven by qualified mechanics, all employed by the CCAA, which would drive to the breakdown locations.

A very common reason for cars breaking down or not starting in the first place was a flat battery. Quite frequently, the motorist needed a new battery. This was not originally part of the charter of the CCAA, which was purely a breakdown service. The mechanics would attempt to recharge the battery to the point at which (at the very least) the motorist could drive home or, if necessary, to a garage and take more remedial action.

After some years, and at the suggestion of some of the mechanics, CCAA contracted certain individuals to provide a round-the-clock battery replacement service. CCAA carefully negotiated the contractor's hours of service availability, duties of service and pay. This ensured that contractors had as much freedom as possible regarding how they arranged their own business. Some of these contractors ran small enterprises such as garages or car repair/maintenance services, while others took on the battery replacement contract as their sole line of business. By having a number of battery replacement service contractors working for them, the CCAA was now able to offer members a 24/7 (24 hours a day/seven days a week) battery replacement service.

Over time, the CCAA examined the possible sources of supply for batteries. After examining prices and the reputations of battery distributors, the CCAA gave a contract to a distributor called Quality Batteries Australia (QBA), a company with substantial warehouses and stocks of batteries in two Australian state capital cities. QBA offered to supply a battery that was a good quality, well-known brand name. QBA undertook to work in concert with contractors to ensure that they had an appropriate stock of batteries available for battery replacement services. This meant some careful logistical planning with contractors in those capital cities without a QBA presence.

Cyber Logistics Australia (CLA) was contracted to transport batteries from QBA warehouses to battery service contractors' sites – as and when required. CLA has a well-known Web page and a good reputation for its round-the-clock fetch-and-carry service for items of all sizes. It had a number of contractors working for the company in all Australian state capital cities. These contractors monitored e-mail requests received by CLA and responded on an internal CLA electronic bidding system. Requests came in on a 24/7 basis, since an 'anytime' service was part of CLA's offering to customers. Contractors would bid for fetch-and-carry business that was reasonably close to their own locations. The bids were for trips that they wished to do at CLA standard prices. If two or more CLA contractors offered to do the same trip the business would go to the first contractor that offered to do the trip within the time and/or other constraints/conditions set by the customer.

A manager in the CCAA breakdown service organization noticed the Web site of Battery Disposals of America (BDA). BDA made money from stripping down dead or unwanted batteries and removing any valuable metals or usable acids. When contacted, BDA was willing to pay for dead batteries arising from CCAA's breakdown service provided these were sent in batches to the USA and that the CCAA arranged shipment. The CCAA contracted CLA to manage the logistics of transporting the batteries. For CLA this meant extending its business internationally. However, it had been planning a move to extend its operations to include Australia's major trading partners. E-mail, fax and telephone contact was established between CCAA, CLA and BDA.

Many CCAA specialist mechanics attending breakdowns had been reporting that, apart from the initial breakdown fault, many of the cars appeared to need various other services. Mechanics often advised clients to get a general service of their vehicle. They felt that it would be helpful (not to say, profitable) if they could service cars using CCAA recommended mechanics. Hence the CCAA began to run a car servicing business. Again this was added to the CCAA list of services with very little additional capital being required. A set of highly competent mechanics was contracted to service CCAA members' vehicles. Part of each of these mechanics' business became servicing CCAA members according to a CCAA specified service. CCAA and the service mechanics meet regularly to agree advertising campaigns, standards of car servicing, education and training needs for the contractors and their employees, and profit sharing in the CCAA car servicing business.

A further set of contractors was organized to fit new windscreens to cars that had broken down on the road or at clients' homes. These contractors were organized in a similar manner to the battery replacement and car service contractors. They increased the set of services that was offered to CCAA members on a seven days a week, round-the-clock basis. The CCAA contracted with Best Windscreens of Australia (BWA) to supply windscreens to the CCAA windscreen replacement contractors. Each of the contractors kept a small stock of windscreens. CLA was contracted to help with the logistics of supplying windscreens to the contractors on a round-the-clock 'as needed' basis. A round-the-clock delivery service was particularly necessary since the stocks of windscreens kept by the contractors were small.

Now consider the structure of the virtual organization of the CCAA, its business partners and the various CCAA contractors. This is illustrated in Figure 10.9.

The organization represented in Figure 10.9 offers more services and value added for clients or customers than can the CCAA alone. Indeed, it probably appears to customers that the CCAA has a larger 'presence' than it actually does. To offer this range of services to its customers the CCAA has had to add very little in terms of real capital structure. The virtual organization depicted can be created relatively quickly in response to perceived customer needs. This can be achieved without the problems of recruiting and training new staff, purchasing new machinery and equipment, or creating new working spaces (and hence possibly erecting new buildings). The role of IT in the CCAA case study is in enabling the necessary communications and hence assisting in the coordination of contractors and business partners.

The structure of the CCAA virtual organization is essentially star shaped, with the CCAA at the hub or centre of the star. Links to

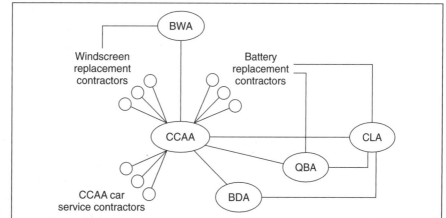

Figure 10.9
The CCAA virtual organization

contractors are highly substitutable and cancelling and/or creating a contract is all that is needed to make or sever linkages with contractors. Links to CLA, QBA, BDA and BWA would require the establishment of more complex business relationships. For these four partners, the services offered are more complex to replace and rearrange than the car service and battery or windscreen replacement offerings. However, each of these companies would be easier to substitute out of the star structure than the hub company CCAA. If the CCAA began to do badly or, even worse, failed, then so too would the virtual organization – and it would be difficult to replace the CCAA. Thus, the star structure does not permit the full flexibility and adaptiveness that is possible in some virtual organizations.

The CCAA, its contractors and alliance partners bring together a range of value-added offerings to people whose cars have broken down. The value chain reworked by the CCAA comprises responding to motorists whose cars have broken down, analysing the breakdown problem, and resolving this problem by enabling the motorist to get to help via repair and replacement services. Previously, if their car had broken down, motorists in Australia relied on the CCAA to get both them and their car to help. For serious breakdowns this is still the case. However, as we saw in the case study, alliance partners and contractors now allow the CCAA to provide a more complete on-the-road, round-the-clock repair and replacement service. The portion of the value chain previously serviced by repair garages is now, in part, offered to CCAA members in the form of a value-added and highly convenient on-the-road service.

This is shown in Figure 10.10, where subchains E-F-G, K-L and M-N involve services to clients that would have previously occurred outside the boundary of CCAA breakdown services. These services would have involved arrangements of much less convenience to motorists whose cars had broken down. Hence, the virtual organization comprising the CCAA, its contractors and alliance partners offer a broader range of products and services that focus on parts of the value chain that were previously outside the narrow focus of the CCAA's basic breakdown service. Thus, the CCAA-based virtual organization has some of the characteristics of the value-alliance model.

Value-alliance model

Value-alliance models bring together a range of inter-related products, services and facilities that are based on an industry value or supply chain. The case study of Wildflowers of Australia explicates this model.

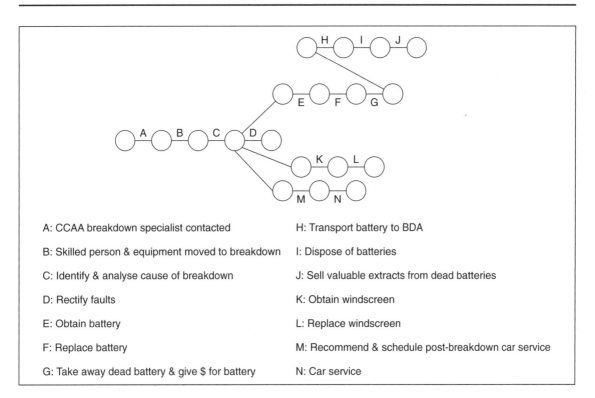

A: CCAA breakdown specialist contacted

B: Skilled person & equipment moved to breakdown

C: Identify & analyse cause of breakdown

D: Rectify faults

E: Obtain battery

F: Replace battery

G: Take away dead battery & give $ for battery

H: Transport battery to BDA

I: Dispose of batteries

J: Sell valuable extracts from dead batteries

K: Obtain windscreen

L: Replace windscreen

M: Recommend & schedule post-breakdown car service

N: Car service

Figure 10.10
The value chain of the CCAA star-alliance

Case study: Wildflowers of Australia

Wildflowers of Australia (WFA) is a national firm that coordinates the ordering, transportation and delivery of flowers in Australia. WFA presents itself as the virtual face to the end consumer and retailer of a number of cooperating partners along an industry supply chain. In terms of actual operations, a number of essential parties are involved, but from the customers' perspective WFA provides a service across the entire value chain. WFA directs and coordinates the orders from retailers and end consumers to growers of Australian wildflowers that can satisfy particular demands.

WFA has extensive information resources regarding the stocks of wildflowers of various types that are being grown and the best (or most appropriate) times for harvesting. Orders from retailers and end customers are accepted via standard electronic forms available on WFA's well-designed Web site. Orders are also accepted by telephone, fax or e-mail. Such orders are transmitted in total or in part to growers who

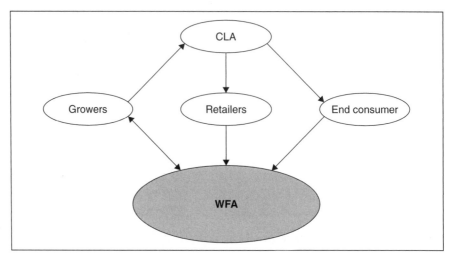

Figure 10.11
Value-alliance model
of WFA

can satisfy them by cutting the appropriate flowers. After cutting the correct flowers in the right quantities, growers call upon Cyber Logistics of Australia (CLA) to deliver the flowers, thus ensuring extra freshness for the end consumer. An overview of the operations of WFA is presented in Figure 10.11.

WFA has arranged for Smart Cards of Australia (SCA) to deal with the recording and processing of transactions within the system of wild-flower provision so that adequate records can be kept and appropriate payments made. Each business and contractor within the virtual organization supplying flowers has a smart card and a device for the input of transaction information. Transaction details are kept on the smart cards. Periodically, SCA downloads and processes the transaction information to give adequate financial accounting and payment details, and the subsequent disbursement of funds for the virtual organization's transactions.

Elements of the re-engineered value chain for WFA are shown in Figure 10.12. Within a number of the organizations shown in this new industry value chain, there are inbound and outbound logistics as well as some handling of the flowers. All these activities take time, which is all the more important given the perishable nature of the product. The value chain for the cut wildflower system coordinated by WFA has a reduced number of steps between grower and end consumer. This ensures less handling of the flowers before final display by the end consumer and, possibly more importantly, less time between when the flowers are cut and displayed. Consequently, the product lasts longer at the point of consumption, giving increased customer satisfaction.

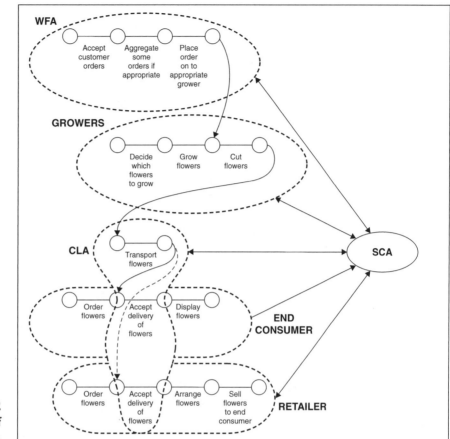

Figure 10.12
Value-alliance of
WFA

WFA and its partners have thus reinvented the cut flower value chain so as to permit an efficient, demand-pull operation that results in increased customer satisfaction. The firms involved in the virtual organization are all specialists, concentrating on their niche market specialisms or core competencies. Logistics has been plucked out of its many places in the traditional value chain and given to a specialist logistics company. The task of recording transaction details, drawing up accounts based on these and making appropriate payments has been taken out of the daily work of a number of players in the industry value chain and given to a specialist smart card-based accounting firm. An essential element of the value-alliance model is that a single virtual organization is presented to the end consumer. In fact, the virtual organization is composed of a number of collaborating and interdependent firms operating along an industry value or supply chain.

Market-alliance model

Organizations based on the market-alliance model come together to coordinate the manufacture, marketing, selling and distribution of a diverse but coherent set of products and services. The market-alliance model differs from the value-alliance model in the sense that several value chains are likely to be involved. From the end customer's perspective, the result is more akin to a marketplace or a community.

Case study: Australian E-Market

Australian E-Market (AEM) provides an online catalogue for consumer durables, including white goods, electrical and electronic goods, and sporting goods. AEM acts as a virtual face to the customer, but serves only to coordinate the marketing, selling and distribution of a coherent set of consumer goods and services. It offers its marketing expertise to the market-alliance members, and has contracted with a number of suitable manufacturers to provide an outlet for their goods and services. AEM also coordinates the logistics requirements for the sale and distribution of these goods with CLA. All payment and transaction processing is arranged in conjunction with SCA. AEM does not purchase the manufacturers' goods itself, but acts as a conduit for a range of goods and services to the end consumer, sharing the profits generated by so doing with the manufacturers and other parties in the market-alliance.

The catalogue is accessible online via the Internet, but is also available to AEM Shoppers' Club members via a CD-ROM and a printed catalogue. AEM Shoppers' Club members pay an annual membership fee of A\$50 and a small charge if they wish to have the CD-ROM and/or paper-based catalogue. Over 100 000 products are available at very attractive discounts. After purchase, and for a small fee, products are delivered from the manufacturer to the customer by CLA. The smart card systems specialist, SCA, takes care of transaction records and payment systems for the AEM operation. The core of the AEM operation consists of its database and its reputation for good deals. Its essence is the provision of information to consumers. The manufacturers who are members of the virtual organization provide the goods that are purchased, and CLA provides the logistics of getting the goods to customers. Thus, AEM has the characteristics of a market-alliance. Figure 10.13 shows the structure of this virtual organization.

Schwartz (1997) provides another example of a market-alliance. Cendant Corporation, the CUC-HFS market-alliance of Walter Forbes and Henry Silverman, is a similar virtual organization to AEM.

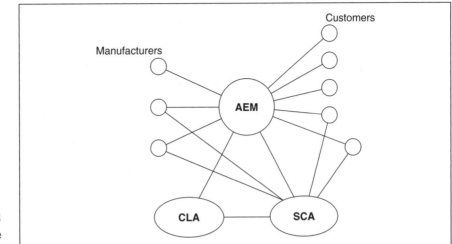

Figure 10.13
The market-alliance
of AEM

CONCLUSION

The virtual organization can obviously take on an infinite array of structures. This chapter has described a number of generic models (co-alliance, star-alliance, value-alliance and market-alliance) and illustrated each of these by way of an original case study. Each case study is an attempt to illustrate the major characteristics of the virtual organization as defined in the earlier sections of this chapter. The case studies are also an attempt to illustrate the criticality of the success factors for virtual organizing (as discussed earlier).

In the Perth Consulting Services (PCS) case study, success depends upon the shared purpose and shared goals of partners. They must trust each another implicitly. They must also recognize that, given their mutual interdependence, any benefit that is derived from their co-alliance virtual organization must be equal. Risk must be seen and accepted as shared among the players. Notwithstanding, they face further significant challenges. Arguably, the nature of their enterprise or innovation is essentially systemic and information and knowledge flows are primarily tacit. Mechanisms for resolving conflicts among the partners – entrepreneurial self-starters used to acting from motives of self-interest – are completely informal, and totally reliant on a trusting relationship. Not surprisingly, therefore, it can be concluded that the people involved, the relationships they construct and the strategies they adopt in operating as a virtual organization are essential to the success of this enterprise (Stafford, 1998).

In the Capital City Automobile Association (CCAA) case study, it could be argued that the potential dominance of the central player means that while a shared purpose is obviously vital, there may be a slightly lower requirement for high levels of trust than in the PCS example. The enterprise or innovation in the CCAA case seems more autonomous than systemic, with information and knowledge flows involving more codified than tacit knowledge. The large established central player would be expected to have well-defined mechanisms for conflict resolution. Such mechanisms could possibly be offered throughout the virtual organization should any disruption occur. Notwithstanding, in some senses, disruption may be less likely to occur; the nature of the business operation may make it easier to specify contractually various outcomes and expectations.

The value-alliance model in the Wildflowers of Australia (WFA) case study stems from the clear mutual benefits derived from this partnering arrangement. Each of the players 'needs' the others in order to provide the requisite level of customer service. As in the CCAA example, the enterprise or innovation involved in WFA is essentially autonomous, involving the transfer of codified information and knowledge. While the partners in the WFA virtual organization may not have any well-defined arrangements for conflict resolution, in all other senses they meet the criteria for successful virtual organizing set down by Chesbrough and Teece (1996).

In the market-alliance model of Australian E-Market (AEM), as in the value-alliance case, there are clear benefits to be derived individually through enacting the shared vision and purpose. In much the same way as with WFA, it seems reasonable to conclude that there are sufficient indicators to suggest that their operation is suitably supported by a virtual organizing strategy.

Given the appropriate conditions and context, the virtual organization offers many attractive benefits as an organizing strategy for the modern enterprise. However, the strengths and potential benefits of virtual organizing need to be weighed against the potential risks and negative impacts. Notwithstanding, the virtual organization may prove to be a low-cost, highly responsive, adaptable and flexible way to organize and compete in modern business environments. New information technologies offer exciting possibilities for new organizational forms and structures into the twenty-first century. This chapter has attempted to characterize the essential features of the virtual organization, considering typical types of processes and activities. However, it has also clearly delineated some of the challenges of virtual organizing, and has argued that caution needs to be exercised in assessing a business opportunity as appropriate for a virtual organization. Certain conditions and criteria would seem to underpin a successful virtual organization venture.

REFERENCES

Benjamin, R. and Wigand, R. (1995). Electronic markets and virtual value chains on the information superhighway. *Sloan Management Review*, 36 (2), 62–72.

Black, J. and Edwards, S. (2000). Emergence of virtual or network organizations: fad or feature. *Journal of Organizational Change Management*, 13, 567–576.

Burn, J., Marshall, P. and Wild, M. (1999). Managing change in the virtual organization. *Proceedings of the 7th European Conference on Information Systems*, Copenhagen, June.

Chesbrough, H. W. and Teece, D. J. (1996). When is virtual virtuous? *Harvard Business Review*, 74 (1), 65–73.

Coutu, D. L. (1998). Organization: trust in virtual teams. *Harvard Business Review*, 76, 20–21.

Czerniawska, F. and Potter, G. (1998). *Business in a Virtual World.* Macmillan.

Dani, S., Burns, N., Backhouse, C. and Kochhar, A. (2006). The implications of organizational culture and trust in the working of virtual teams. *Proceedings of the I MECH E Part B Journal of Engineering Manufacture*, 220, 951–960.

Elliot, S. (2006). Technology-enabled innovation, industry transformation and the emergence of ambient organizations. *Industry and Innovation*, 13, 209–225.

Fenwick, M. and De Cieri, H. (2004). Inter-organizational network participation. *The Journal of Management Development*, 23, 798–817.

Friedman, L. G. (1998). The elusive strategic alliance. In *Web-Weaving: Intranets, Extranets and Strategic Alliances* (P. Lloyd and P. Boyle, eds), Butterworth-Heinemann.

Goldman, S. L., Nagel, R. N. and Preiss, K. (1995). *Agile Competitors and Virtual Organizations: Strategies for Enriching the Customer.* Van Nostrand Reinhold.

Grenier, R. and Metes, G. (1995). *Going Virtual: Moving Your Organization into the 21st Century.* Prentice Hall.

Hedberg, B., Dahlgren, G., Hansson, J. and Olve, N. (1994). *Virtual Organizations and Beyond: Discover Imaginary Systems.* Wiley.

Henning, K. (1998). *The Digital Enterprise: How Digitisation is Redefining Business.* Random House.

IMPACT Programme (1998). *Exploiting the Wired-Up World: Best Practice in Managing Virtual Organizations*, IMPACT.

Kierzkowski, Z. (2005). Towards virtual enterprises. *Human Factors and Ergonomics in Manufacturing*, 15, 49–69.

Lin, L. and Lu, I. (2005). Adoption of virtual organization by Taiwanese electronics firms. *Journal of Organizational Change Management*, 18, 184–200.

Lipnack, J. and Stamps, J. (1998). Why virtual teams? In *Web-Weaving: Intranets, Extranets and Strategic Alliances* (P. Lloyd and P. Boyle, eds), Butterworth-Heinemann.

Magretts, J. (1998). The power of virtual integration: an interview with Dell Computer's Michael Dell. *Harvard Business Review*, 76 (2), 73–84.

Marshall, P., Burn, J., Wild, M. and McKay, J. (1999). Virtual organizations: structure and strategic positioning. *Proceedings of the 7th European Conference on Information Systems*, Copenhagen, June.

Metes, G., Gundry, J. and Bradish, P. (1998). *Agile Networking: Competing through the Internet and Intranets*. Prentice Hall.

Pfeffer, J. (1998). *The Human Equation*. Harvard Business School Press.

Preiss, K., Goldman, S. L. and Nagel, R. N. (1998). *Co-operate to Compete*. Van Nostrand Reinhold.

Schwartz, E. I. (1997). Its! Not! Retail! *Wired Magazine Online*, 5 November. http://www.wired.com/wired/archive/5.11/cuc.html

Siebel, T. M. and House, P. (1999). *Cyber Rules: Strategies for Excelling at e-Business*. Currency-Doubleday.

Sor, R. (1999). Virtual organizations: a case study of the housing construction industry in Western Australia. *Proceedings of the Australasian Conference on Information Systems*, Wellington, December.

Stafford, E. R. (1998). Using co-operative strategies to make alliances work. In *Organizational Transformation through Business Process Reengineering: Applying the Lessons Learned* (V. Sethi and W. R. King, eds) pp. 315–329, Prentice Hall.

Thorne, K. (2005). Designing virtual organizations? Themes and trends in political and organizational discourse. *Journal of Management Development*, 24, 580–606.

Turban, E., McLean, E. and Wetherbe, J. (1999). *Information Technology for Management*. Wiley.

Upton, D. M. and McAfee, A. (1996). The real virtual factory. *Harvard Business Review*, 74 (4), 123–133.

Walker, H. (2006). The virtual organisation: a new organisational form? *International Journal of Networking and Virtual Organisations*, 3, 25–41.

Walters, D. (2005). Performance planning and control in virtual business structures. *Production Planning and Control*, 16, 226–239.

Wiesenfeld, B. M., Raghuram, S. and Garud, R. (1998). Communication patterns as determinants of organizational identification in a virtual organization. *Journal of Computer Mediated Communication*, 3 (4). http://jcmc.indiana.edu/vol3/issue4/wiesenfeld.html

CHAPTER **11**

Web services as an enabler for virtual organizations[1]

Oliver Prokein, Titus Faupel
and Daniel Gille

INTRODUCTION

Few other technologies have been so keenly discussed in recent years as Web services. A Web service is a software system based upon the e**X**tensible **M**arkup **L**anguage (XML) and is designed to support inter-operable machine-to-machine interaction over a network. In order to support intercompany cooperation, the Internet, as an existing infra-structure, can be used. As a result of automated transactions, Web services promise a reduction of transaction costs, especially within the settlement phase (Löwer and Picot, 2002). Thus, Web services possess the potential to effectuate an increase in efficiency and effectiveness within intercompany cooperation. This potential, in turn, offers new possibilities for enabling a further move towards the realization of virtual organizations.

However, due to a lack of knowledge about the application and associated problems of Web services, these opportunities are often not attained in practice. As a case in point, only a few empirical articles exist that analyse the employment and related problems of Web services (Cap Gemini Ernst & Young, 2002; Roger, 2004). This chapter presents the results of an intersectoral survey within German industry and aims at analysing the employment and the principal associated problems of Web services for intercompany cooperation. The results can be seen as a first step for evaluating the potential of Web services to facilitate a more flexible way of intercompany cooperation, thereby providing the foundation for a further 'virtualization' of companies.

The survey was completed in November 2004. It addressed companies which, as we knew from case studies, use Web services, and locations where we assumed that they employ Web services. Thus, business-to-business services and financial services possessed the largest share of the sample, each with 15.6 per cent. A total of 77 questionnaires were analysed, whereby 57.1 per cent of the surveys were completed by members at the first or second management level within each firm.

In the next section we first describe the basics of virtual organizations and possible reasons for their largely insufficient realization in practice. Subsequently, the basic properties and functions of Web services and their implications on transaction costs are presented as a means for further enabling virtual organizations. Thereafter, the results of the survey are presented, and we examine where and why Web services were employed within the companies in the context of intercompany cooperation. In addition, we consider the related barriers. Subsequently, these barriers are analysed more specifically; by means of an exploratory factor analysis, we identify the main problems in the use of Web services for intercompany cooperation. Thereupon, we weigh these identified problems and discuss them. The chapter ends with a summary and conclusions.

VIRTUAL ORGANIZATIONS AND INFORMATION TECHNOLOGY

Definition of virtual organizations

The notion of virtual organizations is based on the simple idea of 'running a business without having to run a business'. According to this idea, the core of a virtual organization concentrates on developing and/or owning the fundamental business idea as well as orchestrating the whole process, while the different steps of the creation of value are delegated to external partners (Semich, 1994). Besides this somewhat utopian and convenient idea, in reality the tendency towards virtual organizations can also be derived from the necessities of increasingly volatile and competitive markets which require the large-scale outsourcing of processes (Klein, 1994). Furthermore, this concentration on core competencies connected with the deputation of major processes of value creation to other corporations is supported by the new possibilities of information technologies, which are widely regarded as the main enabler and success factor of virtualization (Klein and Kronen, 1995).

According to this visionary idea and its concrete manifestations, one can define a virtual organization as a type of cooperation of independent enterprises that deliver performance on the basis of a common vision. Each unit participates by yielding its core competence and the entirety of units acts towards third parties as a uniform corporation. Centralized management functions for designing, controlling and developing the virtual organization are abandoned. Instead, the need for coordination and adjustment is covered by adequate information and communications systems (Arnold *et al.*, 1995; Mertens *et al.*, 1998).

A simple model for the development of virtual organizations

The development from a 'traditional' enterprise towards a virtual organization can be described by deploying a straightforward five-step development model (Mertens *et al.*, 1998). Starting from a fully integrated corporation (phase 0), the regional concentration of activities leads to a reduction in the number of business units (phase 1). The development of legally independent business units as a result of outsourcing or the separation of individual departments leads to the case where two independent corporations deliver common performance on the basis of mutual economic dependency (phase 2). In a third step, suppliers and customers are integrated via the application of information and communications systems (phase 3). Finally, the consequent continuation of phase 2 leads to a subsequent outsourcing of all processes until the core competence of the initial corporation consists of leading and coordinating the virtual organization (phase 4) (see Figure 11.1).

In practice, the transitions from phase 0 to phase 1 as well as to phase 2 and 3 are phenomena that can be easily and widely observed in the modern economy: due to the increasing pressure of market requirements, companies start to concentrate their business activities in certain areas, source out parts of their value generation that do not belong to their

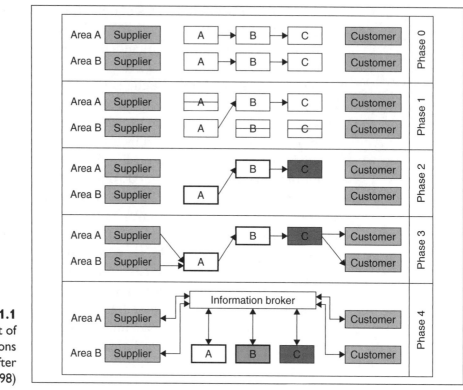

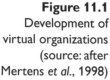

Figure 11.1
Development of
virtual organizations
(source: after
Mertens *et al.*, 1998)

core competencies and get increasingly connected to their suppliers and customers. The main drivers for this development are information and communications technologies like the Internet or EDI (electronic data interchange) which contribute to a substantial decrease in the transaction costs necessary for coordinating the value-creating activities (Müller *et al.*, 2003). For example, the integration of suppliers via EDI has been a common practice in the retail and automotive sectors for more than two decades (Strassner, 2005). Furthermore, electronic tools like workflow or project management systems facilitate the cooperation and coordination of independent enterprises or business units that pursue a common goal (Mertens *et al.*, 1998).

However, examples of fully 'virtualized' corporations (phase 4) are still hard to find. One of the reasons for this observation can be found in the complexity of such arrangements: in the final stage of 'virtualization', a corporation acts as a broker of information, competencies and resources. Due to multiple relationships with cooperation partners, suppliers and customers, coordination is conducted by the deployment of *market mechanisms* (Klein, 1994). The application of market mechanisms for sourcing out business activities, in turn, requires a substantial decrease in external compared to internal transaction costs (Coase, 1937). Even though the general potential of 'traditional' IT systems such as the Internet for decreasing transaction costs is undisputed, it can be argued that it has not been fully sufficient for enabling the complete virtualization of firms. More powerful and flexible forms of IT are needed to further take advantage of the benefits of virtual organizations by supporting the establishment of market mechanisms.

Web services can be seen as a new technology for improving intercompany cooperation (Hagel and Brown, 2001). They facilitate spontaneous connections with unknown transaction partners, are platform independent and can be easily combined in order to meet increasingly complex business and coordination tasks. Therefore, the notion exists that Web services have a great potential for further decreasing transaction costs especially in intercompany application scenarios (Löwer and Picot, 2002). In order to evaluate the potential of Web services for the realization of virtual organizations, the following question arises: 'To what extent are Web services able to further decrease transaction costs compared to other forms of IT?'. After a short description of the basics of Web services, this question will be addressed in the following section.

BASICS OF WEB SERVICES

Definition and characteristics of Web services

The W3-Consortium defines Web services '... as a software system designed to support interoperable machine-to-machine interaction over a network. It has an interface described in a machine-processable format (specifically Web Services Description Language (WSDL) – see Christensen et al., 2001). Other systems interact with the Web service in a manner prescribed by its description using Simple Object Access Protocol (SOAP) (Gudgin et al., 2003) messages, typically conveyed using HTTP with an XML serialization in conjunction with other Web-related standards' (Booth et al., 2004). The services are published in the service registry Universal Description, Discovery and Integration (UDDI) which can be employed within the Internet, extranet and intranet. The service registry UDDI is divided into so-called white, yellow and green 'sides'. The white sides contain information such as the name and address of the enterprise. The yellow sides contain information regarding the industry classification. The green sides contain technical information (e.g. the specific protocol) (Bryan et al., 2002).

249

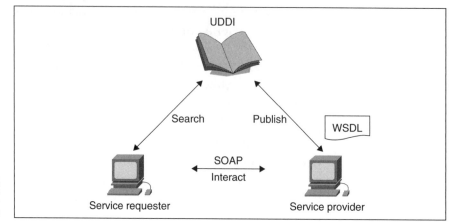

Figure 11.2
Service-oriented
architecture

WSDL, SOAP and UDDI are all based upon the open standard XML. The Web services framework intends to provide a standards-based realization of the service-oriented architecture (Figure 11.2) (Curbera *et al.*, 2003). Typically the service provider publishes a WSDL description of its Web service. The requester accesses this description using a UDDI or other type of registry and requests the execution of the Web service by sending a SOAP message to it.

In the preliminary stages of the deployment of Web services, a set of goals was pursued, whereby some of the goals are reflected in the characteristics of this technology (Alonso *et al.*, 2004; Löwer and Picot, 2002; Newcomer, 2002; Zimmermann *et al.*, 2003):

- *Standardization and openness.* WSDL, SOAP and UDDI are open standards and developed by different consortia for provider-independent deployment.
- *Interoperability.* Web services can be employed independently of hardware platforms and operating systems.
- *Encapsulation.* Web services are self-contained services which are described by their description files and perform a clearly defined task.
- *Loose coupling.* The published functionalities of the defined interfaces enable coupling without complex integration. Furthermore, this implicates the usage of Web services of unknown transaction partners. The messages can thereby be exchanged either synchronously or asynchronously.
- *Service composition.* Business Process Execution Languages (e.g. BPEL) enable the composition of a set of single Web services into new Web services representing entire business processes.

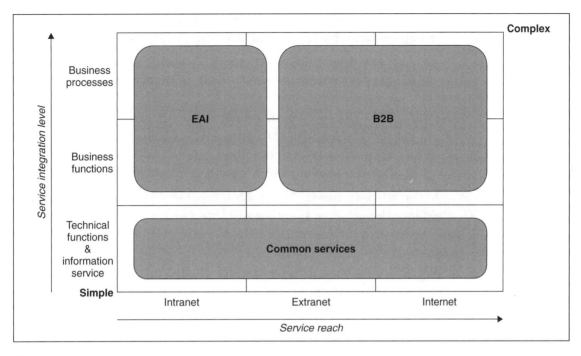

Figure 11.3
Usage scenarios of Web services (source: Zimmermann *et al.*, 2003)

■ *Reuse and flexibility.* Existing applications can be reused and easily integrated into existing or new systems. This implies high flexibility and makes it possible for enterprises to maintain their existing heterogeneous systems landscape.

These characteristics offer the possibility for spontaneous and cheap connections and thus support the development of virtual organizations. After defining Web services and their substantial characteristics, we now describe their usage scenarios.

Usage scenarios of Web services

Basically, one can differentiate between the three scenarios of Web services – enterprise application integration (EAI), business-to-business (B2B) and common services (e.g. a company-wide address service).

As illustrated in Figure 11.3, the usage scenarios can be placed within an application-to-application (A2A) complexity matrix (Zimmermann *et al.*, 2003). The two dimensions of the matrix are the service integration level and service reach. Both dimensions are divided into three sections.

In the vertical axis, the integration level is mapped. Thereby one can distinguish between (Zimmermann *et al.*, 2003):

1. Elementary functions:
    (a) *Information services*, which normally perform read-only access;
    (b) *Technical functions* such as basic general-purpose utilities;
2. *Business functions* with transactional behaviour (i.e. read-write access to service data); and
3. *Business process* externalization along the value chain.

On the abscissa, the service reach is represented, which can be classified into the intranet, extranet and Internet.

The essence of this A2A complexity matrix is that the internal implementation of Web services is significantly easier to achieve than a worldwide B2B undertaking. Since the aim of this contribution is to analyse whether Web services are an enabler for virtual organizations, we focus on the use of Web services for intercompany cooperation (B2B).

The effect of Web services on transaction costs

The above analysis pointed out that the growing importance of external transaction costs, which is associated with increasing virtualization, is one of the main obstacles for virtual organizations. In this section, the effects of Web services on transaction costs that exceed those of 'traditional' Internet technology are examined with special regard to B2B scenarios. In general, a transaction can be differentiated into five specific phases which are presented in Figure 11.4. Costs emerge in each of these phases, which add up to the entire transaction costs.

It can be shown that Web services can decrease these costs in all phases (Löwer and Picot, 2002; Löwer, 2003):

■ *Initiation.* Internet technology can already decrease the costs of the initiation of a transaction (e.g. inquiry and comparison of propositions by means of a search engine). UDDI offers further potential for cost reduction. Thereby, a detailed description

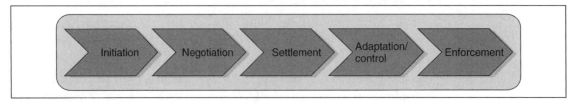

Figure 11.4
Transaction phase model

and an automated search of services and their providers are possible.

■ *Negotiation.* Within the scope of the negotiation phase, price, achievement and completion must be settled. By specifying the services (such as the specification of the message, which is to be exchanged) and the description how these services can be accessed on a technical level (such as the protocol used), WSDL offers outstanding support for this. Further important information, such as the costs of the service and the legal address of the provider, can be supplemented by UDDI.

■ *Settlement.* SOAP and the process-oriented concept BPEL allow the automated settlement of transactions. The automated settlement of transactions is the most important source of transaction cost reductions through Web services, since in many applications manual work can be extensively eliminated.

■ *Adaptation/Control.* The available transparency of the electronic settlement in Web services can decrease control costs. This transparency (e.g. log files) enables an objective and simple assessment of the achievements and possible deviations of a service.

■ *Enforcement.* Finally, it is conceivable that in the case of a necessary enforcement (e.g. in case of service failure) the automatic search for an alternative service can decrease transaction costs. However, human intervention will probably still prevail in this case.

As a result, Web services allow cost reduction in all transaction phases and thus can help in reducing the costs of virtualization. Consequently, it can be assumed that Web services will be an enabler for virtual organizations. Compared to theory, however, everyday business life frequently appears quite different. In order to assess the current deployment of Web services and the corresponding opportunities and problems, we performed an empirical study, the results of which are presented in the following section.

DESCRIPTIVE PRESENTATION OF THE EMPIRICAL RESULTS

Base data of the empirical study

The following analysis is based on data from a survey about the deployment of Web services in German industry (Prokein and Sackmann,

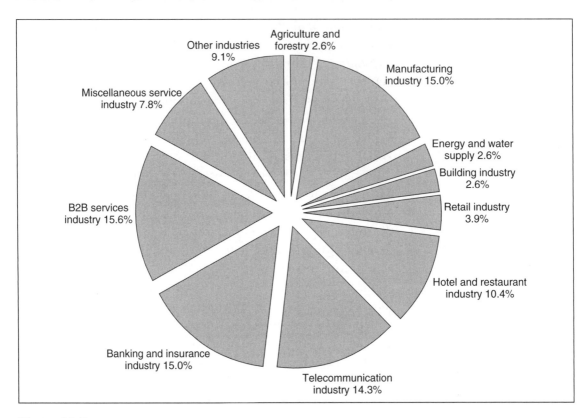

Figure 11.5
Distribution of industry classification in the sample (*n* = 77)

2005). Since the use of the World Wide Web (WWW) is prevalent in German industry, the survey took place by means of an online questionnaire. The answering of the questionnaires took place between the beginning of October and beginning of November 2004. Overall, 77 enterprises were involved in the study. The survey addressed companies which, as we knew from case studies, use Web services, and locations where we assumed that Web services are employed. Thus, the sample was comprised predominantly of enterprises which already use Web services and can make statements about their experiences. Figure 11.5 presents the distribution of the industry classification in the sample. Addressees of the survey were decision makers at upper management levels. The questionnaire was answered by 41.6 per cent of decision makers at the highest management level and by 15.6 per cent at the second management levels. The enterprises in the sample were 27.8 per cent small enterprises, 25.0 per cent medium-sized enterprises and 47.2 per cent large enterprises.[2] The content of the survey was specified after a detailed literature review and a number of expert interviews.[3]

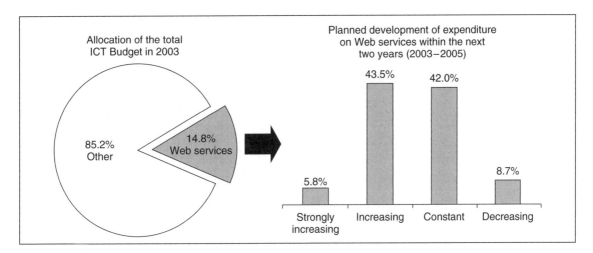

Figure 11.6
Investments in Web services

Investments in Web services

In the year 2003, the interviewed companies declared that they invest 8.2 per cent (basis $n = 50$) of their total expenditures in ICT.

From this investment, 14.8 per cent was spent on Web services (Figure 11.6). It can be assumed that this proportion will increase in the year 2005. With 49.3 per cent (basis $n = 64$), almost every second company plans to increase their investment in Web services, whereas 42.0 per cent plan to maintain and only 8.7 per cent plan to decrease expenditure. The high share of companies that will increase their investments can be seen as a success indicator of Web services.

Employment of Web services

Web services can generally be used for in-plant and cross-plant networking. About two-thirds (66.7 per cent, $n = 51$) of the interviewed companies use Web services for in-plant networking and 64.6 per cent of these plan to extend this activity within the next two years. In the context of cross-plant networking, one can differentiate between the supply and the demand of Web services. Some 59.3 per cent (basis $n = 54$) demand Web services from other companies and of these 46.8 per cent plan to expand this activity within the next two years. In contrast to the demand of Web services, only 46.2 per cent (basis $n = 52$) supply their own Web services to other companies. However, 54.1 per cent of these firms plan to increase this activity within the next two years.

255

Previous surveys found that Web services are primarily employed within in-plant networking (Cap Gemini Ernst & Young, 2002). Contrary to these results, it can be shown that Web services are no longer dominating only in-plant networking, but also cross-plant networking. Furthermore, 61.7 per cent (basis $n = 60$) of the companies interviewed declared that Web services will become more important for cross-plant networking in the future.

In order to evaluate the employment and importance of Web services for intercompany cooperation we modified the value chain of Porter (1985a; 2001). The value chain disaggregates the firm into its distinct activities, whereupon a distinction between *primary* and *support activities* is made. The primary activities are those involved in the physical creation of the product, its marketing and delivery to buyers, and its support and servicing after sales (Porter, 1985b), whereas the support activities provide the inputs and infrastructure that allow the primary activities to take place. Although the application of Porter's value chain does not apply for completely virtualized enterprises (phase 4), it is a suitable instrument for analysing the current deployment of Web services as long as the final phase is not reached. In our modified value chain, the primary activities are composed of *logistics, operations, marketing and sales* and *after sales services.*[4] Within the support activities, we widely retained the original structure. However, Porter subsumes networking under the activity 'Firm Infrastructure'. We factored out networking in order to distinguish between in-plant and cross-plant activities. For this reason, we substituted the original activity of Firm Infrastructure by the residual factors *accounting, control, finance, executive board and miscellaneous organization*. The further support activities are *human resource management, research and development* and *procurement*.

The respondents had the possibility to evaluate the employment of Web services for each activity on a scale of 1 to 4 (1 = high degree of importance; 2 = relatively high degree of importance; 3 = relatively low degree of importance; and 4 = low degree of importance). The results listed in Figure 11.7 present the sum of responses for *high* and *relatively high* degrees of importance.

It can be shown that the companies attach a (relatively) high degree of importance to the use of Web services for intercompany cooperation within *accounting, control, finance, executive board and miscellaneous organization* (39.0 per cent, basis $n = 59$), *human resource management* (14.3 per cent, basis $n = 56$), *research and development* (17.2 per cent, basis $n = 58$) and *procurement* (37.3 per cent, basis $n = 59$).

Within the primary activities, our results indicate that of highest importance for the use of Web services are *marketing and sales* and *after*

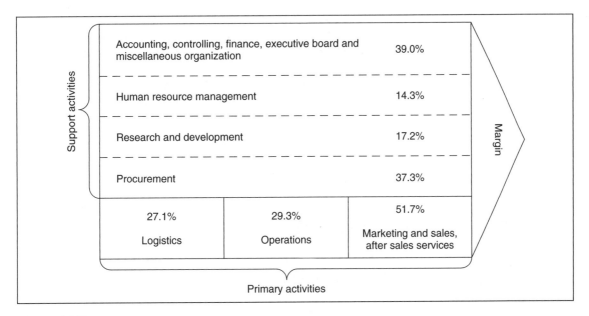

Figure 11.7
Employment of Web services for intercompany cooperation (sums of 'high' and 'relatively high' degrees of importance)

sales services (51.7 per cent, $n = 58$), whereas only 29.3 per cent (basis $n = 58$) attach a (relatively) high degree of importance to *operations* and 27.3 per cent (basis $n = 59$) to *logistics*.

After illustrating the deployment of Web services within companies, we now further examine the applications of Web services for intercompany cooperation.

Applications of Web services for intercompany cooperation

On the basis of the completed expert interviews and a comprehensive literature search, we identified six main applications of the use of Web services for intercompany cooperation. The respondents had the possibility to evaluate these on a scale from 1 to 4 (1 = high degree of importance; 2 = relatively high degree of importance; 3 = relatively low degree of importance; and 4 = low degree of importance). The listed results in Figure 11.8 present the sum of responses for both *high* and *relatively high* degrees of importance.

The primary application of Web services is *payment transactions*. With 58.8 per cent (basis $n = 44$), the companies interviewed attach the greatest degree of importance to the use of Web services within the scope of *payment transactions*. Due to the characteristics of encapsulation

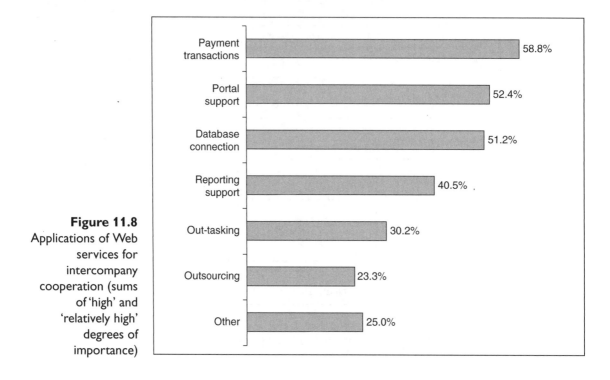

Figure 11.8
Applications of Web services for intercompany cooperation (sums of 'high' and 'relatively high' degrees of importance)

and loose coupling, the Web services of other companies can be easily integrated into portals (Puschmann and Alt, 2004). Some 52.4 per cent (basis $n = 42$) attach a (relatively) high degree of importance to the use of Web services in order to *support a portal*. The results further show that Web services are well suited for *database connection* (51.2 per cent, basis $n = 43$) and *reporting support* (40.5 per cent, basis $n = 42$). Surprisingly, only 30.2 per cent (basis $n = 43$) attach a (relatively) high degree of importance to *out-tasking* and *outsourcing* (23.3 per cent, basis $n = 43$). Thus, it can be argued that Web services have not fully developed their potential for an extensive virtualization of German industry thus far. In order to grasp the relatively low importance of Web services for out-tasking or outsourcing we will analyse the barriers to intercompany deployment in the following section.

Barriers to intercompany deployment of Web services

As well as the applications of Web services we identified 15 barriers on the basis of expert interviews and a comprehensive literature search. The respondents could evaluate the barriers on a scale from 1 to 5 (1 = high degree of importance; 2 = relatively high degree of importance; 3 = relatively low degree of importance; 4 = low degree of importance; and 5 = no importance). The results in Table 11.1 present the sum of responses pertaining to *high* and *relatively high* degrees of importance.

The results are based upon the answers of companies that indicated they were familiar with the technology of Web services. Surprisingly, *insufficient standardization* was rated as the largest barrier. About 77.6 per cent (basis $n = 49$) of the companies attach a (relatively) high degree of importance to this barrier. This contradicts one of the main goals of the technology, namely standardization. As the second and third largest barriers, the companies rated the *complex integration of IT infrastructure* (66.0 per cent, basis $n = 50$) and *small spread of customers* (55.1 per cent, basis $n = 49$) respectively. Astonishingly, not even every second company attaches a (relatively) high degree of importance to *insufficient security of Web services* (48.0 per cent, basis $n = 50$). The lowest degree of importance is attached to the two barriers *retention of*

Table 11.1

Barriers to the intercompany deployment of Web services

Variable	Percentage of 'high' or 'relatively high' responses
Insufficient standardization	77.6%
Complex integration of IT infrastructure	66.0%
Small spread of customers	55.1%
Complex integration of existing processes	54.0%
Other security problems	52.0%
Legal problems	49.0%
Insufficient security of Web services	48.0%
Lack of know-how of the employee	44.9%
Loss of control of own data	41.7%
Unobservability of malpractice by transaction partner	38.6%
Insufficient quality of service	38.3%
Costs exceed benefits	36.2%
Existing network is sufficient	34.8%
Retention of information by transaction partners	27.7%
Information abuse by transaction partners	17.0%

information by transaction partners (27.7 per cent, basis $n = 47$) and *information abuse by transaction partners* (17.0 per cent, basis $n = 47$).

Overall, it appears that a large number of barriers to using Web services for intercompany cooperation still exist. In order to tap the full potential of this technology, it is important to deal with these barriers and search for a solution to overcome them. For this reason, a closer view of the barriers listed in Table 11.1 is presented in the following section.

INVESTIGATION AND INTERPRETATION OF THE BARRIERS TO INTERCOMPANY COOPERATION

Investigation of the barriers using factor analysis

The descriptive view is well suited to obtaining a ranking order for the barriers. However, due to the multitude of barriers, there are several interpretation problems. The multitude of barriers leads, for example, to a high degree of complexity. Furthermore, it is not warranted that all the barriers are independent from each other. If the barriers are not independent from each other, this could lead to errors within the analysis of interactions.[5]

In order to approach these problems, we used an exploratory factor analysis. The starting point of this method is a large number of variables, of which it is *a priori* not known, if and in which manner, they are correlated to each other (Backhaus *et al.*, 2003). In the context of the factor analysis those variables which correlate in the statistical sense are grouped together into a factor. Thus, we use exploratory factor analysis[6] in order to analyse the correlations between the 15 identified barriers (Table 11.1). The result is a reduced number of independent determinants (factors) of barriers.

However, before the exploratory factor analysis can be executed, the set of data must be examined to see if the method can be applied. Therefore, we use the variable-specific test of measure of sampling adequacy (MSA). According to the evaluation of Kaiser and Rice (Kaiser, 1970; Kaiser and Rice, 1974), exploratory factor analysis can be applied to data whose MSA value is 0.5 or greater. Having applied the MSA test to our set of data, we discovered that – except for the variable *small spread of customers/suppliers* (MSA = 0.46) – every variable takes a value greater than 0.5. Thus, the variable *small spread of customers/suppliers* has to be excluded.[7] The MSA value for the entire sample is 0.76. Kaiser and Rice rate this value as 'middling' (Kaiser and Rice, 1974) for factor-analytic purposes. Applying the Bartlett test[8] to the data shows that it is well suited to a factor analysis.[9] Thus, the requirements for executing the exploratory factor analysis are regarded as fulfilled. This also means that the remaining barriers are dependent on each other.

Using the Kaiser criterion[10] (Kaiser, 1958), we could retain four independent factors (Tables 11.2 to 11.5) with eigenvalues greater than 1. In the next step, the barriers have to be assigned to the identified factors. Thereby, a barrier is assigned to one factor if the factor loading[11] of a barrier is greater than 0.5 (Backhaus *et al.*, 2003).

Table 11.2
Factor 1 – security problems

Variable	Factor loading
Other security problems	0.86
Insufficient security of Web services	0.91
Loss of control of own data	0.75
Information abuse by transaction partners	0.85

Table 11.3
Factor 2 – technical and economic integration problems

Variable	Factor loading
Insufficient standardization	0.80
Complex integration of IT infrastructure	0.79
Complex integration of existing processes	0.59
Lack of know-how of the employee	0.82
Costs exceed benefits	0.85

Table 11.4
Factor 3 – not named

Variable	Factor loading
Complex integration of existing processes	0.67
Insufficient quality of service	0.57
Existing network is sufficient (e.g. EDI)	0.90
Retention of information by transaction partners	0.53

Table 11.5

Factor 4 – distrust towards transaction partners

Variable	Factor loading
Legal problems	0.85
Unobservability of malpractice by transaction partners	0.80
Retention of information by transaction partners	0.52

In the following, we present each factor that is derived from the exploratory factor analysis.

Factor 1 summarizes such barriers that, in particular, reflect statements about technical security problems and the risk of the loss or abuse of personal data (Table 11.2). This factor is therefore interpreted as 'security problems'.

As one can see, the factor loadings for all the four barriers take a value greater than 0.5. This implies that all the barriers are related to factor 1. The barrier *insufficient security of Web services* has the highest factor loading of 0.91. The barriers *other security problems* (factor loading of 0.86) and *loss of control of own data* (factor loading of 0.75) also have a high correlation to the factor but less than that of the barrier *insufficient security of Web services*.

Factor 2 summarizes barriers that are particularly associated with the integration of the technology into the company (Table 11.3). This factor can therefore be interpreted as 'technical and economical integration problems'. As one can see, the barrier *costs exceed benefits* has a high positive correlation with this factor; therefore, we can conclude that the cost/benefit ratio primarily depends on technical and economical integration problems.

The interpretation of factor 3 (Table 11.4) is more complicated in that the four listed barriers cannot be classified as unambiguous. With regard to the two barriers *insufficient quality of service* (e.g. availability) and *existing network is sufficient* (e.g. EDI), one could interpret this factor as 'insufficient performance' of Web services. However, the other two barriers cannot be subsumed under 'insufficient performance'. For this reason, factor 3 is not clearly interpretable. By reason of the fact that this factor is not interpretable, we will no longer consider and analyse this factor.

Factor 4 (see Table 11.5) includes barriers that deal with aspects of distrust towards the transaction partner and the uncertainty concerning legal problems. Thus, this factor is interpreted as 'distrust towards transaction partners'.

Table 11.6
Ratings of the identified factors

Variable	Percentage of 'high' or 'relatively high' responses
Technical and economic integration problems	80.0%
Security problems	62.0%
Distrust towards transaction partners	59.2%

Weighing the identified factors

Having identified the four factors we weighed them among each other in order to rate the different factors. Therefore, we examined the portion of companies that ascribe at least one of the listed barriers for a factor a (relatively) high degree of importance. The results are presented in Table 11.6.

One can see that the most important factor is *technical and economical integration problems*. Some 80.0 per cent (basis $n = 50$) of the companies attach a (relatively) high degree of importance to at least one of the barriers listed in Table 11.3.

The second most important factor is *security problems*. According to the barriers listed in Table 11.2, 62.0 per cent (basis $n = 50$) attach a (relatively) high degree of importance to at least one of the barriers.

The least important factor is *distrust towards transaction partners*. About 59.2 per cent (basis $n = 49$) of the companies attach a (relatively) high degree of importance to at least one listed barrier in Table 11.5.

Discussion of the identified factors

In this section, we discuss the identified factors. Therefore, we examine those companies that: (1) use Web services for intercompany cooperation; and (2) ascribe a (relatively) high degree of importance to at least one of the listed barriers in the corresponding factor table.

Technical and economical integration problems

According to Brynjolfsson (2003), companies cannot realize an increase in efficiency merely by investments in new technologies; in order to realize an increase in efficiency in terms of productivity growth, it is necessary to further invest in organizational changes (Brynjolfsson and Hitt, 2000).

Organizational changes can comprise business process re-engineering, work practices or changes in the whole organizational structure. Changes in work practices consist of increased delegation of authority to individual teams, increased investments in training and screening for education as well as incentive systems that reward and encourage high team performance (Brynjolfsson and Hitt, 1998). However, these investments are up to four times larger than the investments in the technology itself (Brynjolfsson, 2003).

Our survey shows that 94.1 per cent (basis $n = 33$) of the companies react with further training of staff. Almost every third company (32.4 per cent, basis $n = 33$) regarded it as necessary to employ new staff. Furthermore, 24.2 per cent (basis $n = 33$) indicated that they had to carry out a reorganization of their organizational structure. We thereby discovered that the longer Web services are established within an enterprise, the more reorganization is conducted.

Security problems

IT security is often a key success factor for the acceptance of a technology. Areas of application and economic benefits can only be developed if, through the implementation of technical security mechanisms, critical and important data can be prevented from attacks and misuse (Müller, 2006a; 2006b). However, in the past, one could see that the development of security mechanisms follows the development of technology (Eggs and Müller, 2001). Although Web services are still an emerging technology, several ambitious efforts are being made to develop uniform security standards. Over the past few years, several standards bodies (e.g. W3C, OASIS and Liberty Alliance) have been developing standards and specifications in order to provide secure schemes for Web services (Atkinson et al., 2002). Security is provided if each of the four security goals of confidentiality, integrity, accountability and availability are satisfied (Müller et al., 2003).

The survey states that 87.0 per cent (basis $n = 23$) of the companies are likely to increasingly invest in IT security technologies. Furthermore, 72.7 per cent (basis $n = 22$) declared that it was necessary to develop and introduce additional IT security directives for their staff.

Distrust towards transaction partners

From an economics perspective, the problem of distrust towards transaction partners can be explained using the Principal Agent Theory

(Kieser and Walgenbach, 2003; Richter and Furubotn, 2003). The starting point of the Principal Agent Theory is the assumption that information is asymmetrically distributed (Mas-Colell *et al.*, 1995). This can lead to adverse selection and moral hazard problems (Kräkel, 1999; Kreps, 1990). Both adverse selection and moral hazards can be explanations for the existence of *distrust towards transaction partners*. In order to limit adverse selection, the better informed (agent) can signal the quality of his Web services, e.g. by the use of the indication of references of former cooperation partners (i.e. signalling). Another possibility is that the worse informed (principal) tries to get information about the quality of the supplier (i.e. screening). Moral hazard problems can be limited by countermeasures after a deal is closed. There are two solutions to this problem. The worse informed can monitor the actions of the better informed (i.e. monitoring). Monitoring has the purpose of circumscribing the behaviour of the better informed. The other solution is *bonding*. Bonding refers to actions or arrangements that seek to align the interests of agents with those of principles. The supplier of a Web service (i.e. agent) can, for example, assume liability if his service fails and damage is caused at the service demander (i.e. principal).

A possible indication that distrust towards a transaction partner exists is the fact that the companies mainly connect to well-known transaction partners. Half of the companies (50.0 per cent, $n = 22$) use Web services solely for bilateral networking. Furthermore, no company publishes its Web services in the public UDDI, whereas 12.1 per cent (basis $n = 33$) use the UDDI within the scope of their extranet.

SUMMARY AND CONCLUSIONS

The underlying goal of this chapter was to assess the potential of Web services for enabling a further virtualization of companies beyond the scope of previous forms of IT. We provided a detailed analysis of the current state of the application and perceived importance of Web services in practice. On the basis of an empirical study within German industry, it was pointed out: (1) where Web services are employed in companies for intercompany cooperation; and (2) what main problems can be identified and analysed that are associated with this deployment.

The survey indicates that almost 50 per cent of the companies that already invest in Web services plan to increase their investments within the next two years. This can be seen as a success indicator for Web services. With regard to the primary and support activities of a company, we discovered that Web services are primarily deployed within the primary activity of *marketing and sales and after sales services* (51.7 per cent). The least number of Web services are employed within the support activity of *human resource management* (14.3 per cent). In our analysis regarding the application of Web services we ascertained that Web services are primarily used for the support of *payment transactions* (58.8 per cent) and least used for *outsourcing* (23.8 per cent). The latter result implies an inferior importance of Web services for the formation of virtual organizations.

In order to identify the main problems of Web services for intercompany cooperation we used an exploratory factor analysis. In doing so, a multitude of barriers could be reduced to four independent factors (where one factor is not interpretable). The companies face their main challenges in *technical and economical integration problems* (80.0 per cent). In this context we discovered that a large part of the companies saw it as necessary to invest in further education and training, whereas only a few companies reorganized their organizational structure. The second most important factor is *security problems* (62.0 per cent). Some 87.0 per cent of the companies indicated that they increased investments in IT security technologies and 72.7 per cent saw the need to develop and introduce additional IT security directives for their employees. The factor *distrust towards transaction partners* (59.2 per cent) is, compared to the other factors, less important. In this regard, we discovered that Web services are primarily used for connection with well-known transaction partners. This can be interpreted as a consequence of the distrust towards unknown transaction partners.

The results indicate that in order to tap the full potential of Web services and thereby enable the formation of fully 'virtualized' companies, many problems still have to be addressed, such as technical and economical integration problems, security problems and distrust towards the transaction partner. Companies that plan to invest and employ Web services in the future should pay close attention to these identified problems. Within the scope of this chapter, general methods of resolution have been briefly discussed. However, there is a need for future work in order to derive concrete suggestions for action as to how to counteract these problems in order to make the vision of 'doing business without doing business' a reality.

ENDNOTES

1. This contribution is an enhanced and revised version of Prokein and Faupel (2006).

2. The classification of small, medium and large enterprises is accordant to the classification of the European Commission (2003).

3. Cp. e.g. Hagel and Brown, 2001; Newcomer, 2002; Zimmermann *et al.*, 2003. Expert interviews were conducted with IBM UK, Microsoft Research Germany, SAP AG as well as with the ISI Fraunhofer Institut.

4. Originally Porter distinguishes between *inbound logistics, operations, outbound logistics, marketing and sales* and *after sales services.*

5. It can particularly lead to errors if further multivariate methods are used. For instance, the regression analysis premises independence between the variables (Backhaus *et al.*, 2003).

6. The following factor analysis will be conducted by a principal component analysis with Varimax rotation (Backhaus *et al.*, 2003).

7. This means that the variable *small spread of customers/suppliers* is independent from the other variables.

8. Via the Bartlett test, it can be verified whether intercorrelations exist between variables.

9. H0 (= variables are uncorrelated) is rejected at the 1 per cent significance level. Furthermore, the Dziuban–Shirkey criterion is fulfilled for the analysed correlation matrix.

10. The Kaiser criterion suggests that one should only retain factors whose corresponding eigenvalues are greater than 1. If the eigenvalue of one factor is greater than 1, this factor explains more of the total variance of the sample than one variable alone.

11. The factor loading is a measure that represents a connection between a barrier and the factor. Thereby the factor loading ranges between -1 and $+1$. A value near zero means that the connection between the barrier and the factor is small. The threshold takes the value 0.5 and is a convention typically used in the literature (Backhaus *et al.*, 2003).

REFERENCES

Alonso, G., Casati, F., Kuno, H. and Machiraju, V. (2004). *Web Services: Concepts, Architecture and Applications.* Springer.

Arnold, O., Faisst, W., Härtling, M. and Sieber, P. (1995). Virtuelle unternehmen als unternehmenstyp der zukunft? *HMD – Theorie und Praxis der Wirtschaftsinformatik*, 32 (185), 8–23.

Atkinson, R., Della-Libera, G., Hada, S., Hondo, M., Hallam-Baker, P., Klein, J., LaMacchia, B., Leach, P., Manferdelli, J., Maruyama, H., Nadalin, A., Nagaratnam, N., Prafullchandra, H., Shewchuk, J. and Simon, D. (2002). *Web Services Security.* April. ftp://www6.software.ibm.com/software/developer/library/ws-secure.pdf

Backhaus, K., Erchison, B., Plinke, W. and Weiber, R. (2003). *Multivariate Analysemethoden.* Springer.

Bellwood, T. (ed.) (2002). *UDDI Version 2.04 API Specification.* July. http://uddi.org/pubs/ProgrammersAPI-V2.04-Published-20020719.pdf

Booth, D., Haas, H., McCabe, F., Newcorner, E., Champion, M., Ferris, C. and Orchard, D. (2004). *Web Services Architecture.* February. http://www.w3.org/TR/ws-arch/

Bryan, D., Draluk, V., Ehnebuske, D., Glover, T., Hately, A. and Husband, Y.L. (2002). *UDDI Version 2.04 Specification.* July. http://uddi.org/pubs/ProgrammersAPI-V2.04-Published-20020719.htm.

Brynjolfsson, E. (2003). The IT productivity gap. *Optimize Magazine,* July, 26.

Brynjolfsson, E. and Hitt, L. (1998). Beyond the productivity paradox. *Communications of the ACM,* 41 (8), 49–55.

Brynjolfsson, E. and Hitt, L. (2000). Beyond computation: information technology, organizational transformation and business performance. *Journal of Economic Perspectives,* 14 (4), 23–48.

Cap Gemini Ernst & Young (2002). *Der Markt für Web services.* April. http://www.at.capgemini.com/servlet/PB/show/1004620/Web-Services.pdf

Christensen, E., Curbera, F., Meredith, G. and Weerawarana, S. (2001). *Web services Description Language (WSDL) 1.1.* March. http://www.w3.org/TR/wsdl

Coase, R. (1937). The nature of the firm. *Economica,* 4 (16), 386–405.

Curbera, F., Khalaf, R., Mukhi, N., Tai, S. and Weerawarana, S. (2003). The next step in Web services. *Communications of the ACM,* 46 (10), 29–34.

Eggs, H. and Müller, G. (2001). Sicherheit und vertrauen: mehrwert im e-commerce. In *Sicherheitskonzepte für das Internet* (G. Müller and M. Reichenbach, eds) pp. 27–44, Xpert Press.

European Commission (2003). Commission Recommendation of 6 May 2003 Concerning the Definition of Micro, Small and Medium-Sized Enterprises. Recommendation 03/361/EG. European Commission.

Gudgin, M., Hadley, M., Mendelsohn, N., Moreau, J. and Frystyk Nielsen, F. (eds) (2003). *SOAP Version 1.2. Part 1: Messaging Framework.* June. http://www.w3.org/TR/soap12-part1/

Hagel III, J. and Brown, J. S. (2001). Your next IT strategy. *Harvard Business Review,* 79 (9), 105–113.

Kaiser, H. F. (1958). The varimax criterion of analytic rotation in factor analysis. *Psychometrika,* 23, 187–200.

Kaiser, H. F. (1970). A second generation Little Jiffy. *Psychometrika,* 35, 401–415.

Kaiser, H. F. and Rice, J. (1974). Little Jiffy – Mark IV. *Educational and Psychological Measurement,* 34, 111–117.

Kieser, A. and Walgenbach, P. (2003). *Organisation.* Schäfer Poeschel.

Klein, S. (1994). Virtuelle organisation. *Wirtschaftswissenschaftliches Studium,* 23 (6), 309–311.

Klein, S. and Kronen, J. (1995). IT-enabled cooperation: a resource-based approach. *Proceedings of the 3rd European Conference on Information Systems,* Athens, June.

Kräkel, M. (1999). *Organisation und Management.* Mohr Siebeck.

Kreps, D. (1990). *A Course in Microeconomic Theory*. Prentice Hall.

Löwer, U. M. and Picot, A. (2002). Web Services: technologie hype oder strategie-faktor. *Information Management and Consulting*, 17 (3), 20–25.

Löwer, U. M. (2003). *Verschieben Web Services Unternehmensgrenzen? Erklärungs-beiträge zweier Theorien der Unternehmungen*. Working Paper, Ludwig-Maximilians-Universität, Munich.

Mas-Colell, A., Whinston, M. and Green, J. (1995). *Microeconomic Theory*. Oxford University Press.

Mertens, P., Griese, J. and Ehrenberg, D. (1998). *Virtuelle Unternehmen und Informationsverarbeitung*. Springer.

Müller, G., Eymann, T. and Kreutzer, M. (2003). *Telematik- und Kommunikationssysteme in der vernetzten Wirtschaft*. Oldenbourg.

Müller, G. (ed.) (2006a). *Emerging Trends in Information and Communication Security*. Lecture Notes in Computer Science, Vol. 3995. Springer.

Müller, G. (2006b). Privacy and security in highly dynamic systems. *Communications of the ACM*, 49 (9), 28–31.

Newcomer, E. (2002). *Understanding Web Services*. Addison-Wesley.

Porter, M. E. (1985a). *Competitive Advantage*. Free Press.

Porter, M. E. (1985b). How information gives you competitive advantage. *Harvard Business Review*, 63 (4), 149–174.

Porter, M. E. (2001). Strategy and the Internet. *Harvard Business Review*, 79 (3), 62–78.

Prokein, O. and Sackmann, S. (2005). *Der Einsatz von Web Services in Deutschen Unternehmen: Eine Empirische Untersuchung*. Working Paper, Institut für Informatik und Gesellschaft, Telematik, Universität Freiburg.

Prokein, O. and Faupel, T. (2006). Using Web services for intercompany cooperation: an empirical study within German industry. *Proceedings of the 39th Hawaii International Conference on System Sciences*, Hawaii, January.

Puschmann, T. and Alt, R. (2004). Process portals: architecture and integration. *Proceedings of the 37th Hawaii International Conference on System Sciences*, Hawaii, January.

Richter, R. and Furubotn, E. G. (2003). *Neue Institutionenökonomie*. Mohr Siebeck.

Roger, S. (2004). *IDC's Web Services Software Study: Trends in Adoption and Use Cases*. IDC.

Semich, J. W. (1994). Information replaces inventory at the virtual corp. *Datamation*, 15 (7), 37–42.

Strassner, M. (2005). *RFID in Supply Chain Management*. DUV.

Zimmermann, O., Tomlinson, M. and Peuser, S. (2003). *Perspectives on Web Services*. Springer.

CHAPTER 12

Cross-cultural knowledge management at virtual interfaces

David J. Pauleen and Nigel Holden

INTRODUCTION

Globalization of the economy challenges everyone to become more internationally aware and cross-culturally adroit. Globalization is not just an economic matter; it is more concerned with issues of cultural meaning, and in particular the mediation of meaning, identity and intention. At the individual level, success in understanding and working with those from other cultures depends on effective communication practices, which themselves are based on relevant knowledge, skills and abilities. Foremost of these is the ability to develop and manage relationships. Relationships and concomitant interaction with other individuals embedded in globe-spanning corporate networks create access to information and knowledge on an unprecedented scale. This information and knowledge represents an invaluable organizational asset, a global resource sustained on organizational learning for reaping competitive advantage.

Over the last two decades, managing cultural exchange between individuals and between organizations, if it were managed at all, was usually an exercise in anticipating and preparing for 'problems'. A vast industry in cross-cultural consulting and training developed to highlight the differences between cultures and how to cope with them. Holden (2002: 49) summed up the attitude that has permeated this thinking as *cultural scare-mongering*, in which:

C1 + C2 = Culture shock, friction, misunderstanding

Holden (2002: 49) has proposed a new perspective: one that incorporates the current realities of both economic globalization and the globalization of cultural meaning – trends that have been tremendously encouraged by the global interconnectivity fostered by information and communication technologies. From this perspective:

C1 + C2 = C3, where C3 is a new cultural hybrid

In cross-cultural organizational contexts, the creation of C3 may occur in a team, a group such as a community of practice, or in the organization itself.

With this as the new starting point, culture and knowledge of culture can be seen as an organizational resource, i.e. *a knowledge asset*. Thus, cross-cultural management then becomes the way to apply this asset. In this sense, as Holden (2002) has argued, cross-cultural management becomes a form of knowledge management.

This chapter addresses the challenge of how new ways to understand, manage and learn from cross-cultural interaction can be developed, particularly in the context of new workplace forms such as geographically distributed, electronically mediated, multi-cultural project teams.

Our specific aim is to frame this challenge through a discussion of the main concepts of culture, cross-cultural management, knowledge management and virtual environments. This will set the scene for a case study which will demonstrate how an appreciation of these factors pinpoints the competencies necessary for effective cross-cultural knowledge management at virtual interfaces.

DEFINING CULTURE – THEN AND NOW

There is a seemingly inexhaustible array of definitions of culture, with over 160 definitions identified as long as 50 years ago (Kroeber and Kluckhohn, 1963). There is good reason to point out that attempts to define culture 'can be compared to exploring the ocean' (Schneider and Barsoux, 1997: 18). Indeed the word culture has its own culture-specific variations. In Finnish the word *kulttuuri* strongly suggests 'the intellectual side of civilization and society' (Koivisto, 1999: 55); the Japanese word *bunka* 'focuses attention on literary or artistic production' (Holden, 2002: 23), while German culture cannot be understood without accounting for the German 'obsession with economics' (James, 2000: 246).

For our purposes we will suggest that culture is composed of three main elements: content, construction and sustainability. In terms of content, culture has been defined as 'a system of ideas' (Namenwirth and Weber, 1987: 8), 'a distinctive, enduring pattern of behaviour and personality characteristics' (Clark, 1990: 66), and 'collective programming of the mind that distinguishes the members of one group from another' (Hofstede, 1984: 21). In essence, the content of culture consists of a set of underlying norms and values of behaviour, shared by a group of people tied together by powerful affiliations or bonds.

The construction of culture, according to Schein (1985), results from the interaction of people and their environment. In particular, Schein emphasized the aspect of problem solving in culture, which is considered to be a valid way of thinking in order to respond to the surrounding environment. That is, culture is a set of valid knowledge, created and shared by a group of people, to solve their problems faced in their environment. This is similar to the view of culture that we put forth below.

In terms of sustainability, culture is transmitted by symbols, rituals and stories, passed on from one generation to another (Kroeber and Kluckhohn, 1963). The implicit (or even tacit) part, as well as the explicit part, of cultural knowledge is sustained and transferred through information expressed in various ways. In this vein, Hall and Hall (1990) view culture as a system for creating, sending, storing and processing information.

However, Barham and Heimer (1998) point out that the standard anthropologically-derived concepts of culture are out of touch with the 'connectivities' and networks of the modern global economy. In a further break with tradition, recent research highlights people's reaction to dynamic contexts and their role as active participants in creating, modifying and even contesting the nature of culture (Giddens, 1984; 1990; Myers and Tan, 2002; Walsham, 2002). Holden (2001: 162), for his part, has called for 'a paradigmatic shift in the way culture is viewed and suggests that researchers reframe culture as infinitely overlapping and perpetually redistributable habitats of common knowledge and shared meanings'.

273

VALUES-BASED CULTURAL TAXONOMIES AND NEW WAYS OF VIEWING CULTURE

A significant number of theories and models have informed cross-cultural research, both methodologically and philosophically. Many of these focus on the concept of national culture and are based on dichotomies or continuums of values, such as: individualism/collectivism (Hofstede, 1980); high and low context (Hall, 1976); and monochronic/polychronic (Lewis, 1996). These value-based models attempt to predict individual and group attitudes and behaviours based on national culture. Such models have been criticized by Corbitt *et al.* (2004) who suggest that such structural frameworks may be too reliant on categorical descriptions that ignore differentiation within cultures, as well as the individual exceptions likely to be found to any general rule.

Several studies have identified national culture in terms of work-related attitudes and values – to distinguish groups of people from other groups (Hofstede, 1980; Ronen and Shenkar, 1985; Smith *et al.*, 1996). Hofstede (1980; 1988) proposed five dimensions of national culture: individualism/collectivism, masculinity/femininity, power distance, uncertainty avoidance, and long-term vs short-term orientation. Some researchers have used this model to account for knowledge management processes and found that the cultural dimensions expressed by the Hofstede model might play a role in the knowledge management processes (Ford and Chan, 2003; Rossen, 2003).

However, the legitimacy of the concept of 'national culture' remains in question as evidenced by the continuing debate in the literature. Scholars argue that globalization has enabled the emergence of the global society, both collocated and virtual, where members of different regional and ethnic groups live and work in the same shared environment. Therefore an identity based upon the notion of a nation state does little to reflect regional and ethnic differences (Holden, 2001; Myers and Tan, 2002). Indeed, McCrone (1998) asserts that the quest for regional identities and decentralization reflects the need for the idea of national cultural identities to be challenged and usurped. The concept of national sovereignty has been linked to the notion of a national cultural identity and it has been suggested that as globalization and economic, political and cultural pressures further negate the importance of national sovereignty, this will affect the idea of a national cultural identity (Castells, 1996; 1997; Featherstone, 1990; Waters, 2001). Hall (1992) contends that instead of thinking of national cultures as unified, they should rather be regarded as a discursive device representing difference as unity or identity.

Most authors agree that nations may contain different cultures or sub-cultures within national borders and that those national borders do not necessarily represent culturally homogeneous populations (Groeschl and Doherty, 2000). Rather than emphasize single national cultural identities, the challenge is developing theory that furthers understanding of heterogeneous cultures (Mercer, 1992). Doney *et al.* (1998) stress their view that national culture is not a characteristic of individuals or nation states but of a large number of people conditioned by similar background, education and life experiences. Based on the social construction of reality theory (Berger and Luckman, 1967), Corbitt *et al.* (2004) argue that national culture can be more accurately understood by seeking out the dominant social codes that frame a society's values, attitudes and behaviours. Weisinger and Trauth (2002), through a combination of theoretical argument and practical research, suggest that culture is, in fact, locally situated, behavioural and embedded in everyday social negotiated work practices: a view also subscribed to by Holden (2001). We suggest that locally-situated culture manifests itself right down to the level of groups and teams.

The debate between proponents of national cultural models and those who favour a more discrete or localized understanding of culture is unlikely to be resolved soon. National culture models certainly help to simplify cross-cultural research, while a more localized view of culture will more likely reflect the culture under study and yield results more pertinent to the individuals under study.

CROSS-CULTURAL MANAGEMENT – THEN AND NOW

Cross-cultural management (CCM) traditionally describes organizational behaviour within countries and cultures and compares organizational behaviour across countries and cultures. CCM seeks to understand and improve the interaction of co-workers, team members, managers, executives, clients, suppliers and alliance partners from countries and cultures around the world (Adler, 2002: 11). Much of cross-cultural management depends on values-based taxonomies as discussed above and its focus is on anticipating and overcoming the differences that might be present in any given cross-cultural encounter – be it an expatriate manager with local staff, an international negotiation, a multicultural team project, or similar.

Although managing (i.e. coping with) culture in this way will provide benefits, the overall tenor of such efforts is negative, with its emphasis on differences that need to be managed and possibly negated. Generally, there is very little appreciation of the differences that make various cultures unique, or of the unique contributions that different cultures can make.

More recently a new vision of cross-cultural management has emerged. In this view, according to Holden (2002), culture becomes an organizational resource, a knowledge asset. From this perspective, global and multi-cultural organizations, with their culturally diverse workforces, suppliers and customers, have access to large amounts of significant and culturally diverse knowledge. The challenge for organizations is how to learn from and utilize this knowledge. In Holden's view, the main task of CCM is to facilitate and direct synergistic interaction and learning at interfaces, where knowledge, values and experiences are transferred into multi-cultural domains of implementation (Holden, 2002).

In this chapter, we suggest that the environment that epitomizes the challenges in which organizations have to manage culturally diverse knowledge is in internationally distributed work environments, i.e. global (and multi-cultural) virtual teams.

KNOWLEDGE MANAGEMENT

Knowledge management (KM) concerns the management of knowledge, and as with culture, there are numerous definitions of knowledge and descriptions and definitions of what it means to manage knowledge. The lack of agreement in defining knowledge and KM may reflect the fact that KM is based on a wide range of disciplines. These include, but are not limited to, sociology, management science, information technology, psychology and philosophy (Hazlatt *et al.*, 2005; Nordin *et al.*, 2006).

Notwithstanding, KM now seems to be split between two primary disciplines – those of information systems and management. These have been termed the computational paradigm and the organic paradigm (Hazlatt *et al.*, 2005). One is techno-centric and focuses on the 'hard' aspects such as the deployment and use of appropriate technology; the other is people-centric and relies on the management of people and processes (Sveiby, 2001). This dichotomy in theory and practice has led some researchers to suggest that KM is still in a pre-science stage (Kuhn, 1977), that is, a field in which there is still no coherent and accepted overarching theory to tie KM together. While this chapter does not attempt to offer an overarching theory to KM, examining knowledge management in virtual environments does highlight the way in which technology and management work together and may lead to further progress in the area of theory development.

Regardless, we need as a starting point a working definition of KM that will at least be sympathetic to the objectives of this chapter. Alavi and Leidner (2001) suggest that KM should effectively apply an organization's knowledge to create new knowledge to achieve and maintain competitive advantage. Nonaka's SECI model (Nonaka, 1994), the most widely referenced KM model, specifically addresses the issue of organizational knowledge creation, predicated on a comprehensive system of knowledge sharing. Pauleen *et al.* (2007) believe that the fundamental goal of organizational KM should be the development and nurturing of the individual employee who is willing and able to share knowledge. Sharing behaviour is what makes knowledge available to other individuals and the organization as a whole. Competent, thoughtful management is needed to nurture the development of the 'sharing' employee.

In terms of cross-cultural research, there are still relatively few studies that examine the relationship between national culture and KM, even though the importance of national culture in KM has recently been recognized (Pauleen, 2007). In one previous and exceptional study of published reports of KM systems, Mason (2003) found that the national culture and ethnic background of users are rarely mentioned, with only one case directly discussing the importance of national culture. Mason suggested that KM designers may be implicitly adopting the 'culture-free' hypothesis as a basis for design. Arguments against the culture-free hypothesis stress the often overwhelming but unrealized influence of culture on many aspects of systems design, implementation and use (Pauleen and Murphy, 2005; Pauleen *et al.*, 2006).

CROSS-CULTURAL MANAGEMENT AS KNOWLEDGE MANAGEMENT

If we accept, as argued above, that culture represents a form of organizational knowledge then we can now accept the idea that CCM is a form of KM and we can now speak of cross-cultural knowledge management (CCKM). We define CCKM as the systematic and purposeful management of culture as an organizational knowledge asset. In an organization with a multi-cultural workforce, a diverse or international customer base, international suppliers and global competitors, the potential for culture to become a significant organizational knowledge asset is great indeed – one that needs conscientious management. According to Holden (2002), the need for CCKM is apparent in three significant organizational activities: Interactive Global Networking, Teamworking and Communities of Practice, and Organizational Learning.

Networking is an important organizational knowledge resource as personal and organizational networks provide pathways to a variety of resources, including human resources, special knowledge, rare competencies, sources of finance and forms of influence. Networking is a form of boundary crossing, which enhances the flow of information from the external environment. Making the knowledge accumulated by the employees – through environmental scanning, networking or other activities – available throughout the organization is a critical management task (Von Krogh *et al.*, 2000).

Interactive global networking exemplifies CCKM because in a global environment, and in particular global organizations, networking inevitably takes place across cultures. The most valuable knowledge is found in the heads of people scattered all around the world. Sending employees to conferences and overseas work assignments supports network building. The nearly everyday use of communications technology in the form of e-mail, Internet-based video conferencing, search engines, and so on is accelerating networking opportunities. CCKM seeks to manage and enhance these opportunities for the benefit of individuals and the organization.

Globalization and the increasing use of ICTs also increase the likelihood of employees working in internationally distributed work environments. These include communities of practice (CoPs), virtual teams, global meta-project teams (Fernandez, 2004), and so on. In each of these cases, the relationships formed between organizations, parts of the same organization and individuals within organizations create opportunities to share knowledge in the present and for future years through webs of enterprise and arrays of networks (Holden, 2002).

If growing involvement in global networks brings individuals and organizations access to knowledge, especially cross-cultural knowledge, then the next question must be how do they take the fullest advantage to learn from these opportunities? One avenue is the concept of the learning organization. Allee (2003) suggests that the key to learning lies in the social interactions between people within the organization and outside of it. She goes on to say that organizational learning is about the collective ability of the organization to make sense of its environment and become more adaptive. According to

Keegan, what sets the global company apart is the capacity to develop and implement global strategies that leverage worldwide learning and make the greatest use of the talents of every employee (Keegan, 1999). Learning from others requires the development of shared mental models (O'Keefe, 2002), a point we will return to shortly.

GLOBAL VIRTUAL TEAMS: AN INTERFACE OF CULTURE, TECHNOLOGY AND KNOWLEDGE

Virtual teams are playing an increasingly important role in organizational life and are often assigned the most important tasks in an organization, such as multi-national product launches, negotiating mergers and acquisitions among global companies, and managing strategic alliances, as well as complex design and development projects (Fernandez, 2004; Maznevski and Chudoba, 2000). In spite of their critical and increasing use, the management of virtual teams has outpaced our understanding of their dynamics and unique characteristics (Cramton and Webber, 2000).

Virtual teams by definition work across time and distance through the use of information and communications technology (Townsend *et al.*, 1998). Virtual teams may communicate and work synchronously or asynchronously through an increasing variety of technologies such as electronic mail, bulletin boards, audio/video/data conferencing, automated workflow, electronic voting, collaborative writing and mobile technology. The practical effect of working across distance means that teams can and do comprise members from different departments, head and branch offices, different organizations, as well as different countries and cultures. Indeed, quick and relatively easy access to the knowledge found in different organizational, functional and cultural perspectives is a key reason for using virtual teams (Pauleen and Rajasingham, 2004). However, the boundary-crossing inherent in working across functions, organizations and cultures is also one of the greatest challenges in working virtually.

Pauleen and Rajasingham (2004) summed up the challenge of managing knowledge sharing across boundaries in virtual environments as one of mediating complexity. Some of the challenges are similar to those found in face-to-face teams but are of a higher order as they must be negotiated through electronic communication channels. The difficulties of building consensus or coordinating the activities and efforts of individual team members are magnified many times when they take place across time and space. But these are just the obvious challenges.

Much more insidious are the issues that most (virtual team) managers are barely aware of, including the use of culturally biased technologies and management practices. Culturally biased technologies that may be used in virtual teams include group decision support systems, Web-based intranets and even e-mail (Pauleen and Murphy, 2005). Culturally biased management favours rules of interaction and the language of communication of one dominant culture. Even conceptualizations of knowledge and expectations of how knowledge will be expressed and shared within the team are culturally biased (Nisbett, 2003).

Clearly, managing at virtual interfaces, such as virtual teams, exemplifies the challenge and the potential of CCKM. The following case illustrates some of the key cultural challenges to be found in virtual teams.

A CASE OF EMERGENT TEAM CULTURE

The case presented here illustrates how culture, technology and knowledge sharing were managed in a semi-virtual team environment. The case specifically highlights how a team culture can emerge through extensive relationship building and the development of shared meanings between the team members. The case features the negotiation of historical claims between a national government and an indigenous group. A full description of the methodology and findings of this case has been published (Pauleen, 2003b); in this chapter only the points most salient to the discussion here are included. It involved many team members, organizations and cultures, with large amounts of money and land at stake, and all taking place within a historical and political context. Table 12.1 lists the core government team members, the indigenous claimant team members, extended team members and various stakeholders in this case. All together, there were approximately

Table 12.1

The extended team membership (source: Pauleen, 2003)

Core team members (government)	Claimants	Extended team members	Key stakeholders
Representatives from the Office of Treaty Settlements; Department of Conservation; Treasury	Principal negotiator; other negotiators appointed by the mandated body	Other departments (e.g. Fisheries, Education); lawyers; specialists; consultants	Ministers; claimant community; local authority; the public

eight members on the core team, ten extended team members and several key stakeholder groups.

The Office of Treaty Settlements (OTS) is a part of the Ministry of Justice of the national government. The OTS's key responsibility is the settling of historical treaty claims made by indigenous groups. This project involved the negotiation and settlement of a treaty claim by one indigenous group. The project was essentially a negotiation between two parties, the government and the claimants. This project was unique because although two sides were involved in the negotiation, the government and the claimant side, it was basically a collaborative rather than a confrontational negotiation. So in a real sense the project consisted of two teams working toward a common goal: in this case, a legal and political settlement. Representatives of the claimant side generally had the use of phones, fax and e-mail.

The wider government team, which consisted of a number of government departments – including the OTS, the Department of Conservation, the Ministry of Fisheries and the Treasury – as well as consultants, had access to a greater range of virtual technologies.

Table 12.2 highlights the nature of the team issues, the extensive cross-cultural issues that needed to be addressed, and the policies and resources of the organizations that were involved.

Within OTS itself, all permanent staff are located in the capital city. The OTS also works with numerous consultants, such as negotiators

Table 12.2
Conditions present at start-up of the virtual team (source: Pauleen, 2003)

Key issues	Related issues	Specific conditions

Team issues	Project goal
	
	Time frame
	Team membership
		• Complex
		  ○ Negotiate a historical treaty settlement
		• Long-term with a deadline
		• Members from different organizations
		• Virtual team experience
		  ○ Some with experience of electronic
		    communication channels, others with none

Boundary crossing	Organizational
	
	Culture/language
		• Claimants and government; different government
		  departments
		• Different cultures; different languages on
		  occasions

Organizational policies and resources (including technology)	Policies
	
	Resources
		• Policies on e-mail; quality assurance policies on
		  letters sent outside the office
		• Unaware of what electronic resources were
		  available to claimants

and environmental specialists, from around the country. There is no policy regarding working virtually, but in practice what typically happens is that these consultants visit the capital city for an initial meeting and then continue work via phone and e-mail. Weekly meetings may occur when negotiations are moving very fast. According to the team leader, this department appears to be generally unaware of the influence that ICT may be currently having in its organization.

The defining condition in this project was the amount of boundary crossing that needed to be addressed – not only the cultural differences between the government and the claimants, but also the organizational differences among members of the government team, which consisted of a number of government departments, consultants and specialists. The team leader summed up the cultural crossing between the government and claimants as follows:

> There are two sorts of cultures that we need to bring together, between the claimant negotiators and the key government negotiators, who are going to meet and be making hard judgements based on what we were telling them. And that requires a huge level of trust, which we were able to build up through a whole lot of face-to-face meetings over long periods of interaction – two years.

In essence, there was a tremendous need for culturally led relationship building to take place and fortunately there was the opportunity for extensive face-to-face meetings in which to build relationships. The team leader noted that at the very beginning of the negotiations process with the claimants, they visited the capital and had a face-to-face meeting with the OTS side even though no meeting was really required. They reported on what they had been doing and asked a few questions. The team leader concluded:

> I guess they just wanted to meet with us. It was more than was required and more than what any other claimant groups had done. But it built up some sort of rapport. It was just a little bit unusual at the very outset. Face-to-face was much more relevant than might otherwise have been the case. It's the way that they operate, by talking and looking at you.

Although face-to-face communication was critical in these negotiations, several other channels were also used and towards the end of the project assumed a critical role. The team leader explained:

> The last four weeks before the signing of the Heads of Agreement was frantic and involved a different way of working together virtually. After a series of critical face-to-face meetings to work out some difficult points and with just a couple of days to go, communication took place primarily by phone and e-mail. Important issues, normally dealt with face-to-face, were resolved virtually and they performed admirably on their side under that regime.

The factors that drove the selection and use of communications channels are summarized in Table 12.3.

By the end of this negotiation, the government and the claimants had managed, through a long process of face-to-face relationship building, to build up a great deal of trust. This trust allowed them to operate virtually when necessary. From a CCKM viewpoint the two

Table 12.3
Driving factors in the selection and use of communication channels (source: Pauleen, 2003)

Communication channel	Driving factors for selection and use by government side	Driving factors for selection and use by claimant side
Face-to-face	• Get core business done • Discuss and resolve key issues • Get people to do things • Convey negative responses to claimants • Allow for credible, but inconclusive dialogue	• Build relationships • Get core business done • Raise key issues • Get government to focus on claimant's issues
Letters	• Provide formal official response (must be quality assured)	• Provide formal, written records of every step of the process • Move things along and generate responses
Telephone	• Deal with matters under some urgency • To discuss issues informally (before or after sending a formal letter)	• To check on progress and keep up momentum • To discuss issues informally (before or after sending a formal letter)
E-mail	• Used primarily within the government side • Interdepartmental e-mail discussion on issues relating to the negotiations • Confirm and clarify details • Possesses speed of a phone call with the paper trail of a written response • Used to quickly transfer working documents back and forth in template form	E-mail was not used between OTS and the claimants until the end of the negotiations when time constraints forced its use

sides were able to develop shared patterns of meaning and interpretation (Holden, 2002). In a sense, they were able to negotiate a shared culture – culture 3 in Figure 12.1 – which needed time to emerge. The nature of that emergent culture was summed up by the team leader:

> We have got to the position where they can trust us as government negotiators to be acting in their best interests. We are not going to be running them short, to try to get something from them. That requires a close cultural melding in a sense.

The significance of this case is that it demonstrates how culture can be managed in a way that strengthens relationships, improves trust and facilitates knowledge sharing. Time, commitment and a clear sense of what motivates the people involved in the team are all critical elements that have a cultural basis and need to be managed.

This case specifically demonstrates the importance of face-to-face relationship building, and it was very clear that the claimants considered both relationship building and face-to-face communication absolute prerequisites before task-based negotiations could continue. With relationships and trust established, the negotiations could continue in an increasingly virtual environment.

There are many cultures around the world that insist on face-to-face relationship building and the development of significant interpersonal trust before beginning negotiations or engaging in meaningful teamwork. In such cases it would be foolish and counterproductive for one side, or the team manager or leader, to abruptly insist on getting 'down to business'. Even with people who are comfortable in totally virtual

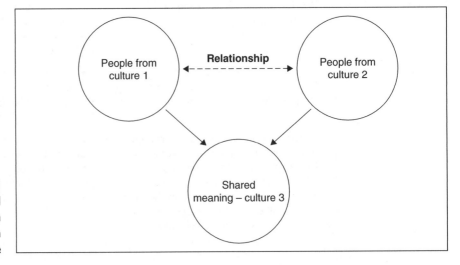

Figure 12.1
Building shared meaning through social interaction over time

environments, a virtual team manager may still need to devise strategies to build appropriate levels of relationship with and among team members (Pauleen, 2003a).

Knowing how to cultivate the ground in multi-cultural contexts is an important lesson in CCKM. Knowing which communications channels are most appropriate and how to select them is another important lesson that still needs to be learned by all those who operate in global, multi-cultural and virtual environments.

CONCLUSIONS AND IMPLICATIONS

Following up on the discussion of culture, CCM, KM and CCKM and taking the lessons of the case into consideration we can conclude that, to a significant extent, it is possible for local culture to manifest itself when relationship and context are successfully managed. However, context is ever changing and relationship building is very much a human and hence unpredictable activity. Therefore, it would be safe to say that outcomes of cross-cultural collaboration and integration processes cannot be predicted with certainty. Indeed, any cross-cultural activity, particularly in a virtual context, represents something akin to a complex adaptive system (Shoham and Hasgall, 2005).

Managing – or perhaps it would be more truthful to say coping with – complex systems requires special knowledge, skills and abilities (KSA). The objectives of CCKM should not only be to try to foster the ability to effectively participate in cross-cultural contexts, but also to learn from them. This learning can be at the level of the individual, the team and the organization.

At an individual level a form of practical wisdom may be necessary. Fundamental to wise practice is the ability to engage in reflexive thought. Rooney and McKenna (2005: 314) define reflexivity as an aspect of wise practices that:

- acknowledges the ambiguous, fragmented and contested nature of knowledge, but does not prevent a determination of the understood 'facts' in a matter;
- acknowledges that there are multiple perspectives to any phenomenon, each with their own vocabularies, theories, interpretations and frames; and
- understands as far as possible one's own subject position individually and as a member of a community of practice, and that this will influence the perception of the object.

If a manager can cultivate these practices, it is likely that a broader appreciation of the complexity inherent in CCKM will result and this may allow more effective and creative solutions to emerge.

However, anyone participating in cross-cultural interactions should at least possess the qualities and characteristics of: an open mind, a flexible and non-judgemental attitude, a tolerance for ambiguity and the ability to communicate respect, display empathy and personalize knowledge and perceptions. Excellent interpersonal skills, language competency and area knowledge of the cultures one is working with should also be a given.

At the team and organizational level, the main lessons from the literature and the case point to some obvious macro-managerial strategies. These are summarized in Table 12.4.

In sum, when it comes to managing culture two options appear to exist. One is to subscribe to culture shock and the like, and to create high hurdles. The second is to embrace the diversity of culture as an organizational resource to respond to the demands of the global economy, reap the benefits of cross-border alliances and enhance organizational learning (Schneider and Barsoux, 1997). Organizational renewal for the global, knowledge-based economy is directly linked to the 'organization's willingness and capacity to integrate best practices and experience from as many of the in-company loci of common knowledge as possible' (Holden, 2002: 222). Virtual teams and networks provide the potential for rapidly bringing together diverse, organizational (and

Table 12.4

Lessons learned and managerial responses

Lesson learned	Management response
The importance of relationship building in multiple boundary-crossing teams	Allow sufficient relationship-building time and activities in project timelines (Pauleen and Yoong, 2001); up to two years has been recommended to support the transfer of knowledge in business projects (Fink and Holden, 2005)
The need to consciously select and use appropriate ICT channels	Provide access and training to a wide range of ICT channels and negotiate appropriate channel selection and use with team members (Pauleen, 2003)
The usefulness of cross-cultural training in appropriate KSA *with* the emphasis that ultimately individual and group behaviour may be flexible and negotiable based on a range of contextual elements	Provide member training in multiple boundary-crossing interaction (Hall, 1976; Hofstede, 2000); foster cross-cultural learning and participation within the organization (Myers and Tan, 2002); use trained cultural facilitators in complex, multiple boundary-crossing project work (Holden, 2002)

extra-organizational) knowledge, but they require proactive and 'advanced' CCKM to be successful.

REFERENCES

Adler, N. (2002). *International Dimensions of Organizational Behavior*. Third Edition. South-Western.

Alavi, M. and Leidner, D. (2001). Knowledge management and knowledge management systems: conceptual foundations and research issues. *MISQ Review*, 25, 107–136.

Allee, V. (2003). *The Future of Knowledge: Increasing Prosperity through Value Networks*. Elsevier Science.

Barham, K. and Heimer, C. (1998). *ABB. The Dancing Giant. Creating the Globally Connected Corporation*. FT Pitman Publishing.

Berger, P. and Luckman, T. (1967). *The Social Construction of Reality*. Anchor/ Doubleday.

Castells, M. (1996). *The Information Age: Economy, Society and Culture*. Volume 1: *The Rise of the Network Society*. Blackwell.

Clark, T. (1990). International marketing and national character: a review and proposal for an integrative theory. *Journal of Marketing*, 54 (4), 66–79.

Corbitt, B., Peszynski, K., Intranond, S., Thanasankit, T. and Hill, B. (2004). Culture, information and code systems. *Journal of Global Information Management*, 12, 65–85.

Cramton, C. and Webber, S. (2000). Attribution in distributed work groups. In *Distributed Work: New Research on Working across Distance Using Technology* (P. Hinds and S. Kiesler, eds) pp. 191–212, MIT Press.

Doney, P., Cannon, J., Mullen, M. and Michael, R. (1998). Understanding the influence of national culture on the development of trust. *Academy of Management Review*, 23, 601–621.

Featherstone, M. (1990). *Global Culture: Nationalism, Globalization and Modernity*. Sage.

Fernandez, W. (2004). Trust and trust placement process in metateam projects. In *Virtual Teams: Projects, Protocols and Processes* (D. Pauleen, ed.) pp. 40–70, Idea Publishing Group.

Ford, D. and Chan, Y. (2003). Knowledge sharing in a multi-cultural setting: a case study. *Knowledge Management Research and Practice*, 1, 11–27.

Giddens, A. (1984). *The Constitution Society: Outline of a Theory of Structuration*. Polity Press.

Giddens, A. (1990). *Consequences of Modernity*. Polity Press.

Groeschl, G. and Doherty, L. (2000). Conceptualizing culture. *Cross-Cultural Management*, 7, 12–17.

Hall, E. (1976). *Beyond Culture*. Doubleday and Company.

Hall, E. and Hall, M. (1990). *Understanding Cultural Differences*. Intercultural Press.

Hall, S. (1992). The question of cultural identity. In *Modernity and its Futures* (S. Hall, D. Held and T. McGrew, eds) pp. 273–325, Polity Press.

Hazlatt, S., McAdam, R. and Gallagher, S. (2005). Theory building in knowledge management: in search of paradigms. *Journal of Management Inquiry*, 14, 31–42.

Hofstede, G. (1980). *Culture's Consequences: International Differences in Work-Related Practices*. Sage.

Hofstede, G. (1984). *Culture's Consequences: International Differences in Work Related Values*. Sage.

Hofstede, G. (1988). Confucius and economic growth: new trends in culture's consequences. *Organizational Dynamics*, 16, 4–21.

Holden, N. (2001). Knowledge management: raising the spectre of the cross-cultural dimension. *Knowledge and Process Management*, 8, 155–163.

Holden, N. (2002). *Cross-Cultural Management: A Knowledge Management Perspective*. Pearson Education Limited.

James, H. (2000). *A German Identity: 1770 to the Present Day*. Phoenix Press.

Keegan, W. (1999). *Global Marketing Management*. Prentice Hall.

Koivisto, J. (1999). *Cultural Heritages and Cross-Cultural Management: Cross-Cultural Synergy and Friction in Finno-Japanese Management*. Ph.D. thesis. Helsinki School of Economics and Business Administration.

Kroeber, A. and Kluckhohn, C. (1963). *Culture: A Critical Review of Concepts and Definitions*. Vintage Books.

Kuhn, T. (1977). Second thoughts on paradigms. In *The Essential Tension* (T. Kuhn, ed.) pp. 293–319, Chicago University Press.

Lewis, R. (1996). *When Cultures Collide: Managing Successfully Across Cultures*. Nicholas Brealey Publishing.

Mason, R. M. (2003). Culture-free or culture-bound? A boundary spanning perspective on learning in knowledge management systems. *Journal of Global Information Management*, 11 (4), 20–36.

Maznevski, M. and Chudoba, K. (2000). Bridging space over time: global virtual team dynamics and effectiveness. *Organization Science*, 11, 473–492.

McCrone, D. (1998). *The Sociology of Nationalism*. Routledge.

Mercer, N. (1992). Culture, context and the construction of classroom knowledge. In *Context and Cognition* (P. Light and G. Butterworth, eds) pp. 28–46, Harvester-Wheatsheaf.

Myers, M. and Tan, F. (2002). Beyond models of national culture in information systems research. *Journal of Global Information Management*, 10, 24–32.

Namenwirth, J. and Weber, R. (1987). *Dynamics of Culture*. Allen and Unwin.

Nisbett. R. (2003). *Geography of Thought: How Asians and Westerners Think Differently … and Why*. The Free Press.

Nonaka. I. (1994). A dynamic theory of knowledge creation. *Organizational Science*, 5, 14–37.

Nordin, M., Pauleen, D. and Gorman, G. (2006). Broadening our understanding of KM by examining its antecedents: the case for KM in the criminal justice system. *Proceedings of Knowledge Management in the Asia Pacific 2006,* Hong Kong, December.

O'Keefe, T. (2002). Organizational learning: a new perspective. *Journal of European Industrial Training,* 26, 130–141.

Pauleen, D. (2003a). An inductively derived model of leader-initiated relationship building with virtual team members. *Journal of Management Information Systems,* 4, 227–256.

Pauleen, D. (2003b). Lessons learned crossing boundaries in an ICT-supported distributed team. *Journal of Global Information Management,* 11, 1–19.

Pauleen, D. and Rajasingham, L. (2004). Mediating complexity: facilitating relationship building in start-up virtual teams. In *Virtual Teams: Projects, Protocols and Processes* (D. Pauleen, ed.) pp. 255–279, Idea Publishing Group.

Pauleen, D. and Murphy, P. (2005). In praise of cultural bias. *Sloan Management Review,* 46, 21–22.

Pauleen, D., Everisto, R., Davison, R., Ang, S., Alanis, M. and Klein, S. (2006). Cultural bias in IS research and practice: 'are you coming from the same place I am?' *Communications of the Association of Information Systems,* 17, 354–372.

Pauleen, D. (2007). Introduction. In *Cross-Cultural Perspectives on Knowledge Management* (D. Pauleen, ed.) pp. 3–20, Libraries Unlimited.

Pauleen, D., Wu, L. L. and Dexter, S. (2007). Exploring the relationship between national and organizational culture and knowledge management. In *Cross-Cultural Perspectives on Knowledge Management* (D. Pauleen, ed.) pp. 3–20, Libraries Unlimited.

Ronen, S. and Shenkar, O. (1985). Clustering countries on attitudinal dimensions: a review and synthesis. *Academy of Management Review,* 10, 435–454.

Rooney, D. and McKenna, B. (2005). Should the knowledge-based economy be a savant or a sage? Wisdom and socially intelligent innovation. *Prometheus,* 23, 307–323.

Rossen, E. (2003). Cross-cultural inequality in IS: a preliminary exploration of Scandinavia and France. Cross cultural workshop at the *International Conference on Information Systems,* Seattle, December.

Schein, E. (1985). *Organizational Culture and Leadership.* Jossey-Bass.

Schneider, S. and Barsoux, J. (1997). *Managing across Cultures.* Prentice Hall.

Shoham, S. and Hasgall, A. (2005). Knowledge workers as fractals in a complex adaptive organization. *Knowledge and Process Management,* 12, 225–236.

Smith, P., Dugan, S. and Trompenaars, F. (1996). National culture and the values of organizational employees. *Journal of Cross-Cultural Psychology,* 27 (2), 231–263.

Sveiby, K. (2001). *What is Knowledge Management?* Sveiby Knowledge Associates. http://www.sveiby.com/Portals/0/articles/KnowledgeManagement.html

Townsend, A., DeMarie, S. and Hendrickson, A. (1998). Virtual teams: technology and the workplace of the future. *Academy of Management Executive,* 12, 17–29.

Von Krogh, G., Ichijo, K., and Nonaka, I. (2000). *Enabling Knowledge Creation: How to Unlock the Mystery of Tacit Knowledge and Release the Power of Innovation.* Oxford University Press.

Walsham, G. (2002). Cross-cultural software production and use: a structurational analysis. *MIS Quarterly,* 26, 359–380.

Waters, M. (2001). *Globalization.* Second edition. Routledge.

Weisinger, J. and Trauth, E. (2002). Situating culture in the global information sector. *Information Technology and People,* 15, 306–320.

CHAPTER 13

Achieving advanced supply chain management through Internet-based electronic commerce

Robert B. Johnston, Horace Cheok Mak and Sherah Kurnia

INTRODUCTION

The use of electronic commerce (EC) technologies to improve the efficiency of supply chains has been widely promoted in the retail and general merchandising industry. This business-to-business EC makes use of standardized product numbering, automatic identification technologies, electronic data interchange (EDI), electronic marketplaces (Kaplan and Sawhney, 2000) and data synchronization hubs (GS1 Australia, 2006) as its essential core technologies (Johnston, 1998; 1999; Mak, 1998; Turban *et al.*, 2006). Most large retail chains now make use of EC with their larger, technologically sophisticated suppliers to control a significant proportion of their replenishment transaction value. To that extent, EC can be thought to have reached significant adoption levels in the industry. Direct operational savings accrue from the elimination of data rekeying, through the speed and accuracy of application-to-application transfer of machine-readable data, and via the automatic identification of products and shipments. However, in keeping with the Pareto principle, the remaining transaction value is spread over a large proportion of non-EC-compliant suppliers, usually small- to medium-sized enterprises (SMEs) who are technologically unsophisticated.

Furthermore, it is increasingly being realized that the greatest benefits of supply chain EC are to be derived through its role in enabling advanced replenishment and distribution techniques which require strong coordination between the operational activities of various supply chain parties. To be practical, such tight coordination of activities demands 100 per cent compliance to EC. Thus, despite their small contribution to transaction value, the existence of a large proportion (by number) of non-EC-enabled suppliers creates a barrier for large retailers and distributors in implementing supply chain reforms. Unwillingness on the part of SMEs to adopt EDI in particular has proved to be a problem for large retailers. These SMEs typically do not have enough to gain from the application-to-application functionality and global connectivity offered by the traditional approach to EDI to justify its high cost (Iacovou *et al.*, 1995; Kurnia and Johnston, 2003; Mak and Johnston, 1998; Mehrtens *et al.*, 2001). In being the most transient and least strategic-thinking sector of the economy they have also proved difficult to coerce.

Increasing interest is being shown by large retail players in new Internet-based EC methods for the exchange of electronic trading documents with unsophisticated small suppliers (Mak, 1998; Mak and Johnston, 1999). The latest development is the commercial promulgation of AS2 (Internet Engineering Task Force, 2006) as a secure transport layer for document exchange over the Web, largely led by Wal-mart's initiatives with its suppliers (Barlas, 2002). Not only is the Internet a global network of networks with high throughput and low cost, it brings through the Web new open and highly standardized data exchange protocols that are ideally suited to the transfer and presentation of digital business documents (Mak, 1998; Turban *et al.*, 2006). A large number of products and services have recently appeared purporting to support Internet-based EDI and a significant target for these products has been the particular requirements of small trading partners (Mak and Johnston, 1997; 1998).

The aim of this chapter is to elaborate on the way in which these Internet-based supply chain EC products and services are transforming the prospects for universal supply chain EC compliance in the retail industry. We illustrate this analysis using a case study of the EC infrastructure used by Australia's leading supermarket chain, Coles Myer Limited (CML), which makes use of these Internet-based EC products. CML's aim is to leverage their considerable existing EC investment by achieving 100 per cent supplier compliance to EC, thereby enabling advanced supply chain reforms.

We begin by describing in detail the concept of cross-docking as an example of a distribution technique used in advanced supply chain management. Cross-docking is currently being widely advocated in the grocery industry, for instance as part of the influential Efficient Customer Response (ECR) concept (Hoffman and Mehra, 2000; Kurnia and Johnston, 2001; Kurt Salmon Associates, 1993). Improving existing cross-docking operations and extending the concept to wider product ranges forms one of CML's main motivations for 100 per cent EC compliance by suppliers. Additionally, cross-docking affords an excellent example of the basic paradigm shift of advanced supply chain reforms in general – away from islands of automation and towards the use of a high quality data communications channel between trading parties to deal with operational complexity. This shift brings high operational efficiencies, but demands EC compliance in the construction of such a channel for coordinated activity. The analysis of cross-docking also sets the scene to discuss the contribution that Internet EC can make to enable these reforms.

We then discuss in detail why the traditional approach to EDI was unable to deliver 100 per cent EC compliance. We also analyse two key ideas that Internet-based EC products and services have contributed that appear to overcome these difficulties. We then present the case study of CML's EC infrastructure, which strongly incorporates these ideas, and discuss the further development of the underlying concept of EC infrastructure. In our concluding remarks we describe the latest trend in this area toward process-driven EC using service-oriented architectures (SOA). We also note the emergence of a new conception of supply chain EC that features a richer choice of network topology, delivery media and message types commensurate with the variety of participating trading partner capabilities, in order to improve supply chain visibility and end-to-end process integration.

CROSS-DOCKING AS AN EXAMPLE OF EC-ENABLED SUPPLY CHAIN REFORM

Cross-docking (Abdolvand and Kurnia, 2005; Kurnia and Johnston, 2001; Luton, 2003) is a new method, currently being advocated in the grocery and general merchandise retailing industry, of distributing goods from a large number of manufacturers to a large number of retail outlets via a centralized distribution centre (DC). As an innovation it typifies new approaches to supply chain acceleration and buffer stock reduction, which employ greater coordination of the activities of participating parties by means of EC.

The traditional approach to distribution of high variety products via a distribution centre, the so-called 'pick-and-pack' approach, relies on a buffer stock of each product at the DC. (In the following discussion we use CML's terminology for various distribution techniques since across the industry there is some variation in the use of various terms.) Goods are generally ordered from the DC frequently and in small quantities by the retail store in order to minimize its stock levels. However, replenishment of stocks from the manufacturers is triggered by reorder point methods. In the interests of economies of scale these orders are generally large and infrequent. There is thus little coordination between the replenishment by the retailers of goods *from* the DC and the replenishment of goods from the manufacturers *by* the DC. This lack of coordination of activities has several consequences. First, it results in large stocks of products at the distribution centre. This problem becomes worse as a retail chain tries to distribute a greater variety of products. Managing this stock requires both a large area for storage and sophisticated systems. Managing stocks within a finite warehouse capacity under variable demand requires sophisticated computerized warehouse management systems, forecasting systems and inventory management systems. To some extent it also requires double handling of goods since these are put away in store and then picked at a later time. Finally, since replenishment orders are consolidated at the distribution centre, the manufacturer is effectively denied sight of events at any individual store. The manufacturer, therefore, cannot gauge consumer buying patterns. The advantage of the method is that it is able to provide rapid replenishment to stores at low risk.

Cross-docking, by contrast, seeks to eliminate all DC buffer stocks by converting the distribution problem into one of sortation. Retailers place frequent small replenishment orders directly with manufacturers, preferably using EDI. Manufacturers deliver goods, generally for several stores, to the distribution centre for immediate distribution. Shipments are broken down to individual store level and sorted by destination, preferably using bar-coded destination information and electromechanical means, and then repacked by the store for dispatch. Radio frequency identification (RFID) is set to have a role in this area too (Sarma, 2001). Such an approach achieves a much more efficient use of space, requires no double handling of goods and sortation can be accomplished with relatively low technology. However, it requires strong coordination between the activities of the retail stores and the manufacturers. Such coordination can generally only be achieved through speed-of-light digital communication. This is accomplished first by using EDI purchase orders between the retailers and manufacturers. It is also necessary to simplify, as much as possible, the processing of goods at the distribution centre. The minimum technical requirement to automate sorting is the use of manufacturers' barcoding on cartons from which the destination store can then be machine read. However, the additional requirement to check actual articles against orders can be further reduced by the use of other electronic commerce technologies such as the GS1 standardized product numbering scheme (GS1, 2006) and automatic identification technologies (bar-coding or RFID), to increase data accuracy through procedures at the manufacturers' dispatch site. For example if, as goods are packed, an EDI advanced shipping notice (ASN) message is created by scanning product bar-codes (so-called 'scan-packing') and this is sent to the DC ahead of the shipment, and a unique shipment number for the ASN is bar-coded on the cartons, the contents of the cartons can be retrieved at the DC by scanning the shipment number. Individual item checking can be automated or eliminated.

Thus, while cross-docking promises operational and infrastructural cost savings it presents a new range of system implementation issues that require cooperation across the boundaries between retailers, distributors and manufacturers (Abdolvand and Kurnia, 2005; Kurnia and Johnston, 2001; 2003). The pick-and-pack approach uses sophisticated physical and computer systems to deal with the complexity of distributing a high variety of products between multiple manufacturers and retail stores, essentially by predicting and planning the future. By contrast, cross-docking relies heavily upon electronic commerce technologies for the establishment of a high quality communication channel between participating parties to achieve coordinated action, since the use of paper-based control documents provides insufficient processing speed, accuracy and data integrity. The level of technology involved in establishing such a communication channel is fairly low.

The key challenge is not the technology itself but achieving 100 per cent participant compliance to the technology. Thus, advanced supply chain reforms, which incorporate electronic commerce, can be seen as part of a general paradigm shift. This fundamental shift is in the perception of the role of IT in business performance improvement. It is a shift from the earlier vision of computers as intelligent logic engines (to be applied to problem solving and planning), to a view of computers as a medium for communication and coordination between parties and business transactions.

THE FAILURE OF TRADITIONAL EDI IN ADVANCED SUPPLY CHAIN MANAGEMENT

Prior to the commercial use of the Internet, the standard method for implementing electronic business information exchange in a large-supply chain was via EDI. This used the services of a value-added network (VAN), which provided store and forward facilities for messages transmitted over private wide-area networks (WANs), which they frequently owned (Emmelhainz, 1990; Johnston, 1998; Turban *et al.*, 2006). Outputs from diverse business applications operating on diverse platforms were translated into standard EDI transaction sets using mapping software – again often provided by the VAN. This use of industry-wide, national or international EDI message standards ensured that the EDI network was open since it allowed potential participants to choose mapping software and VAN services independently. It was assumed that these EDI messages would be transmitted from computer application to computer application, in order that the maximum operational benefits from labour reduction, increased accuracy and greater speed would be realized through the elimination of unnecessary data re-entry.

This traditional vision of EDI has changed in three ways. First, the Internet has largely replaced private networks as a transport medium for EDI messages, although post-Internet private TCP/IP networks such as ANX (ANX, 2006) have also emerged for applications requiring high security and high reliability. Second, eXtensible Markup Language (XML) has been widely hyped as a superior syntax for structuring EDI messages (Huemer, 2000), although replacement of traditional EDI messages by XML structured ones has not been as universal as initially anticipated (Kanakamedala *et al.*, 2003). Finally, the AS2 standard has simplified transmission of messages (either traditionally structured or using XML) over the Internet in a simulated point-to-point connection by making use of open encryption and handshaking protocols. Despite these changes in the favoured transportation network, the transport layer and the message formatting layer, the basic business concept of traditional EDI, which is to send a standardized message between trading partners running diverse applications, remains.

In the grocery and general merchandise retailing industry, this traditional approach to EDI has been widely adopted by the larger, more technically sophisticated retailers and manufacturers. Since interactions between these sophisticated players represents perhaps 80 per cent of all transactions in the supply chain, from the point of view of the value of transactions controlled, traditional EDI can be thought of as having achieved considerable penetration in the industry. This translates into considerable direct cost saving in the replenishment cycle. However, a large number (perhaps 80 per cent) of all suppliers, who are technically unsophisticated and generally small, fail to use EDI. Their non-compliance is not a significant barrier to achieving the direct benefits of EDI, since their transaction value is small. However, it does nevertheless present an obstacle to achieving the more significant benefits obtainable from EC as an enabling technology for supply chain reform initiatives such as cross-docking, which do not run smoothly with less than 100 per cent EDI compliance. The size of this obstacle is measured in terms of the number of firms that have to be persuaded to come onboard, rather than their transaction value.

It is now clear to many large retail chains that have the most to gain from advanced supply chain management that 100 per cent EC compliance cannot be achieved using the traditional approach. In the early EDI era, it was generally believed that small suppliers could be brought into the EC network through mutual benefit, coercion or critical mass effects (Emmelhainz, 1990; Sarich, 1989; Zinn and Tahac, 1988). However, as a result of the persistence of the non-compliance problem, it is now recognized that these ideas are flawed and new solutions are being sought. The problem is that these traditional approaches to achieving compliance are not compatible with the profile of the typical SME (Iacovou et al., 1995; Mak, 1998; Mehrtens et al., 2001). Small to medium-sized enterprises typically interact with a small number of trading partners (Johns et al., 1989; Mehrtens et al., 2001), and often have only one large customer. They therefore have little to gain from the global connectivity offered by the traditional EDI open network. The system purchase, installation and running costs of the traditional approach are high. Such firms typically have simple (often manual) operational and financial systems (Iacovou et al., 1995; Rodwell and

Shadur, 1997) and therefore have little to gain from the application-to-application connectivity offered by the traditional approach (Scala and McGrath, 1993; Turban *et al.*, 2006). Thus, both the initial set-up costs and ongoing operating costs of the traditional approach cannot generally be justified by any operational benefit to SMEs. These businesses would need to bear these costs simply to protect themselves against the threat of 'de-sourcing' (Zinn and Tahac, 1988). Moreover, small enterprises are the most transient and least strategically-oriented segment of the economy, which makes them difficult to influence on this basis. Finally, because the VAN offerings were designed to interact with existing applications on diverse platforms they were usually general purpose rather than turnkey in nature, and to install and operate them generally required higher levels of technical sophistication than is typically present in SME organizations.

USE OF INTERNET EC TO FACILITATE SUPPLY CHAIN REFORMS

The large EDI players with the most to gain from supply chain reforms are increasingly looking to non-traditional Internet-based EDI solutions as a means of resolving the problem of EDI non-compliance of small unsophisticated trading partners. To comply with their EDI-enabled trading partner's information requirements, non-EDI-enabled trading partners can use a Web browser to fill in a form-based Web page representing a business document. To access the Internet they need only a personal computer, a modem and an Internet Service Provider (ISP). They require little more computer expertise than that which is fast becoming common knowledge.

The last decade has seen a large number of new software products and services that enable Internet-based EDI. These products have been conceived in response to the new cost structure of the Internet, the access to a global market it creates, and the reduction of the stranglehold of the traditional VANs upon EDI software and services that this new global public network has afforded. Mak and Johnston (1997; 1998) propose a classification of these Internet EDI products. Some of these products merely translate the traditional approach to the new Internet transport medium. For instance, message-mapping software is available to translate application output to traditional standardized EDI messages. These EDI messages are then sent between parties using Internet protocols such as Simple Mail Transport Protocol (SMTP),

Multipurpose Internet Mail Extensions (MIME), File Transfer Protocol (FTP) and/or Secure/HyperText Transfer Protocol (HTTP/HTTPS). More recent products use AS2 standards, which bundle these Web standards with encryption to produce a fully endorsed secure message transport vehicle over the Web. Small traders can gain access to the Web through ordinary ISPs or through Application Service Providers specializing in EDI, variously called Internet Value-Added Networks, Integrated Value-Added Networks (IVANs) or Internet Value Added Services (IVAS). These are often commercial offshoots of the transitional VANs (for instance, GXS Trading Grid).

A significant proportion of the new products differ markedly in their approach from traditional EDI. Two important new concepts are increasingly being embodied in this group of non-traditional Internet EDI products that are crucial to a new match between EDI requirements and SME capabilities. These are:

1. The provision of a *new* mode of distribution and collection of electronic business documents between large players and their small unsophisticated trading partners that is more appropriate to the capabilities and requirements of the small players. These products (for example, see Mak and Johnston, 1998) generally provide the tools to build a hub-and-spoke network between the large player and its small suppliers using Web-based client/server technology. Since these products generally require that the client and server programs are built with the proprietary tools provided, these subnetworks are not open in the traditional EDI sense, and often use proprietary or Web messaging standards rather than traditional EDI standards. These products feature the capability to tailor business documents and document handling processes to the needs of the large player while providing a cheap, easy-to-use and turnkey client package to the small trader. These products recognize the inadequacy of the one-size-fits-all approach of traditional EDI, which was only appropriate for interactions between sophisticated trading partners.
2. The recognition of the need for large players to support and efficiently manage *multiple* modes of delivery and receipt of electronic business documents appropriate to the existence of multiple kinds of trading partners. This requirement is addressed in 'intelligent gateway' products (Mak and Johnston, 1998) which are capable of receiving application flat-file, XML or EDI message inputs, and route the data to trading partners

using various formats and media based on a profile of the trading partner. The reverse process is also supported. The media supported include private VAN networks, the Internet, public telephone lines and dedicated connections. The formats supported include traditional standards-based EDI messages intended for sophisticated trading partners, XML-based EDI messages, proprietary or Web-form messages of the type described above intended for unsophisticated partners, formats based on popular software packages including Excel, proprietary formats specific to use in high-volume exchanges between cooperating trading partners, and fax for non-EDI-enabled trading partners.

Intelligent gateways provide a link between the traditional open EDI network of sophisticated trading partners, who value global connectivity and application-to-application functionality, and the hub-and-spoke networks specifically catering to large players' needs and small players' capabilities. Thus, what is emerging is a new vision of universal business-to-business EC based on a richer network which explicitly recognizes the existence of multiple kinds of trading partners and trading relationships, multiple delivery modalities and message formats, and a fairer distribution of costs, benefits and risks between participating parties. From the large traders' point of view these new products allow them to leverage their considerable investment in traditional EDI by achieving the benefits of 100 per cent EDI compliance at a relatively small extra cost. We would argue that the emergence of these new EDI concepts is at least as important a contribution of the Internet to advanced supply chain management as the more heavily hyped electronic marketplace concept (Kaplan and Sawhney, 2000).

CASE STUDY – COLES MYER LIMITED

Coles Myer Limited is Australia's largest retail store chain and is the country's largest non-government employer, with over 165 000 staff and annual sales of over A$36 billion. CML operates eleven retail brands through 2600 stores in Australia and New Zealand including Coles, Coles Express, Bi-Lo, Kmart, Target, Fosseys, Liquorland, Theo, 1st Choice, Harris Technology and Officeworks. CML spends over A$27 billion each year on buying merchandise and services (Coles Myer Limited, 2006). At the time of the case study in 1997, CML had more than 15 000 suppliers (including grocery, general merchandise and service suppliers): 1800 suppliers used the traditional EDI approach, while the remainder used conventional paper-based document processes via regular mail, phone calls or fax, to exchange business data with CML.

This case study describes how CML is making use of Internet-based EDI products to enable them to handle all their grocery and general merchandise replenishments (from approximately 10 000 suppliers) through a single centralized EC system. CML is aiming for 100 per cent compliance to electronic purchase orders and ASNs by using the system, which includes an Internet-based component tailored to the needs of small suppliers. The following account of the EC infrastructure at CML and its significance in enabling cross-docking is based on a number of data sources. These sources include: semi-structured interviews and follow-up communications with the Electronic Trading Coordinator; company documents; participation in CML's original 'proof of concept' project as observer; and involvement in the product and Internet EDI strategy evaluation for CML's front-end Internet EDI system as an independent evaluator.

An in-depth case study and participatory research method was chosen to gain deep access to the practices of a significant industrial player. In keeping with the limitations of this research method (Galliers, 1992; Yin, 1989), it has been used mainly to generate novel propositions concerning the role of the Internet in advanced supply chain management that will be tested empirically in future research.

CML has various business applications for different retail brands, running on different system platforms. In the past, there were a number of translators mapping flat-file outputs from these applications into traditional EDI messages that were sent via the store-and-forward facilities of a VAN to EDI-enabled trading partners using the VAN's private network. In addition, there were multiple manual systems to send and receive trading documents to and from non-EDI-enabled suppliers via regular mail, phone calls or fax. The previous EDI infrastructure is shown in Figure 13.1.

This EDI infrastructure presented a number of problems for CML, both in achieving direct operational cost saving through EDI and in implementing EC-enabled supply chain reforms such as cross-docking. First, there is the basic undesirability of maintaining multiple document distribution systems, including manual ones. Second, manual systems offer little opportunity to control the integrity of delivery data received from non-EDI-enabled suppliers. When preparing a manual delivery docket from a CML purchase order (PO), suppliers can easily alter the quantity, price or the ordered item itself, either intentionally or by

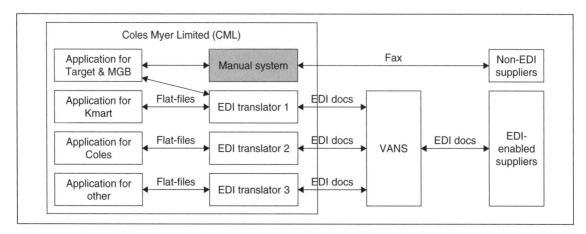

Figure 13.1
The previous EDI infrastructure at CML

error. Ideally, CML would like suppliers to base an electronic ASN upon data received in the electronic PO in order to improve data integrity. The principle at work here is the data turnaround principle (Johnston, 1999) which states that data received by a trading partner is likely to be more accurate if it is derived from data sent earlier by that trading partner. Accuracy would further increase by providing some intelligent data checking to the supplier's interface and by using bar-code scanning to acquire product numbers direct from the packed items.

Due to reliance on the traditional VAN-based approach, CML experienced difficulty over many years of EDI operation in bringing small suppliers into the network. Small suppliers lack the technical, financial and human resources to develop a traditional EDI system to handle all the functionality required by CML. According to the Electronic Trading Coordinator at CML, the conventional VAN-based EDI development costs for small suppliers, including the costs of purchasing and EDI translator and communication software, are in the range of A$5000 to A$20 000. Transferring 10 kilobytes of data via a VAN might cost a small supplier, at list price, A$4 per document, plus a monthly VAN subscription fee of A$100. While these costs may be justifiable for a larger supplier who can gain mutual benefit from the investment, small suppliers generally have primitive in-house business systems (often manual) and cannot use the potential benefits from application-to-application transfer of data from the VAN-based EDI approach to justify the decision. With very few customers, they also gain little from the global connectivity of traditional EDI.

Finally, two further issues prevented CML from reaping the full benefits of cross-docking operations within the previous infrastructure: a lack of data accuracy resulting from the use of paper-based trading documents, and operational complications resulting from the existence of non-EC-compliant suppliers. While it is possible to use cross-docking without EC compliance, it incurs labour-intensive activities at the distribution centre, such as manual bar-coding of cartons and manual inspection and verification of carton contents. Such activities can be substantially reduced when all suppliers are compliant to standardized product and shipment numbering schemes, such as the EAN numbering system, bar-coding and electronic ASNs.

Based on a need to overcome these problems and extensive experience with the capabilities of small suppliers, CML determined the following requirements for the new system:

1. The systems need to support existing VAN-based EDI. Both CML and its larger suppliers have a considerable investment in the existing VAN-based infrastructure and it was decided that investment in the new Internet system should leverage this existing investment rather than replace it.

2. There should be a single centralized system to handle business documents from all retail brands.

3. Use of the Internet should be part of the system because of its ability to deliver documents to small suppliers at low cost and in user-friendly form. According to the Electronic Trading Coordinator at CML, the incremental cost of transferring a 10 kilobyte message over the Internet is about A\$0.50 (mainly associated with telecommunication costs, such as telephone call charges), plus, typically, a A\$25 monthly subscription fee for an ISP. Small suppliers could use a CML-provided Web-form Internet application as a data entry system, not necessarily using the traditional EDI standard format needed for application-to-application data transfer. However, this use of the Internet requires issues of security and reliability to be considered. It was decided that mission critical transfers should continue to be made via the VAN network. Thus, the transfers to be made via the Internet component were not subject to high security and reliability requirements. Nevertheless, the security of HTTPS using the Secure Socket Layer (SSL) – which enables point-to-point data transmission without storage at the ISP site – together with the password protection and document control facilities provided routinely by third party Internet EDI development software, will provide a secure and reliable transport mechanism for these Web forms and other file

types. Eventually, this may provide a low-cost alternative transport system even for standard EDI files.

4. A limit was placed on the system so that the cost of participation to small suppliers should be no more than A\$500 for a basic system and A\$1000 for a system with extra bar-code scanning and label printing facilities. The monthly running cost should not be greater than A\$25 for an ISP subscription plus phone calls. Suppliers must also provide a PC, a modem and a printer.

5. The requirement to keep operating costs down to these low levels has led to an additional requirement that the front-end used by the small suppliers must be capable of running offline from the central CML system while shipments are packed. Otherwise ISP charges might become prohibitive.

6. In order to facilitate cross-docking distribution the system should provide for the highest quality data about impending shipments. This led to the requirement that the system should make use of the electronic turnaround document concept and scan-packing. A paper-based turnaround document is one that is expected to be returned by the receiver to the sender with certain data added. From the viewpoint of data integrity, this approach is superior to receiving a separate manual response, since it does not require transcription of data on the original document. In electronic form this means that a document message sent by a small supplier to CML can only be constructed based on the contents of the original document source from CML to which it is a response. Scan-packing means that any data used to construct the ASN should be entered by directly scanning the EAN product number barcodes on the products as they are packed.

To satisfy these requirements, CML developed a new EC infrastructure that makes use of both the intelligent gateway concept and an Internet-based hub-and-spoke network for use by small unsophisticated suppliers. The intelligent gateway replaces the multiple translators of the current system and transfers flat-file outputs to and from the various brands' application programs. It translates these flat-files to various formats, determined from a trading partner profile database, including fax, traditional EDI and Web-forms, which are also routed via various communications media including the private network of their VAN, the Internet, telephone lines and point-to-point fixed connections. The new EC infrastructure at CML is shown in Figure 13.2.

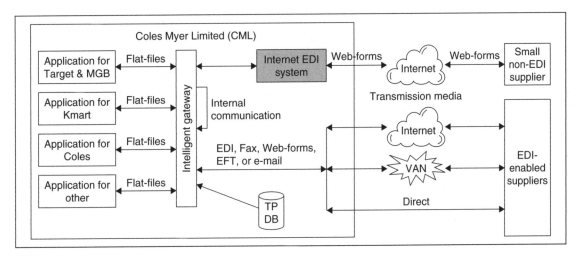

Figure 13.2
The new e-commerce infrastructure at CML

An important component of the new infrastructure is the Internet EDI hub, shown shaded in Figure 13.2. There are many products now available for exchange of business documents over the Internet using a wide range of approaches (Mak and Johnston, 1997; 1998). These differ mainly: in their use, or non-use, of traditional EDI standards; in whether they involve third-party Internet sites; and in whether they force the use of software from the same provider at both sender and receiver sites. The choice between these various options should be made on the basis of the degree of system integration (application-to-application or application-to-person) and the degree of connectivity (global or hub-and-spoke) required of the Internet EDI system (Mak, 1998). On the basis of their evaluation process and 'proof of concept' project, CML chose an approach which uses software from a single provider to create both the CML hub and the small supplier front-end data entry application. This allows for document exchanges that are not structured using traditional EDI standards, and facilitates the participation of SMEs in the EC network, without needing full EDI translation facilities.

For this Internet EDI subsystem, CML chose to use client/server technology. The server interfaces with business applications via the intelligent gateway and distributes business documents as Web-forms that can be displayed by the small suppliers using a client program incorporating a Web browser. CML produces customized form-based document templates using tools provided by the software vendor, and these are distributed with the suppliers' front-end program.

CML had to choose between so-called 'thick client' and 'thin client' approaches. In the thin client approach, nearly all the data processing operations are performed by the server (hub) program and the client software may consist of little more than a Web browser. In the thick client approach, the client program has some capability for processing the exchanged data, independently of the hub. A typical example is where the client program performs data editing without needing to refer back to data stored at the hub. This would generally result in duplicate storage of data at the hub and client. A thick client approach is more suitable when the business running the client program wishes to use the exchanged data in their own applications, because in this instance the well-known problems that attend data duplication might be justified. Hence, we would normally associate the choice of thick client approaches with a desire for application-to-application system integration.

CML had an additional requirement that the small suppliers should be able to perform much of their data entry offline – that is, while not connected to their ISP. Consequently, motivated by the desire for a high standard of data integrity, CML chose to adopt a thick client approach in order to enable extensive data editing to be performed while processing offline. While not a primary requirement, this choice also reserves the opportunity for suppliers to integrate their in-house applications with the front-end data entry system by reusing the local database or exporting the data from the front-end system.

The Internet EDI subsystem incorporates the 'data turnaround' principle. Purchase orders are received by the hub program from the application programs via the gateway and are converted to Web-forms. These can be retrieved by the client front-end program over the Internet using HTTPS and can be displayed or printed. Upon despatch of goods these purchase orders form the basis for the creation of an ASN and a bar-coded carton label. The original purchase order is stored temporarily at the client site and is used as a basis for edit checks upon packed quantities and product numbers. In the scan-packing process, the product numbers and quantities for the ASN are entered by actually scanning the EAN product number bar-codes on the items being packed. A label for the shipment carton is also printed which shows, among other information, a bar-coded Serial Shipping Container Code (Application Identifier '00') using the EAN/UCC128 label standard, and a bar-coded destination store number (Application Identifier '90'). Figures 13.3 to 13.5 show the purchase order, the ASN entry interface and the carton label. The ASN is transmitted via the Internet as a Web-form to the server program and the receiving applications are updated via the

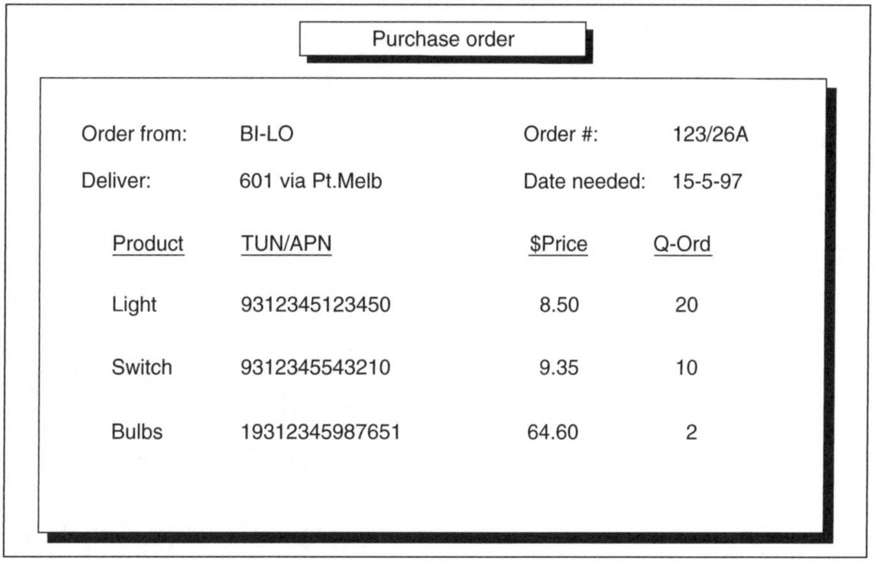

Purchase order

| Order from: | BI-LO | | Order #: | 123/26A |
| Deliver: | 601 via Pt.Melb | | Date needed: | 15-5-97 |

Product	TUN/APN	$Price	Q-Ord
Light	9312345123450	8.50	20
Switch	9312345543210	9.35	10
Bulbs	19312345987651	64.60	2

Figure 13.3
Sample purchase
order displayed or
printed from the
Web browser

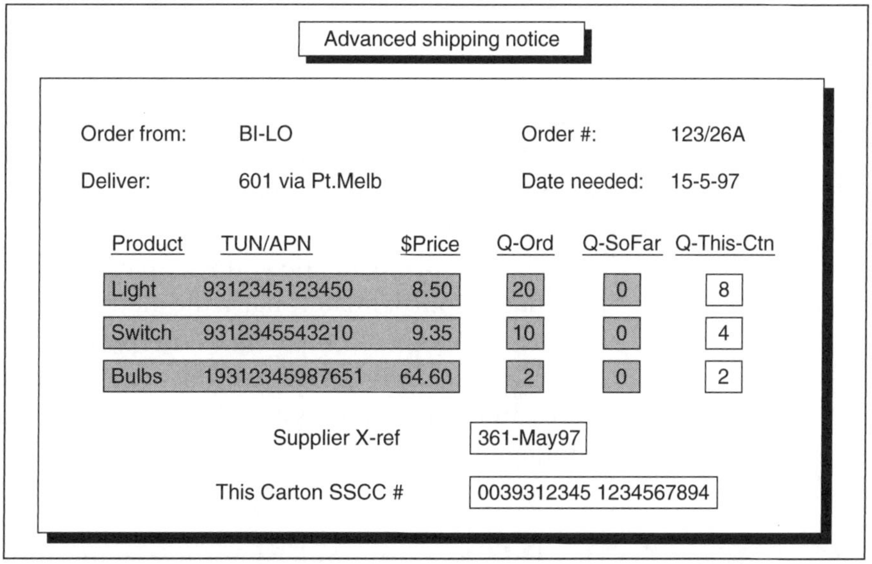

Advanced shipping notice

| Order from: | BI-LO | | Order #: | 123/26A |
| Deliver: | 601 via Pt.Melb | | Date needed: | 15-5-97 |

Product	TUN/APN	$Price	Q-Ord	Q-SoFar	Q-This-Ctn
Light	9312345123450	8.50	20	0	8
Switch	9312345543210	9.35	10	0	4
Bulbs	19312345987651	64.60	2	0	2

Supplier X-ref   361-May97

This Carton SSCC #   0039312345 1234567894

Figure 13.4
Sample form for
turnaround ASN
data entry (entry-
enabled fields are
boxed)

gateway to reflect this impending shipment and to facilitate receiving at the distribution centre.

At the distribution centre, the bar-coded shipment number can be scanned and the data are used as the key to retrieving the contents of the shipment via the ASN. Having the packed EAN product numbers available in this way facilitates checking of the shipments. When full EC compliance and scan-packing is in place, the quality of the shipment data will be enhanced and, therefore, checking upon delivery may be

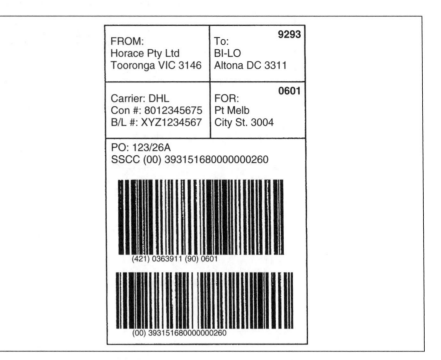

Figure 13.5
Sample shipping
container label

reduced to a low level. Payments can also be made based on this data, referred to as Evaluated Receipts Settlement (Johnston, 1998; 1999), leading to further process simplification. The bar-coded store number is used to control the electromechanical automatic carton sorting facility. With full ASN, bar-code and scan-packing compliance, there is the potential to approximately halve the all-up distribution cost per carton using cross-docking compared to the pick-and-pack method (Kurnia and Johnston, 2001). The main savings are through reduced warehouse and computer system infrastructure and reduced double handling of cartons.

FROM DOCUMENT-DRIVEN TO PROCESS-DRIVEN ELECTRONIC COMMERCE

The new infrastructure at CML is one company's approach to achieving a richer connection to a variety of trading partners through Internet-based electronic commerce. CML chose to purchase and install a gateway product provided by a third-party software provider and also to use third-party software to build their Internet-EDI subnetwork. CML is a sufficiently large player in the industry to justify these outlays in terms of operational benefits and the flexibility that a tailored solution offers them in designing new business processes. However, these same Internet EDI connectivity concepts are also available to sophisticated EDI players in other ways. The new breed of third-party Internet-based EDI service providers, IVANs, also offer services based on these same concepts to allow traditional EDI-enabled players to reach both other EDI-enabled trading partners and small unsophisticated trading partners. Typically, IVANs will receive traditionally structured EDI messages and route them via private networks or the Internet, or convert them into Web-forms or fax for small trading partners. They also support the reverse translation processes. The Perth-based Australian company Atkins Carlyle (Anonymous, 1998) chose this approach to EC with small trading partners. Other examples of this third-party gateway approach include 'AT&T InterCommerce' (AT&T, 1999), an IVAN service that enables SMEs to reach their EDI-enabled trading partners using Web-based solutions.

The initial concept of the intelligent EC gateway and the Internet-based hub-and-spoke network was *transaction/document driven*, where a business transaction initiates the data transformation based on trading partners' profiles including transaction type relationships and communication channels. As large retailers, including CML, have achieved many operational benefits via the enhanced connectivity obtained from document-driven EC through 100 per cent EC compliance in business document exchange while leveraging their traditional EDI investments, they have identified the need for end-to-end business process integration; this is not just with their back-end applications such as ERP, inventory control, order management systems, and so on, but also with their operational management systems such as transportation management systems (TMS) and warehouse management systems (WMS), to enhance business process flows and the visibility of their supply chain operation. Therefore, more recently, the concept of a *process-driven* business-to-business (B2B) EC gateway has interested many organizations wishing to improve their business process integration and supply chain visibility.

Typically, process-driven B2B EC gateways are developed based on Service-Oriented Architecture (SOA) rather than client/server architecture. SOA applications are built using loosely coupled and interoperable services and thus support integration and consolidation activities within a complex enterprise system (Oracle, 2006). B2B solution vendors (see, for example, Sterling Commerce, 2006) have developed process-driven B2B EC gateway products that help organizations to establish the required platform to enable business-to-business collaboration among trading partners with different systems and infrastructures across the supply chain. The concept of process-driven EC should not be considered a completely new concept, but it should rather be seen as a progression of document-driven EC.

Unlike document-driven EC, which only facilitates the exchange of business documents electronically through various channels based on trading partners' profiles, process-driven EC also deals with the entire business process involving transactions or documents exchange. With this process-driven EC concept, visibility throughout the supply chain is enhanced because business processes among trading partners and enterprise supply chain operations systems can be streamlined and integrated. Therefore, organizations can identify any business transactions or exceptional events and respond to them more quickly. In addition, business logic is often embedded into the system to drive or monitor business processes and trigger automated responses. As a result, an improvement in business process management across the supply chains can be obtained. Process-driven EC has become the fundamental infrastructure for achieving the vision for advanced supply chain management and many leading organizations are moving towards it.

CONCLUSIONS

This chapter has analysed the role that Internet-based EC is playing in making advanced supply chain management initiatives, such as cross-docking, achievable in the grocery and general merchandise retailing industry. We have described the problems that the traditional approach to EDI poses to large retailers in achieving 100 per cent EC compliance from small, unsophisticated suppliers. We have also indicated two contributions that new non-traditional Internet-based EDI products are making toward a viable solution to this problem which recognizes the limited capabilities and requirements of small suppliers. In the case study, we have illustrated how these new ideas are being used in a large retail chain in Australia. We have also discussed how the new infrastructure of this large retail chain, which is based on a document-driven EC gateway, has improved connectivity with small trading partners while leveraging the traditional EDI investment with large trading partners. Furthermore, we have briefly discussed the relatively more recent concept of process-driven EC that is seen as a progression from the document-driven EC concept to provide better supply chain integration and visibility.

The traditional vision of EDI was that trading partners would send data seamlessly from their application programs to those of their trading partners – transmitting digital documents structured according to international standards from application to application without manual data entry. Despite changes in the delivery medium (i.e. from private networks to the Internet), in the formatting syntax (i.e. from traditional EDI formats to XML) and in standards (e.g. from UN EDIFACT to ebXML) this traditional EDI approach is still the backbone of inter-organizational system connectivity among large manufacturers, distributors and retailers in the retail industry. The new non-traditional Internet-based EDI products such as EC gateway solutions and low-end form-based EDI compliance solutions now enhance this backbone with proprietary hub-and-spoke networks catering to the particular needs and capabilities of small players. The hubs will be centred on large players or Internet third party sites.

This new EDI network topology involves relaxing a number of rigid and utopian ideas of the traditional, one-size-fits-all EDI approach. In the traditional approach, the universal adoption of internationally regulated message formatting standards was supposed to provide unlimited connectivity between trading partners and to facilitate application-to-application data transfer between diverse application platforms. When used in hub-and-spoke subnetworks, the relaxation of traditional standards requirements by these products may not be a backward step, since it provides greater flexibility to the large players to develop systems quickly that meet their particular needs. Since application-to-application and global business connectivity are not particularly important to small trading partners, proprietary message formats can be used by them in a hub-and-spoke configuration without compromising the global nature of the backbone network. The platform independence of the network that was traditionally supposed to require universal compliance to standards is now achieved in additional ways through intelligent gateways at large player or Internet third-party sites.

Additionally, this richer approach to EDI connectivity embodies more realistic ideas about the nature and relations between trading partners within and along retail supply chains. It recognizes the existence of a variety of levels of technical sophistication and capability among trading partners, but also an uneven distribution of potential benefits from EC among them, particularly from the most advanced supply chain management initiatives. The new range of connectivity options made available by Internet-based EC allows for a more equitable distribution of the costs and risks commensurate with benefits, which, being more in keeping with the political realities of the industry, should enhance the chances of widespread adoption of EC over traditional enforcement approaches.

The increased connectivity will not only benefit large players but also the small players. For the small players this new form of Internet EDI may prove to be a palatable point of entry into electronic commerce with subsequent benefits. With a working familiarity of electronic exchange of data, initially through an application-to-person approach, the benefits of transferring data directly to a simple accounting package may become apparent. Knowledge gained through the use of a single customer EDI system might be leveraged by small suppliers to provide a first-mover advantage over their peers with other customers. An important issue will be the provision of migration paths for small trading partners between these alternative modes of connection, moving to the greater EC network as the sophistication of small players increases.

REFERENCES

Abdolvand, N. and Kurnia, S. (2005). The EPC technology implications on cross docking. *Proceedings of the San Diego International Systems Conference*, San Diego, July.

Anonymous (1998). Technologies to grow electronic trading communities for Atkins Carlyle. *EC Edge: Newsletter of Tradegate ECA*, 3, 13.

ANX (2006). ANX eBusiness: an SAIC company. *ANX.com*, 20 November. http://www.anx.com/

AT&T (1999). *AT&T InterCommerce*. October. http://www.att.net.au/products/interc.html

Barlas, D. (2002). Wal-Mart upgrades EDI model. *E-Business News*, 10 October. http://www.line56.com/articles/default.asp?NewsID=4083

Coles Myer Limited (2006). About us. *Coles Myer Website*, 20 November. http://www.colesmyer.com.au/AboutUs/

Emmelhainz, M. A. (1990). *Electronic Data Interchange: A Total Management View*. Van Nostrand.

Galliers, R. D. (1992). Choosing information systems research approaches. In *Information Systems Research: Issues, Methods, and Practical Guidelines* (R. D. Galliers, ed.) pp. 144–162, Blackwell Scientific.

GS1 (2006). GS1: the global language of business. *gs1.org*, 20 November. http://www.gs1.org/

GS1 Australia (2006). Data synchronization. *gs1au.org*, 20 November. http://www.gs1au.org/services/eannet/data_synchronisation.asp

Hoffman, J. M. and Mehra, S. (2000). Efficient consumer response as a supply chain strategy for grocery industry. *International Journal of Service Industry Management*, 11 (4), 365–373.

Huemer, C. (2000). XML vs. UN/EDIFACT of flexibility vs. standardization. *Proceedings of the 13th Bled Electronic Commerce Conference*, Bled, Slovenia, June.

Iacovou, C. L., Benbaset, I. and Dexter, A. S. (1995). Electronic data interchange and small organizations: adoption and impact of technology. *MIS Quarterly*, 19, 465–485.

Internet Engineering Task Force (2006). *Applicability Statement 2 (AS2)*. http://www1.ietf.org/mail-archive/web/ietf-announce/current/msg01383.html

Johns, B. L., Dunlop, W. C. and Sheehan, W. J. (1989). *Small Busine$$ in Australia*. George Allen and Unwin.

Johnston, R. B. (1998). *Trading Systems and Electronic Commerce*. Eruditions Publishing.

Johnston, R. B. (1999). Principles of digitally mediated replenishment of goods: electronic commerce and supply chain reform. In *Electronic Commerce: Opportunities and Challenges* (S. M. Rahman and M. Raisinghani, eds), Idea Group Publishing.

Kanakamedala, K., King, J. and Ramsdell, G. (2003). The truth about XML. *McKinsey Quarterly*, 3, 9–12.

Kaplan, S. and Sawhney, M. (2000). E-hubs: the new b2b marketplaces. *Harvard Business Review*, 78 (3), 97–103.

Kurnia, S. and Johnston, R. B. (2001). Adoption of efficient consumer response: the issue of mutuality. *Supply Chain Management: An International Journal*, 6 (5), 230–241.

Kurnia, S. and Johnston, R. B. (2003). Adoption of efficient consumer response: key issues and challenges in Australia. *Supply Chain Management: An International Journal*, 8 (2), 251–262.

Kurt Salmon Associates (1993). *Efficient Consumer Response: Enhancing Consumer Value in the Grocery Industry*. Food Marketing Institute.

Luton, D. (2003). Keep it moving: a cross-docking primer. *Materials Management and Distribution*, 48 (5), 29.

Mak, H. C. (1998). *Use of the Internet to Facilitate Electronic Data Interchange between Small and Large Enterprises*. Unpublished Masters Thesis, Monash University.

Mak, H. C. and Johnston, R. B. (1997). A survey of Internet strategies for EDI. *Proceedings of the 1st Annual Collecter Workshop on Electronic Commerce*, Adelaide, Australia, October.

Mak, H. C. and Johnston, R. B. (1998). Tools for implementing EDI over the Internet. *EDI Forum: The Journal of Electronic Commerce*, 11, 44–56.

Mak, H. C. and Johnston, R. B. (1999). Leveraging traditional EDI investment using the Internet: a case study. *Proceedings of the 32nd Hawaii International Conference on Systems Sciences*, Maui, Hawaii, January.

Mehrtens, J., Cragg, P. B. and Mills, A. M. (2001). A model of Internet adoption by SMEs. *Information and Management*, 39, 165–176.

Oracle (2006). *Portals: The Face of Service-Oriented Architectures*. http://whitepapers.techrepublic.com.com/abstract.aspx?docid=174239&promo=300111

Rodwell, J. and Shadur, M. (1997). What's size got to do with it? Implications for contemporary management practices in IT companies. *International Journal of Small Business Management*, 15, 51–62.

Sarich, A. (1989). The outlook for pan-European EDI. *Proceedings of Electronic Messaging and Communications Systems Conference*, London.

Sarma, S. (2001). *Towards the 5c Tag*. Research Report MITAUTOID-WH-006, Massachussetts Institute of Technology, Cambridge MA. http://www.autoidcentre.org/research.asp

Scala, S. and McGrath, R. (1993). Advantages and disadvantages of electronic data interchange. *Information and Management*, 25, 85–91.

Sterling Commerce (2006). *Sterling Commerce Gives You Better Control Beyond the Edge of Your Enterprise: Gentran Integration Suite for B2B Collaboration.* http://www.sterlingcommerce.co.uk/

Turban, E., King, D., Lee, J. K. and Viehland, D. (2006). *Electronic Commerce: A Managerial Perspective*. International Edition. Prentice Hall.

Yin, R. K. (1989). *Case Study Research: Design and Methods.* Sage Publications.

Zinn, D. K. and Tahac, P. F. (1988). *Electronic Data Interchange in Australia: Markets, Opportunities and Developments.* Royal Melbourne Institute of Technology Press.

CHAPTER 14

Collaboration and conflict in the electronic integration of supply networks

Akos Nagy

INTRODUCTION

Supply chain integration (SCI) is gaining increasing attention both from researchers and practitioners as technological developments, increasing competition and ever more demanding customers necessitate the supply chain to be more efficient. The reduction of costs by eliminating waste and delays and the simultaneous improvement of customer satisfaction are goals of lean supply chain performance initiatives (Christopher and Towill, 2001). Agile supply chains, on the other hand, are market sensitive and can embrace change in real demand as well as in the structure of the supply network. Information enrichment, the immediate sharing of marketplace data throughout the supply chain, is the key to acquiring such ability in each case (Mason-Jones and Towill, 1997).

The above practices are able to diminish the bullwhip effect (Morell and Ezingeard, 2002), which is the amplification of demand order variability as orders move up the supply chain (Lee *et al.*, 1997). This approach requires that communications at all levels of the supply chain are effective and timely; therefore, the integration of information systems becomes a necessary component of a successful supply network design.

Interorganizational information systems (IOS) refer to computer and telecommunications infrastructure developed, operated and/or used by two or more firms for the purpose of exchanging information that supports a business application or process (Li and Williams, 1999). IOS enable higher visibility between trading partners and support the struggle to lower demand uncertainty. In the context of supply chains they enable integration between trading partners through faster, more efficient and more accurate data exchange, thus offering ample benefits for companies (Bakos, 1998; Heck and Ribbers, 1999; O'Callaghan *et al.*, 1992; Vlosky *et al.*, 1994).

Despite these benefits there are many organizations that still do not engage in cross-organizational electronic integration. In practice, the ideal scenario of supply chain-wide integration is often not realized and supply chains become fragmented (Watson, 2001). Frohlich and Westbrook (2001) found that some organizations extensively integrate either downstream or upstream, but not in both directions. In this study the following research questions are considered. Why does the electronic integration between trading partners fail? What factors determine the success or failure in IOS adoption?

Firms act strategically when they decide not to adopt a certain IOS (Bouchard, 1993); therefore, we assume that companies act rationally and estimate not only the benefits (Chwelos *et al.*, 2001; Jones and Beatty, 1998), but also the perceived costs (Ekering, 2000) and perceived risks (Kumar and Dissel, 1996) of an IOS project. The successful realization of an integrated supply chain is complicated by the fact that two or more organizations are needed to agree on the adoption of the interconnecting IOS (Chan and Swatman, 1998). This necessitates the study of certain behavioural or social aspects of a relationship, such as organizational power and trust (Hart and Saunders, 1997).

To answer the research questions, we use the Adoption Position model to study several tiers of the supply network of a Dutch manufacturing firm that produces composite panels.

LITERATURE REVIEW

Adoption of interorganizational information systems

Research on the adoption of IOS already has a long history. Electronic data interchange (EDI) has been used for more than 30 years to exchange structured data electronically in a standardized format between organizations (O'Callaghan and Turner, 1995) and has been intensively researched since the mid-1980s (Chan and Swatman, 1998; Somasundaram and Karlsbjerg, 2003).

The diffusion of IOS can be analysed at three different levels: the micro-level analysis focuses on characteristics of individuals and/or organizational units, the macro level examines industry-wide or national regulatory bodies, while the meso level looks in between these two and concentrates on networks of interacting agents (Damsgaard and Lyytinen, 1998). The ideal scenario of the integration of cross-organizational business processes (Nelson and Shaw, 2003) is that the same practices and the supporting IT infrastructure diffuse among the members of the network to ensure smooth information and product flow. The building blocks of such diffusion are the adoption of IOS among dyadic pairs. Therefore, this study is positioned at the meso level.

Due to its long history, the field of IOS adoption has seen several meta-studies that try to distil the literature and describe the development of the field (Somasundaram and Rose, 2003) and the applied philosophical approaches (Somasundaram and Karlsbjerg, 2003), to create an integrative approach (Chatterjee and Ravichandran, 2004) and to validate the constructs across studies (Jones and Beatty, 1998). Probably the most well-known and accepted model is the one developed by Iacovou *et al.* (1995), which was refined by Chwelos *et al.* (2001). However, Nagy (2004) criticizes the IOS literature for not handling the role of power relations between supply chain partners properly. One of his main criticisms is that power is viewed only as a driver to adoption and is not considered to be part of the causes of non-adoption, which we call the inhibiting effect. Building on previous literature, Nagy develops the Adoption Position model to try to overcome this biased view of the role of power in order to give a more complete explanation of the adoption phenomenon.

Conflicting interests

Why do we need to study power relations when the benefits of electronic integration are so well documented? As we mentioned earlier the success of IOS projects largely depends upon the collaboration of the trading partner(s) of the initiating organization, necessitating the co-adoption of the technology. We assume that trading partners rationally evaluate their options when faced with an IOS proposal. The costs and risks of IOS implementation have often been cited as potential barriers to adoption, along with social factors such as a lack of trust (Hart and Saunders, 1997) and lack of coordination and cooperation (Tan and Raman, 2002).

Several factors can lead to the lack of intention for adopting an information system: the company may not see the benefits of the technology or it may not perceive added value by adopting another IOS if it already has a different system in place with other trading partners. Costs of implementing an IOS could discourage firms, especially when it necessitates change in business processes. The perception that the investment has a high risk on the technical, operational or strategic levels negatively affects the intention to adopt as well (Hughes *et al.*, 2004). Such risks are that the technology will become obsolete (Kumar and Dissel, 1996), the trading partner will act opportunistically, the IOS has a high asset specificity (which means that the investment will only have value in one particular function and relationship and less or no value in others) (Williamson, 1979) and the possibility of getting locked in (Lonsdale, 2001).

Gregor and Johnston (2001) find that the adoption of IOS across an industry group is dependent on current industry structure. Forster and Regan (2001) observe that the use of electronic integration as a strategy is limited by the supply chain environment and the quality of the partnership between firms in the supply chain. Despite much of the rhetoric about partnership, the practice of working closer together still has a long way to go (Fernie, 1994). There are two types of inherent conflicts of interest present in supply networks: (1) a conflict between individual firm goals and supply chain-level goals; and (2) a conflict of interest between buyers and sellers.

Type I conflict

We call the conflict of interest between firm- and supply chain-level goals a type I conflict. Competition is increasingly shifting to the supply chain level from the single firm level. This means that members of a supply chain ought to act together towards a common goal in order to remain competitive. These goals are increasing the market share for the product or service the supply chain is producing and the maximization of profit. Supply chains can achieve this by maximizing the value proposition to end customers (typically, lower price, value-added features and value-added services) and by reducing costs internally, thereby maximizing effectiveness and efficiency throughout the supply chain. The philosophical basis of the supply chain integration is that it is necessary for firms to recognize their shared interests and to act in an open, trusting and transparent manner to serve those shared interests (Sanderson, 2004). Moreover, it is argued that only by being truly transparent with one another will the firms in a supply network uncover those activities and processes which are carried out inefficiently (Lamming, 1996).

We assume the rationality of supply chain members and that their primary goal is to maximize their own value appropriation. Each individual company within a supply network has to maximize shareholder value and eventually earn money. If organizations could not make money from producing and delivering goods and services to consumers, then even if people wanted or needed things, it is highly improbable that they would receive them (Cox *et al.*, 2001). In order to satisfy supply chain-level goals some firms might have to perform suboptimally. From an individual firm's point of view this is not desirable and value-maximizing behaviour would still dominate their individual mindset as they strive to increase the value proposition to the end customer. Pursuing supply chain-level goals is often argued to be beneficial to all supply chain members, because it 'increases the size of the pie'. Once the supply network has reached its goal of obtaining a larger pie, it is still faced with the problem of cutting the pie, which is a metaphor for value distribution among the trading partners (Ramsay, 2004). This leads us to type II conflict.

Type II conflict

This type of conflict refers to the value distribution in a dyadic exchange relationship. To understand what a business transaction involves requires a basic understanding of what the goals of buyers and suppliers are when they enter into an exchange relationship. Both parties in general have the same value appropriation goal (i.e. profits), but they have dissimilar operational and commercial goals (Cox, 2004). The buyer is interested in maximizing the value for money it receives from the supplier by increasing functionality and services and at the same time reducing the total cost of ownership. The supplier on the other hand is interested in increasing the share of customer and market revenue while constantly increasing price alongside added functionality to keep returns high.

The ideal outcomes for the buyer and the supplier are not fully commensurable and they are not reachable for both parties in the dyadic relationship at the same time. This, however, does not mean that mutuality does not exist in dyads and that there are no win/win situations. Cox (2004) argues that the assumption that mutuality can only occur with an ideal outcome for both parties (in which both parties fully achieve their goals) needs to be relaxed. This allows us to accept that mutuality and win/win situations can still exist when either one or both parties achieve only partially their value capture goals. 'Loose' outcomes here imply that one or both parties fail to achieve their basic value capture goals – that is, they work with the other party operationally (to provide or receive goods and/or services), but do not achieve their basic commercial goals. Win/lose situations are not sustainable relationships over time. Therefore it is impossible to achieve a complete win/win situation between two trading partners, since there is a payoff between maximizing one's own value capture and that of the trading partner. It follows that type II conflict is always present in dyadic relationships.

This does not mean that collaboration and supply chain integration is unapproachable, rather that it is important to recognize when the underlying power structure enables or hinders integration. Rather than advocating an integrative approach in all cases we should realize when the integrative approach is the appropriate strategy given the circumstances (Cox et al., 2004) and when it is in the real commercial interests of the involved firms (Sanderson, 2004).

Power in the IOS field

The above reasoning makes the study of the role of power in IOS adoption all the more relevant. In recent years, research on the role of power in information systems has gained momentum, with rising interest of researchers in studying behavioural factors as well as purely rationalistic ones (Jasperson et al., 2002). Power relations have been studied on the individual, group, organizational and interorganizational levels. In this chapter we are interested in the last category and we define power as a firm's ability to influence change in another organization that is dependent upon that firm's resources (Hart and Saunders, 1998). To further position the topic we define our approach as having an organizational lens and a pluralist view on power according to the typology developed by the meta-study (Jasperson et al., 2002).

In a previous study (Nagy, 2004) we reviewed the IOS field with respect to its use of the concept of power and we came to the conclusion that the research stream is biased towards adoption and considers non-adoption a failure. Power has only been represented as a force towards adoption – most of the time as the 'external pressure' construct. While this construct shows perfectly the scenario where a powerful member of a supply chain coerces its trading partners to use a particular IOS (Gregor and Johnston, 2001; Kurokawa and Manabe, 2002; Meier, 1995; Premkumar and Ramamurthy, 1995; Webster, 1995) it does not capture the other role of power, namely the ability of a firm to decline an IOS proposal. It is also hard to capture whether power was used coercively, persuasively or rather it triggered a proactive action from a dependent trading partner as a sign of potential power (Hart and Saunders, 1997; Premkumar and Ramamurthy, 1995; Webster, 1995).

According to Emerson (1962), power resides implicitly in others' dependency. Dependence on the trading partner is the most often found interpretation of power in the literature; the studies, however, differ greatly in the further operationalization of this construct.

Firm size is a poor measure of dependence as we will demonstrate with our case study. Rather, we should look at the resource dependence theory (Pfeffer and Salancik, 1978) which broadens the view of dependence to interorganizational relationships and proposes that firms depend on their external environment to the extent of the resources that they need, but do not control, hence they should strive for the acquisition of those resources to decrease their dependence. The supply chain management literature (Cox *et al.*, 2002) extends this view via research on value distribution along the supply chain by defining power as the ability of a firm to own and control critical assets in markets and supply chains that allow it to sustain its ability to appropriate and accumulate value for itself by constantly leveraging its customers, competitors and suppliers. Critical assets are supply chain resources that combine high utility with relative scarcity in a buyer/supplier exchange and in a market context. This definition relies heavily on the resource-based view (Barney, 1991) in identifying the properties of those critical assets and on the work of Emerson (1962), where dependence is a function of availability (i.e. relative scarcity) and motivational investment (i.e. utility).

RESEARCH MODEL

We developed the Adoption Position model to overcome this biased view of the role of power and to give a more complete explanation of the adoption phenomenon (see Figure 14.1a). We are going to apply this model through multiple case studies to show how the (lack of) co-adoption of an IOS contributes to the realization of an integrated supply chain.

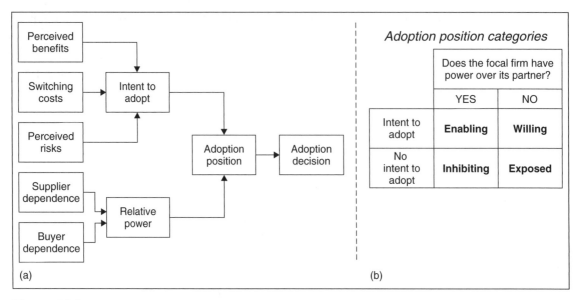

Figure 14.1
The Adoption Position model (source: Nagy, 2004)

The main advantage of the model is that it takes into account both the economic and social factors in decision making and by doing so it becomes possible to separate the intention of adoption from the actual ability of the firm to control that decision. Furthermore, it is an analytical and predictive tool for IOS adoption with which we can map an entire supply network and identify not only the points of fragmentation, but also the reasons for adoption failure.

The adoption decision is a function of the combined adoption position of the two trading partners that are negotiating over a proposed IOS. There are four possible adoption positions that a company can be categorized into based on its intention to adopt and its relative power to its partner (Figure 14.1b). An *Enabling* firm is interested in the adoption and has influence over its trading partner; therefore even when the other firm is resistant it can use its power in different ways to *try* to make the implementation come about. Note that being in an enabling position does not guarantee that the IOS adoption will occur; instead, it only gives the possibility for the firm to try starting the project.

A firm that is interested in the adoption of a certain IOS, but has no power over its trading partner, is termed as being in a *Willing* adoption position. The Willing firm perceives a net positive return on the investment and is willing to share information through the intended electronic linkage, but it is not able to force its trading partner into the

Table 14.1
Propositions table

Supplier's adoption position	Buyer's adoption position			
	Enabling	Willing	Inhibiting	Exposed
Enabling	+	+	±	+
Willing	+	+	−	?
Inhibiting	±	−	−	−
Exposed	+	?	−	−

adoption. A firm with an *Inhibiting* position sees no interest in implementing and using the proposed IOS and has the power to create a barrier to adoption. Those firms that fall into the last quadrant are less fortunate; they see no interest in the adoption and they have no leverage over the trading partner – therefore they are dependent on the other's position. Their adoption position is called *Exposed*.

Determining the adoption position of a focal firm, however, still does not make it possible to predict the outcome of the adoption decision. The cause of this ambiguity is the way in which power positions are categorized between the two firms. Cox (1997) proposes the 'power matrix' as a typology of power relationships between two firms. Next to the two cases where one of the partners dominates (supplier dominance [A > B] or buyer dominance [A < B]), the parties involved can be also interdependent [A = B] or independent [A0B]. This means that knowing whether the buyer has power is still not enough information to decide if it is a case of buyer dominance or interdependence. This method therefore necessitates the analysis of dependence from both sides of the dyad.

When we apply the Adoption Position model to both parties in a dyadic relationship, we get 16 possible combinations for the positions of the supplier and the buyer (see Table 14.1). This typology is addressed in a pair-wise way, such as Enabling-Willing or Inhibiting-Enabling, where the words signify the adoption position of the supplier and the buyer, respectively.

At the intersection of each combination is a proposition for the success of the IOS adoption. A '+' sign means that the particular adoption position pair will hypothetically support the adoption, while a '−'-marked pair does not. In the case of '±' the interdependent parties have opposing intentions and the decision is not straightforward. The '?' sign refers to the equivalently ambiguous outcome of the decision when the parties have opposing intentions, but neither has the leverage to influence the other.

METHODOLOGY

The study reported here was conducted with a positivist mindset using qualitative methods, namely via case studies and field surveys. A large Dutch manufacturer of special wooden panels was selected as the focal company for the case study – further on referred to as the Manufacturer. We have conducted several in-depth interviews with both business and IT managers to understand the internal operations and information systems present at the company. Interviews with supply chain managers and with the customer relations team leader provided information on the immediate tiers in their supply network. These interviews were guided by a case study protocol (Yin, 2003).

A structured questionnaire was developed based on a review of previous studies. The instrument was refined with the help of an expert and via pre-tests during the interviews at the Manufacturer. The questionnaire had four different versions – one specifically for a buyer and one aimed at a supplier in a dyadic relationship, because the measures of dependence and the wording of some question items differ between these two. The other distinctive factor between the surveys was whether it was an *ex post* or *ex ante* IOS adoption case. The appropriate questionnaires were sent out to selected trading partners on both the supplier and customer sides.

The questionnaire was not only a data gathering tool, but also helped us to screen out interesting cases. We visited three of these companies, which were both geographically close and agreed to receive us, in order to triangulate the survey results by interviewing IT and purchasing managers.

The unit of analysis for the research is an IOS proposal within a dyadic relationship; therefore each relationship with a trading partner can be treated as a case and can thus be evaluated in terms of their adoption positions.

COMPARATIVE CASE STUDIES

In this section we are going to describe and analyse ten comparative cases of IOS adoption – all based on relationships in the supply network of the focal manufacturing company.

Focal company

The Manufacturer is an international company in the Netherlands that develops and manufactures high quality composite panelling for façade cladding and interior applications. It has about 600 international buying customers who generate about 60 000 order lines per year. With 550 employees and a €125 million annual turnover it is one of the largest composite panel manufacturers in the world.

The Manufacturer produces four high quality product lines – three for interior and one for exterior applications. The interior lines are resistant to impact and scratching, moisture and stain and can be used for furniture, wall coverings, lockers and cubicles. One of the interior product lines is targeted at laboratory environments due to its highly chemical-resistant surface. The exterior panels are highly durable and sun, rain and rapid temperature changes typically do not affect appearance. This product line can be considered as a luxurious alternative to glass, brick or other exterior building façade materials.

The company is not only innovative in its product design, but it is also a pioneer in supply chain integration in the construction industry. In 1997, it set up an EDI connection with Customer 1, but curiously it was not until 2000 when electronic integration started to gain the attention of senior management. By that time, the company was running on SAP and through the use of the ERP system it became interested in further automating procurement and order processing. Currently the company is using four different IOS messaging standards, namely EDIFACT, bXML (business-XML), xCBL (XML Common Business Library) and standardized text-file (CSV or comma-separated value) e-mail attachments, through three communication channels (HTTPS, FTP and e-mail).

The large diversity of IOS standards required substantial investments from the Manufacturer not only in IT infrastructure and application integration, but also in developing relationship-specific business processes. Despite these efforts, the company still has to maintain manual, fax-based order processing, which results in higher processing costs and errors in the data. The reason for this is that most of the integrated partners are suppliers and customer-side electronic integration is virtually non-existent.

Why is there asymmetry in the degree of integration between the supplier and the customer side? Why does the Manufacturer have to deal with many different IOS standards? What are the reasons behind failures in integration attempts? We try to answer these questions by analysing specific relationships in the Manufacturer's business network

Table 14.2

Case summaries

Relationship	Supplier's intention to adopt	Buyer's intention to adopt	Dependence of supplier on buyer	Dependence of buyer on supplier	Adoption position	Hypothesis	IOS adoption
Supplier 1	Yes	Yes	High	High	En-En	+	+
Supplier 2	Yes	Yes	High	Medium	En-En	+	+
Supplier 3	No	Yes	Low	High	Inh-Will	−	−
Supplier 4	Yes	Yes	High	Low	Will-En	+	+
Customer 1	Yes	Yes	High	Medium	En-En	+	+
Customer 2	Yes	No	Medium	Low	Will-Inh	−	−
Customer 3: Manufacturer initiative	Yes	No	Low	Medium	En-Exp	+	+
Customer 3: Customer initiative	No	Yes	Low	Medium	Inh-Will	−	−
Customer 4	Yes	No	Medium	Low	Will-Exp	?	−
Customer 1: tier 2 customer	Yes	Yes	High	Low	Will-En	+	+

using the Adoption Position model. See Table 14.2 for a list of the discussed cases.

Supplier side cases

Altogether there are around 60 companies that are supplying the Manufacturer, including MRO (Maintenance, Repair and Operating) suppliers. The quality level of the product and the unique production process requires special inputs, which only a few suppliers can provide.

Supplier 1 is a producer of a special carton paper that forms the core material of the product that sits between the surface sheets and it takes the largest share of the procurement budget. Supplier 1 is a large manufacturer of paper- and wood-based products in the USA, employing more than 40 000 people. The Manufacturer procures 75 per cent of its core material from Supplier 1, while Supplier 2 provides the rest. This is due to its dual sourcing strategy to reduce the dependence on a single source in the case of highly specialized, strategic items.

Supplier 1 was the first company on the procurement side that established an IOS with the focal firm. They both use SAP and they set up an

XML-based EDI connection using the business connector (BC) module for automating order handling and advanced shipment notices (ASN). The initiative came from the Manufacturer and it had high perceived benefits in the form of reduced inventory level, improved information quality, improved internal operations and decreased lead times. Costs were high, because this was the first time the IOS was implemented at the focal company and it also had to complete relation-specific message mapping to xCBL message format. However, the benefits were perceived to be higher than the costs and the risks, and both companies had the intention to adopt.

The Manufacturer is clearly dependent on Supplier 1, because of the volume and scarcity of the core material. Recently it has started to experiment with using wood chips as a substitute for the core material; however, the investments needed to increase capacity in this direction were prohibitive at the time of the study. Although Supplier 1 is a much larger company, the Manufacturer is the largest buyer from them in Europe and is the second most important buyer outside the US market. The regularity, frequency and predictability of orders also increases the value of the Manufacturer (Cox *et al.*, 2002). In terms of power structures, this is an interdependent relationship (A = B). Both parties depend on each other and both were interested in the adoption of the IOS. Therefore, the adoption position of this dyad is Enabling-Enabling. This is a supportive structure that resulted in integration and collaboration.

Supplier 2 is a paper, packaging and forest products company with 45 000 employees, producing and selling fine papers, packaging boards and wood products all over the world. It is the secondary supplier of core material to the focal company and is a direct competitor of Supplier 1. Almost the whole ordering cycle is done electronically, including purchase order, order response, ASN, invoice and forecast information. The difference between this and the previous case is that this time the supplier had more dedicated investments in the IOS adoption. For them this was a pilot project, while the Manufacturer already had the BC ready and implemented.

One problem during integration was that Supplier 2 used the standard system of the paper industry, which was not compatible with the BC. Both intention and dependence scored very similar to the previous case, except that the buyer is slightly less dependent on the supplier. This relationship is also an Enabling-Enabling one. This resulted in extensive collaboration, where Supplier 2 set up a dedicated gateway towards the Manufacturer and with its help has done extra, relation-specific data mapping to bXML format, which is the preferred message standard of the Manufacturer. These cases have shown that in an

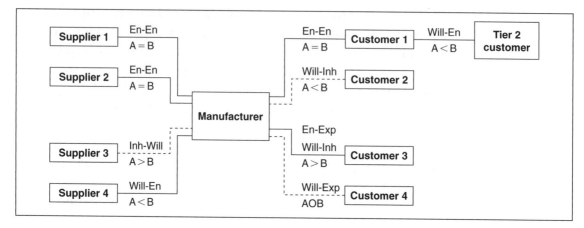

Figure 14.2
Adoption positions and power structures in the supply network of the manufacturer

Enabling-Enabling type of relationship, both firms collaborate and are dedicated to investing in the relationship regardless of being the supplier or the buyer (see Figure 14.2).

Supplier 3 is the single source supplier of the surface material from the chemical sector. The Manufacturer used a dual source strategy in the past until one of the supplier companies took over the other, resulting in the current Supplier 3. It is now the world's leading specialty chemicals and materials company. Currently there is no IOS implemented between the Manufacturer and Supplier 3. The Manufacturer would be interested in establishing a Vendor Managed Inventory (VMI) system; however, its intention has been diminished by several factors. Supplier 3 is exploiting its monopoly position by charging a high price for its product. This lowers trust towards it and raises the value of the perceived risks construct. Moreover, the increase in post-adoption dependence is seen as a real threat to the Manufacturer. As mentioned above, one strategic goal is not to engage in single source partnerships, which in turn lowers the perceived benefits construct.

Supplier 3 is also reluctant to implement VMI due to the costs involved and it sees no benefits from it. The power structure is supplier dominant (A > B). According to the Adoption Position typology this is an Inhibiting-Exposed relationship, which is a prohibitive structure. The proposition of a negative adoption decision in this case is confirmed.

Our last case from the supplier side is the opposite. Supplier 4 is a small, family-owned company in the Netherlands with 60 employees specializing in impregnating paper with resin. The Manufacturer can select from a larger pool of suppliers (15 companies) and switching costs are low. Supplier 4 impregnates 70 per cent of the material rolls of the Manufacturer and was selected due to its reputation and internal automation. Not to jeopardize its automated processes, the Manufacturer decided to initiate an IOS. However, the small supplier does not have an ERP system and the integration required special, relation-specific mapping of the messages into a customized text-file message (CSV) from the Manufacturer's side. This CSV file is then sent by e-mail to the supplier. Investment was necessary for the supplier as well – to program a module that can read the file and upload the contents into its internal system. Both companies had the intention to adopt and the power structure is buyer dominant (A < B). This resulted in a Willing-Enabling relationship, which is a supportive scenario.

Customer side cases

Approximately 600 dealers and OEMs (original equipment manufacturers) from all over the world make up the customer pool of the Manufacturer. The OEMs are mostly furniture manufacturers and use the panels as part of tables, cabinets and hospital beds. Dealers are wholesalers to the construction industry and distribute for both internal and external applications. The product comes in standard sizes and colours, but it can also be highly customized with differing dimensions and various printed surface patterns.

Customer 1 is a large distributor of wood products in the Netherlands. It does not only distribute, but stores the panels and cuts them to custom shapes. It has an internally built ERP system and established an EDI connection with the Manufacturer in 1997. In fact this was the first IOS for the focal company and has remained the only one on the customer side. Interestingly, this is the only EDI connection for Customer 1 on the supplier side as well. The reason is that the adoption positions were Enabling-Enabling. Customer 1 initiated the project, because it saw a lot of benefits in terms of cost reduction and lead time improvement with the Manufacturer. Being the largest customer with the most volume and with highly frequent (daily) and regular orders, the focal company estimated positive benefits as well. Power analysis determined that both parties depend on each other due to the large trade volumes and the unique qualities of the products, which are not easily substitutable and are demanded by architects.

We have visited Customer 1 to find out why they initiated EDI among their customers. We found out that it has a centralized IT department with a sister company that, instead of focusing on the professional construction industry, serves the do-it-yourself consumer market. That market is dominated by a few large players, which mandated the use of EDI to its suppliers. The relationship between the Tier 2 Customer and the sister company of Customer 1 was Exposed-Enabling, and EDI was adopted under trading partner pressure. The availability of the technology at Customer 1 lowered further implementation costs and triggered the EDI initiative with the Manufacturer.

Customer 2 is a distributor and stockholder of a range of specialist sheet materials in the UK. For the Manufacturer it provides a gateway to a niche market for its special product line, which is not sold to many other dealers, making Customer 2 a very important partner. Customer 2 also handles competitive products rendering the focal company more easily substitutable. There is a buyer dominance in this relationship ($A < B$). Customer 2 has been approached with an IOS proposal, but has declined its implementation, because it did not see any added benefits. They would need to make specific investments to convert to the message standard proposed by the Manufacturer. The relationship was Willing-Inhibiting and the hypothesis for a negative adoption decision has been corroborated by this case.

Customer 3 enabled us to analyse two IOS proposals – one initiated by the Manufacturer, the other by the buyer. Customer 3 is a very small OEM manufacturer contributing to 0.08 per cent of total sales. They have been developing a procurement portal, which requires a CSV file exchange in a proprietary format. The Manufacturer did not want to customize for this one customer, because it already had its own standard for CSV files. This put the focal company into an Inhibiting adoption position; while having no leverage, Customer 3 was a Willing company. In accordance with the hypothesis this IOS proposal was rejected. After some negotiations Customer 3 was willing to consider a proposal from the Manufacturer. This created an Enabling-Exposed situation where power played a major role and the IOS was implemented.

The majority of the dealers, however, remained reluctant to integrate electronically. Most of them keep the product as part of their assortment with no particular dedication or dependence on the Manufacturer. Many dealers lack automation and the necessary investments in IT and in business process redesign discourage them from adopting an IOS. Power structures in these cases take more of an independent nature (A0B), where a market situation exists with lots of buyers and suppliers. One example is Customer 4, a medium-sized distributor of construction materials in the Netherlands. The adoption position of the companies in this case is Willing-Exposed. This is an unsupportive situation, which has been confirmed by an unsuccessful attempt to establish an IOS.

DISCUSSION

The case studies enabled the testing of a wide variety of scenarios. We have observed both adoption successes and failures, and the results support the model without exception. There are several points that we would like to emphasize based on the research findings.

Theoretical implications

Studies about the adoption of information systems should also include failures within their scope. This way it becomes easier to identify the critical factors that distinguish a successful project from an unsuccessful one. Our cases suggest that the intention of a single organization to adopt is not a sufficient factor in the overall outcome of an adoption decision. We need to study the underlying power relations as well to get a better understanding of the phenomenon.

This leads to our second point. The main difference between IOS adoption and that of an internal information system is that the decision for an IOS involves more than one organization. Joint decisions are needed on the number and the standard of messages to be exchanged and on the supported shared business processes. This necessitates the inclusion of trading partners in IOS studies. In addition to economic factors – such as perceived benefits and costs – behavioural concepts are also relevant, such as power and trust. It is important to note that power relations are relative and are specific to a trading relationship. Our cases support this notion, where we saw that the same company can be very powerful in one relationship, but on the other hand can be very dependent in another.

The Adoption Position model builds on previous literature and covers many of the already validated constructs in the field. In particular, the intention to adopt construct is affected by a large number of variables. Compatibility of a legacy system with the new IOS (or readiness) is viewed here as the extent of investment needed in the current IS to accommodate the new system. Trust in the trading partner is again an important factor in IOS adoption and it is addressed in the perceived risk construct. Network effects are another factor that could affect adoption, although this is not included in the model directly. We could theorize that the increased necessity to use a certain widely diffused IOS standard in a supply network will lead to an increase in the perceived benefits construct; however, we do not have enough data to establish this connection.

Further research is needed to explore whether there are other factors that affect IOS adoption. We need to collect data from different industries to increase the generalizability of the model and to try to cover all the propositions in Table 14.1. We would like to test whether Table 14.1 is actually symmetric or not, because an asymmetry would highlight interesting differences between the role of suppliers and buyers in the diffusion of IOS standards. Once the model is validated it could be used in future research to generate hypotheses using the adoption position typologies; for example, 'Can a supplier in a Willing-Inhibiting adoption position change the relationship to a favourable one, and if yes, how?' or 'What are the main reasons for being an Inhibitor?'.

Practical implications

What strategies are available for an organization that wishes to introduce a new information system to exchange business documents, but has experienced difficulties in doing so? We can use the Adoption Position model to answer this question as well. Table 14.1 shows those adoption position pairs that are supportive of an IOS adoption decision. A company that wishes to implement a system with its trading partner therefore first has to evaluate the relationship and position itself and its partner in the matrix of Figure 14.1b. There are two ways to change an unfavourable position to a favourable one: either the focal firm has to persuade its trading partner to use the system or it has to increase its power level.

By increasing the benefits or lowering the barriers of adoption the focal firm can positively change the intention of its trading partner. Piderit (2000) found that lowering barriers is more effective. Barriers such as the switching costs of the partner (Nagy et al., 2004) to the new system can be lowered by using standardized applications that can integrate more easily into existing IT architectures or by jointly planning shared business processes, which will require less business process redesign (Nelson and Shaw, 2003).

The second strategic direction for an initiator of an IOS project is to increase its power base or to increase the dependence of the partner firm. This is much harder to achieve as it often requires the redesign of the supply chain (e.g. vertical integration or disintermediation), making significant changes in one's own business (e.g. a higher value proposition for a partner through increased commercial or operational importance; see Cox et al., 2002) or introducing new governance mechanisms (e.g. quasi integration and participation in joint decision making; see Subramani and Venkatraman, 2003).

It is important to note that higher power does not imply it is used coercively. Power can be exercised in a persuasive way or the potential of having power can influence adoption (Hart and Saunders, 1997). Helping suppliers in developing the necessary capabilities to adapt to new business requirements (Krause *et al.*, 1998) will establish trust in the relationship. This increased trust will lower the perceived risks of the IOS and create a positive intention towards adoption.

Thus, a self-assessment of the relative power of a firm will result in different negotiation strategies. A relatively more powerful firm might choose to coercively influence the behaviour of its trading partner or could try to persuade it with a softer approach. A weaker firm could anticipate the requirements of a more powerful partner and employ a proactive strategy (Webster, 1995). So far in this chapter we have assumed a single relationship between supply chain members; however, these relationships are often multi-faceted (Wiseman, 1988). In such situations firm A might be dependent on firm B on one side, but could have the upper hand on another. Negotiation strategies become even more important in these cases, but a further discussion is beyond the scope of this chapter.

CONCLUSION

The cases in this chapter suggest that the electronic exchange of information between trading partners depends not only on their intention to adopt the system, but also on the underlying power structure. A conflict of interest in IOS adoption coupled with an unsupportive power structure could lead to inefficiencies in the supply network and can indirectly thwart efforts to realize an integrated supply chain. At the same time we have identified the type of relationships that are supportive towards collaboration. It is important for practitioners to recognize their own position in their relations with trading partners in order to formulate strategies on how to move from an unfavourable position to a favourable one.

Using the Adoption Position model we were able to explain why the co-adoption of IOS fails or succeeds. However, the small number of cases does not completely validate our model, and therefore further case studies are needed to test the hypotheses.

By estimating the adoption position of both parties in a dyadic relationship one could predict the outcome of the adoption decision. This has important implications for both researchers and practitioners: researchers are able to map entire supply chains and examine the prospect of supply chain-wide diffusion of a technology; practitioners could benefit from the model by establishing a clearer view of their company's position in the supply network and to evaluate project proposals on different IOS.

REFERENCES

Bakos, Y. (1998). The emerging role of electronic marketplaces on the Internet. *Communications of the ACM*, 41, 35–42.

Barney, J. (1991). Firm resources and sustained competitive advantage. *Journal of Management*, 17, 99–120.

Bouchard, L. (1993). Decision criteria in the adoption of EDI. *Proceedings of the 14th International Conference in Information Systems*, Orlando, December.

Chan, C. and Swatman, P. M. C. (1998). EDI implementation: a broader perspective. *Proceedings of the 11th International Conference on Electronic Commerce*, Bled, Slovenia, June.

Chatterjee, D. and Ravichandran, T. (2004). Inter-organizational information systems research: a critical review and an integrative framework. *Proceedings of the 37th Hawaii International Conference on Systems Sciences*, Hawaii, January.

Christopher, M. and Towill, D. (2001). An integrated model for the design of agile supply chains. *International Journal of Physical Distribution and Logistics Management*, 31, 235–246.

Chwelos, P., Benbasat, I. and Dexter, A. S. (2001). Empirical test of an EDI adoption model. *Information Systems Research*, 12, 304–321.

Cox, A. (1997). On power, appropriateness and procurement competence. *Supply Management*, 2 October, 24–27.

Cox, A. (2004). Business relationship alignment: on the commensurability of value capture and mutuality in buyer and supplier exchange. *Supply Chain Management: An International Journal*, 9, 410–420.

Cox, A., Ireland, P., Lonsdale, C., Sanderson, J. and Watson, G. (2002). *Supply Chains, Markets and Power: Mapping Buyer and Supplier Power Regimes*. Routledge.

Cox, A., Sanderson, J. and Watson, G. (2001). Supply chains and power regimes: toward an analytic framework for managing extended networks of buyer and supplier relationships. *The Journal of Supply Chain Management*, 37, 28–35.

Cox, A., Watson, G., Lonsdale, C. and Sanderson, J. (2004). Managing appropriately in power regimes: relationship and performance management in 12 supply chain cases. *Supply Chain Management: An International Journal*, 9, 357–371.

Damsgaard, J. and Lyytinen, K. (1998). Contours of diffusion of electronic data interchange in Finland: overcoming technological barriers and collaborating to make it happen. *Journal of Strategic Information Systems*, 7, 275–297.

Ekering, C. F. (2000). *De Specificiteit van EDI.* Ph.D. Thesis. Katholieke Universiteit Brabant, Dutch University Press.

Emerson, R. M. (1962). Power-dependence relations. *American Sociological Review,* 27, 31–41.

Fernie, J. (1994). Quick response: an international perspective. *International Journal of Physical Distribution and Logistics Management,* 46, 274–285.

Forster, P. W. and Regan, A. C. (2001). Electronic integration in the air cargo industry: an information processing model of an on-time performance. *Transportation Journal,* 40, 46–61.

Frohlich, M. T. and Westbrook, R. (2001). Arcs of integration: an international study of supply chain strategies. *Journal of Operations Management,* 19, 185–200.

Gregor, S. and Johnston, R. B. (2001). Theory of interorganizational systems: industry structure and processes of change. *Proceedings of the 34th Hawaii International Conference on Systems Sciences,* Hawaii, January.

Hart, P. and Saunders, C. (1997). Power and trust: critical factors in the adoption and use of electronic data interchange. *Organization Science,* 8, 23–41.

Hart, P. and Saunders, C. (1998). Emerging electronic partnerships: antecedents and dimensions of EDI use from the supplier's perspective. *Journal of Management Information Systems,* 14, 87–111.

Heck, E. van and Ribbers, P. M. (1999). The adoption and impact of EDI in Dutch SMEs. *Proceedings of the 32nd Hawaii International Conference on Systems Sciences,* Hawaii, January.

Hughes, M., Powell, P., Panteli, N. and Golden, W. (2004). Risk mitigation and risk absorption in IOS: a proposed investigative study. *Proceedings of the 12th European Conference in Information Systems,* Turku, Finland, June.

Iacovou, C. L., Benbaset, I. and Dexter, A. S. (1995). Electronic data interchange and small organizations: adoption and impact of technology. *MIS Quarterly,* 19, 465–485.

Jasperson, J., Carte, T. A., Saunders, C., Butler, B. S., Croes, H. J. P. and Zheng, W. (2002). Power and information technology research: a meta-triangulation review. *MIS Quarterly,* 26, 397–459.

Jones, M. C. and Beatty, R. C. (1998). Towards the development of measures of perceived benefits and compatibility of EDI: a comparative assessment of competing first order factor models. *European Journal of Information Systems,* 7, 210–220.

Krause, D. R., Handfield, R. B. and Scannel, T. V. (1998). An empirical investigation of supplier development: reactive and strategic processes. *Journal of Operations Management,* 17, 39–58.

Kumar, K. and Dissel, H. G. (1996). Sustainable collaboration: managing conflict and cooperation in interorganizational systems. *MIS Quarterly,* 20, 279–300.

Kurokawa, S. and Manabe, S. (2002). *Determinants of EDI Adoption and Integration in the US and Japanese Automobile Suppliers.* Working Paper, Kobe University. http://www.rieb.kobeu.ac.jp/academic/ra/dp/

l.

Lamming, R. (1996). Squaring lean supply with supply chain management. *International Journal of Operations & Production Management*, 16 (2), 183–196.

Lee, H. L., Padmanabhan, V. and Whang, S. (1997). The bullwhip effect in supply chains. *Sloan Management Review*, 38, 93–102.

Li, F. and Williams, H. (1999). New collaboration between firms: the role of interorganizational systems. *Proceedings of the 32nd Hawaii International Conference on Systems Sciences*, Hawaii, January.

Lonsdale, C. (2001). Locked-in to supplier dominance: on the dangers of asset specificity for the outsourcing decision. *The Journal of Supply Chain Management*, 37, 22–27.

Mason-Jones, R. and Towill, D. (1997). Information enrichment: designing the supply chain for competitive advantage. *Supply Chain Management*, 2, 137–148.

Meier, J. (1995). The importance of relationship management in establishing successful interorganizational systems. *Journal of Strategic Information Systems*, 4, 135–148.

Morell, M. and Ezingeard, J.-N. (2002). Revisiting adoption factors of inter-organisational information systems in SMEs. *Logistics Information Management*, 15, 46–57.

Nagy, A. (2004). The effect of power on the adoption of interorganizational information systems: the Adoption Position model. *Proceedings of the 12th European Conference on Information Systems*, Turku, Finland, June.

Nagy, A., Orriens, B. and Fairchild, A. (2004). The promise and reality of Internet-based interorganizational systems. *Proceedings of the IADIS International Conference on e-Society*, Avila, Spain, July.

Nelson, M. L. and Shaw, M. J. (2003). The adoption and diffusion of interorganizational system standards and process innovations. *Proceedings of the Workshop on Standard Making: A Critical Research Frontier for Information Systems*, Seattle, December.

O'Callaghan, R., Kaufmann, P. J. and Konsynski, B. R. (1992). Adoption correlates and share effects of electronic data interchange systems in marketing channels. *Journal of Marketing*, 56, 45–56.

O'Callaghan, R. and Turner, J. A. (1995). Electronic data interchange: concepts and issues. In *EDI in Europe: How it Works in Practice* (H. Krcmar, N. Bjorn-Andersen and R. O'Callaghan, eds), John Wiley and Sons.

Pfeffer, J. and Salancik, G. R. (1978). *The External Control of Organizations*. Harper and Row.

Piderit, S. K. (2000). Rethinking resistance and recognizing ambivalence: a multidimensional view of attitudes toward an organizational change. *Academy of Management Review*, 25, 783–794.

Premkumar, G. and Ramamurthy, K. (1995). The role of interorganizational and organizational factors on the decision mode for adoption of interorganizational systems. *Decision Sciences*, 26, 303–336.

Ramsay, J. (2004). Serendipity and the realpolitik of negotiations in supply chains. *Supply Chain Management: An International Journal*, 9, 219–229.

Sanderson, J. (2004). Opportunity and constraint in business-to-business relationships: insights from strategic choice and zones of manoeuvre. *Supply Chain Management: An International Journal*, 9, 392–401.

Somasundaram, R. and Karlsbjerg, J. (2003). Research philosophies in IOS research. *Proceedings of the 11th European Conference on Information Systems*, Naples, June.

Somasundaram, R. and Rose, J. (2003). Rationalizing, probing, understanding: the evolution of the inter-organizational systems adoption field. *Proceedings of the 36th Hawaii International Conference on Systems Sciences*, Hawaii, January.

Subramani, M. and Venkatraman, N. (2003). Safeguarding investments in asymmetric interorganizational relationships: theory and evidence. *Academy of Management Journal*, 46, 46–62.

Tan, M. and Raman, K. S. (2002). Interorganizational systems and transformation of interorganizational relationships: a relational perspective. *Proceedings of the 23rd International Conference on Information Systems*, Barcelona, December.

Vlosky, R. P., Smith, P. M. and Wilson, D. T. (1994). Electronic data interchange implementation strategies: a case study. *Journal of Business and Industrial Marketing*, 9, 5–18.

Watson, G. (2001). Subregimes of power and integrated supply chain management. *The Journal of Supply Chain Management*, 37, 36–41.

Webster, J. (1995). Networks of collaboration or conflict? Electronic data interchange and power in the supply chain. *Journal of Management Information Systems*, 4, 31–42.

Williamson, O. (1979). Transaction cost economics: the governance of contractual relations. *Journal of Law and Economics*, 22, 233–261.

Wiseman, C. (1988). *Strategic Information Systems*. McGraw-Hill Professional.

Yin, R. K. (2003). *Case Study Research: Design and Methods*. Sage Publications.

CHAPTER 15

Recognizing the limits of virtual organizations

Lucas D. Introna and Dimitra Petrakaki

INTRODUCTION

The preceding chapters in this section have examined the notion of
virtual organization in a number of respects. However, the predominant view is that of support for this concept. It therefore also seems
appropriate to step back and take a critical perspective. Is the virtual
organization the model for future corporate life or is it merely another
management fad? This must be a substantive question in need of articulation and debate; there is so much at stake for those firms that choose
to embark on this road. Hence, the purpose of this chapter is to develop
a critique of the virtual organization. It is then up to the reader to draw
from both the thesis and the antithesis a set of ideas that will develop
into a sensible judgement about the validity – or not – of the now all
too pregnant concept of a virtual organization. The critique will draw
mainly on the phenomenological and critical schools of thought.

From a phenomenological viewpoint the critique will take the reader back to the implicit and tacit background practices that organize our everyday experience even before conscious awareness – the world of the preconsciousness. This is intended to show that our preconscious rootedness in the world acts in a very fundamental way; providing the context that gives meaning to all conscious social activity – such as communication, learning, and so forth. One could almost say they are the 'spaces' in the social sentences that allow us to parse and make sense of the words/acts. Although they are essentially empty of meaning (as blanks or spaces), and we cannot say much about them as such, we depend – in a very subtle way – on their important contribution to our day-to-day sense making. To neglect these preconscious spaces of our everyday world would be to reduce experience to that which can be represented – that which can be explicitly thought. Such a view would imply a type of reductionism that impoverishes our understanding of the social. Ultimately this path would lead us to embrace contradictory positions when attempting to transform social practices – as seems to be the case with the current thinking about virtual organizations.

From a critical perspective we want to highlight the inherent – always already there – political forces that convert every attempt at transformation into resources for power. If we deny power an adequate role in our discussion of virtual organization, then we overlook some very important issues; in particular, there will be a tendency to end up with idealistic concepts that ignore the messy realities of everyday practice. Clearly such a procedure is perilous. It is believed that the phenomenological and critical perspective will provide a more balanced view of the issues we are facing when trying to establish the new forms of organization and work demanded by the emerging socio-economic context.

TRUST AND CONFLICT

Almost without exception, the proponents of the virtual organization operate with the assumptions of a sociology of regulation (Burrell and Morgan, 1979). Essentially, they are concerned with describing a social reality characterized by social order, social integration, consensus, solidarity, need satisfaction and actuality. In contrast to this seemingly coherent social world there is another, more radical view of the social. This radical view sees the social world as characterized by modes of domination, emancipation, deprivation and potentiality – known as the sociology of radical change. Somehow, proponents of the virtual organization see the chaos, conflict and fluctuation in the environment, but then assume a social reality (such as in the virtual organization) in which individuals will tend to trust each other and cooperate in a cohesive and seamless manner. This paints a picture of society as inhabited only by winners and not losers. This does not quite square with reality. In addition, it seems naive to think that in a post-modern society, where the enlightened idea of institutionalized trust (as embodied in the institutions of the State and the Church, for example) has been deconstructed, that all participants would suddenly embrace the notion of trust on face value. In an age of deep mistrust, to call on this idea as key to the success of the virtual organization seems counterintuitive. However, if trust is indeed an essential element of the virtual organization then we need to understand the ways in which it emerges in the social context.

Although we do not have consensus on the particular ways in which trust emerges and dissipates in social relationships, there is sufficient reason – and intuitive empirical evidence – to believe that trust and mistrust operate within the Kuhnian notion of a 'gestalt switch' and resulting paradigm shifts (Kuhn, 1977). Trust is not merely the exchange of objects. Rather, it emerges as a result of sustained interaction in which the parties continually take note of the coherence between their held paradigm (of trust or mistrust) and the actual behaviour of the partner in the interaction. When two parties engage in cooperative activity in which they are mutually interdependent they tend to start with a particular paradigmatic view of the trustworthiness of the partner. This may be a position of relative trust or mistrust depending on a number of factors including their individual propensity for risk, the cost of failure and past experience. As humans interact they observe others' behaviour and tend to maintain the prevailing paradigm even in the face of a number of anomalies that may suggest their prevailing paradigm is incorrect. Such interactions create feelings of personal responsibility and appreciation, which often 'generate a spiral of rising trust' (Fox, 1974). However, if the anomalies (evidence of trustworthiness or untrustworthiness) accumulate to a point where the prevailing paradigm can no longer be sustained, a gestalt switch occurs. In a gestalt switch, the prevailing paradigm will be completely aborted for a new paradigm (of trustworthiness or untrustworthiness). This means that if the prevailing view is one of mistrust then it will take *a large number of anomalies* to achieve a gestalt switch. Thus, trust is a social capital that may need a significant reciprocal social investment from the partners. If this is the case then it seems that the virtual organization lacks some of the important requirements for trust to emerge.

In the virtual organization, interactions will be short-lived and tend not to provide the shared social space to generate the anomalies required for trust to emerge. Most significant in generating evidence of anomalies is an assessment of the validity claims raised in the exchange of communication (Whitley and Introna, 1996). We tend to believe the claims (e.g. truth, sincerity or normative claims) people make in their communication to the degree that we can validate them. For example, we judge the sincerity of a request by eliciting cues from the context (e.g. the place, situation, facial expression, bodily movements, and so on). If there are limited institutional obligations (such as participants working for the same organization) then generating anomalies (as evidence for a prevailing paradigm) becomes all the more important. Yet, these rely on a shared history and context – exactly that which is lacking in the virtual organization. This is the first paradox in the virtual organization argument; trust is central to the functioning of the virtual organization but the virtual organization often does not have the resources to generate this trust. On the contrary, the lack of face-to-face communication and the short-term orientation of virtual organizations are likely to render people insincere, to create chances for opportunistic behaviour and thus to prevent the development of social relations that may lead to trust building (Jones and Bowie, 1998).

Since virtual organizations lack long-term orientation and partners do not often already share a common historical or cultural background, future behaviour can rarely be predicted with certainty. Risk is an ever-present factor that could potentially disrupt a participant's actions. With reference to this, institutional frameworks are often established with a view to guiding people's conduct and thus reducing uncertainty, complexity and risk (Lewis and Weigert, 1985). In such situations trust is often located in a 'framework of shared obligations and expectations' and/or 'abstract systems' (Luhmann, 1979; Reed, 2001). These systems are elaborate structures of guarantees and guarantors such as laws, policies, norms/values, social roles, regulations, contracts and agreements (such as trade agreements between nation states), and so forth (Fox, 1974). The purpose of such systems is to enforce compliance onto actors (Luhmann, 1979) and, by implication, to create certain expectations about the behaviour of others (Knights *et al.*, 2001; Shapiro 1987). Such systems enable the development of trust because they mitigate risk, discourage misbehaviour, ensure predictability and give 'good reasons why to invest in trust relations' (Knights *et al.*, 2001; Luhmann, 1979). Moreover, they are thought to bring a state of ontological security, which guarantees 'the continuity of things and people' (Giddens, 1990).

In these situations where trust is an outcome of institutionally agreed systems, rather than being an outcome of reciprocity, trust is generated through the notion of constraint. Such a view could render our view of human conduct to be the outcome of a standardized or ordered environment and excludes the subjects' own views, values and beliefs that may require different behaviour. In reality what we find is not just compliance but also resistance – resistance that turns these very attempts to constrain into opportunities for opportunistic behaviour. There is a fundamental tension here. The more we want to create abstract institutional systems as a basis for trust the more we impose limits on the flexibility and situatedness required for virtual cooperation. The development of trust or mistrust happens in and through engagement and conflict rather than simply through abstract systems of law. Where will this happen in the virtual environment?

WHOLES AND PARTS

It is well known in systems theory that combining a number of very efficient and effective parts does not necessarily produce an efficient and effective whole (Ackoff, 1971; Beer, 1966; Bertalanffy, 1968; Churchman, 1968). This may only be the case when all constituent parts act as 'black boxes' (Latour, 1987) (i.e. all behaviour is completely localized) and are linked together in a mechanistic manner in the pursuit of explicit and unambiguous (uncontested) global goals. This is the situation in a typical engineering design context. However, in the case of the virtual organization neither of these requirements is present.

Logically, each partner brings into the whole that which they do best (their core competencies). These constituents are then combined into the virtual operation through a set of processes (as outlined above) with the understanding that synergistic combination of core competencies will render the whole more successful than any of the parts. This may happen, but it also may not. The core competence may not be 'relocatable', for the simple reason that many firms do not necessarily know what it is that they do well. Most of this knowledge may be tacit and distributed. Once a successful unit is dislocated from its context it may cease to be successful. The success of an employee, unit or organization is not only located 'in' them, but in the whole that they draw upon 'in doing' what they do well. In other words, competence isn't a fixed entity that belongs to humans as such; it is not embodied in a person but equally exists in the environment where the person is competent (Law, 1997). This causes a problem in locating the 'competence' (as such). For example, the success of a world-class athlete is not solely 'in' the athlete, or solely 'in' the technology, or solely 'in' the coach, or solely 'in' the facilities, and so on. It is simultaneously in each and all of these. To locate a core competence could be extremely difficult and it would mean going back and trying to capture all the relations and interactions, including the negotiations and the power struggles, that enabled this competence to emerge – hence the problem of black boxes.

A further difficulty is in assuming an explicit unambiguous and uncontested goal. There is no reason to believe that the partners automatically accept and commit themselves to the goals of the virtual organization. It may even be that in the process of integrating partners' core competencies, with the extensive renegotiation and realignment that this implies, that the original goals that are constitutive of the core competencies are lost. Skill actors in the organization are not merely docile bodies; they are more than their competencies, skills and potentialities. They are rather conscious of their actions and their effects, they are driven by ethical considerations and they are always acting in relation to others (Fuller, 1999). Virtual organization rhetoric that suggests that partners are bound together for a single purpose neglects this more political view of human actors; they often assume that human beings are rational and driven by personal aspirations and interests. Partners (and the individual actors) always enter a field where power asymmetries already exist. These asymmetries would lead to resistance and to reformulations of what the 'shared' purpose is. It will also lead to challenges of the various 'technologies' that aim to normalize behaviours in the pursuit of cohesion (Callon, 1986; Foucault, 1977). An existing power game is the ground upon which partners' interests are to be 'translated' into a unity, or rather a 'network', within a flux of interests.

KNOWLEDGE AND LANGUAGE

Organizational knowledge is the most important asset of an organization (Argyris, 1993; Nonaka, 1994; Pentland and Reuter, 1994). However, it is no simple matter to discover where in the organization this knowledge is embedded. It may reside in the technology, in the heads of people, in the information systems, in the organizational structures, and so on. The best answer to this question is to say that it is in each of them and in all of them together. Nevertheless, most authors on organizational knowledge – such as Nonaka (1994), Pentland and Reuter (1994) and Von Krogh and Roos (1995) – agree that the most important source of organizational knowledge is tacit knowledge (Polanyi, 1973).

Tacit knowledge is that we can apply *in doing* but which, when asked, we may not be able to articulate. It is a truism to say we do not know what we know, we only know in the sense that we can apply knowledge or demonstrate how to apply it (riding a bicycle being an often cited example). The tacit basis of organizational knowledge has many implications for the virtual organization concept. We will limit ourselves to two aspects.

If tacit knowledge is the most important source of organizational knowledge, how is this to be 'located' in a way to make it available to partners in the virtual organization? This problem was touched upon above. Even if we assume we can locate it, how do we make it accessible to our virtual partners? It is well known that tacit skills can only be transferred through a process of socialization, i.e. working and collaborating together in a local site (such as in the master/apprentice relationship) (Law, 1994). If virtual partners need to draw on this source of tacit knowledge, as one would expect, where and when will this socialization be realized – unless we see partners as black boxes (an option ruled out above)? We would therefore argue that unless the partners really do things together for a reasonable period of time (in some time/space dimension) the exchange of expertise in the partnership would tend to be limited to concrete explicit knowledge (such as technology artefacts). In such a case one might ask whether this could instead be bought in the 'market'. Why, indeed, enter into a partnership at all? This, however, assumes that knowledge is discovered; that it can be reduced to the facts which exist 'out there' and can be found and picked up (Law, 1994). Without sharing this significant organizational knowledge resource the partnership merely becomes a legal or financial entity and not an *organizational* entity. Let us remember the notion of an organization requires that the elements 'work' together – i.e. they engage in cooperative activities. Without significant sharing and co-creation of organizational knowledge the idea of a virtual organization is simply a meta-entity. Moreover, this is nothing new, as the financial markets indicate.

To share a world is to share a language (Maturana and Varela, 1987). Wittgenstein (1956) argues that language is invariably already situated. We understand each other because we *already share a world*, a form of life. The language of doing in everyday work is 'constructed' intrinsically as part of *what we do*; the 'language and the actions into which it is woven' are fused together (Wittgenstein, 1956). Similarly, Latour (1987: 25) has argued that 'By itself a given sentence is neither a fact nor a fiction; it is made so by others later on'. As Foucault (1969) has argued, to speak a language is not solely to construct and utter grammatically good sentences. Nor is it merely to construct a proposition that is governed by a specific logic. We always speak *in a situation* as part of doing something. Speaking, like doing, always assumes a shared world, a form of life. We have 'lawyer-speak', 'nurse-speak', 'shopping-speak', 'fishing-speak', and so on. These are all 'forms of life', each with its own language-game – here understood as a collection of words and associated ways of using these words that make sense to those that participate in that form of life. For example, there is a language-game – a particular way of speaking – which a theatre nurse may use to instruct a ward nurse to 'prepare this patient for the operating theatre' in the form of life called 'nursing'; this could be something such as 'do a prep on her!'. The 'rules' – or way of talking about the world – in each language-game evolve in and through situated action and interaction. The way we speak about the world is the way we think about the world, and thus is the way we do things in the world. The statements we utter are, in other words, 'speech acts' (Foucault, 1969). This notion implies that speaking goes hand-in-hand with acting and acting is accompanied by our utterances. These two are constitutive of each other. Speaking, thinking and doing are fused together in and through action and interaction – separating these facets for technical design may be analytically valid but does not ring true in day-to-day organizational practice.

Moreover, each language-game is, by its nature and in some absolute sense, incommensurate with the others. Obviously, in a practical sense one would tend to try to 'work it out' utilizing all sorts of heuristics – but this working out takes time and involvement. To become a 'native speaker' of a form of life is not merely a matter of constructing a dictionary. If this were the case then we could learn a language through studying a dictionary, and creating ordinary language translation software would be a simple affair. Nevertheless, it is only when one becomes a 'native speaker' in a form of life, through one's interactions with the others (Law, 1994), that subtle and important tacit knowledge can be shared; one can only fully participate in a culture once 'native speaker' status is reached. In addition, it is this very cultural background that provides the subtle meanings which give a language its expressive power. This means that the notions, terms and ideas that really matter do not just move from one form of life to another without losing the meaning (or sense) that is local to that form of life. If that was the case then the sense we would make out of this local knowledge would be both *simplified* and *translated*, to use Law's terms (Law, 1994): simplified, because we only relate to that which is directly given, and translated in that we always come to it from our own context.

When we make statements in organizational context, as part of our work, we do not simply talk or chat. We tend to make claims we want others to take seriously. We might say: 'this project is over budget' or 'you are not doing our work'. The validity of a claim is inseparable from the context within which it is uttered, the people who utter it, the tools they use to systematize it, the institutions within which they belong, the positions they occupy, the other related statements of the past and the present and upon various criteria that trigger the choice for the prevalence of these specific statements (Foucault, 1969). Contrary to a grammatical sentence or a logical proposition, which 'always remains a sentence or a proposition and can always be recognized as such' (Foucault, 1969: 109), organizational statements or better speech acts are inseparable from the context of use. They *bring into operation* and they *make possible* a space of which they are at the same time an outcome. Therefore, if each partner has a locally situated language that captures what and how they do things, and if these languages are incommensurable, then the only option available is to develop a new language-game that situates the discourse of the different partners into a new combined context. This implies that they have to share a form of life, i.e. they have to do things together for a reasonably extended period of time in a shared space. Hence, it seems that notions such as the quick 'in-and-out', flexibility and adaptability, and high degree of electronic mediation – as put forward by the proponents of the virtual organization – do not seem to take note of the complexity of everyday practices.

BEING-IN-THE-WORLD AND UNDERSTANDING

We understand the world because we are 'in' the world (Heidegger, 1962). This does not imply the idea of inclusion in the sense of the chair being 'in' the room. Being 'in' the world implies that we are involved in the world; we are 'in' the world because we do things in it. In our involvement, our actions make sense because they refer to other actions (in the past, present and future). Our projects, actions and equipment weave together in a seamless world available for our use – merely there: like the chair, door and table. They are merely there in our preconscious as possibilities for sitting, or for entering, or as a surface for placing things. We use them as part of what we do. In using them they slip into the background of our focal attention. As available, our bodies deal with them in the way they deal with a step that is suddenly there, or not there. Further, in a similar manner to everyday objects, so too with language, supposition, categories and the like. As we engage them in our world they slip into the background as possibilities for doing, saying and thinking.

This tacit, preconscious world is the whole that situates and renders individual actions meaningful – for those involved in that world. It provides the rationale and intention that ground our action. Similarly, an involved actor 'knows' what to do without necessarily being able to make it explicit why. This is because an 'involved actor' acts impulsively; thinking and acting happen simultaneously and are the outcome of not only reason and purpose but intuition, faith, luck and innumerable other factors. The logic for action is not only a matter of cognition, but emerges as coherence between conscious thought and involved action in an already there world in which we find ourselves already immersed. We dwell in this world and find ourselves entangled – always already entangled. As such, it provides both our possibilities and our limits, enables both planned and improvised actions and paves the way for both routine and enraptured decisions to be made.

Thus, to be-in-the-world, according to Heidegger (1962), means that we always already understand – or have a sense of that world – even before thinking about it. We understand it because we are immersed 'in' it through our everyday doing. Any explicit understanding (or knowledge) always assumes this already present familiarity with the world – our being-in. Our knowledge and past experiences enable our sense making and trigger our spontaneous actions. In this understanding of the world we do not normally make decisions or explicitly think about what we are doing, we simply do what is available for doing. This is the tacit and available pool of understanding that makes up our common sense of how to do things, in doing what we do well. To share this understanding is to share this world – a referential whole. This is why it is possible to tell someone who shares your world, 'I understand', without needing to make the 'what' of that understanding explicit.

As was the case with the tacit knowledge concept of Polanyi (1973), the question now becomes: 'how will this shared understanding evolve when the virtual partners do not share a world?'. These partners may think they understand, but since this understanding is always only implicit, how will this be validated? (Normally this will be done in shared action at moments of breakdown.) One may find that the initial saving realized by pooling core competencies will be neutralized by a whole series of efforts to try to render coherent worlds that do not intersect. Even with extensive planning and prior decision making, common understanding of that which is said and done is transferred with difficulty. The good practices, as Ciborra (1999) would argue, are often those that circumstances allow. Improvisation and human judgement intervene even in the most standardized work environment and reinvent it. The foundation of all organizational interactions is this *always already shared* world that is sustained through shared action. There is no quick 'cut-and-paste' solution for this shared understanding. The organizational discourse makes sense (i.e. is deeply meaningful) to its participants because they share a referential whole (i.e. a world) that makes it sensible (Introna, 1997). Without this referential whole the dialogue can only be superficial; it must, by necessity, refer to very general, widely understood, notions. Even with extensive planning and prior design, common understanding of that which is said and done is grasped and transmitted with difficulty. This is because, as Ciborra (1999: 77) argued, 'in the background of impromptu action, as well as of a more authentic notion of time, lies what is missing from the managerial models in good currency: human existence and experience', and in our discussion here, *common* human existence and *shared* experience. We would argue, therefore, that there is a large underestimation of the effort needed to share knowledge in the world. Furthermore, there seems to be no short-cut. It also seems problematic to think that we can mediate content-rich communication without some fairly significant level of shared action in a shared world. The split between cognition and action may hold on a superficial level, but it will not hold when it comes to sharing the extremely subtle understanding that is the very source of our expertise. The current thinking – as espoused by proponents of the virtual organization – is simply too naive about the complexity of cognition and action in the world.

SYNTHESIS AND CONCLUSIONS

In the first chapter of this section, the main proponents of the virtual organization concept made the claim that it could become the predominant organizational metaphor for the next century. The arguments being put forward are that socio-economic forces are pushing all organizations into this almost inevitable position of having to become fast, flexible and fluid – and therefore virtual. There is no doubt that the pressures articulated are substantive and real. There are many dynamic forces at play, and these have long since been recognized by many commentators, both academic and populist (Drucker, 1978). It is also easy to see why the idea of a virtual organization seems to be the 'right' answer for the issues at hand; on an obvious level it makes a lot of sense. However, we believe the concept of the virtual organization is a little naive and somewhat mechanistic. Our antithesis suggests that there is much more to 'organizations' than meets the eye; organizations are not black boxes that one could simply tie together in an obvious and non-problematic way. Many questions have been raised that create doubt over the legitimacy that the idea seems to have in academic and popular circles.

The Ameritech case study is frequently cited (Graves, 1994; Grenier and Metes, 1995; Kupfer, 1994) as a model of the virtual corporation. Seemingly, the essence of the partnership is built around organizational knowledge in the form of explicit technological artefacts. Cooperation of this sort is not new. In such instances the core competence can, to a large extent, be located and made explicitly available (through disciplines such as configuration management). Here, the issues of virtual organization become a technology transfer issue, for which there exist many examples of success and failure (such as the transfer of technology to developing countries).

Without wishing to unduly simplify an obviously complex issue, and by way of an example only, we want to propose a situation where the virtual organization may be feasible (see Figure 15.1). For instance, this could occur where the core competency consists of explicit technological artefacts, and the level of integration between the core competencies (in the virtual operation and product) is fairly low or unproblematic due to, for example, existing industry standards. This is demonstrated by area A in Figure 15.1. Also, there may be some feasibility in the idea of a virtual organization where the core competency is tacit but where very limited integration is required in the virtual

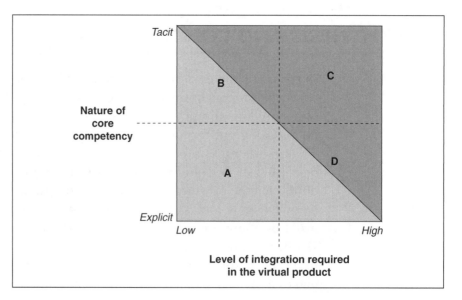

Figure 15.1
The space of possibilities for the virtual organization

product (as indicated by area B in Figure 15.1). In such a case the virtual organization may merely become an entity that is meta-legal or financial. An example of this could be a firm of consultants (each with their own expertise) that serve a common customer base but function relatively independently from each other. However, from our discussion above, it seems that where the core competence of the partners is tacit and the level of integration in the virtual process and product is high (as shown in area C in Figure 15.1), the barriers to virtualization are immense and perhaps impossible to overcome. Further, in the situations indicated by areas B and D in Figure 15.1, we would expect a large amount of effort to make virtualization possible, if at all. We would suggest – based on the above discussion rather than from empirical work – that some of the following conditions would tend to improve the probability of success:

- *A limited number of participants.* The greater the number of participants the greater the effort needed to create a common language game (i.e. native tongue) to express and share knowledge.

- *Strong and shared values.* The presence of strong and shared values would increase the probability that the tacit dispositions of participants coincide. In other words, there would be an 'already there' common sense to work from.

- *A strong incentive to share expertise.* Even if there are shared values there must also be significant incentive for participants to make the sharing of knowledge a priority. This may imply incentives for collaborative efforts – even if they are not strictly functionally needed.

- *A limited presence of strategic action.* The greater the level of strategic action – that is, action directed at self-interest – the lower the levels of trust and the incentive for sharing knowledge.

- *A strong culture of experimentation and reflection.* Since most of the important knowledge would be tacit, it would be necessary for the participants to engage in experimentation and reflection. Thus, through processes of experimentation and subsequent reflection, taken-for-granted practices can be accessed and articulated.

Obviously there are many other aspects that may, or may not, influence the success of a virtual venture. The point is simply this: conditions for virtual organization success may be so varied and contingent, and the space of possibilities so limited, that there is no reason whatsoever to think of the virtual organization as *the* organizational metaphor for the future. This is not to say that it has no possibilities at all, merely that these possibilities are far more limited than the proponents would like to suggest. Furthermore, the idea is so complex that it may represent a very high risk organizational strategy for those who enter it without a full understanding of the issues involved.

REFERENCES

Ackoff, R. L. (1971). Towards a system of systems concepts. *Management Science*, 17, 83–90.

Argyris, C. (1993). *Knowledge for Action*. Jossey-Bass.

Beer, S. (1966). *Decision and Control*. John Wiley and Sons.

Bertalanffy, L. von (1968). *General Systems Theory*. Braziller.

Burrell, G. and Morgan, G. (1979). *Sociological Paradigms and Organizational Analysis*. Heinemann.

Callon, M. (1986). Some elements of a sociology of translation: domestication of the scallops and the fishermen of St Brieuc Bay. In *Power, Action and Belief* (J. Law, ed.) pp. 196–233, Routledge and Kegan Paul.

Churchman, C. W. (1968). *The Systems Approach*. Delacorte Press.

Ciborra, C. (1999). Notes on improvisation and time in organizations. *Accounting, Management and Information Technologies*, 9, 77–94.

Drucker, P. F. (1978). *The Age of Discontinuity: Guidelines to Our Changing Society*. Harper and Row.

Foucault, M. (1969). *The Archaeology of Knowledge*. Routledge.

Foucault, M. (1977). *Discipline and Punish: The Birth of the Prison*. Penguin Group.

Fox, A. (1974). *Beyond Contract: Work, Power and Trust Relations*. Faber and Faber Limited.

Fuller, S. (1999). Why science studies have never been critical of science: some recent lessons on how to be a helpful nuisance and a harmless radical. *Philosophy of the Social Sciences*, 30, 5–32.

Giddens, A. (1990). *The Consequences of Modernity*. Stanford University Press.

Graves, J. M. (1994). Bye-bye, smarties. *Fortune*, 130, 12–13.

Grenier, R. and Metes, G. (1995). *Going Virtual: Moving Your Organization into the 21st Century*. Prentice Hall.

Heidegger, M. (1962). *Being and Time*. Translated by J. Macquarrie and E. Robinson. Basil Blackwell.

Introna, L. D. (1997). *Management, Information and Power: A Narrative of the Involved Manager*. Macmillan.

Jones, M. and Bowie, N. (1998). Moral hazards on the road to the virtual corporation. *Business Ethics Quarterly*, 8, 273–292.

Knights, D., Noble, F., Vurdubakis, T. and Willmott, H. (2001). Chasing shadows: control, vulnerability and the production of trust. *Organization Studies*, 22, 311–336.

Kuhn, T. S. (1977). *The Essential Tension: Selected Studies in Scientific Tradition and Change.* University of Chicago Press.

Kupfer, A. (1994). New bedfellows on the Infobahn. *Fortune,* 129, 9–10.

Latour, B. (1987). *Science in Action: How to Follow Scientists and Engineers through Society.* Harvard University Press.

Law, J. (1994). *Organising Modernity.* Blackwell.

Law, J. (1997). *The Manager and His Powers.* Working Paper, Centre for Science Studies, University of Lancaster. http://www.lancs.ac.uk/fss/sociology/papers/law-manager-and-his-powers.pdf

Lewis, D. and Weigert, A. (1985). Trust as social reality. *Social Forces,* 63, 967–985.

Luhmann, N. (1979). *Trust and Power.* John Wiley and Sons Ltd.

Maturana, H. and Varela, F. (1987). *The Tree of Knowledge: The Biological Roots of Human Understanding.* Shambhala.

Nonaka, I. (1994). A dynamic theory of organizational knowledge creation. *Organization Science,* 5, 14–37.

Pentland, B. T. and Reuter, H. (1994). Organizational routines as grammars of action. *Administrative Science Quarterly,* 39, 484–510.

Polanyi, M. (1973). *Personal Knowledge: Towards a Post-Critical Philosophy.* Routledge and Kegan Paul.

Reed, M. (2001). Organisation, trust and control: a realist analysis. *Organisation Studies,* 22, 201–228.

Shapiro, S. (1987). The social control of impersonal trust. *The American Journal of Sociology,* 93, 622–658.

Von Krogh, G. and Roos, J. (1995). *Organizational Epistemology.* Macmillan.

Whitley, E. A. and Introna, L. D. (1996). How do you make a deal when you can't shake hands? *Telecom Brief,* June, 32–34.

Wittgenstein, L. (1956). *Philosophical Investigations.* Translated by G. E. M. Anscombe. Basil Blackwell.

Index